Paul Simpson has written on a wide variety of topics, with his recent books including an acclaimed overview of conspiracy theories, a history of spying since the Second World War, an anthology of prison breaks, and examinations of the careers of J. R. R. Tolkien, C. S. Lewis, and Stephen King as well as the world of L. Frank Baum's Oz. A keen traveller, he currently oversees news and reviews website Sci-Fi Bulletin from his home in a small village north of Brighton, England.

THE MAMMOTH BOOK OF

Air Disasters and Near Misses

Paul Simpson

RUNNING PRESS
PHILADELPHIA · LONDON

ROBINSON

First published in Great Britain in 2014 by Robinson

A CIP catalogue record for this book
is available from the British Library.

ISBN 978-1-78033-828-6 (paperback)
ISBN 978-1-78033-829-3 (ebook)

Typeset in Plantin by Hewer Text UK Ltd, Edinburgh
Printed and bound in Great Britain by CPI Mackays

Robinson
is an imprint of
Constable & Robinson Ltd
100 Victoria Embankment
London EC4Y 0DY

An Hachette UK Company
www.hachette.co.uk

www.constablerobinson.com

First published in the United States in 2014 by Running Press Book Publishers,
A Member of the Perseus Books Group

Books published by Running Press are available at special discounts for bulk purchases in
the United States by corporations, institutions, and other organizations. For more
information, please contact the Special Markets Department at the Perseus Books Group,
2300 Chestnut Street, Suite 200, Philadelphia, PA 19103, or call (800) 810-4145,
ext. 5000, or e-mail special.markets@perseusbooks.com.

US ISBN: 2013953380
US Library of Congress Control Number: 978-0-7624-4942-2

9   8   7   6   5   4   3   2   1
Digit on the right indicates the number of this printing

Running Press Book Publishers
2300 Chestnut Street
Philadelphia, PA 19103-4371

Visit us on the web!
www.runningpress.com

In memory of Robin Marshall and Bob Stewart, two great influences on my life, who both loved to travel.

For want of a nail, the shoe was lost.
For want of a shoe, the horse was lost.
For want of a horse, the rider was lost.
For want of a rider, the battle was lost.
For want of a battle, the kingdom was lost,
And all for the want of a horseshoe nail.

– Old proverb, quoted by Benjamin
Franklin, *The Way to Wealth*

"In the airline business, safety comes only from a kind of total paranoia – that is, always believing that you are not safe."
– *Time* correspondent Jerry Hannifin, 1979

CONTENTS

Part 2: Ground Collisions and Near Misses

Part 3: Death Comes On Swift Wings: Bird Strikes

Part 4: A Fatal Icy Touch

Part 8: An Explosive Situation: Bombings on Board

Part 9: Shootdowns

Part 10: Your Life in Their Hands – Suicidal Pilots

Part 11: Take-Off to Disaster

Part 12: Disaster and Triumph

INTRODUCTION

There's no question about it – there is something unnatural about putting a motley collection of people into a long metallic tube, sticking wings and some engines to it, and flying it into the sky. According to the old saying, "If God had meant Man to fly, he would have given him wings". But right back to ancient times, humanity has sought to get away from the confines of the ground.

However, as the myth of Daedalus and Icarus was just the first story to demonstrate, there are many dangers inherent in flying. Even before powered flight became possible at the start of the twentieth century, there were accidents, injuries and deaths connected to attempts to fly – and we have always been fascinated by them, as the success of reality series like the Cineflix show *Mayday* (US)/*Air Crash Investigation* (UK), or movies such as *Airport* and its ilk have proved.

The Mammoth Book of Air Disasters and Near Misses doesn't try to be encyclopaedic – a quick perusal of the databases for just the British or American air-accident investigation services reveals that there are unfortunately far more instances of things going wrong than there are paragraphs in this book. The sections comprise a cross-section of some of the most common types of air disasters, and the entries chosen have made their mark in some way on aviation history – whether because they represent the first time that some particular problem was encountered; or the accident or incident in question led to alterations in the way we fly today; or occasionally because of the people involved, either as passengers or crew.

Much as I would have liked to include some of the incidents involving ballooning and airships (the R101 and the *Hindenburg* disasters in particular), even a Mammoth Book has its space limitations (not to mention its deadlines), so this volume confines itself to powered aircraft. The first such aviation accident occurred on 17 September 1908, with original pioneer Orville Wright at the controls; a perusal of Google News shows that there is an incident of some sort on most days. The majority of incidents relate to commercial aircraft, rather than military; there are many volumes available which deal with the disasters that the world's armed forces have faced. Inevitably there are some disasters and near-misses which are not covered (notably those involving controlled flights into terrain), but the contents pages list the major events contained in each chapter, referenced by flight title, date and location or other aide-memoire.

Where they are available, the official accident investigation reports have been studied, likewise the transcripts of the "black box" data from the flight recorders and the cockpit voice recorders. Contemporary reports, both in the mainstream press and trade magazines such as *Flight International*, have been incorporated into the narrative, and the terminology of the entries reflects the way in which they were presented then – cabin personnel in particular have gone through many changes in nomenclature over the years, and it would be jarring to read someone described one way in the text, and differently in the sources quoted. Wherever a direct quote is given in the narratives, it is sourced from the official released transcripts from the cockpit voice recorders and other recordings. (Because English is the official language of aviation, these reports are nearly always released in an "official" English translation.)

At the end of each section of the book, a comprehensive list of sources is given; barring the occasional piece of historical news footage, I have tended not to draw on the televised documentary/dramas of these events, as these have often had to conflate or expand material to fit within the strict one-hour nature of the programmes.

Inevitably, at times there are conflicts of testimony, and the narratives in these pages are largely drawn from the work of the various accident investigation authorities worldwide, who, in most cases, had the opportunity to take eyewitness statements from those involved. As anyone who has been a witness to an accident will know, no two people see things alike – the Vancouver Canucks ice hockey team had just landed at Los Angeles back in 1991 when a 737 crashed into a smaller aircraft and then careered off into a derelict fire station. "It's funny sometimes how you can all watch something and come out with different stories," coach

Pat Quinn told the *Los Angeles Times* the next day. "When we were standing around waiting for our bags, some players said they thought they saw the plane on fire before it landed, but we later found out that was not the case." People's immediate reaction to incidents can be revealing, and where at all possible, each account here incorporates comments from those involved as passengers, not just the flight crew.

The causes of the various incidents within these pages are many and varied, and there are those who will maintain that there is no such thing as pilot error (except in really exceptional circumstances, such as the Russian pilot who misguidedly allowed his teenage children to sit in the pilots' seats, and put their hands on the controls, thereby disengaging the autopilot). Speaking after the Überlingen mid-air collision in July 2002, Stuart Matthews, president of the Flight Safety Foundation, commented, "[I]t is for certain that no one thing causes an accident, it's always a chain of events . . . I don't necessarily blame the pilot because I don't know all the facts, but at the end of the day he was the last link of the unbroken chain." As some of the accounts in here show, there is sometimes very little that a pilot can do faced with a catastrophic mechanical failure – whether that's caused by someone taping over an inlet, which affects the functioning of the aircraft, or following a collision. However, there have been many occasions where pilots have been able to snatch victory from the jaws of defeat, and save the lives of some – and sometimes, all – of those aboard their aircraft, against all the odds.

The National Transportation Safety Board (NTSB) investigator and pilot Brian S. Richardson is quoted on the website regarding the Aloha Airlines flight in which part of the roof of the aircraft was blown away, commending all those who warn about the dangers. "The industry needs to be constantly reminded of the past so they can be ever vigilant in the future," he wrote in April 1998. "Believe me, as one who makes his living in the environment, I'm acutely aware that neat little 10 to the minus ninth probabilities [one in a billion chance] aren't worth a shit if you are on the airplane when the numbers don't work out."

Everyone has had their own brush with aviation disaster, either personally or vicariously through friends and relatives. I was travelling from Heathrow to Los Angeles less than two weeks before

9/11 when the doors on the aircraft remained open, rather than being closed in preparation for take-off; about forty-five minutes later, my travelling companion and I were a little perturbed to see the cabin crew leaving the aircraft, and coming back after a briefing, clearly surprised by what they had heard. Rumours inevitably started spreading around the cabin, and it transpired that a threat had been received against an aircraft; when it became clear that it was a specific threat against the flight that we were on (rather than a general one against the airline as had happened a few times in preceding months), we decided discretion was the better part of valour, and elected to join those deplaning. As it transpired, the flight left, albeit two and a half hours late, and arrived safely; when we checked in the next day for the revised flight, we learned that a particular target of extremist hatred had been on board our aircraft the previous day. Apparently it was the last time that the person in question was allowed on that airline's flights. However, what impressed me most was that the staff on the flight didn't hesitate: they continued with their duties, irrespective of their personal concerns. (As Cristina Jones, one of the flight attendants who tackled Richard Reid, the shoe bomber three months after this incident, told *Time* magazine, "As a flight attendant, you learn to leave your feelings at the door.")

The Mammoth Book of Air Disasters starts with a look at incidents with some of the highest potential for disaster, when two aircraft come into collision, either mid-air or on the ground. After that, the following sections deal with natural phenomena, particularly bird strikes and ice. Explosive decompression and fire are the causes of our next batches of accounts, with manmade problems – hijackings, bombings, attacks on aircraft and even suicidal pilots – forming our penultimate part.

The book concludes with three difficult take-offs, and then with an account of one particular incident, which was referred to by more people within the aviation industry to whom I spoke during the preparation of this book than any other: the emergency landing of United Airlines Flight 232 into Sioux City on 19 July 1989. What could go wrong did go wrong on that flight – and yet 185 from the 296 people on board survived, despite the pilots dealing with a situation that was "virtually impossible".

With a book like this, there is always a danger that the reader – and the author – can become inured to the reality of what is being discussed. There are many television documentary series about aircraft crashes – a large number of episodes of *Mayday/ Air Crash Investigation* have been uploaded to YouTube – and many of these include interviews with survivors or the relatives of the victims. Within these pages, the sudden deaths of many hundreds of people are recounted. It is to the memory of all those who died or were injured in the events related herein that this book is also respectfully dedicated.

Paul Simpson
May 2014

AUTHOR'S NOTE

Timings in the narratives are usually given in the format adopted by the official report, most of which adopt UTC (Universal Time Clock) or GMT (Greenwich Mean Time) as standard. Where a time is given as 0000.01, this indicates 1 second past the time given in the twenty-four-hour clock format – given the speed at which so many of the incidents in this volume occur, such a breakdown is often essential.

Part 1:
Mid-Air Collisions

THE MORE THINGS CHANGE . . .

The very first recorded collision between aircraft (or airships as they were called in contemporary reports) took place on 3 October 1910 at the Milano Circuito Aereo Internazionale. You might have thought at this stage, when aviation really was in its infancy, that the odds of two aircraft being in the same place at the same time should have been astronomical, but unfortunately, M. Rene Thomas in his Antoinette monoplane and Captain Bertram Dickson in a Henry Farman biplane achieved it. *Popular Mechanics* magazine commissioned a full-page depiction of the event; *Flight* magazine reported that "Capt. Dickson during the week had been very popular because of his splendid gliding flights from high altitudes, and on Sunday afternoon, after a glide downwards, he was once more rising when Thomas, who had been flying very high and very fast, commenced to plane down at a fast speed. He was unable to see Capt. Dickson, and also the noise of his own motor drowned that of the British airman, and to the horror of the spectators, the Antoinette monoplane crashed on to the biplane, both machines falling to earth a mass of broken planes and tangled wires. Thomas escaped serious injury but Capt. Dickson was not so fortunate." The British captain never flew again.

The first known fatal collision followed twenty months later, on 19 June 1912 at Douai in northern France. A wire press report noted that Captain Dubois and Lieutenant Albert Peignan, "both officers of the French army, and trained airmen, were killed this morning when the biplanes they were piloting around the military flying ground, collided with terrific force in mid-air. The two officers, who were close friends, were unable to perceive each other while flying through the early morning haze. In making a curve their machines collided with an awful impact, the wire stays and canvas wings became interlocked and the two biplanes crashed to the ground. Lieut. Peignan was taken dead from among the debris. Capt. Dubois died within an hour."

There were, of course, many collisions between airplanes during the Great War. German ace Fritz Rumey, who was reputed to be even more fearless than the Red Baron, was brought down when he overlooked the presence of South African Lieutenant Bruce Lawson in a dogfight. When he pulled up to avoid Lawson's guns, the top of his Fokker collided with Lawson's undercarriage. Rumey undid his seat belt, and jumped from his machine, hoping that his parachute would save him. It failed to open and he plummeted to his death. On another occasion, two American flyers collided during a particularly heavy bombing raid as they tried to avoid accurate anti-aircraft fire.

The first mid-air collision involving a passenger aircraft took place on Friday 7 April 1922. As described by *Flight*, it was "an extremely regrettable and unusual accident [which] marred the running of the London Continental Air service, which has hitherto been remarkably free from serious disasters." Eyewitnesses who spoke to the *New York Times* said that it was about 1.15 p.m. "when the drone of a big machine was heard by the villagers" of Thieulloy-St. Antoine, 27 kilometres north of Beauvais. They were used to seeing the aircraft flying towards London."

A thick fog was covering the whole landscape, accompanied by a steady drizzle of rain. "Suddenly a huge machine appeared as if coming out from behind a curtain at a height of about 150 meters, proceeding in the direction of London. It was the Goliath. Hardly had it appeared when a smaller machine shot forth from behind the fog screen, flying toward Paris. Those watching had not time to think before a sinister crash resounded through the air, and the next thing they saw were masses of debris – broken wood and bent metal – hurtling to the ground. The two airplanes had telescoped each other, and after staggering blindly for a few short seconds crashed burning to the earth."

The Compagnie des Grands Express Aériens (CGEA) Farman F.60 Goliath was carrying a pilot and mechanic, and three passengers, two of whom were honeymooning Americans who had made a last minute change of plans to fly rather than travel by rail and boat. The other aircraft was a mail carrier from Daimler Airway, whose service from London to Paris had only begun on the preceding Monday. Both on board – the pilot, R. E. Duke, and a cabin boy, Hesterman – were both killed. Hesterman survived for a short time, but succumbed to his injuries; all on the Goliath died instantly.

The tragedy led to a meeting between many of the world's aviation authorities including CGEA, Compagnie des Messageries Aériennes, Daimler Airway, Handley Page Transport, Instone Air Line and the Royal Dutch Air Service, where key rules, such as aircraft offsetting to the right when going around landmarks, and also turning to the right if on a collision course, were established. The first airway systems – the systems of levels of flight dictated by the direction of travel – were also devised.

The United States hadn't long been involved in the Second World War when the pilot of an US Army Air Forces B-34 bomber was blamed for the downing of a Douglas DC-3 belonging to American Airlines on 23 October 1942 – or to be more accurate, according to the Civil Aeronautics Board (CAB), the cause of the crash was "the reckless and irresponsible conduct of Lieutenant William N. Wilson in deliberately maneuvering a bomber in dangerous proximity to an airliner in an unjustifiable attempt to attract the attention of the first officer (copilot) of the latter plane." (Not for the first, and certainly not for the last time, the report of the CAB was challenged by other authorities – Lieutenant Wilson was cleared of responsibility for the crash at a subsequent court martial.)

American Airlines Trip 28 (as flights were then known) was eventually bound for New York; the B-34 was heading between bases at Long Beach, California, and Palm Springs. The pilot of the bomber, Lt. Wilson, was a friend of the first officer of the AA aircraft, Louis Reppert, Jr, and when the pair had met the previous evening, they realized that they were going to be "going out" at about the same time the next day. The two had trained together several months previously and Lt. Wilson explained to the CAB that they had thought it would be "pleasant to 'see each other in the air'". They had discussed the idea of clicking their radio microphones to say hello, but when they determined that they'd be on different frequencies, the idea was dropped. However, the co-pilot on the bomber, Staff Sergeant Robert Reed Leicht, testified that Lt. Wilson had explained that he "would like to thumb his nose" at the airliner's co-pilot.

Captain Pedley, the AA pilot, was unaware of the friendly rivalry between his first officer and the USAAF lieutenant, and took off from Burbank Airport (just north-east of Los Angeles) on schedule around 4.36 p.m. The bomber had left Long Beach ten minutes earlier, but Lt. Wilson wasn't planning on heading straight for Palm Springs. He went to a point north and west of March Field near Riverside, California, and circled round, telling his co-pilot to look out for the AA airliner.

When they spotted the DC-3, Wilson climbed from 4,000 feet to 9,000 feet, and passed around 1.5 to 2 miles to the left of the passenger service. Wilson rocked the wings of his bomber to identify himself to Reppert, but there was no response from the AA aircraft. By this point, Wilson was well ahead of the airliner, so crossed over its line of flight, then throttled back, waiting for it to overtake him on his left. However, as it did so, Wilson felt that he was still too far from AA 28 to identify his friend, so decided to approach it and get closer.

And he came too close. Realizing that he was much closer than he had planned, he started a right turn. "It was while in this right bank that the impact occurred," he told the CAB. He thought he had been in the turn "for a long enough time that I felt perfectly clear and far away and on my way back to the airport". He maintained that he "had throttled my left engine up a couple of inches and was getting my nose down a little bit, and I was ready to trim it up and prepare for my letdown when the impact occurred".

Staff Sergeant Leicht said that the DC-3 was immediately below and ahead of them at impact – the bomber's propeller had hit the DC-3's rudder, destroying three-quarters of it. The DC-3 "then appeared to rise about ten feet above them, hover momentarily, fall off to the left and disappear". Wilson heard a "noise, and a wrenching of my ship up and to my left", and realized the bomber was handling sluggishly.

Burbank control received a message: "Flight 28 from Burbank . . . correction Burbank from Flight 28" but that was the last anyone heard from the passenger service. Witnesses on the ground had noted that the two aircraft had "looked like one plane, they were so close" before impact.

The wreckage of the aircraft was found about two miles west of the Army Airport at Palm Springs, three miles south of the centre of the airway, scattered over an area about two miles long and three-quarters of a mile wide. It had burst into flames on impact and burned for around five hours. Three crew members and nine passengers, including the songwriter Ralph Rainger, were killed.

Lieutenant Wilson's court-martial board were more taken with the testimony of Private Roy West than the CAB had been – the aviation experts had discounted his version, since he seemed to think that if the DC-3's nose had come down, then the tail would rise as if it was on some sort of fulcrum. The minor damage to the bomber was repaired, but it was involved in another crash on 5 August 1943, in which all three crew members were killed.

No one could have guessed at Lieutenant Wilson's antics in the bomber; when the crash initially occurred, there were suggestions that the bomber had tried to "hop on and off the airlines' beam without reporting positions to traffic controls". *Time* commented that "this was one time when there must be abundant, clear-cut evidence".

There was a further incident at the end of the war involving a DC-3, this time belonging to Eastern Air Lines. Flight 45 from Boston, Massachusetts, to Miami, Florida, was also in collision with a bomber, an A-26 engaged in a local practice flight. One person on board the DC-3 died as did two of the Army personnel, but the majority of those on the Eastern flight survived to tell the tale. Senior pilot G. D. Davis was commended for his actions by an army public relations officer: "except for the masterful handling of his plane by Pilot Davis, it is almost certain that the 17 passengers and three crewmembers of the airliner would also have perished".

The DC-3 was scheduled to stop at New York; Washington DC; Columbia, South Carolina; and Jacksonville, Florida, on its way to Miami, and the flight, on 12 July 1945, was uneventful until two hours into the leg from Washington. Captain Davis was concerned about the possibility of heavy military traffic close to Florence Army Air Field, so decided to deviate from the airway, and at 1436, five minutes after he reported in over Florence, he was in fact eight miles west of where he should have been. He was then starting his descent into Columbia.

While the captain had the discretion under the rules of the air to deviate, this did mean that the Eastern passenger aircraft might not be where military flights out of Florence would expect it to be. At 1315, an Army A-26 had taken off for a two-hour training mission. After carrying out various manoeuvres within the designated test area, the pilot, First Lieutenant Stephen G. Jones, started to head back to base. Along the way he decided to practise aural null procedures, checking for a change in signal to indicate the relative bearing of the Florence radio range station from his aircraft. At around 1436, Jones entered a left turn of 15 to 20 degrees of bank at an airspeed of 220 mph. He was in this turn for sixty to ninety seconds – and when he rolled out of the turn, Eastern 45 was almost directly in front of him.

The two pilots had approximately a second to react. Captain Davis saw the A-26 heading in a direction almost at right angles to that of his aircraft, and pulled back on his controls. First Lieutenant Jones pushed his controls forward, trying to pass beneath the airliner. It was too late – the two aircraft collided.

The vertical fin of the bomber hit the leading edge of the DC-3's left wing, and travelled along it until it struck the left engine nacelle (the housing holding the engine to the wing), tearing the engine loose. Its propeller still rotating, the engine moved to its right, and the propeller cut into the DC-3 fuselage, just behind the baggage-compartment door. The top four to five feet of the bomber's fin and rudder were broken off, and hit the DC-3 fuselage, making more holes. The DC-3's right propeller severed the bomber forward of the empennage, and the A-26 turned over. The pilot ordered his crew to bail out.

Only First Lieutenant Jones made it. The forward gunner was not able to get out of the aircraft, and was killed in the crash. The tail gunner was hit by one of the DC-3 propellers and was killed.

Captain Davis was thrown against the left-hand side of the DC-3 cockpit, and was temporarily stunned, yet, still woozy from the knock, managed to maintain control of the aircraft by gliding steeply. He realized to his horror that he had no power available, since the left engine was gone completely, and the blades had been torn off the right engine propeller. Bringing the aircraft in as a glider, he managed to land it in a cotton field, after a twenty to thirty second descent with flaps and wheels up, although it then ground-looped about 170 degrees to the right – and the right engine fell off. A two-year-old boy suffered head injuries and died on his way to hospital; his mother and two other people were seriously injured but recovered.

The CAB found that "the probable cause of this accident was the lack of vigilance on the part of the pilots of both aircraft resulting in the failure of each pilot to see the other aircraft in time to avoid collision". The bomber pilot shouldn't have been practising manoeuvres away from the designated test area; the DC-3 might have possessed the right of way, but Captain Davis shouldn't have deviated from the airway.

POST-WAR TENSIONS

In the period immediately after the Second World War, tensions began to rise between the Western powers and those in the Eastern bloc. They might have been allies during the fight against Hitler, but cracks in the alliance grew when Marshal Stalin's designs on the countries of Eastern Europe became clear. The German capital, Berlin, had been divided into sectors controlled by different governments, and was always likely to be a potential flash point. When a British European Airways (BEA) Vickers Viking airliner collided with a Soviet Yakovlev Yak-3 fighter, there were those on both sides who read far more than a simple accident into events.

Because Berlin was situated in the heart of East Germany, aircraft travelling from the Western nations had to follow a very clearly delineated air corridor over the Communist states. BEA operated a regular service between RAF Northolt and the RAF station at Gatow, in the borough of Spandau in the south-west part of Berlin. The former Luftwaffe staff and technical college (now the General Steinhoff-Kaserne and home of the Luftwaffe museum) received six flights a week from the UK.

Easter Sunday 1948 fell on 28 March, and in the days following, Soviet fighters engaged in a game of "buzzing" the American and British passenger airplanes which were travelling to Berlin. The Russians warned the other occupying powers that "an unusually large number of their fighter craft were in the air over and around the corridor from the Western zones and that everyone should watch out". What this meant became abundantly clear on the afternoon of 5 April.

The daily scheduled BEA Viking was approaching the airfield at around 2.30 p.m., and was just levelling off to land when a Soviet Yakovlev Yak-3 fighter approached it from behind. For no readily apparent reason, it then dived underneath the Viking, then rose sharply, and its starboard wing collided with the other aircraft's port wing. Both aircraft lost the colliding wing, and the

BEA aircraft came down as a mass of wreckage around 2.5 miles short of the airfield, killing the ten passengers and four crew members. The Yak was also downed near a farmhouse just inside the British Zone, its pilot instantly killed.

Eyewitnesses were not certain whether the Soviet fighter had been shadowing the BEA Viking, or whether it had simply arrived near the landing field – in those days before cockpit voice recorders, the deaths of all involved meant the truth would probably not become clear. At the time of the incident, the possibility was mooted that the Russian was trying to land at Dallgow, a Soviet airfield adjacent to Gatow, and it was a terrible misjudgement. (The undercarriage was still locked up, so this idea was dismissed later.)

Russian troops reached the crash site first, refusing to allow RAF ambulances and fire engines to approach the wreckage to salvage bodies or luggage; they also sent a sentry into the British zone to guard their own aircraft – which was surrounded by British troops. The stand-off was only resolved when General Sir Brian Robertson, the British commander, had a meeting with his Soviet counterpart, Marshal Vassily D. Sokolovsky. The Russian apologized, and said that "no interference with the passage of British planes through the agreed corridor to Berlin was 'or is' intended". Sokolovsky then ordered the Russian troops to let the British remove their dead; they had already removed the body of their own pilot.

The incident led to renewed tensions: for part of the day, fighter escorts had been provided for British and American airplanes entering Berlin. "A very serious view is taken in London of today's air crash in Berlin," the British Foreign Office announced. "The Foreign Secretary is in close touch with the commander-in-chief who is ascertaining all the facts." A spokesman went on the record to express the government's view that "the British do not believe the presence or manoeuvering of the Soviet fighter was accidental despite the Russian disclaimer".

A joint British-Soviet commission of enquiry was established five days after the crash, but Soviet Major-General Alexandrov claimed that he would only hear testimony from Soviet or British witnesses, since Germans or Americans would be unreliable. *The Spectator* issue of 15 April 1948, headlined the story and noted: "The history of the inquiry into the Gatow air disaster is quite sufficient to show that reasonable behaviour, or even common decency following the death of innocent people, cannot be expected from the Russian authorities. The accusation that the British Viking transport swooped on the tail of the Russian Yak fighter is fantastic; the Russian acceptance of the invitation to co-operate in the inquiry contained a plain indication that an objective view of the case would not be taken; and the subsequent refusal to hear German or American witnesses ended even the pretence that the Russians wish to recognise the facts."

The British refused to take part under the conditions laid down by the Soviets, and set up their own court of enquiry under General Robertson. They found that the crash was accidental, and "the collision was caused by the action of the Yak fighter, which was in disregard of the accepted rules of flying and, in particular, of the quadripartite flying rules to which Soviet authorities were parties".

The Russians refused to accept this and published their own version, which claimed that the Viking had emerged from low cloud and crashed into the fighter. (The Viking was at 1,500 feet, with cloud cover at 3,000 feet.) The British response to this was summed up by the Secretary of State for Foreign Affairs, Christopher Mayhew in the House of Commons on 26 April: "I have seen the text as published in the Soviet-controlled press. I have no wish to comment on this document, except to say that the account given of the disaster and of its causes is totally inaccurate. The accusation in it that the British court of inquiry manipulated the evidence is also totally false and unfounded."

Less than three months after the Gatow disaster, the Russians blockaded Berlin, and the air corridors became the beleaguered city's only chance of survival. For all Marshal Sokolovsky's protestations, Josef Stalin was determined to force the Westerners out of his domain.

One of the worst disasters in British aviation history occurred the same year, with the deaths of thirty-nine people in the mid-air collision between an SAS DC-6 and an RAF Avro York near RAF Northolt on 4 July 1948. As a direct result of the incident, the minimum stacking level over British airports was increased from 500 feet to 1,000 feet.

The SAS DC-6 was heading to Northolt from Stockholm with twenty-five passengers and seven crew; the six crew of the Avro York C.1 transport from RAF 99 Squadron were bringing Sir

Edward Gent, the High Commissioner for the Federation of Malaya, back from Malta to London. The DC-6 entered the Metropolitan Control Zone over Luton beacon at around 2.19 p.m. with the York entering the Zone at 2.32 p.m. at Woodley Beacon (near Reading). Both were held at 5,000 feet in heavy cloud.

At 2.48 p.m., the tower controller gave the DC-6 permission to descend to 2,500 feet, and four minutes later, the pilot reported: "Just passed 2,500 feet, going down." The controller told him to remain at 2,500 feet; he had not been given clearance to go lower.

At 2.54 p.m., the York was cleared to descend to 3,000 feet, and ordered to call when it had reached that height. At 2.56 p.m., Northolt acknowledged receipt of a message from the RAF aircraft saying, "Roger, 3,000 feet", but it was not clear whether the York crew were simply confirming that they had received the instruction, or that they were informing the tower that they were at the correct height.

At 2.59 p.m., the SAS crew decided that they were abandoning the landing at Northolt because of the poor weather conditions, and informed the tower that they were going to proceed to Amsterdam. At 3 p.m., the tower told them that they were cleared out of the zone via Stapleford at 2,500 feet, but there was no confirmation that they received this.

At 3.05 p.m., the York was cleared to descend further to 1,500 feet but they never received the instruction. Two minutes earlier, the York and the SAS aircraft had collided about four miles north-north-west of the airfield. There were no survivors.

It wasn't as if there were large numbers of aircraft above Northolt that afternoon. According to *Flight*'s report on the accident, there were only four airplanes stacked: the DC-6 at 2,500 feet, the York at 3,000 feet, and two others above them.

The Minister of Civil Aviation set up a Court of Inquiry, which confirmed that the York was above the DC-6 at the time of the accident, and that the DC-6 had been climbing. The DC-6's starboard wing penetrated the York on the starboard side, behind the freight door, and detached the RAF aircraft's tail unit. Both aircraft burst into flames on impact, although the rudder and tail-plane of the DC-6 remained intact for investigation.

The Court found that the "cause of the loss was in all probability to be found in the field of human fallibility on the part of those responsible for the control of the aircraft from the ground, or the flight of the aircraft in the air", which was rather hedging their bets. They found that the air traffic control system was satisfactory for purpose, but that there had been errors of detail or bad practice which could have either caused or contributed to the disaster. These included errors relating to the setting for the altimeters: an error in setting the pressure of one millibar affected the height by 28 feet. The figures hadn't been provided to the aircraft at the right time, or in the right way. They also were concerned about the proximity of aircraft in the stack, and recommended the increase from 500 feet distance to 1,000, which was made official by the Ministry of Civil Aviation on 10 November 1948.

Some accidents simply can't be explained other than as human error. The collision of a BEA DC-3 with an RAF Avro Anson T21 on 19 February 1949 was ascribed to "failure on the part of the captain of each aircraft to ensure the maintenance of an effective lookout". The BEA aircraft was flying the 0905 service to Glasgow, with six passengers and four crew on board. It took off from Northolt at 0913, under VFR conditions and at 0922 Captain McDermott requested permission to contact the Northern Flight Information Region Control Centre, as he was flying over Rugby at 4,500 feet. Permission was granted at 0944, and that was acknowledged – but that was the last anyone heard from the DC-3.

The Anson had left RAF Middleton St. George in Yorkshire at 0800, and was on a cross-country navigational training flight, heading toward Chatteris. Both aircraft were flying at about 4,500 feet, the DC-3 heading north-west, the Anson east-south-east. At 0945, above the village of Exhall, near Coventry, the two collided, and the wreckage from both aircraft fell near a local old peoples' home, the Exhall Lodge Hospital.

There seemed to be no obvious reason for the crash relating to the condition of the aircraft or the pilots involved. The weather at the time was reported to be cloudless, with a bright sun providing visibility for around six miles. Yet no avoiding action was taken by either pilot. Eventually the Chief Inspector of Accidents had to conclude "that the pilot of the Anson did not see the Dakota and that the pilots of the Dakota did not see the Anson".

"MAKE BOLIVIA FAMOUS"

While the SAS disaster at Northolt provided one of the UK's worst accidents, the incident at Washington National Airport involving Eastern Air Lines Flight 537 and a Lockheed P-38 Lightning was the deadliest aviation event in American history to that point. Although initial newspaper reports suggested that perhaps only twenty-three people had died, all fifty-five passengers and crew aboard the Eastern DC-4 perished; the pilot of the P-38, the Bolivian Air Force test pilot Erick Rios Bridoux, survived.

Exactly what happened on 1 November 1949 was open to some question; Bridoux's version of events differed quite dramatically from that of the tower controllers and other involved parties. The CAB had little option but to decide which set they were going to believe, with their eventual report containing both a "History of the Flights", recounting both versions, and a "Reconstruction of Events". It might be worth noting the comment in Eleanor Roosevelt's diary about the disaster: "According to reports last night, Eric (sic) Rios Bridoux, pilot of the military P-38 that caused the accident, wanted only to die. He had been told that he was the only survivor. It is a natural reaction for him not to want to live to carry about the feeling that he was responsible for so many deaths, but one hopes that he will be able to tell what happened." Was Bridoux desperate not to be blamed for events for which he knew he was responsible? Certainly, the CAB determined that "the probable cause of this accident was the execution of a straight-in final approach by the P-38 pilot without obtaining proper clearance to land and without exercising necessary vigilance".

Erick Rios Bridoux (who is referred to as Rios throughout the CAB report) took off from Runway 3 at Washington National Airport at 1137, Eastern Standard Time. The P-38 was a war surplus aircraft, which was being put through its paces by Bridoux, an expert pilot, and the Director of Civilian Aviation in his home country, Bolivia. The Air Force was considering purchasing the P-38, and Bridoux was the obvious person to test it: he had trained with the US Army Air Force during the Second World War, and had eighty hours' experience of flying P-38-type aircraft. He was being observed by representatives of his government.

Eastern Flight 537 was flying from Boston to New Orleans via various stopovers along the way, including Washington DC. At 1138, Captain George Ray contacted Washington Control Tower and was cleared to enter a left traffic pattern, going counter clockwise around the airport, for landing on Runway 3. Visibility around the airport was 15 miles; the ceiling was 6,500 feet with scattered clouds at 3,500 feet, and there was a surface northeasterly wind of 20 to 25 miles per hour.

Bridoux climbed to around 300 feet, turned left and continued to climb on a westerly heading. However, as he turned, the right engine of the P-38 became erratic, and he decided to return to the airport as soon as possible, although it wasn't bad enough to warrant declaring an emergency. After reaching 3,500 feet, he levelled off and then turned south. It then seems that he became disoriented regarding his location and was circling at a high altitude about five miles south of National Airport. A P-38 was certainly seen by a flight instructor at Hybla Valley Airport, near Alexandria (south of Washington) flying with its landing gear up at about 3,000 to 4,000 feet in the vicinity of Alexandria that then made a long final approach toward National Runway 3. (The Bolivian claimed that he had contacted the tower and informed them of his emergency, but received no reply and so circled the field.)

At 1143, a USAF B-25 made a practice instrument approach to Runway 36, passing over the field without landing. A minute later, Eastern 537 was cleared to land number one on Runway 3; the DC-4 was at this point on its downwind leg, west of the field. It made a continuous turn from that leg to a final approach to Runway 3.

Bridoux was told to enter left traffic pattern, and to call the tower when he was west of the field. There was no acknowledgement from the P-38. Instead, Bridoux continued his high straight-in approach – to Runway 3. In the tower, traffic controller Glen T. Tigner desperately called to warn him. "Bolivia 927 . . . Bolivia . . . Bolivia . . . turn left . . . turn left . . . Traffic, Eastern DC-4 on final approach and below!" The DC-4 was now only three-quarters of a mile from landing on Runway 3; the P-38 simply didn't respond to the frantic entreaties.

With seconds before the collision was clearly going to occur, Tigner changed frequencies and told the DC-4 crew to turn left because the P-38 was on the approach behind them. The captain immediately applied power, levelled off and turned left − but before more than five degrees of turn had been made, the two aircraft collided at an altitude of 300 feet, around half a mile from the approach.

Witnesses to the collision described the P-38 hurtling like "a huge explosive shell" into the packed DC-4, the fighter's twin propellers chewing through the larger aircraft, and breaking its back. After its left propeller hit the DC-4 just forward of the trailing edge of the wing, the P-38 ricocheted off, plummeting into the river Potomac, as the DC-4 was torn in two in mid-air. The tail section scattered debris and bodies as it fell to earth, smashing into the riverbank, just missing the Mount Vernon Memorial Highway, near Four Mile Run. The front hit the water.

Civilians helped to drag bodies and possessions from the river, including one woman, who was found floating face down. She was bleeding from the mouth but didn't survive long, one of seven people who survived the impact for a short time. Ambulances and crash trucks from the airport were quickly at the scene, and USAF officials from the base at Bolling Field, on the other side of the Potomac, also came to assist. Among the victims were Congressman George Bates of Massachusetts, *New Yorker* cartoonist Helen Hokinson, and Michael Kennedy, a former Congressman from New York.

Bridoux was severely injured but survived the crash. Sergeant Morris Flounlacker from Bolling Air Force Base jumped into the freezing cold waters of the Potomac to save him, just as the Bolivian lost consciousness. He had a broken back, crushed ribs and severe concussion. The Bolivian ambassador visited him and told the *New York Times* "the pilot told him he had been occupied with engine difficulties and apparently did not hear the final warning from the control tower."

The CAB assessed the various testimonies, and faithfully recorded Bridoux's account – including his claims that he took off from a different runway initially, and that he saw other aircraft on approach to the airport during his flight, neither of which tallied with the official logs, and that he was cleared to land on Runway 3 with no indication that there was anyone ahead of him. He also admitted that he heard the instruction to "clear to the left" but claimed the tower didn't use any call sign, so he didn't realise that it was meant for him. When he was challenged about the course he had taken, he could not describe any landmarks in the area he said that he had been: according to him, navigation by landmarks "is not my way to fly. I do not take care of the small details on the ground." In as polite official language as possible, the CAB made it clear that they simply didn't believe Bridoux's story. (They also noted that the tower could have responded differently, although they accepted that the controller took action that he believed would rectify the situation.)

The *Time* report on the incident, which made clear that they weren't blaming Bridoux "until the CAB finished its exhaustive inquiry", made one telling remark about the Bolivian pilot. "He had burned for years, said friends, to perform some Lindbergh-like feat of aerial derring-do which would 'Make Bolivia famous'." Unfortunately, he achieved infamy.

THE GRAND CANYON COLLISION

Although the death toll in the 1949 Washington disaster was horrific, it was exceeded only seven years later in the collision between United Airlines Flight 718 and TWA Flight 2, when 128 people lost their lives. The "Grand Canyon collision" as it became known was a catalyst for change within the aviation industry. "The Federal Aviation Administration was created out of the ashes of that Grand Canyon crash," Sid McGuirk, an associate professor of air traffic management at Embry-Riddle Aeronautical University, told the *Los Angeles Times* in 2006. It was by no means the first mid-air collision since the Washington incident: according to *Time*, 254 commercial and private planes collided in flight between 1948 and 1955, and there was an average of four near misses a day by September 1956.

At the time that the Grand Canyon collision occurred on 30 June 1956, airspace was not as well controlled as it is today. Flights operating under instrument flight rules (IFR) were more regulated than those on visual flight rules (VFR), but there were areas – particularly over places like the Grand Canyon – that were outside air traffic control's jurisdiction, where the pilots had more latitude than they do now. In the case of this collision, where it seemed as if one plane was operating under IFR, the other effectively on VFR, this led to one crew receiving initial blame for the collision, but it highlighted a fundamental flaw in the system – and with increasing numbers of aircraft in flight at any one time, and the advent of jet aircraft imminent, more accidents were seen as inevitable.

TWA Flight 2, a Lockheed L-1049 Super Constellation, should have left Los Angeles at 0830 Pacific Standard Time, but minor problems had delayed departure, and it didn't take off from runway 25 until 0901, with Captain Jack S. Gandy and Co-pilot James H. Ritner at the controls. Its destination was Kansas City, Missouri, and its IFR flight plan took it via controlled airspace on Green Airway 5 and Amber Airway 2, then at Daggett turning towards the radio range at Trinidad (Colorado), then towards Dodge City, before entering controlled space again on Victor Airway 10 coming into Kansas City. Their assigned cruising altitude was 19,000 feet, and they anticipated a true airspeed of 270 knots.

United Airlines Flight 718 was a DC-7 Mainliner, flown by Captain Robert Shirley, First Officer Robert Harms, and Flight Engineer Gerard Fiore. Its destination was Chicago, and it took off from Los Angeles three minutes behind TWA 2, at 0904. It was also on an IFR flight plan, using Green Airway 5 to reach a point near Palm Springs, where it would then turn towards the radio range at Needles, California, and from there to the range at Painted Desert just beyond the eastern end of the Grand Canyon and various other ranges until it reached controlled airspace around Chicago. The assigned cruising altitude was 21,000 feet, with a true airspeed of 288 knots. Their departure time should have been 0845.

As the United DC-7 climbed to 21,000 feet (under VFR conditions, as requested by the Los Angeles controller) the pilots made regular reports back on its position. These were relayed to the air traffic controllers. As it passed over Palm Springs, they estimated the aircraft would reach Needles at 1000 and the Painted Desert at 1034. They actually reached Needles two minutes ahead of schedule, and corrected their estimate for the Painted Desert to 1031.

By this time, Captain Gandy had requested a change in flight plan. They had climbed to 19,000 feet (also under VFR conditions, at the controller's request), and because of thunderheads in the vicinity, asked to use Victor Airway 210 to reach Daggett. This was a routine request, and approved accordingly. At 0921, they requested to increase their altitude from 19,000 feet to 21,000 feet. Air traffic control refused permission because of other traffic – United 718 – so Captain Gandy changed the request and asked for a clearance of "1,000 feet on top". What this meant was that TWA 2 would fly a thousand feet above the clouds, until such time as they could properly ascend to 21,000 feet. At the time Captain Gandy asked, 19,000 feet was already 1,000 on top of the cloud level. Air traffic control approved the request with a proviso: "ATC clears TWA 2, maintain at least 1,000 on top. Advise TWA 2 his traffic is United 718, direct Durango, estimating Needles at 9:57." This 1,000 on top put TWA 2 under VFR rather than IFR. Air traffic control had no responsibility for the separation of the flights, since they should be able to see each other. (The manual was clear: "During the time an IFR flight is operating in VFR weather conditions, it is the direct responsibility of the pilot to avoid other aircraft, since VFR flights may be operating in the same area without knowledge of ATC.") There was no requirement to inform United 718 of the potential presence of TWA 2 – and the controller hadn't told TWA 2 about United's presence as a traffic advisory, but simply to explain why he was refusing permission to ascend to 21,000 feet.

At 0959, a minute after United 718 had provided its revised estimate of 1031 at the Painted Desert line, TWA 2 confirmed that it was 1,000 on top, and therefore at 21,000 feet, and expected to be at the Painted Desert checkpoint at 1031. For the next half hour, the two flights flew towards each other, neither realizing that they would arrive simultaneously in the same area at the same height. The only person who had this information was the controller in Salt Lake City, who received notification about TWA 2 at 1001, and United 718 at 1013, but, as was later explained, the Painted Desert line of position was nearly 175 miles long with no definite position within that distance. The estimates of the flights did not necessarily mean they would converge, but "merely that both would pass the line eastbound at that time". (The CAB noted that "the existing control concept, Air Traffic Control policies and procedures, and the express duties of a controller" did not require the controller to notify the two aircraft.)

At 1031, a radio transmission was picked up in both Salt Lake City and San Francisco. At the time it was unintelligible, but after the recordings were analysed, it became evident that it was the final message from the United DC-7. First Officer Harms' voice could be heard: "Salt Lake, United 718 . . . ah . . . we're going in." Further investigation revealed someone else, probably Captain Shirley, had been picked up on the recording screaming something like "Pull up!" The CAB report noted "both general voice patterns, particularly as to pitch, showed the speakers were under great emotional stress, indicating that they were already in serious trouble."

That was an understatement. High above the Grand Canyon, the two aircraft had collided. The DC-7 was banking to the right and pitching down, but its upraised left wing just clipped the top of the TWA Constellation's vertical stabilizer. The lower surface of the wing hit the upper aft fuselage of the Constellation with sufficient force to completely destroy the fuselage, and the structural integrity of the left wing outer panel. The aircraft were passing each other laterally, so the left fin leading edge of the Constellation and the left wing tip of the DC-7 made contact, tearing pieces off from both. The United's propeller started to cut into the aft baggage compartment of the TWA aircraft. All of that took just half a second to occur.

The TWA's fuselage had been ripped open from the main cabin door to the tail, and its empennage separated. The aircraft pitched down and fell to the ground in two main pieces. The United DC-7 had lost most of its left outer wing, and its horizontal stabilizer was hit by debris from the Constellation. With restricted aileron control, the DC-7 fell rather less steeply.

The forward part of the TWA aircraft hit the north-east slope of Temple Butte, around sixteen miles north-east of Grand Canyon Village, at around 3,400 feet, and the wreckage was scattered along the Colorado river. The tail landed nearly intact. The DC-7 hit the south face of Chuar Butte, near the confluence of the Colorado and Little Colorado rivers, at around 4,040 feet, and disintegrated on impact. Much of the wreckage was – and remains to this day – inaccessible. The impacts carved two black burns into the buff-coloured terrain of the canyon.

Frantic calls were made by the airlines' ground communications teams to their respective aircraft on every frequency that the crews might be using, but there was no reply. At 1151, a missing aircraft alert was issued, and a search and rescue operation mounted.

Although *Time* magazine initially suggested that debris was spotted around 1200, it was actually early evening before the wreckage was found. Palen Hudgin ran Grand Canyon Airlines, providing tours of the area, along with his brother Henry; Palen recalled seeing some light smoke rising from the canyon earlier in the day, but, as his brother explained around the fiftieth anniversary of the crash, "[t]here was a lot of lightning that morning so he didn't think much of it". However, when he realized that there wasn't that much vegetation around to burn, the brothers flew back. "We saw the United Airlines plane in a crevice and the TWA on a slope on one of the peaks," Henry Hudgin recalled. "The thing that amazed us was the United fuselage was fully intact, although the wings and tail were sheared off. And there wasn't much smoke around it . . . We were both really surprised the next morning when we flew out there to see it was totally burned up." At the time, he told reporters, "From the amount of stuff and the distribution of it and the way the planes were demolished, it looked like there wouldn't be any life there."

The next day, they returned to confirm the sighting, accompanied by the Coconino County Deputy Sheriff, and then a helicopter crew fought turbulent air to land beside the wrecks. They confirmed that everyone was dead. All those who saw the position of the wreckage were in little doubt about the cause of the accident: Captain Byrd Ryland from March AFB in California, in charge of the search and rescue mission, told reporters that the aircraft "must have" collided in the air. Nine Army helicopters were on standby to bring the bodies out, along with ground vehicles; the problem was that there was only one highway through the region, at an altitude of about 6,000 feet, but it was 20 miles west of the crash scene.

The conditions were so bad that thirteen people had to spend the night of Monday 1 July in the canyon after a helicopter had nearly hit a plane. These included specialists from the Civil Aeronautics Administration who were assisting the CAB. When they found paint from the DC-7's propeller on the Continental's door, the cause of the accident was confirmed. In all, seventy-six trips were made over the next ten days, in conditions that some pilots compared unfavourably with those they later experienced in Vietnam. To try to retrieve the bodies from the United DC-7, a specially trained mountain rescue and recovery team were brought in from Switzerland, assisted by two American climbers, including Dave Lewis from Colorado. "I walked to the edge of the flat ground and I was suddenly staring at a steep gully packed with blackened wreckage and all surrounded by spectacular scenery," Lewis recalled. "It's indescribable if you've never seen a plane crash that burned. It's just chaos. How do you describe particular brands of chaos?"

Sixty-six of those on TWA 2 were interred in a mass grave at the Flagstaff Citizen's Cemetery on 9 July; sixty-three of these were unidentified. Four others who were identified were sent back to their homes for burial. The next day, efforts to recover bodies from the United DC-7 had ceased, with half the victims identified and shipped home; the other remains were buried in three caskets at Grand Canyon Cemetery on 12 July.

The CAB investigation began immediately, and the discovery of the paint from the propeller confirmed their suspicions. What they could not explain was how both flights were off-course, as revealed by the crash site, unless the pilots were independently providing a scenic view of the Canyon for their passengers – California Representative Carl Hinshaw went so far as to announce within two weeks of the crash that the accident happened because "they were too close because they were both looking at the Grand Canyon".

Initially, the CAB blamed the TWA crew for the crash, saying that because they were on VFR, flying 1,000 on top, they bore the responsibility to see and be seen. This was challenged by the Board's own Bureau of Safety Regulations who pointed out that both flights were in uncontrolled air space. The controllers' manual made it clear that "Clearances authorize flight within control zones and control areas only; no responsibility for separation of aircraft outside these areas is accepted". United company procedures meant that their aircraft was also flying under VFR, rather than under IFR, so both pilots had the responsibility. Analysis of the weather conditions prevalent at the time showed that there might have been cumulus-type clouds in the accident area, but these shouldn't have affected the crews' ability to see each other, although it could have reduced the collision avoidance time.

The CAB's final report came with a heavy rider: the Board "has learned all that existing methods of investigation and evaluation enabled it to do. This was done without the assistance of survivors or eyewitnesses whose testimony is considered imperative to a complete knowledge and to single conclusions in the collision-type accident." With that in mind, they determined that the probable cause was that "the pilots did not see each other in time to avoid the collision". Why that was, they couldn't determine, but it was from one or a combination of: "Intervening clouds reducing time for visual separation, visual limitations due to cockpit visibility, and preoccupation with normal cockpit duties, preoccupation with matters unrelated to cockpit duties such as attempting to provide the passengers with a more scenic view of the Grand Canyon area, physiological limits to human vision reducing the time opportunity to see and avoid the other aircraft, or insufficiency of en route air traffic advisory information due to inadequacy of facilities and lack of personnel in air traffic control."

Action was demanded, and many changes were implemented to increase safety in the air; however, military and civilian flights were still independently controlled, and it was only after United Airlines 736, a DC-7, collided with a USAF North American F-100F-5-NA Super Sabre fighter jet on 21 April 1958 near Las Vegas, with the loss of 49 lives, that the situation was resolved. As the editorial in the *Deseret News* pointed out the next day: "There is so much room up there, it would seem all but impossible for two planes to come together at the same spot at the same time. Yet it has happened again . . . The Las Vegas crash provides grim emphasis to the argument vigorously pressed by the *Deseret News* last year, that all military student-training flights be performed out of bounds of commercial airways . . . What's the answer to the mid-air crash enigma? Two moves should be made: 1 – Bring the nation's air traffic control system up to date, and 2 – designate areas for commercial plane travel and entirely separate areas for jet-training navigation. Anything less is not enough for the flying public's safety and peace of mind."

Four months later, the Federal Aviation Act was signed into law, giving the Federal Aviation Agency total authority over American air space. Despite all the changes, it was not enough to stop one of the largest losses of life in American aviation history from happening two years later over New York City.

FALLING FROM THE SKY

"I remember looking out the plane window at the snow below covering the city. It looked like a picture out of a fairy book. Then all of a sudden there was an explosion. The plane started to fall and people started to scream. I held on to my seat and then the plane crashed. That's all I remember until I woke up."

So said eleven-year-old Stephen Lambert Baltz, the only survivor of the deadliest air disaster to hit America to that date, talking to doctors in Methodist Hospital where he had been taken suffering extensive burns. It was the first major collision of the jet age, as United Airlines Flight 826 – a DC-8-11 – hit TWA Flight 266, a Lockheed L-1049 Super Constellation, on the morning of Friday 16 December 1960. The United aircraft fell to earth in Brooklyn, devastating the neighbourhood of Park Slope; the TWA's final resting place was the grass runway at Miller Army Airfield on Staten Island. Including Baltz, who succumbed to his injuries less than 24 hours after the crash, 136 people lost their lives.

The "Coding Apparatus For Flight Recorders And The Like" had been patented by Professor James J. Ryan at the University of Minnesota in 1959, and the investigation into the cause of the mid-air collision was one of the first times that data from a "black box" was available. From this, the exact time and location of the accident could be ascertained, as well as other key pieces of information. (Cockpit voice recorders weren't patented until the following year.)

TWA 266 began its journey in Dayton, Ohio, with Captain David A. Wollam and First Officer Dean T. Bowen at the controls. After a stop at Columbus, Ohio, the Constellation was en route to LaGuardia Airport in Queens, New York, with thirty-nine passengers on board, for a flight that should have taken ninety-two minutes. Its flight plan was changed by clearances that allowed it to cruise at 19,000 feet, and at 1005 Eastern Standard Time, it reported in to the New York Air Route Traffic Control Center

(ARTCC) over Selinsgrove at 19,000 feet. It was cleared to descend in stages, and to cross Allentown, Pennsylvania at 11,000 feet. At 1019, TWA 266 reported that it had reached Allentown at the instructed altitude, and New York ATC confirmed it had the aircraft on radar, cleared it to the next intersection, and asked it to stand by for descent. At 1021, New York Center cleared the Constellation to descend to, and maintain, 10,000 feet.

United 826 was heading from Chicago's O'Hare Airport for New York International Airport in Jamaica, New York (better known then as Idlewild, and now as JFK). Captain Robert H. Sawyer and First Officer Robert W. Fiebing were in charge of the jet, and had already flown it from Los Angeles to Chicago before taking a two-hour stopover. They departed from Chicago at 0911 with seventy-six passengers. The flight to New York was uneventful, cruising at 27,000 feet. They contacted New York ARTCC at 1012 and were told "radar service not available" and to descend to and maintain flight level 250 (25,000 feet). At 1015, they were given a set of clearances for their pattern over New York, and told to "maintain flight level 250". They acknowledged.

At 1021, United 826 contacted the radio company who operated United's systems, and informed them that "No. 2 navigation receive accessory unit inoperative", which meant that it was harder for them to navigate in IFR conditions. The information about the VOR unit (the part of the navigational system which wasn't working) was passed to United, but not to anyone else.

A few seconds later, New York ARTCC contacted the jet giving clearance to descend to 13,000 feet, but Captain Sawyer preferred to "hold upstairs". The controller passed responsibility for the United flight to another controller, who confirmed radar contact with them at 1022. The United crew explained that they'd rather "hold upstairs than down" if there was going to be a delay, that they were "going to need ¾ of a mile", and requested the weather.

TWA 266 also needed a weather report, and received this at 1023. Over the next three minutes, New York Center cleared the Constellation to descend to and maintain 9,000 feet, and to report leaving 10,000 feet. This was acknowledged at 1026. A minute later, they advised they were over Solberg, New Jersey, and were told to contact LaGuardia Approach Control, which they did at 1026.22. They were told to maintain 9,000 feet.

United 826 was over Allentown at 25,000 feet at 1023 and had received the weather report for Idlewild at 1024. A few seconds later they announced that they were "starting down". At 1025, they were given a revised clearance, which shortened their route to the Preston checkpoint, near South Amboy in New Jersey, by approximately 11 miles. At 1026.49, they were cleared to descend to and maintain 11,000 feet.

Over the next seven minutes, something went seriously wrong – far from holding over Preston, as both the pilots and controllers believed they were doing, they were in fact over Staten Island. United 826 only had one radio receiver operative (unknown to the controllers) and to use the aircraft direction-finding equipment would require some rapid mental calculations which pilots under pressure could easily get wrong. When responsibility for the flight was handed to Idlewild Approach Control, United 826 stated they were approaching Preston at 5,000 feet – in fact they had gone past Preston, the holding limit, several seconds before, and were several miles beyond where they should have turned into the oval-shaped holding pattern. They simply should not have been in the skies over New York at that point. Nor should they have been going at more than 360 miles per hour.

TWA 266 had gone through a standard descent, and was preparing for its touchdown at LaGuardia, descending to 1,500 feet at 1033.14, and acknowledging an instruction to turn left to heading 130 at 1033.23. Three seconds later, an urgent message was sent to the Constellation. "That appears to be jet traffic off your right now 3 o'clock at one mile, northeast-bound." At 1033.33, six seconds of open microphone sound were heard.

The radar at LaGuardia confirmed that two targets had merged about a mile west of Miller Army Air Field, in New Dorp, Staten Island. However, because there was no indication of altitude, they were unable to tell immediately whether this simply meant that the two aircraft had passed over each other.

It didn't. In the fog, the United jet had slammed into the right-hand side of the Constellation, effectively running it over from behind. The engine nearest the end of the United's right wing crashed through the fuselage of the TWA aircraft then broke off. One of the passengers on board the Constellation was sucked into the engine of the DC-8. Divided into three by the impact, the Constellation spiralled down onto the army field, disintegrating as it fell, with some parts landing in New York Harbour. Witnesses said that it sounded like "a thousand dishes crashing from the sky".

One blip on the screen continued north-east for about eight miles – it was the DC-8 falling 60 feet per second. Whether by a miracle or thanks to some last ditch efforts by the pilots, it banked to the right just before it would have hit St Augustine's Academy on Sterling Place below Sixth Avenue, in Park Slope, Brooklyn. The dying jet lost altitude completely above Sterling Place, and at roughly 200 mph, the right wing hit the roof of the brownstone at number 126, leaving two feet of the tip protruding through the roof. The fuselage veered to the left and crashed into the local evangelical church, Pillar of Fire. The aircraft exploded, killing those passengers in one section of the cabin, as well as the church's ninety-year-old caretaker, Wallace E. Lewis.

The left wing, now ablaze, sheared into an apartment next to the church, and the other section crashed into McCaddin's Funeral Home on the corner of Seventh Avenue and Sterling Place. The tail section fell upright into that intersection, to become the most obvious visual symbol of the crash. A stream of jet fuel ignited into flame, setting off the gasoline tanks of the cars parked nearby. Two men selling Christmas trees on a corner, a man shovelling snow, a doctor walking his dog and an employee at a local butcher's were also killed. Screams could be heard emanating from the fuselage, but no one bar Stephen Baltz survived for more than a few moments. Ten four-storey tenement buildings as well as the church were set ablaze by the crash, with more than 250 firemen and fifty pieces of fire apparatus rushed to the scene.

Baltz had been hurled to a soft landing in a snow bank, but was seriously burned – to the extent that local resident Dorothy M. Fletcher thought the young Caucasian was an African-American. He was still conscious, but in shock, as he was taken to Methodist Hospital. New Yorkers rallied behind him, particularly after a photo of him lying in the snow, sheltered from the falling snow by an umbrella as passers-by tried to comfort him, appeared on the front page of the newspapers. They were desperately hoping for another miracle, but Baltz's injuries were far too severe, and although he had drifted in and out of consciousness throughout the night, at one point asking if there was a television he could watch, he died at 10 a.m. The nurse who tended him, Barbara Stull, hadn't realized that he was too badly burned to live: "I was probably the only person who thought he might make it," she commented years later.

The TWA Constellation had narrowly missed a housing development as it – along with the wing from the United jet – fell onto the recently vacated airfield. Local residents tried to pull people from the burning wreckage before trained rescue workers arrived. Once the bodies were recovered, the investigators set to work, with representatives from the Federal Aviation Agency, Civil Aeronautics Board and the FBI, with FAA Administrator Elwood Quesada racing to New York to direct the investigation. Within a week, "educated guesswork by trained observers" (as *Time* called it) had deduced that the United flight had flown beyond the holding area into the LaGuardia approach.

The CAB took its time over the investigation, and released its report on 18 June 1962. The probable cause of the accident was that United 826 proceeded beyond its clearance limit and the confines of the airspace allocated to the flight by Air Traffic Control. Contributing factors included "the high rate of speed" of the DC-8 as it approached (what it thought was) the Preston intersection, and the change of clearance that reduced the en route distance by approximately 11 miles. Some called the verdict a whitewash, claiming that United had an unsatisfactory training programme, and that the airline routinely falsified air safety records.

Lawsuits totalling over $300 million were filed; United was held responsible for 61 per cent of the claims, TWA 15 per cent, and the US government the remaining 24 per cent, since the airplanes' instrument landing approach had been guided by FAA controllers.

Changes that resulted from the collision included a speed limit of 250 knots below 10,000 feet, and a requirement for pilots to report all problems with navigational equipment to controllers. Tower controllers were also now required to acknowledge transfer of responsibility for aircraft.

A WING AND A PRAYER

Not every mid-air collision resulted in the deaths of all involved; when TWA Flight 42 hit Eastern Flight 853 on 4 December 1965, all aboard the TWA Boeing 707 survived, and there were only four casualties among the passengers and crew of the Lockheed L-1049C Super Constellation, including its captain, who returned to the burning wreckage to try to save one of the passengers and paid for his bravery with his life.

TWA 42 was on its way from San Francisco to New York's John F. Kennedy Airport, heading on an IFR flight plan at an assigned altitude of 11,000 feet. EA 853 was on a short hop from Boston, Massachusetts, to Newark Airport, New Jersey, also on an IFR flight plan, but at 10,000 feet. Both were approaching the VORTAC navigation beacon situated at Carmel, New York at their designated heights – but as they saw each other, both sets of flight crews believed that they were on a collision course.

The 707 was being flown on autopilot with the altitude-hold feature engaged, but Captain Thomas H. Carroll had his left hand on the yoke. As they neared the beacon, Carroll saw a white and blue aircraft at his 10 o'clock position. It seemed to him that it was heading straight for him, and he disengaged the autopilot by thumbing the switch (which worked the same way as tapping the brake or accelerator in a car to disengage cruise control), put the wheel hard over to the right and pulled back on the yoke. His co-pilot, First Officer Leo M. Smith, did the same. The aircraft rolled to the right, but the pair realized that this wouldn't be sufficient to avoid collision, so they tried to reverse the wheel to the left and both pushed on the yoke. However, before the 707 could respond, they felt two shocks and the jet began a steep dive.

The first order of business was to regain control of the aircraft, which Captain Carroll quickly did, and the crew began to assess the damage, without alerting the passengers to what had happened. The crew could see that the left wing tip was missing, so they contacted New York ATC, and declared an emergency since they had collided with another aircraft. Clearance was given to land the 707 but before Captain Carroll could do so, he flew a large 360-degree left turn south-east of the airport to confirm that the landing gear hadn't been affected by the collision and was fully down. He then brought the 707 in at around 1640. About 25 feet of the wing was missing and an engine had impact abrasions, but hadn't detached from the aircraft. There were other signs of damage to the aircraft, but no one on board was hurt.

The Constellation crew and passengers weren't so lucky. Forty-nine of them received injuries of some description during the incident, as well as the quartet who died. First Officer Roger I. Holt Jr had observed the TWA jet coming towards them as they emerged from a puff of cloud, and put his hands on the control wheel. Exclaiming, "Look out!" he made what he described as "a very rapid application of up elevator simultaneously with the captain". The g-forces invoked were sufficient to pull the crew into their seats. And it provoked the accident that they were trying to avoid. (One of the passengers had spotted the 707 coming towards them and was trying to take a picture of the jet but couldn't do so because the Constellation pulled up and started a left turn.)

The Eastern aircraft collided with the 707 and continued to climb. It then shuddered and began a left turning dive. In the cockpit, Captain Charles J. White tried to ascertain what was available to him. There was no response from the controls or trim tabs, so the only way he could regain control of the aircraft was by power application. Once the aircraft had descended through the solid clouds, recovery was made with the use of throttles, and White and Holt zoomed into the clouds to discover a power setting which could give them some form of descent and level attitude with a degree of consistency.

Eastern 853 flew over Danbury Airport in Connecticut at a height of around 2,000 to 3,000 feet but they couldn't make an approach: an airspeed of between 125 and 140 knots had to be maintained. The nose would rise when power was added, and fall when it was removed, and a rate of descent of around 500 feet per minute could be achieved; if they tried to descend faster, the aircraft would stall.

They needed to find somewhere to land rapidly, and Captain

White decided that they would have to use an open field. On the Connecticut–New York border most of the fields had stone walls around them, but the captain saw a pasture halfway up Hunt Mountain which would fit the bill. Using asymmetric thrust to line the aircraft up, he warned the passengers to brace themselves (they'd already been warned that there had been a collision and a crash landing was imminent), and headed towards the hillside with wheels and flaps retracted. He knew that the nose would smash into the hill on the current path, so he would need to use some power to lift it just as they touched down – but if he applied the power too early, the aircraft would rise, miss the field, then stall and drop in a flaming heap. At precisely the right instant before impact, White revved the engines to full power, and in what fellow Constellation pilot Gary Holt described as "one of the most magnificent feats of airmanship in the history of flying" he managed to get the belly of the ship skimming above the grass.

The left wing hit a tree just before touchdown, then hit a second one which tore it off completely. The remainder of the aircraft slammed into a gully, then skidded up the hill, pieces ripping off and falling down into the field. The aircraft was on fire by this point, as all four engines broke loose, followed by the tail. The stub of the left wing dug into the ground, acting as a pivot, yanking the fuselage around to the left, and it cracked beneath the strain into three pieces.

The passengers got out of the aircraft as quickly as they could through whatever hole in the fuselage they could find, or the cabin doors. The stewardesses did their best to assist, but both of them had been injured – one had a crushed spinal disc, the other had five broken bones in her back.

Local residents quickly came to the scene and ambulances took the co-pilot and flight engineer to hospital – the latter with little memory of anything after the final approach. Although there was no conclusive evidence to prove it, it seemed that following the crash landing, Captain White went into the passenger cabin to assist a soldier whose seat belt had jammed. Safety investigator Jack Carroll said shortly afterwards: "In my personal opinion, there is little doubt that Captain White had deliberately gone back to the cabin to help the young soldier." Both the pilot and the soldier were overcome by the poisonous fumes. Two other passengers died in hospital at Danbury from their injuries, but fifty people survived the accident.

But if both aircraft had been at their allotted height, as seemed to be the case, why did the crew of Eastern 853 believe they were about to hit the 707? As the CAB report noted, "the primary device used to provide orientation with respect to the horizontal and vertical planes, depth and distance is the eye", and they determined that the sort of cloud tops through which the Constellation was flying produced an optical illusion. The probable cause was "misjudgement of altitude separation by the crew of EA 853 because of an optical illusion created by the up-slope effect of cloud tops resulting in an evasive maneuver by the EA 853 crew and a reactionary evasive maneuver by the TW 42 crew".

According to Captain White's nephew, John Frasca, "My incredible uncle was buried with full military honours at Arlington Memorial Cemetery and with a long line of Eastern captains in full uniform saluting him. Many of the survivors also attended. People were stopping their cars alongside a nearby freeway and stood there in respect and silence." It was a fitting tribute to a masterful piece of flying.

CONFLICT OF INTEREST?

The collision over Hendersonville, North Carolina could easily have cost more lives than it did, given that the aircraft involved crashed very near summer camps – only 50 yards away, according to the Associated Press' contemporary report. It was one of the first major incidents that the newly formed National Transportation Safety Board (NTSB) investigated, and became the subject of some controversy three decades later when the NTSB's decision was challenged by an amateur local historian.

John T. McNaughton, who had just been named Secretary of the Navy, as well as his wife and son, were on board the Boeing 727-22 which collided with a twin-engine Cessna 310 on 19 July 1967, a mere four months after Piedmont Airlines had begun using jet aircraft. They were among the seventy-nine fatalities on the jet, in addition to the three who lost their lives on the Cessna. Captain Ray F. Schulte was in charge of the 727, with First Officer Thomas C. Conrad and Flight Engineer Lawrence C. Wilson alongside him in the cockpit.

In the Cessna were pilot Dave Addison, and insurance executives Ralph Reynolds and Robert Anderson, heading from Charlotte, North Carolina to the Asheville Municipal Airport. After they had received the weather report for their route, Addison had requested an IFR clearance to "on top" (i.e. go under instrument conditions through the cloud layer, and once on top of the clouds, to operate under VFR conditions). The Cessna left Charlotte at 1130 Eastern Daylight Time, and climbed to 8,000 feet. At 1151, it was cleared by Atlanta ATC "to the Asheville VOR, descend and maintain seven thousand, expect ILS approach at Asheville". The Cessna contacted Asheville Approach Control and reported that it was passing the 340-degree radial of the Spartanburg VOR.

Five minutes later, at 1156.28, Approach Control gave this clearance to the Cessna pilot: "Three one two one Sugar cleared over the VOR to Broad River, correction make that the Asheville radio beacon . . . over the VOR to the Asheville radio beacon. Maintain seven thousand, report passing the VOR." The Cessna acknowledged the instruction a few seconds later.

Departure time for the Piedmont 727, Flight 22, should have been 1128, but the flight had been delayed after it had left Atlanta late, so it was running half an hour behind when it eventually started its take-off roll on Asheville's Runway 16. The time was 1158.07, and Captain Schulte had been instructed to maintain the runway heading until reaching 5,000 feet. This was to ensure that it kept separated from the Cessna – the 727 would stay on a south-easterly course until the Cessna had reported being over the VOR.

Thirteen seconds into the take-off roll – and of course, unknown to the captain of the 727 since, following standard practice, they were on different radio frequencies – the Cessna reported that it "just passed over the VOR, we're headed for the . . . [four second pause] . . . for . . . ah . . . Asheville now." (The question of what, if anything, was said during those four seconds became critical later.) Approach control acknowledged that the Cessna was "by the VOR" and ordered it to "descend and maintain six thousand." The Cessna confirmed it was "leaving seven now".

That was sufficient for the tower to clear Piedmont 22 at 1159.44 to "climb unrestricted to the VOR, report passing the VOR". The acknowledgment of that report was the last communication with the 727. The aircraft began to bank on its journey to Roanoke.

At 1200.02, the Cessna was cleared for "an ADF-2 approach to runway one six, report the Asheville radio beacon inbound." The Cessna pilot simply said, "Roger", without repeating back the instructions.

Watching from the ground, twelve-year-old Alden Conner was following the jet's progress through the sky – still something of a novelty. "Look, Daddy," he told his father, "that little plane is gonna hit it." To his father, Thomas, it looked as if "the little plane [was] coming up under the big one".

Witness William N. Ford saw the whole incident play out in front of him as he sat eating his lunch. "As I was taking in the sight of this graceful aircraft [the 727] heading to the south-east,

I noticed a black dot moving to the south-west and growing ever larger until it became identifiable as a twin-engine private aircraft. I glanced back and forth, with the odd sense that a piece of transparent graph paper had suddenly been placed in front of my eyes. I was studying the relative vectors of the planes. I judged that they would, from my vantage point, appear to cross the same point at the same time. But I felt confident that they were separated vertically by at least a thousand feet [as the FAA required at that time]. Then, in a split second, I realized that there was no vertical distance at all between them. The Cessna slammed into the side of the 727 and exploded, a mushroom of flames and debris."

The two aircraft had collided at an altitude of 6,132 feet, eight miles south-east of the airport. For some reason, instead of turning right at the beacon and heading north-west, the Cessna had turned left, heading south-west. After the impact, no one saw the Cessna again – but the fall to earth of the 707 was observed by dozens. The NTSB determined that "the jet continued straight ahead momentarily, then nosed over and fell rapidly to the ground", although there were some eye witnesses who told newspapers at the time that it was under control for a few seconds as the pilots tried to bring it down onto the nearby highway, Interstate 26. However, after a second explosion, the 707 was in various pieces: the body fell nose first, hitting the ground about 200 feet from the interstate. Smaller pieces, and the bodies thrown from the plane by the explosion landed in nearby areas.

Over 400 emergency personnel were called to the site, but there was no possibility of any survivors. By chance, no one on the ground had been injured. The NTSB's chief investigator, Tom Saunders, was immediately sent to the site, and began work assembling the pieces of the two aircraft to assist with the enquiry. The FAA announced immediately that the Cessna "was about 12 miles south of where it should have been", and it became clear that the Cessna pilot was likely to be held responsible.

The NTSB report indeed found that "probable cause of this accident was the deviation from its IFR clearance resulting in a flightpath into airspace allocated to the Piedmont Boeing 727. The reason for such deviation cannot be specifically or positively identified. The minimum control procedures utilized by the FAA in its handling of the Cessna were a contributing factor." In other words, the ATC should have realized that the Cessna effectively was lost, and assisted earlier.

Questions were raised over the NTSB findings particularly since they could not determine why the Cessna pilot had made such a fundamental error – even if the air traffic control, as Piedmont Airways' Don Collins noted, "didn't do their job". During the hearings, there had been some doubt as to who was actually flying the Cessna at the time of impact – although the recordings certainly seemed to indicate that Addison, who was fully qualified, was piloting, there was evidence that one of the passengers might have been at the controls. But Addison himself wasn't familiar with the area, and – at least according to the NTSB report – "engaged in poor flight planning". It was perhaps also indicative that the maps and approach charts found at the site were three years out of date.

Local historian Paul Houle helped to raise funds for a memorial to the crash victims in 2004, and decided to investigate the causes of the accident. "Once I started looking into the factual circumstances of the collision, the NTSB's findings didn't seem entirely truthful, and certainly not fair and just to the three men from Missouri. I just had to try to set the public record straight for those guys and especially their families," he explained in 2007. He believed that because the NTSB was still a new agency at the time, and not independent from the Department of Transportation, they had not been as critical of the FAA as they should have been, making public the tower recordings which showed that in the supposed "four-second gap" the Cessna pilot could clearly be heard given a course heading, which the tower did not correct.

He also learned that examination of the cockpit voice recorder from the 727 revealed that during the run-up to the collision, the crew were dealing with a smouldering cigarette; Houle argued that this would have diverted the pilots' attention and perhaps had they been focusing elsewhere they would have spotted the Cessna. He suggested that the restricted movement order was breached by the crew and that they should not have begun a turn, insinuating that they were trying to make up the lost half-hour. (This particularly incensed Captain Schulte's fellow pilots.)

Houle further discovered that the lead investigator, Tom Saunders, was the brother of Piedmont Airlines Vice President, Zeke

Saunders. "Even the appearance of impropriety was just as bad as impropriety," Houle pointed out. However, it did appear as if this had been dealt with at the time: Tom Saunders' name was next in line for an investigation, while his brother Zeke stepped down from any involvement in the enquiry, leaving Piedmont's Director of Flight Operations to answer questions on behalf of the airline. Houle accepted that this happened, but still maintained in his petition to the NTSB that "The omission from the final report of vital evidence that would have been highly beneficial to Lanseair [the owners of the Cessna] and extremely detrimental to Piedmont can only lead one to assume that (Thomas) Saunders did not act with the objectivity required of an investigator."

In March 2005, Houle filed a petition with the NTSB for reconsideration of the facts, and fourteen months later, they agreed. In September 2006, US Airways, who had taken over Piedmont, filed an inch-thick report containing documents that even the NTSB hadn't kept on file, which countered Houle's allegations. On 2 February 2007, the NTSB said that it was standing by its original report: those reviewing it had voted 3-1 that his arguments were unsubstantiated. One of the five-member board had been a Piedmont/US Airways pilot, so recused himself. Houle was disappointed by the response, since he felt that all the NTSB had done was review their old investigation, rather than open a new one. "All they did was reaffirm evidence from 40 years ago – evidence that was collected by the brother of a Piedmont vice-president." However, he accepted that any further steps would need to be taken by family members of those who died. None has so far been taken.

TIME RUNS OUT

Collisions between jets and light aircraft continued to occur far more frequently than they should have done in the early years of jet aviation, particularly when the radar systems installed at airports were simply not always capable of picking up the tracks of the smaller machines. The old "see and avoid" concept that had ruled for so many years was also coming to the end of its usefulness – if one of the aircraft was travelling so much faster than the other, there simply wasn't time for pilots to react. Animations created by the NTSB and others demonstrated just how little leeway there was in many of these accidents, and contemporary studies demonstrated that fifteen seconds was the absolute minimum time for detection, evaluation and evasive action if a collision was to be avoided.

The collision between Allegheny Airlines Flight 853, with a Piper PA-28 on 9 September 1969, near Fairland, Indiana was a case in point. Eighty-three people lost their lives when the two aircraft hit each other at a relative speed of approximately 350 mph – and according to the NTSB's assessment of the weather conditions prevalent at the time, the maximum warning that either pilot would have had was fourteen seconds. In its report on the incident, *Time* magazine noted: "It was the 19th time this year that two planes have collided and the 58th time since the start of 1968."

Allegheny Airlines' DC-9 was flying from Boston to St Louis via Baltimore, Cincinnati and Indianapolis. Its journey from Boston to Cincinnati was uneventful, but there was a delay on the ground once there. Sixty-four people were waiting for the TWA flight to New York that was running late; the airline therefore offered passengers the chance to transfer to the Allegheny flight. This meant that instead of departing from Cincinnati at 1457, Flight 853 left at 1516. Thirty-eight people who weren't supposed to be on the DC-9 were now in the Allegheny aircraft, which had filed a flightplan under IFR, at an altitude of 10,000 feet.

At approximately the same time, a Piper PA-28, belonging to the Forth Corporation, which had been leased to Bob Carey, an advanced flying student, took off from Brookside Airport, 20 miles north-east of Indiana. The weather conditions were not good, with low-level cloud, so Carey amended his plans to complete a solo cross-country flight to Perdue University Airport, and instead filed a flight plan under VFR, for Bakalar AFB, which was roughly 40 miles south of Brookside. He would be cruising at approximately 3,500 feet. As was the custom then, the Piper didn't have a transponder or any form of black box.

As far as Captain James Elrod and First Officer William Heckendorn were concerned, the approach into Indiana's Weir Cook Airport was perfectly normal. At 1525, Allegheny 853 reported leaving 10,000 feet and was instructed to contact Indianapolis Approach Control. Two minutes later, the approach controller advised them of the approach heading ("two eight zero radar vector visual approach three one left"), which the aircraft acknowledged, and was then ordered to descend to 2,500 feet and report once it was reached. At 1527.29 they confirmed this instruction.

The cockpit voice recorder shows First Officer Heckendorn reporting "out of 35 for 25" at 1529.13, to which the captain confirms, "I'm going down." As he said that, the front left side of Bob Carey's Piper impacted with the top front right section of the DC-9's vertical stabilizer, just beneath the horizontal stabilizer. The impact point on the Piper was just forward of the left wing root, inches from where Carey was sitting. The father of six was killed instantly as the Piper was bisected by the collision, the vertical stabilizer slicing it in two at a 45-degree angle across the cockpit. The engine, propeller, engine compartment and right wing of the Piper continued on past the vertical stabilizer then across the underside of the left half of the horizontal stabilizer – the propeller was still spinning. The remainder of the Piper – including the left wing, the fuselage and about three-quarters of the cockpit that held Bob Carey's body – scraped along the underside of the right half of the horizontal stabilizer.

The tail assembly of the DC-9 sheared off completely. In the next twelve seconds, the aircraft plummeted from the sky. There was just time for the first officer to ask, "What'd ya hit up there?" before the DC-9 hit the ground. The Piper dropped like a stone, leaving Bob Carey's as the only body that was found intact. The jet, however, was still travelling at 400 mph, and everything inside it was destroyed.

The wire report noted that "the two planes plunged out of the sky into a soybean field near the small town of London, Indiana, showering a nearby trailer park with debris" and quoted one of the trailer park residents, James Shields: "I think the pilot – if he were still alive after the collision – tried to hit the open spot away from the trailer court area." Eight witnesses saw the collision and told the NTSB later that there was "broken-to-scattered cloud in the area" but that both aircraft were below the clouds and were clearly visible at the time of the collision.

At approach control, Merrill McCammack had received Allegheny 853's acceptance of the landing instructions, then looked at another screen to deal with Allegheny's Flight 820. When he looked back, "I noticed that the target was no longer visible on Allegheny 853," he told the public enquiry into the collision. "This was not of immediate concern to me inasmuch as it's not particularly unusual to miss an aircraft for two or maybe three sweeps. I initiated a transmission to Allegheny 853, which was in effect, 'What is your altitude?' I didn't necessarily care in this instance what his altitude was; it was just a method of trying to establish communications. I wanted to hear his voice." McCammack did not see the Piper on his radar scope – tests showed that it would not have registered, and the NTSB concluded that it was not visible. (This statement of fact held no sway with a later jury apportioning damages in a civil court, who found that it *was* visible, and that McCammack should have seen it.)

The residents of the trailer park rushed to try to assist, but there was little anyone could do. The NTSB sent a ten-man investigation team to the scene and as well as examining the wreckage, they held a three-day inquiry. As Steve Delaney, the NBC's reporter at the inquiry, noted: "Lawyers representing a half-dozen different aviation interests have questioned the witnesses. They have spent most of their time trying to protect their agencies from blame for last month's mid-air collision, as a result there has been little agreement as to what caused it, and even less agreement on how to prevent the next one."

The NTSB blamed the ATC system, rather than the specific

controllers, for the crash. "The Board determines the probable cause of this accident to be the deficiencies in the collision avoidance capability of the Air Traffic Control system of the Federal Aviation Administration in a terminal area wherein there was mixed instrument flight rules and visual flight rules traffic. The deficiencies included the inadequacy of the see-and-avoid concept under the circumstances of this case; the technical limitations of radar in detecting all aircraft; and the absence of Federal Aviation Regulations which would provide a system of adequate separation of mixed VFR and IFR traffic in terminal areas."

They were nearly investigating a double tragedy. According to *Time*, two days after the disaster (September 11) "the very same flight – Allegheny 853 – came perilously close to another mid-air collision with a light plane while departing Greater Cincinnati Airport." Luckily on that occasion, the smaller aircraft suddenly showed up on radar when the two were "within five to ten seconds of crashing" which provided time for the controllers to warn the jet away.

There are two unusual footnotes to this incident: a jury in 1975 were presented with the evidence, and asked to apportion the blame for the "negligence" which caused the collision between various parties: Allegheny 22 per cent (the flight was supposedly descending too rapidly; if it had followed ordinary procedures there would have been time to spot the Piper, and in any case they were below cloud cover so should have seen him); Carey 21 per cent (since he should have seen the DC-9); Forth Corporation (the owners of the Piper, who had operated the facility which taught him) 21 per cent; and the United States of America (as represented by the air traffic controllers) 36 per cent.

The crash site has also been the subject of various paranormal investigations, notably by the Paranormal 911 group, whose visit was featured on the A&E reality show, *My Ghost Story*. According to them, a male voice could be heard asking a simple question, "Did we crash?"

THE USUAL PATTERN

Various recommendations were made as a result of the Allegheny Airways collision that helped to improve safety, including the provision of better radar facilities. However, some areas needed to get better quicker, and there were still conflicts of interest between military and civilian needs in the air. Military flights were continuing to operate under Visual Flight Rules and didn't necessarily show up on air traffic controllers' radar – as demonstrated by the case of the F-4 involved in a collision with a Hughes Air West DC-9 on Sunday 6 June 1971. As one of the investigators sent to the scene, Oscar M. Laurel, told the press two days later, it "may be a good time to take another look" at the VFR regulations.

Even before the accident not far from Los Angeles, there had been debate about the need to tighten up the rules. In March 1971, the NTSB produced a major study of mid-air collisions over the previous decade, predicting that over the next ten years "528 persons will die in airline disasters in midair if today's odds aren't reduced". As another study pointed out, somewhere in the United States, on an almost daily basis at that point, a jetliner had a close brush with a private plane in what was officially termed a "near miss". Los Angeles was the most dangerous area; New York ran a close second. The NTSB strongly argued against permitting combinations of flights operating under IFR and VFR near airports, but the necessary safety discussions kept getting entangled in power politics between the now-independent NTSB and the FAA, whose top officials were privately briefing the press that the NTSB was both headline-grabbing and power-grabbing.

The crash on 6 June fit what the NTSB described as "the usual pattern – clear weather with good visibility, one plane either climbing or landing, a second plane using visual rules while within range of a major airport". Added to this were allegations that the second plane in question – the F-4 – had been indulging in aerobatics shortly before the collision, and given that the surviving member of the crew admitted that they had definitely performed a 360-degree turn not long before the fatal incident, a lot of attention was focused on the enquiry.

Hughes Air West 706 was flying from Los Angeles to Seattle, Washington, with stopovers in Salt Lake City, Utah; Boise, Idaho; Lewiston, Idaho; Pasco, Washington; and Yakima, Washington. Captain Theodore Nicolay and First Officer Price Bruner were in charge of the DC-9, which was scheduled to depart from Los Angeles at 1800 (Pacific Daylight Time), and actually took off at 1802. It should have been a perfectly routine flight. However, nine minutes after take-off, it collided with the F-4B-18-MC Phantom II (known as 458 from its military bureau number, 151458). First Lieutenant James R. Phillips was pilot, with First Lieutenant Christopher E. Schiess as co-pilot and Radar Intercept Officer. Both men were part of the Marine Fighter Attack Squadron 323, Marine Aircraft Group 11, 3rd Marine Air Wing, and based at the Marine Corps Station at El Toro AFB, in Orange County, south-east of Los Angeles.

Phillips and Schiess had been bringing the F-4 back to El Toro, after it had developed a radio fault during a cross-country flight of two aircraft to McChord Air Force Base, Washington. Both F-4s suffered transponder failure during the onward journey on 4 June, and the next day, during the return leg, it was discovered that 458 also had an inoperative radio, an oxygen system leak and a degraded radar system. Maintenance personnel at Mountain Home AFB fixed the radio, but couldn't check the transponder, repair the oxygen leak, or upgrade the radar. Phillips and Schiess managed to get the plane to the Naval Auxiliary Air Station at Fallon in Nevada, but technicians there were unable to assist, and so, on 6 June, Phillips was ordered to proceed back to El Toro at low altitude.

The crew filed a VFR flight plan, but couldn't depart until 1716 because El Toro was closed that afternoon for an airshow. Their route took them via Fresno, Bakersfield and Los Angeles to El Toro. They climbed to 15,500 feet to clear the mountains and clouds 50 miles from Fallon, then descended to 5,500 feet until they reached Bakersfield. After reporting their position and receiving a weather report for El Toro when they were 15 miles north of the Bakersfield Flight Service Station, they decided to change course, to avoid the heavy air traffic over Los Angeles.

They flew at a minimum of 1,000 feet above the ground until they were 15 miles north-west of Palmdale (north-north-east of Los Angeles). Because visibility was poor, they climbed to 15,500 feet, and after levelling off, the VORTAC indicated they were 50 miles from El Toro. Phillips then executed a 360-degree aileron roll – turning the aircraft through a full circle on its axis to check for anything in the vicinity which might otherwise be in blind spots – while Scheiss was operating the radarscope, looking down at his instruments which were scanning the ground.

About seventy seconds after Phillips completed the roll, Scheiss looked up, and saw a DC-9 in his peripheral vision. It was about 50 degrees to the right, and slightly beneath the F-4. Phillips reacted as Scheiss began to shout a warning, and tried to initiate an evasive roll. It was too late.

The two aircraft collided over Mount Bliss. It took some time for the investigators to work out exactly what had happened – the nose of the DC-9 wasn't recovered for some time, and its cockpit voice recorder was destroyed in the crash. Initially, all they had to go on was the witness statements – and these were completely at odds.

"After impact – the airliner hit us – we tumbled violently four or five times," Scheiss told a press conference the day after the incident. He was the sole survivor: he had waited for about five seconds, but after seeing numerous warning lights in his cockpit, he had ejected from the F-4, and parachuted to the ground with only minor injury. Phillips was unable to eject, and died when the F-4 impacted.

Witnesses on the ground said that the DC-9 cartwheeled "like a shooting star" as it fell, with articles streaming from the jet as it plunged towards the mountainside in the Angeles National Forest, around 20 miles north-east of Los Angeles. Luggage was also seen falling from the hole in the side of the aircraft. The wreckage was strewn over a mile in highly inaccessible terrain, and the County Fire Division Chief, who flew several times over the 2,000-feet-deep gorge in which it lay, said that if there were any other survivors than Scheiss, "it will be the greatest miracle I've ever seen". A sheriff's spokesman added: "There was no room for it to skid. It went straight in."

Over sixty witnesses gave their testimony to the investigators, who represented the NTSB, the Marine Corps, Hughes Air West and the Airline Pilots Associated. Not all of it tallied with the radar officer's account of events. While Schiess maintained that the DC-9 hit the F-4, Jeff Whittington told the NTSB investigators that he and a friend saw the F-4 "do a spiral and a loop and disappear behind the ridge where they crashed. I saw the left wing of the fighter strike the centre of the fuselage of the Air West. The military jet went straight down."

The investigators had a number of questions to answer: Why did the DC-9 take no evasive action? Did it hit the F-4 as Schiess claimed? Why didn't the F-4 spot it earlier and avoid it? Did Phillips really carry out an aileron roll as Schiess stated, or were the impressions of the many witnesses on the ground accurate and it was "stunting"?

By a process of reassembling the wreckage of the aircraft, they were able to deduce that the tail and right wing of the F-4 had slashed through the cockpit and the front of the passenger section of the DC-9. If Phillips' evasive manoeuvre had started a fraction of a second earlier the two would have missed each other – according to George R. Baker, the chief of the NTSB team, he only needed to be ten feet further away. Duplicating the flight paths of the F-4 demonstrated that Phillips was carrying out an aileron roll, as Scheiss had said; ironically, if he had been performing a barrel roll, as suggested by the eye witnesses, the F-4 would have been less far advanced along its route, and would have missed the DC-9.

The duplicate flights also allowed the investigators to examine the role of the air traffic controllers in the collision. The antiquated equipment (which some said dated back to the Second World War) was not capable of spotting the F-4, particularly given its transponder problems. (If, of course, the F-4 pilot had contacted the civilian air traffic control and advised them of their route, particularly given their damaged aircraft, the controllers would have been able to tell the F-4 and the DC-9 of each other's presence – but this wasn't standard procedure at this time.) As to whether the crews on each aircraft should have spotted the other, it became clear from the investigation that no blame could be ascribed, given the conditions prevalent at the time.

As the NTSB final report stated, the "probable cause of this accident was the failure of both crews to see and avoid each other, but recognizes that they had only marginal capability to detect, assess, and avoid the collision. Other causal factors include a very high closure rate, comingling of IFR and VFR traffic in an area where the limitation of the ATC system precludes effective separation of such traffic, and failure of the crew of BuNo458 to request radar advisory service, particularly considering the fact that they had an inoperable transponder." They strongly recommended that the FAA and the Department of Defense should work on a way to avoid such collisions in future. The next of kin sued Hughes Air West and the US government, who agreed not to contest the issue of liability, and various settlements were agreed.

The investigation into the collision over the Los Angeles Forest was far from concluding when the world's worst air disaster to that point occurred over the mountains of Northern Japan on 30 July 1971. All Nippon Airways Flight 58 piloted by Captain Saburo Kawaniski was returning from Sapporo, on the Japanese island of Hokkaido, to Tokyo, carrying seven crew and 155 passengers, most of whom were members of a tour group from Fuji City of relatives of the Second World War dead. They were flying at 26,000 feet.

Half an hour after take-off, at 2.04 p.m. local time, Kawaniski found himself closing in on an F-86 Sabre jet, piloted by Sergeant Yoshimi Ichikawa, who had been practising formation turns. The young trainee recalled that he received an order from his instructor, Captain Tamotsu Kuma, to climb and turn. He "saw a civilian plane approach from the rear and felt a jolt in my tail" after he failed to break away in time.

The jolt came from the 727 as its horizontal stabilizer impacted with the leading edge of the F-86's right wing. Straight after impact, Captain Kawaniski bellowed, "Emergency! Emergency! Emergency! This is All-Nippon! All-Nippon! Unable to control! Unable to control!" That was the last message received from the 727. Both aircraft disintegrated, and debris showered down on the village of Shizukuishi. Sergeant Ichikawa ejected and landed in a rice paddy.

"I heard something like a clap of thunder and I looked up into the sky," recalled school teacher Masataka Kato. "High in the air, I could see a lot of smoke. There were five columns of white smoke coming from the wing of a big plane flying eastward. Then I saw the fuselage going down in the mountains near here. Up above I could see what seemed to be parts of the plane."

The next day, Lt. Gen. Tsyrayuka Ishikawa, the Vice Chief of Staff for the air Self Defence Forces, blamed Ichikawa and Kuma for a serious error, and both were arrested on a charge of negligence resulting in death. Ichikawa was tried, but acquitted. On 2 August, Keikichi Masahara, the Director-General of the Defence Agency, resigned, taking responsibility for the disaster. As a result of the collision, military aircraft were banned from commercial air lanes.

LETHAL STRIKE ACTION

The importance of professional, competent personnel, trained in all aspects of their job became abundantly clear during the investigation into a collision over France in March 1973. French civilian air traffic controllers began strike action on 20 February, which they initially expected only to last four days. However, when it continued, the Clément Marot Plan was put into effect on 24 February by the French government's Secretariat Général à l'Aviation Civile. This was a military contingency system designed to replace civil air traffic services; in some cases, this meant that temporary routes replaced the established airways system, so that the military radar units could control the area adequately.

There were also two other consequences of the decision: the military controllers weren't as familiar with the usage and terminology employed by civilian aircraft (and particularly the predominance of English), and the equipment they were using wasn't as up to date. (The British Air Lines Pilots' Association were particularly concerned about this.)

Iberia Flight 504 was travelling from Palma to London on 5 March. The DC-9 carried sixty-one passengers and seven crew, headed by Commander Luis Cueto Capella as it flew over France at flight level 310 (31,000 feet), heading for the Nantes VOR. As normal they contacted the Marina Control Centre at Mont-de-Marsan at 1219 to confirm they were following route W 132, and at 1225 reported that they expected to reach the VOR at Nantes at 1252. Responsibility for the flight would then pass to Menhir Control Centre at Brest. However, at 1227, Menhir informed Marina that Iberia 504 would need to cross the VOR at flight level 290 (29,000 feet). At 1232, they were asked to descend accordingly.

Meanwhile, a Convair CV-990 charter flight heading from Madrid-Barajas for London, operating as Spantax 400, was also expecting to be at the Nantes VOR at 1252. At 1230, they were told to climb from flight level 260 (26,000 feet) to flight level 290. This meant that within the space of two minutes, Marina Control Centre had told two separate flights to assume the same altitude, knowing that they were both anticipating arriving at the same spot at the same time. In a debate in the House of Commons a few years later, when he was summarizing the sequence of events, Robin Hodgson MP stated that "From that moment on, a collision was inevitable."

That wasn't completely true. A discussion followed between the air traffic control centres, and it was decided that the Spantax should delay its arrival at Nantes by eight minutes, and therefore arrive there at 1300. (For some reason, which was never adequately explained, the controllers didn't want to be monitoring flights at separate levels, so rather than separate the two aircraft by space, they decided to separate them by time.) This wasn't communicated to the Spantax flight until 1240 – meaning that they somehow had to do the flying equivalent of twiddling their thumbs for eight minutes when they were only twelve minutes away from the VOR. Worse, when Spantax Captain Antonio Arenas-Rodriguez requested confirmation of the instruction, he was told to "standby". Without absolute confirmation, he could not proceed to follow the instructions. (As it transpired, to the controller the words "standby" didn't mean "wait" – they meant "proceed with the instructions".) Three minutes later, with just nine minutes left to go, the confirmation was given, and Captain Arenas-Rodriguez started to slow the Convair down.

Totally unaware of all this, the Iberian DC-9 was continuing towards the Nantes VOR at flight level 290. At 1241, it had reported that it was going to be a couple of minutes later at Nantes than anticipated – now getting there at 1254.

At 1249, the Spantax captain realized that he wasn't going to be able to slow down in time, and therefore needed to carry out a racetrack manoeuvre, properly known as a 360-degree turn. This means that the aircraft turns to starboard out of the traffic lane, flies back down the outside of the lane, and rejoins it when they have lost the requisite time – so to arrive eight minutes late, they needed to go "backwards" for four minutes then retrace their steps for a further four. At that point, Captain Arenas-Rodriguez was told to change radio frequencies so he could contact the correct centre, but he believed that this meant he should do it *after* they had passed the VOR rather than immediately. He therefore contacted Marina control centre rather than Menhir with his request to make the racetrack turn but because Marina was now so far behind him, communications were almost impossible, and he received no reply.

Captain Arenas-Rodriguez called twice more before he reported that he would have to make the turn. And when he did so, in thick cloud, he flew straight into the DC-9 which was coming up behind him. From the ground, it looked as if "[s]uddenly a streak of red light appeared and part of the aircraft came down with bodies flying out," according to Max Chevalier, the British Honorary Vice-Consul at Nantes. The DC-9 broke up.

One of the passengers on the Convair recalled that "There was an enormous bump and then everything seemed to fall about. No-one knew what was happening except that the aircraft was falling fast." The Convair had lost an outboard portion of its port wing, but Captain Arenas-Rodriguez was able to maintain control of the aircraft, and issued a Mayday call. A French Air Force T33 was instructed to intercept the Convair, and to guide it in to Tours. However, they were unable to establish radio communication. At 1318, Bordeaux Approach was able to take it under radar control, and was about to begin the approach to Bordeaux, in sight of Cognac base, when the Air Force base crew fired green pyrotechnic signals and the Convair was brought in for a heavy landing at Cognac. All eight crew and ninety-nine passengers escaped uninjured.

While the investigation proceeded, an almost total prohibition of commercial flights followed within French air space (Laker and British Midland continued to use it). The French Minister of Transport, Robert Galley, stated that the air traffic controllers were not at fault, but Captain Arenas-Rodriguez disagreed and claimed that he didn't think that the controllers understood English clearly enough. General Claude Grigaud, chief of staff of the French Air Force, said initial investigations suggested pilot error was to blame. Captain Arenas-Rodriguez had disobeyed the order to slow down and made his turn "without warning".

The official French report by the French Secretariat of State for Transport was reprinted by the British Department of Trade

Accidents Investigation Branch, since so many Britons were on board the destroyed aircraft. Released in July 1975, it noted that the emergency plan needed "strict compliance" with its special regulations in order to succeed. When the two aircraft were due to arrive at Nantes at the same time, a conflict arose and the solution proposed "necessitated either particularly precise navigation by the crew of [the Convair] or complete radar coverage, and, in both cases, trouble-free communication facilities, conditions which were not realised. The continuing progress of the flight was affected by delays attributable in part to the control, in part to the crew and also to difficulty in air/ground radio communications resulting in complete failure of the crew and the control to understand one another. At the critical juncture, the crew, unmindful of their exact position, commenced a turn in order to lose time, without having been able to obtain the agreement of the control, as a result of which the aircraft intersected the adjacent route."

The air traffic controllers' strike lasted until 21 March 1973. In April 1979, the French government were still prevaricating over paying compensation over and above that due under the Warsaw convention (around £9,000) despite affirming their "commitment to accept responsibility for their obligations and duties in this matter, in accordance with the principles of French law".

SCAPEGOATING THE CONTROLLER

British Airways' worst accident occurred on 10 September 1976 when Flight 476 collided with Inex-Adria Airways Flight 550 when an air traffic controller's desperate attempt to prevent them from hitting each other went catastrophically wrong. There were no survivors from the 176 people on board the two aircraft; one person on the ground also died. As a result, eight air traffic controllers and supervisors were brought to trial, with one of them treated as a scapegoat.

The merger of BEA, BOAC, Cambrian Airways and Northeast Airlines in 1974 had created one national British carrier (it wasn't privatized until 1987), and the Trident Three flight from London to Istanbul should have been routine. The Yugoslav DC-9's journey from Split to Cologne should have seen it pass the British jet safely across the crowded Yugoslav skies. However, at 1014 GMT, the two aircraft were both on flight level 330 in exactly the same place, over the town of Vrbovec, north-east of Zagreb.

The end five metres of the left wing of the DC-9 cut through the base of the forward windows on the Trident's flight deck and then broke through the fuselage by the forward passenger compartment. The resultant decompression meant the fuselage disintegrated, and part of that struck the Trident's own rudder, which fell from the aircraft to the ground. The destroyed Trident fell to the ground with no forward movement, landing on its tail, a mile south of Gaj village.

The DC-9's wing was completely cut, and part of it (or possibly the Trident fuselage debris) reached the DC-9's left engine. The impact broke the compressor blades, which fell from their housing, and struck the left side of the stabilizer, the rudder and a lower left side of the elevator. The cone and the tail broke off, and the rest of the aircraft slammed to the ground right wing first, half a mile east of Dvoriste village.

Although the Yugoslav Federal Committee for Transportation

and Communications' second commission of inquiry found that the accident was in part caused by "non-compliance with regulations on continuous listening to the appropriate radio frequency of ATC and non-performance of look-out duty from the cockpits of either aircraft" – a finding with which the UK's accredited representative to the commission disagreed strongly enough to append an official addendum to the Committee's report – the main cause was "improper ATC operation".

Within a few days of the collision, it was clear that the air traffic controllers' behaviour was going to come under intense scrutiny. The preliminary opinion of Vjeceslav Jakovac, the Yugoslav judge heading the investigation, was that the controllers probably had incorrectly assessed the altitude of the planes, and five of them were taken into custody for questioning. It quickly became clear that the staff at the Zagreb ARTCC had been under considerable, if not intolerable, pressure.

There were only thirty people working in what was the second busiest ARTCC in Europe by 1976, with most experts reckoning that at least double that number would have been needed. It wasn't as if they were working with the most modern equipment either – although a radar flight-control system had been installed in 1973, it still wasn't in full use, after it kept going wrong. Procedural control was the standard operating method: pilots transmitted their positions from specified points, which were then monitored by the radar, using flight progress strips which were updated as the aircraft moved through the area. There were three high-level airways intersecting over Zagreb beacon – Upper Blue 5 (UB5), Upper Blue 9 (UB9) and Upper Red 22 (UR22) – as well as Upper Blue 1 (UB1) which ran slightly to the south, and Upper Amber 40 (UA40), which ran directly from Zagreb to Sarajevo. The airspace was divided into three levels – upper (above 31,000 feet), middle (25,000–31,000 feet) and lower (beneath 25,000 feet) – with the top two directed by a single controller, Supervisor Julije Dajcic.

On the morning of 10 September, BA 476 was flying on UB1 at 33,000 feet (flight level 330) at 0948 at the same time as Inex-Adria JP 550 took off from Split. Both were due to cross the Zagreb beacon. At 1004, the crew contacted Zagreb control and told them they were estimating reaching the beacon at 1014.

They were instructed to call control as they passed Zagreb at flight level 330, and to squawk Alpha 2312 as their transponder code. Their confirmation of this order was the last heard from the BA flight.

JP 550 should have been climbing up to its planned flight level of 310, but its progress was delayed because a flow of east-west traffic was blocking levels above 260. When they asked for a higher flight level, they were offered 350, which they accepted "with pleasure". The controller, Bojan Erjavec, needed permission to confirm this instruction, and waved a hand at Gradimir Tasić, the upper level controller – who had given BA 476 clearance a few moments earlier. Tasić was handling other aircraft, and couldn't be interrupted. Another middle sector controller, Gradimir Pelin, was told to coordinate the handover of JP 550 from the middle sector to Tasić in the upper sector.

At 1007, Pelin took the flight progress strip for JP 550 and asked Tasić if JP 550 could climb to flight level 350. They waited for another aircraft to cross, and then Tasić gave permission for the DC-9 to proceed. At 1012, JP 550 contacted Bojan Erjavec to confirm that the aircraft was out of flight level 310. They were given the frequency for the upper level controller, Tasić, and to stop squawking the assigned code.

The flight crew didn't contact Tasić until 1014.04, when they had reached the Zagreb VOR and were climbing through flight level 325. At 1014.17, they told Tasić they were at 327. The controller immediately saw the problem: the British Airways Trident was above the beacon, as was the DC-9, which was rapidly climbing. The combined airspeed was 920 knots – faster than the muzzle velocity of a .44 Magnum handgun. The radar screen indicated that BA 476 was at 335 (in fact, it was lower – it was actually at 330), and Tasić hoped that if he kept the DC-9 where it was, then the two aircraft would come very close, but not actually collide.

Speaking in Croatian, Tasić hastily told Captain Krumpak on the DC-9 to hold his present height. When the captain asked what height, Tasić stammered, "The height you are climbing through because . . . er . . . you have an aircraft in front of you at [unintelligible on the tape] 335 from left to right." Captain Krumpak said he would remain at 330.

Three seconds later the two aircraft collided. The only coherent words from the DC-9 after impact came from First Officer Dusan Ivanus: "We are finished," he said, "Goodbye. Goodbye."

The controllers and supervisors were charged with violation of air traffic regulations, negligent supervision of air traffic, inadequate organization and failure to maintain discipline and safe work loads. British lawyer Richard Weston's girlfriend had been one of the cabin crew on the BA flight, and he attended the trial as one of the prosecutors. It became evident to him that the men standing trial were in fact being made scapegoats for the system's inefficiency. The problems with the Zagreb ARTCC were laid bare in the court room: the authorities admitted that thirty to forty more controllers were needed, that funds for training and updating equipment were being cut by 30 per cent each year, and that refresher courses had been scrapped. Weston ended up using his closing speech to the court as an argument for the defence.

All bar Tasić were acquitted, but the young controller was sentenced to seven years' imprisonment. The other air traffic controllers, helped by Weston, petitioned President Tito for Tasić's release and on 29 November 1978, after he had spent nearly two years and three months in prison since the accident, he was freed. A Granada TV movie based on the case, *Collision Course*, starred Antony Sher as Tasić; Weston later wrote a detailed account of the accident and its aftermath.

FLYING UNDER THE RADAR

American airlines and aviation personnel were hoping that the many changes that were being implemented during the 1970s as a direct result of earlier incidents, including the Hughes Air West disaster in Los Angeles (see page 44), would mean an end to serious mid-air collisions. Unfortunately, although they were certainly less frequent, there were still some major incidents.

"It's not that we want to exclude them from airspace," United Airlines Captain Bay Lahr said of smaller aircraft in the wake of the tragedy that hit San Diego on the morning of 25 September 1978, when preliminary indications suggested that a Pacific Southwest Airlines (PSA) jet had hit a Cessna during its landing approach. "It's just that we don't want to crash into them."

At 0816 Pacific Standard Time on that bright sunny September morning, a Cessna 172 belonging to Gibbs Flight Centre left Montgomery Field, California, on an instrument training flight. Martin Kazy Jr, a flight instructor with 5,000 hours of experience, was at the controls, giving a lesson to Marine Sergeant David Lee Boswell, who wanted to upgrade his commercial pilot's licence to include instrument flight training. Kazy sat in the right front seat of the four-seater, Boswell in the left. Although Boswell would need to wear a special hood during his training, to ensure that he concentrated completely on flying by instrument rather than by what he could see, Kazy had full visibility, and dual controls – if there was any problem, he could take over the aircraft immediately.

Eighteen minutes later, at 0834, PSA 182 set off for the short hop from Los Angeles to San Diego's Lindbergh Airport. The flight had originated in the Californian state capital, Sacramento, departing from there at 0700, and when it left Los Angeles, there were 128 passengers on board, including a large number of PSA employees, as well as a crew of seven, led by Captain James E. McFeron, First Officer Robert E. Fox and Flight Engineer Martin J. Wahne, all of whom had thousands of flight hours' experience.

With them was another company pilot, Spencer Nelson, who was catching a free ride (deadheading) back to San Diego. This meant there were four experienced sets of eyes in the cockpit of the 727.

The jet flew southward along the Pacific tracked by the controllers at Los Angeles, then by the FAA controllers at Miramar Naval Air Station near San Diego. At 0853.10 they reported to San Diego approach control at 11,000 feet, and were cleared to descend to 7,000 feet preparatory for a landing on Runway 27. Because of the prevailing wind direction, commercial traffic was using Runway 27: the PSA jet would therefore have to fly eastwards, parallel with the runway, then turn south, and finally back westwards for the touchdown.

The Cessna had carried out its two practice runs making an instrument approach on Runway 9 (the same physical runway as Runway 27, but with the traffic going in the opposite direction – east rather than west). At 0857, the Cessna began to climb out from Runway 9 to the north-east; at 0859.01, the tower controller cleared the Cessna pilot to maintain VFR conditions and to contact San Diego approach control.

The 727 had been given clearance for a visual approach to runway 27 at 0857, and at 0859.28, the approach controller advised the PSA flight that there was "traffic [at] twelve o'clock, one mile northbound." Five seconds later, the pilot confirmed that they were looking.

Eleven seconds after that the approach controller told them that "additional traffic's twelve o'clock, three miles, just north of the field, north-east bound, a Cessna one seventy-two climbing VFR out of one thousand four hundred." At 0859:50, the co-pilot replied, "OK, we've got that other twelve." A few seconds later, San Diego approach control contacted the Cessna, and told them to "maintain VFR conditions at or below three thousand five hundred, fly heading zero seven zero, vector final approach course." (As this was happening, the off-duty captain in the PSA cockpit was relating an anecdote.)

At 15 seconds past 0900, approach control advised PSA 182: "Traffic's at twelve o'clock, three miles out of one thousand seven hundred." The first officer scanned the skies, telling the captain at 0900:21 he'd "got 'em" and the captain told the approach controller, "Traffic in sight."

In light of this, the controller cleared the 727 to "maintain visual separation" and to contact Lindbergh tower. At 0900:28, the captain replied, "OK." The approach controller's final contact with either aircraft came at 0900:31, seventy-six seconds before the accident: "Traffic at six o'clock, two miles, eastbound; a PSA jet inbound to Lindbergh, out of three thousand two hundred, has you in sight." Martin Kazy Jr simply confirmed receipt of the information. As far as he knew, the much larger jet knew exactly where he was, and would take all necessary measures to stay out of his way.

That's not what happened. The captain contacted Lindbergh tower at 0900.34 and told them they were "downwind". The tower controller also reminded them that there was "ah, traffic twelve o'clock, one mile, a Cessna". Hearing that, the captain asked the first officer if the tower was referring to the same aircraft they'd been looking at before. "Yeah, but I don't see him now," First Officer Fox replied, at 0900.43, and a second later the captain told the tower, "OK, we had it there a minute ago." The tower "roger"-ed that, and at 0900.50, the captain said, "I think he's pass (sic) off to our right." Critically, the tower controller didn't hear the words "I think" – as far as he knew therefore, the Cessna and the PSA were sufficiently far apart since the light aircraft was *passing* off to their right.

At 0901.07 the tower gave the 727 clearance to land. The first officer was still concerned: "Are we clear of that Cessna?" he asked at 0901.11, with the others saying that they guessed so, before the captain noted at 0901.21: "Oh yeah, before we turned downwind, I saw him at about one o'clock, probably behind us now."

Seven seconds later, the conflict alert warning began to sound in the San Diego Approach Control Facility, suggesting that the flight paths of the 727 and the Cessna were about to enter the computer's warning parameters. By the time that an approach controller contacted the Cessna to alert of "traffic in your vicinity, a PSA jet has you in sight, he's descending for Lindbergh", it was all over.

At 0901.31, three seconds after the alert had sounded on the ground, the first officer confirmed that gear was down. Seven seconds after that, he said, "There's one underneath," to which the reply from one of his colleagues couldn't be made out on the cockpit recording. "I was looking at that inbound there," First Officer Fox then said at 0901.39.

The 727 overtook the Cessna, which was beneath it, and at 2,600 feet, at 0901.47, the two aircraft collided. The nose wheel of the 727 had hooked the Cessna, and flipped the lighter craft against the 727's lowered right wing. This broke the wing and the empennage to pieces. The Cessna's vertical stabilizer had been torn from the fuselage, and the light aircraft plummeted to the ground. The engine and propeller separated from the aircraft and landed near the rest of the wreckage, about 3,500 feet north-west of the 727's final resting place.

Flight 182 began a shallow right descending turn, with a vapour coming from its right wing. A bright orange fire erupted near the wing as the fuel tank erupted, which increased as the aircraft fell towards the ground. In the cockpit, the crew desperately tried to regain control. "We're hit man, we are hit," the first officer confirmed six seconds after the collision. "Tower we're going down," Captain McFeron said flatly. The tower told them they'd call "the equipment" for them, but the PSA flight was never going to reach the landing field.

"This is it, baby," Captain McFeron said at 0901.59. Four seconds later he told the passengers to brace themselves. There was time for two of the other crewmen to say final words for loved ones that they knew the voice recorder would pick up. And then, at 0902.04, the 727 hit the ground, three miles north-east of Lindbergh field, in San Diego's North Park, just west of the 805 freeway, and a few metres north of the intersection of Dwight and Nile streets. In less than a quarter of a minute, two aircraft had gone from collision to fiery wrecks, what one air traffic controller described as "an aluminum shower" falling on the streets of San Diego. Both of the aircrafts' descents to earth were captured by photographers.

It was obvious to everyone who witnessed the crash that no one was going to survive. Five women and two boys on the ground were also killed, and twenty-two houses were damaged or destroyed. Horrific orange and black smoke surrounded everything, as the wreckage of the aircraft and its occupants burned. At St Augustine High School, Father Anthony J. Wasko was worried that the 727 would land on top of its buildings and the 575 boys within, but when it missed, he opened its gymnasium as a temporary mortuary. Firemen fought the blazes for two hours, and the police had to deal with scavengers, including twenty-eight people who were arrested either for refusing to leave the area, or for stealing watches and wallets from the passengers' remains.

The NTSB was notified of the accident within ten minutes of its occurrence, and dispatched an investigative group to the scene. Nearly a hundred investigators came from the FAA, PSA, Gibbs Flite Center, the Southwest Flightcrew and Flight Attendants Association, Boeing, Cessna, the Professional Air Traffic Controllers Organization, Pratt and Whitney, the Air Line Pilots Association, and the Aircraft Owners and Pilots Association to probe the wreckage of the aircraft and take statements from 221 people in an effort to discover what went wrong. The possibility that the crew of the PSA had seen a different Cessna to the one they struck was looked into; the blind spots of the two aircraft were carefully examined. A five-day public hearing followed in November and the NTSB report was issued on 20 April 1979.

Investigations established that the Cessna pilot failed to maintain the 070-degree heading which he had been following, and therefore had gone into the 727's path. (At no point was this relayed to the PSA flight crew.) However, local rules stated that the 727 should have maintained 4,000 feet until it was clear of the Montgomery Field Airport traffic area, which the approach controller should have advised them to do. The crew of the PSA jet failed to clearly inform the tower control that they had lost sight of the Cesssna, and the advisories issued to them by the controller didn't meet the requisite standards. The controller failed to warn the two pilots after the conflict warning alert because he believed the conflict was already resolved – and in the circumstances, since he had the capability to provide lateral or radar separation to either aircraft, he should have done so.

The report determined that the probable cause was "the failure of the flightcrew of Flight 182 to comply with the provisions of a maintain-visual-separation clearance, including the requirement to inform the controller when they no longer had the other aircraft in sight", with the air traffic control procedures contributing to the accident.

Unusually, there was a dissenting statement appended to the report: Francis H. McAdams felt that "the inadequacies of the air traffic control system" should have been cited as a probable cause, and pointed out that the majority opinion agreed that if the lateral or vertical separation had been used, the two aircraft would not have collided. He was a strong opponent of "see and avoid" in a busy area such as San Diego, and he was also concerned that there might have been another aircraft in the vicinity, as some witnesses had suggested. If that were the case, it would explain why the pilot of the 727 thought he had seen the Cessna at the 1 o'clock position, when in fact it would have been at the 11 o'clock position.

McAdams' probable cause – which was adopted by the NTSB officially in August 1982 – was "the failure of the flightcrew of Flight 182 to maintain visual separation and to advise the controller when visual contact was lost; and the air traffic control procedures in effect which authorized the controllers to use visual separation procedures in a terminal area environment when the capability was available to provide either lateral or vertical radar separation to either aircraft." Contributory factors were the failures of the air traffic control in other areas, as well as the failure of the Cessna to head in the assigned direction, and the possible misidentification of the Cessna by the PSA crew.

As a direct result of the PSA crash – as well as another collision between a Falcon jet and a Cessna over Memphis, Tennessee, the previous May – there was intense criticism of the FAA's ATC programme, and the lack of progress in developing an airborne collision-avoidance system. Eastern Air Lines Pilot Jack Howell asked,"I wonder how many more San Diegos we will have before we get an efficient system?" The FAA argued that "there would be whistles and buzzers going off constantly in the cockpit and this would not serve the interests of air safety".

On 27 December 1978, FAA Administrator Langhorne Bond and Secretary of Transportation Brock Adams announced a regulatory programme to reduce the risk of mid-air collisions by 80 per cent – but this received a massive negative reaction. In June 1981, the FAA decided to adopt the Threat Alert and Collision Avoidance System, soon renamed the Traffic Alert and Collision Avoidance System (TCAS) that worked in conjunction with the aircraft's transponders.

UNCONTROLLED IN THE CONTROL AREA

The next major incident occurred in 1986, but a near miss on 18 October 1984 could have rewritten history – Air Force Two, carrying the Vice-President, George H. W. Bush, had to take evasive action after they failed to sight an aircraft which was flying under visual flight rules. There were two major near misses near Washington DC on 9 June and 24 September 1985, and the FAA acknowledged that near misses had been increasing during the first quarter of 1985 – although they noted that the statistic had been compiled using improved methods.

In the immediate aftermath of the collision between Aeromexico Flight 498 and a Piper Cherokee Archer over Cerritos, Los Angeles, on 31 August 1986, the Sunday of Labor Day weekend, one unnamed 747 pilot told *Time* magazine, "You get below 10,000 ft., and it becomes almost suicidal not to devote a tremendous amount of attention outside the cockpit. I can't tell you how difficult it is to pick up a small airplane." Eighty-two people – including fifteen on the ground – died as a result of the accident, which occurred after the smaller aircraft strayed into the protected Traffic Control Area (TCA) around LAX.

Although many accounts of the accident suggest that the cause of the collision was the pilot of the Piper, William Kramer, suffering a heart attack, and his aircraft then inadvertently flying into the TCA, this was conclusively proved not to be the case by the NTSB investigation. The fifty-three-year-old pilot did suffer from "generalized arteriosclerosis, slight to moderate and coronary arteriosclerosis, moderate to focally severe with complete proximal occlusion of the main right coronary artery", according to autopsies and heart examinations carried out both by the Los Angeles county coroner, and the Armed Forces Institute of Pathology, but there were no signs of "necrosis or other evidence of acute myocardial infarction". In other words, he did have heart problems, which might have caused him difficulties later in life, but he did not have any form of heart attack or stroke while flying the Piper – and certainly, there is no evidence to back up the assertion that his wife and daughter, who were killed along with him in the crash, were trying to revive him, and that was why the Piper wasn't where it was meant to be. (All three of those on board the Piper were found with their seat belts still fastened.)

Kramer and his family took off from Torrance Municipal Airport, California, around 1141 Pacific Daylight Time, on a VFR flight towards Big Bear Lake, some 90 miles to the east. Kramer had held a licence for six years, but had spent most of his 231 hours' flying time in the Spokane, Washington area – since December 1985 he had only flown seven flights in the LA area, logging around five and a half hours. He was described as a conscientious and careful pilot, who one friend noted was "old-maidish" with his pre-flight checklist, "too careful" about rules, and aware of his comparative inexperience as a pilot.

The retired business executive had filed a flight plan via Long Beach, California, then direct to the Paradise, California VORTAC, and then direct to Big Bear, flying at 9,500 feet. This flight plan was advisory only; there was no requirement for him to follow it. The ATC data, based on the working transponder on board the four-seater Piper, showed that Kramer had not flown towards Long Beach, but instead had adopted an easterly heading, towards the Paradise VORTAC, soon after take-off. This took him into the LA TCA, which he entered without clearance. It wasn't as if Kramer didn't know it was there – earlier that morning, he had bought an up-to-date map showing the TCA boundaries (it was found in the wreckage open to the correct place), but maybe he didn't realize that he had to keep beneath 6,000 feet.

Aeromexico Flight 498 was a regularly scheduled DC-9 operating between Mexico City, Mexico and LAX, via Guadalajara, Loreto and Tijuana. It left Tijuana at 1120, with fifty-eight passengers and six crew, headed by Pilot Arturo Valdes Prom. The routine flight into Los Angeles saw it leave 10,000 feet at 1144.54, and at 1146.59, five minutes and ten seconds before impact, it was ordered to contact Los Angeles Approach Control. Half a minute later, it did so, reporting it was level at 7,000 feet. It was cleared for the ILS runway "two five left", and at 1150.05, the controller, Walter White, requested it to reduce airspeed to

210 knots indicated airspeed (KIAS). At 1150.46, he advised Flight 498 that there was "traffic, ten o'clock, one mile, northbound, altitude unknown" – this wasn't Kramer's Piper – which the DC-9 acknowledged. At 1151.04, they were cleared to descend to 6,000 feet, and reduce airspeed to 190 KIAS.

The controller's attention was then taken by a Grumman Tiger's pilot who contacted ATC asking for flight-following services (i.e. that air traffic control were aware of its presence and would notify it of any problems). This seemed as if it might cause a potential hazard and at the same time, White was informed that there was a potential runway change for Flight 498. He therefore instructed the DC-9 at 1151.57: "We have a change in plans, sir. Stand by." At precisely 1152, Flight 498 confirmed that they would maintain a speed of 190. It was the last transmission from the Aeromexico flight.

Over the next half a minute, the controller dealt with the Grumman – who misheard the instructions for the transponder squawk – and gave him a stern telling off for entering the TCA. He then tried to find Flight 498 on the radar screen, but it had vanished. He tried to make radio contact but received no reply. "He was hoping against hope that a transponder had gone out or there was something wrong with the radar – anything but a crash," Karl Grundmann, another controller on duty at the time recalled. "He was looking anguished. We knew something was wrong."

At 1156.05, Walter White contacted American Airlines 333, and asked them to "look around at eleven o'clock and about five miles" since he "just lost contact with a DC-9". At 1156.26, the AA flight crew reported, "I see a . . . very large . . . smoke screen off on the left side of the aircraft abeam . . . the nose of the airplane right off our left. It is a very large smoke . . . column . . . caning from it, and . . . emanating from the ground, and at our altitude, at eight thousand feet, there's another smoke column vertically overhead. It looks like it something smoked up . . . ahead and then went down."

It was the first confirmation of what those on the two aircraft and on the ground already knew. Flight 498 had been descending through about 6,660 feet on a north-westerly track; the Piper was heading east. Despite the skies being clear, and a visibility of around 14 miles, the Piper was about 8 to 10 feet above the top of the DC-9's fuselage, and about 15 to 17 feet above its wings when it struck the front of the DC-9's vertical stabilizer. The jet's horizontal stabilizer then hit the top of the Piper's fuselage, shearing off its roof, and decapitating the three Kramers. The Piper's engine smashed into the horizontal stabilizer's main support structure, causing that to fail, and the stabilizer to separate from the rest of the DC-9. This left Captain Valdes Prom with no longitudinal control.

The DC-9 dropped its nose and rolled to its left, before twisting upside down and plummeting to earth, picking up speed as it fell. Captain Valdes Prom tried his best, throwing the engines into reverse thrust, but it was futile. The DC-9 smashed into the suburban area of Cerritos, blocking out the sun from the houses as it passed over, sending flaming aviation fuel all around. In the fire that followed, eleven homes were destroyed and six damaged on Ashworth Place, Holmes Avenue and Reva Circle. Fifty-three fire units from six agencies, five fire helicopters and nineteen ambulances responded to the scene.

Among the fifteen people killed on the ground were a father of four who was talking on the telephone, two mothers and their children moving into a new house around the corner, and a woman who was waiting for her son to return home with her car. A number were from the Comanche, Kickapoo and Sioux Native American tribes, congregating for a family holiday party. All sixty-four passengers and crew on the DC-9 died – the cockpit voice recorder registered the captain simply commenting, "Oh shit, this can't be . . ."

What was left of the Piper fell onto the unoccupied playground at Cerritos Elementary School, just missing the congregation of Concordia Lutheran Church across the street who were leaving after morning service. "For just a moment," California Highway Patrol Officer Lyle Whitten recalled, "I couldn't believe it was a real airplane. It looked like a toy . . . but then it hit the ground and you could see it wasn't a toy, and then for a moment I just wanted to cry."

Investigators were keen to discover why White hadn't spotted Kramer's Piper and warned the DC-9 of its presence. It transpired that the type of transponder Kramer was using didn't transmit altitude information, and John Lauber from the NTSB noted that "if [the controller] doesn't have altitude information, then it's a reasonable assumption for him that the aircraft is not operating in the terminal control area". As a result of this crash, the FAA began requiring Mode C transponders to be fitted on small planes near busy airports, which broadcast both position and altitude – giving the controllers the vital data they need at a glance, rather than just blips on a radar screen. Additionally, in this case, atmospheric temperature inversion meant that the radar might not have displayed the transponder reading properly.

The NTSB investigators' findings severely criticised the failings of the ATC system, determining that the probable cause was the "limitations" of the ATC system "to provide collision protection". The continued reliance on "see and avoid" – there was no evidence that either pilot had tried to evade the collision – and Kramer's inadvertent and unauthorized entry into the TCA were deemed contributory factors. (Chairman Jim Burnett made a dissenting statement, making clear that he felt it was Kramer's failure to see and avoid, rather than all parties', which was a contributory factor.) They made multiple recommendations to the FAA including the expedition of development, operational evaluation and final certification of a Traffic Alert and Collision Avoidance System (TCAS), and a requirement that this be installed on aircraft.

In the year that followed, the rules governing the Los Angeles TCA were tightened up, so that no small aircraft could cross the control area without contacting controllers. In Cerritos, they came to fear cloudy days: "We can't see the planes," local resident Sue Nelson explained around the first anniversary of the tragedy. "All the neighbours take a look at planes overhead to see if everything is OK, but on cloudy days it is just unnerving. It always scares me. It sounds louder when there is a cloud cover."

Court cases were brought and a Federal jury found in April 1989 that the air traffic controller and Kramer were equally responsible for the collision. The relatives of the victims had also added Aeromexico to the action, but the jury cleared them of blame, with jurors explaining after the verdict that they believed Kramer had acted negligently, and that Walter White should have steered the DC-9 away from the smaller aircraft. $56.5 million was divided among the plaintiffs, including nearly one tenth to Theresa Estrada, who lost her husband and two teenage children.

Although it was the last major loss of life in the United States caused in a mid-air collision, the worst was yet to come.

CONGESTION OVER INDIA

"We were in the clear when a cloud to our two o'clock position lit up," USAF Captain Timothy J. Palace stated in an affidavit sworn three days after two aircraft collided above the village of Charkhi Dadri, west of New Delhi, India, on 12 November 1996.

"The light was orange in colour and its intensity continued to increase. We were somewhere between flight level 12,000 ft and 14,000 ft [estimate]. The cloud, from what I saw as it lit up, was about 20 to 40 miles from us, about 20 to 30 miles in length in a line about even with or slightly below our altitude.

"As the cloud lit up, I remarked that it must be a rocket launch. The intensity continued to increase and involve the entire cloud. Then a plume of fire came out of the cloud on the right, followed shortly after by one on the left.

"The direction of movement was hard to determine and we were trying to identify what we were witnessing. I remarked, 'That's not a missile, is it?' I think this was just prior to or about the same time the second plume appeared.

"Captain Marks was flying in the right seat and started to bank the aircraft to the left. After a short while (about ten seconds), it became evident the plumes were descending to the ground.

"Finally, the glow of the cloud diminished, and the two plumes reached the ground, continuing to burn as two distinct fires. That's when we realized that it might have been a mid-air collision.

"Captain Incerpi was working the radius from the left seat and he informed the controller of what we had just witnessed. The controller made several attempts to contact the two aircraft with no replies."

Three hundred and forty-nine people in total were aboard the Saudi Arabian Airlines Boeing 747 Flight 763 travelling from New Delhi to Dhahran, Saudi Arabia, and the Kazakhstan Airlines Ilyushin Il-76 Flight 1907 coming in to New Delhi from

Shymkent, Kazakhstan. All of them perished in the deadliest mid-air collision ever, with the third-highest fatality count in aviation history. And while TCAS and better radar equipment could have helped to prevent the crash, it became clear that the cause was human error.

At the time, flights in and out of Indira Gandhi International Airport at New Delhi were using one air corridor out of a potential four. This was mainly because the military were keeping the others for their own use, despite protestations at the risks this presented. In order to prevent collisions, arrivals and departures were kept at separate altitudes, with arriving aircraft often flying over departing ones. That's what should have happened on the night of 12 November: the Kazakhstan Airlines Ilyushin was directed to stay at flight level 150 (15,000 feet) while the Saudi 747 had been deliberately held at flight level 140, a thousand feet below, by air traffic controller V. K. Dutta until the two aircraft had passed. For reasons that only became clear during the investigation – and despite claims to the contrary from representatives of Kazakhstan Airlines – the Ilyushin had not been anywhere near the correct flight level.

The 747 had left Delhi Airport at 1833 Indian Standard Time, and was in the middle of its climb to cruising level. On board the flight to the Persian Gulf were twenty-three crew and 289 passengers, many of whom were Indian workers returning to jobs as drivers, cooks and housemaids in the Middle East. The Kazakhstan Ilyushin had twenty-seven passengers and ten crew, and was around 70 nautical miles from Delhi Airport when it had reported passing through flight level 230 for flight level 180. Dutta cleared it to continue descent to flight level 150.

As far as Dutta was concerned, when the Ilyushin confirmed that they were at 150, he was simply giving them a warning that there was "traffic 12 o'clock reciprocal Saudi Boeing 747, 14 miles" – there was another plane heading towards them at a lower level. The crew queried the distance, but then confirmed receipt of the information.

However, the Ilyushin wasn't flying at flight level 150 at all. It was continuing to descend, and, as analysis of their flight data recorder and cockpit voice recorder would show, the aircraft wasn't where the radio operator, who was communicating with

Dutta, believed it to be. They were in fact already around flight level 145, and in the few seconds before the collision they had descended a further 310 feet. Radio operator Igor Repp had passed on the instruction to "keep the 150, not descending", but when he saw the altimeter reading showing that they were dangerously low, he screamed at the pilot to "get to 150!" As Gennadi Cherepanov tried to regain altitude, the Saudi 747 appeared – and, at 1840, the two aircraft collided. On the ATC screen, the two blips merged, but then failed to separate before disappearing completely.

The Ilyushin's tail cut through the 747's left wing and horizontal stabilizer, and Saudi Airlines Captain Khalid Al Shubaily and First Officer Nazir Khan quickly lost control of the jet. The 747 went into a rapidly descending spiral, fire trailing from its wing. In the cockpit, the crew recited the prayer required by Islamic law for those who are facing certain death. The plane ploughed into a mustard field. Unlike the 747, the Ilyushin remained mainly intact as it rapidly descended towards a cotton field, around five miles from the wreckage of the Saudi jet. About 200 bodies were taken to a hospital, and more were scattered within a one-mile radius of the smouldering Saudi jet; there were reports that three or four people had survived the initial impact but no living patients were received at any of the local hospitals.

Suspicion immediately fell on air traffic controller Dutta. "Under air-traffic control they are told what to do. Provided they did what they were told to do, it was an air-traffic control error," David Rider, editor of *Jane's Air Traffic Control*, told the *Independent*. "Otherwise, it was pilot error – if an aircraft was told to turn right and turned left, for example." Within two days, however, the *Times of India* was reporting that the accident was "probably due to the Kazakh pilot's error." The black boxes from both aircraft were found the day after the crash, and a judicial enquiry was set up the same day by the Indian government. Within three days, it was already clear from the transcript of the conversations between ATC and the pilots that Dutta was not at fault – he had provided information to the flight crews as required – and he was allowed to return to work.

Examination of the wreckage revealed the angle of impact between the two aircraft, and that for some reason the Ilyushin had come up from beneath the 747. This didn't seem to make sense, since the Kazakh flight should have been above the Saudi, so the data from the black boxes was going to be critical. However, the analysis of the flight data and cockpit voice recorders took longer than anticipated, since agreement couldn't be reached between the various parties as to who should transcribe the information. Eventually, the black boxes for the Saudi 747 were taken to the Farnborough Aviation Research Centre in Britain, and the Kazakhstan aircraft's devices went to a similar research facility in Moscow.

With blame clearly being placed on their crew, the Kazakh authorities tried to claim that the descent from 15,000 feet had been caused by turbulence. This seemed to be borne out by Captain Palace's affidavit, quoted at the start of this chapter, which also stated that there were heavy cumulus clouds for 20 to 30 miles in length on a line approximately parallel to the path of the collision. However, the Airports Authority of India, the Directorate General of Civil Aviation, the Air Traffic Controllers Guild, Boeing and Saudi all disagreed, and said that there was no bad weather. The Kazakhs countered that the flight data from the Ilyushin showed that it had been "bouncing" during the turbulence – the black box seemed to indicate that the aircraft had undergone a number of sharp falls in the period immediately before the collision. The experts at Farnborough were able to explain this: the equipment on the Ilyushin had been faulty, and had jammed from time to time. This gave the appearance of bouncing when in fact the aircraft had been in a controlled descent.

The cockpit voice recorder on the Ilyushin showed that the situation had been made worse by the apparent lack of clear understanding by the Kazakh pilots of the instructions they were being given. The radio operator spoke English, but he didn't have his own set of flight instruments – he relied on looking across the cockpit at the altimeters in front of the pilot and co-pilot, which may have been the cause of the inaccurate information passed to the ATC about their flight level. Dutta's traffic advisory of the Saudi aircraft at flight level 140 may have been misinterpreted by the pilots as an instruction to descend to that level. Either way, the investigation decided that "the root and approximate cause of the collision was the unauthorised descending by the Kazakh aircraft to FL140 and failure to maintain the assigned FL150", with a contributory factor being the "disregard of ATC instructions by the Kazakh aircraft".

The Court of Inquiry also made various recommendations: separate air corridors should be created in to and out of New Delhi; a secondary ATC radar with aircraft altitude data should be installed – this had in fact been purchased, but at the time of the collision had not been taken out of its boxes according to air traffic controllers (Indian officials claimed that the changes had run into "technical problems"); mandatory collision avoidance equipment on commercial aircraft operating in Indian airspace; and reduction of the airspace around New Delhi that was controlled by the Indian military. Collision avoidance equipment was quickly made obligatory on all aircraft. Never since has there been such a loss of life in a mid-air collision.

DOUBLE DESCENT

But for the sharp eyes and movements of the pilot of an aircraft over Yaizu in Japan's Shizuoka Prefecture on 30 January 2001, an even worse collision could have occured. Makoto Watanabe, the pilot of Japan Airlines Flight 907, reported at 1610 that he had "taken near-miss evasive action to avoid a collision", and because passengers and crew had been injured, he returned to Haneda Airport in Tokyo. The near-collision had come about because of conflicting information coming to the pilots of the two aircraft from the local air traffic controllers and their TCASes, resulting in both aircraft entering a descent to "avoid" the incident – and thereby creating it. If the aircraft had collided, it is highly unlikely that any of the 677 people on board could have survived; instead nine people received serious injuries, with ninety-one minor cases also reported.

Flight 907, a 747, was on its way from Tokyo International Airport (Haneda) to Naha International Airport on Okinawa, while Japan Airlines Flight 958, a DC-10, was travelling between Gimhae International Airport in Pusan, South Korea, and Narita International Airport in Tokyo. If all had gone according to the flight plans, the two aircraft should have passed each other separated by 2,000 feet.

Twenty minutes after Flight 907 left Haneda, it was climbing towards 39,000 feet. Its TCAS sounded at 1554.19 Japanese Local Time, a second after its counterpart on the DC-10 had done the same. In air traffic control, trainee controller Hideki Hachitani saw the situation on his screen and made a potentially catastrophic error. At 1554.27, he mistakenly ordered Flight 907, rather than Flight 958, to descend. Not realizing that the order wasn't really meant for him, Captain Watanabe followed the instruction and began to descend. However, at 1554.34, the DC-10's TCAS had issued an RA (resolution advisory) to descend, which its crew complied with. A second later, the TCAS on the 747 issued an RA telling it to ascend. If both Watanabe and

DC-10 pilot Tatsuyuki Akazawa had followed the TCAS instructions, there wouldn't have been a problem.

However, Watanabe was still following the instructions from ATC and descending. When Hachitani looked at his screen again at 1554.38, he saw that Flight 958 wasn't changing altitude, so ordered it to turn right and go on heading 130 degrees. There was no response. Eight seconds later, Hachitani sent another urgent instruction to take heading 140 degrees. Neither message was acknowledged or acted on by the 958 pilot. Hachitani's supervisor, Yasuko Momii, therefore intervened and ordered "Japanair 957" to climb. This just added to the confusion, since there was no "Japanair 957" in the skies nearby – and neither 907 nor 958 took any notice of the instruction. Both aircraft were still descending and heading for collision. At 1555.02, ATC ordered Japanair 907 to "climb and maintain flight level 390", but by that point it was too late.

At 1555.11, the two aircraft came within 35 feet of each other, according to Watanabe, with the 747 passing underneath the DC-10. Both pilots had reacted instinctively and avoided each other, but the steep dive into which Watanabe entered sent passengers, luggage and the food service carts crashing into the 747's ceiling. One woman received a broken leg, others were burned. "I have never seen a plane fly so close," one unidentified passenger told NHK, Japan's semi-public television network. "I thought we were going to crash." Once he realized the extent of the injuries aboard, Watanabe decided to return to Haneda, reaching there at 1647; the wounded were taken to local hospitals, and the flight was rescheduled to depart at 1915 that evening.

The controllers involved were immediately blamed, and the official Aircraft and Railway Accident Investigation Commission concluded that the air traffic controllers' error and the pilots' decision to follow air traffic control instructions instead of the TCAS Resolution Advisory (RA) were the two main causes. However, when a case against the controllers for professional negligence came before the Tokyo District Court in March 2006, presiding Judge Hisaharu Yasui decided that the mistaken instructions they had given were not the direct cause of the accident. "Hachitani's instruction [to Flight 907 to descend rather than 958] at that time was not a dangerous move that would have caused a collision," the judge noted, adding, "It's unwarranted to hold the air traffic controllers and the pilot criminally accountable." He did however note that Hachitani was not aware of the severity of his responsibility as an air traffic controller." The Tokyo District Public Prosecutor's Office appealed, and Judge Masaharu Suda revoked the not-guilty verdicts, finding that the mix-up of the flight numbers was a "rudimentary error".

Hachitani was sentenced to a year's imprisonment, his supervisor Momii to eighteen months. They, in turn, appealed, but the Supreme Court upheld the guilty verdict. Their prison sentences were suspended, but Japanese public service regulations required that they were dismissed from their jobs.

BLOOD FEUD

Eighteen months after the incident over Yaizu, a conflict between the TCAS and ATC instructions did not resolve as successfully, and an extra name was added to the tally of those who died as a result of the first major mid-air collision of the twenty-first century when the air traffic controller who was deemed partly responsible for the tragedy was murdered by a relative of three of those who lost their lives. There were many in his community who felt sympathy for Vitaly Kaloyev's actions – and on his release from prison for the murder, he was appointed his country's deputy minister of architecture and construction.

Despite the incident in Japan – and a couple of others which had occurred over Europe in the months following that near miss – it was still not obligatory for pilots to follow the instructions from the TCAS. Indeed, for the crew of the Tupolev involved in the collision over Überlingen, their manual stated that when an RA came to "climb, climb", this was to be treated as a "recommendation to the crew". When they continued to obey the ATC instruction to descend, it led to the deaths of all seventy-one aboard their aircraft and the DHL Boeing 757 with which they collided.

The two aircraft collided at 2135 GMT on 1 July 2002. Bashkirian Airlines Flight 2937, a Tupolev Tu-154M, was carrying nine crew and sixty passengers, the majority of whom were schoolchildren from the city of Ufa in Bashkortostan heading out to Barcelona for a trip to a music festival on the Costa Daurada organized by UNESCO. They shouldn't have been there at all: they had arrived in Moscow just too late to catch their flight to Spain, but the airline had put on a special charter flight so they wouldn't miss the festival. It was also useful for the airline: it provided an opportunity for an assessment of Captain Alexander Mihailovich Gross by their chief pilot, Oleg Pavlovich Grigoriev, who acted as first officer for the flight but was effectively in charge. Gross's normal first officer, Murat Ahatovich Itkulov, was also aboard, as were a flight engineer and flight navigator.

The DHL 757 was heading northbound on a flight from Bahrain via Bergamo to Brussels, piloted by Captain Paul Phillips and First Officer Brant Campioni. Both were flying at flight level 360 (36,000 feet) and their paths intersected over Lake Constance, an area which came under Zurich air traffic control, operated that evening by Peter Nielsen, who at the time was working on his own. The 757 had received the instruction to climb to that flight level at 2126.36, reaching there at 2159.50 (although they failed to confirm to the ATC that they had done so). Twenty-one seconds later, the Tupolev crew contacted ATC Zurich and informed controller Nielsen that they were at flight level 360. For the next four and a half minutes, everything seemed normal to the two flight crews; on the ground, Neilsen was dealing with other traffic.

First Officer Campioni saw this as a good time to take a toilet break, and at 2134.24 he handed over control to Captain Phillips. Eighteen seconds later, the TCAS on both the 757 and the Tupolev issued a traffic alert, warning of conflicting traffic – purely an advisory at this stage. However, Campioni returned to his seat. Seven seconds later, Nielsen urgently instructed the Tupolev to descend to flight level 350 – "Expedite – I have crossing traffic," he warned them. The crew began their descent immediately.

It was now 2134.56, at which time the TCAS on both aircraft issued RAs to their crews. The 757 was ordered to descend, and the crew instantly obeyed. The Tupolev was told to climb – but this order was coming a mere two seconds after they had been told the exact opposite by the ATC. First Officer Itkulov realized the dilemma quicker than anyone else, and said pointedly, "It says 'climb'." Chief Pilot Grigoriev believed that "he is guiding us down". Seven seconds later, they received clarification from ATC: "Descend level 3-5-0, expedite descent."

As the Tupolev crew acknowledged the instruction and continued their descent, the TCAS on the 757 was reacting to the situation, and ordered "Increase Descent!" A second thereafter, at 2135.13, Nielsen advised the Tupolev, "We have traffic at your 2 o'clock position now at 3-6-0." This was wrong: relative to the Tupolev's current position, the 757 was at the 10 o'clock position – on the other side of the aircraft from where the crew started urgently looking. They spotted it at 2135.24 as their TCAS ordered them to "Increase climb!"

There were only eight seconds from that moment until the vertical stabilizer of the 757 sliced straight through the main fuselage of the Tupolev. The cockpit voice recorders on both aircraft register swearing and a final desperate attempt by the DHL crew to "Descend hard!" During that time, Peter Nielsen was responding to a call from another aircraft and didn't realize what was happening 34,890 feet up in the air.

The 757 had bisected the other aircraft just ahead of its wings. The Tupolev exploded, with forty of the sixty-nine on board thrown out into the cold night air as the aircraft broke up into four pieces. Eighty per cent of the vertical tail of the 757 was torn off by the impact. "I heard a loud bang and thought there might be a thunderstorm and when I looked out of the window the whole sky was red and orange. One of the planes suddenly passed over and I heard an explosion a second afterwards," local resident Edward Lloyd told reporters, while another told the BBC website, "There was one piece of a plane bursting like a rocket into a forest and exploding there." Local photographer Dirk Diestel told ABC news, "I heard what sounded like thunder, but it wouldn't stop . . . I looked up and saw four or five giant fireballs shooting directly over me."

The debris from the two aircraft was scattered over seven main sites in an area of about 350 square kilometres. The main part of the 757 was found about a kilometre from the village of Taisersdorf, with the tail around five kilometres away. The forward part of the fuselage of the Tupolev crashed in the area of Brachenreuthe, with the left wing in a garden by a golf course in Owingen, nearly two kilometres away. The tail section had fallen straight to earth, landing some 300 metres from the forward part, near a boarding school for mentally handicapped children. The right wing fell into a corn field nearly a kilometre away from the main crash site.

More than 800 rescue workers carried out an intensive search, some using helicopters equipped with infrared cameras and sonar-equipped boats on Lake Constance. The aircraft parts were then removed to a hanger at Friedrichshafen Airport for examination. Teams from the German Federal Bureau of Aircraft Accidents Investigation (the BFU) worked in conjunction with Russian investigators and a team from the NTSB.

Multiple theories proliferated in the media, increasingly focusing attention on Skyguide, the operators of Zurich ATC. "My theory is that it is the fault of the air traffic controllers, they put the planes on the same path," Nikolai Odegov, a director of Bashkirian Airlines, said soon after the crash. "There were no reasons to say that the pilots didn't handle the plane properly."

It transpired that a short-term conflict alert (STCA) system had been taken offline for maintenance at the time of the collision; Nielsen should therefore have given instructions to the Tupolev earlier, since a wider lateral separation requirement was in effect with no STCA operational. (An aural STCA system was working, but it only delivered a warning thirty-two seconds before the collision, far too late to be of any practical use, even if anyone had heard it.)

However, Nielsen was dealing with five different aircraft on two radar screens, as well as on two different radio frequencies. His colleague was on a break – a practice that was condoned by Skyguide if skies were quiet. The company had originally claimed that this wasn't the case but they had to backtrack in the first of many volte-faces by Skyguide.

Additionally, one of the German air traffic controllers based at the Karlsruhe ATC centre, had spotted the potential collision, and had tried to call Skyguide repeatedly – but the Swiss firm's main phone line was out of order, and Nielsen had been using the back-up line to call the tower at Friedrichshafen regarding one of the other aircraft he was handling.

Skyguide themselves were already the subject of investigation, following a couple of previous near misses, according to the German newspaper *Der Spiegel*, who said that a Swiss report published the week before the accident noted "insufficiencies in its radars and serious problems in its co-ordination with neighbouring countries and military air controllers".

Peter Nielsen admitted the week after the accident that it was "his duty and responsibility to prevent such accidents happening", and in a statement he wrote: "On the night of the accident I was part of a network of people, surveillance equipment, and regulations. All these pieces must work together seamlessly, and be coordinated. The tragic accident shows that errors cropped up in this network."

What also became clear in the discussions was that there was no absolute rule regarding the priority that should be given to either TCAS or ATC where their instructions were in conflict. The International Civil Aviation Organization rules stated that "nothing in these rules shall relieve the pilot-in-command of an aircraft from the responsibility of taking such action, including collision avoidance manoeuvres based on resolution advisories provided by ACAS equipment, as will best avert collision."

The BFU report was released in 2004, and noted: "This accident happened because many actions and failures to act came together that, viewed on their own, might only have a small significance for air safety." Rather than giving causes, with contributing factors, as the NTSB does, the BFU's report divided the causes into two groups – immediate and systemic – which were given equal weight. The immediate causes were that the "imminent separation infringement was not noticed by ATC in time. The instruction for the [Tupolev] to descend was given at a time when the prescribed separation to the [757] could not be ensured anymore"; and that "the [Tupolev] crew followed the ATC instruction to descend and continued to do so even after TCAS advised them to climb. This manoeuvre was performed contrary to the generated TCAS RA."

The systemic causes were that the TCAS system wasn't properly integrated, particularly as the "regulations of national aviation authorities, operational and procedural instructions of the TCAS manufacturer and the operators were not standardized, incomplete and partially contradictory"; that the "management and quality assurance of the air navigation service company did not ensure that during the night all open workstations were continuously staffed by controllers"; and that Skyguide had tolerated the practice of one controller retiring to rest "during times of low traffic flow at night".

Skyguide accepted full responsibility for the errors after the report was published and asked relatives of the seventy-one victims for forgiveness. But by this point there was already a seventy-second death connected to the crash: Peter Nielsen's mea culpa following the crash brought architect Vitaly Kaloyev to the door of his home in Kloten, near Zurich. Kaloyev had been working in Barcelona, and was waiting for his wife and two children to visit. Instead, he had helped with the recovery of their bodies from the crash site; he had found one of his daughter's necklaces before locating her body in a tree. He had a nervous breakdown following their deaths, and spent much of the first year afterwards building a shrine to them.

At the memorial service held for the first anniversary of the crash in 2003, Kaloyev had asked Skyguide representatives for a meeting with the controller but received no reply. He had therefore hired a private detective to track Nielsen down, and in February 2004, he went to the controller's home, where he claimed that he showed Nielsen pictures of his children. "I went to Nielsen as a father who loves his children, so he could see the photos of my dead children and next to them his kids, who were alive," he told a court in Zurich. However, he lost control when Nielsen hit him on the hand. He stabbed the controller multiple times, and the man bled to death. Kaloyev was held on remand until October 2005 when he was sentenced to eight years in prison, although he was released in November 2007. Returning to his home in Ossetia, an area where blood feuds are a traditional way of sorting out disputes, he was hailed as a hero.

However, when Kaloyev tried to attend the tenth anniversary memorial, he was detained by German border authorities: "The German authorities apparently do not want to let me attend the mourning ceremony," he told the Interfax news. "They think for some reason that my presence there is unnecessary, although all my family perished in the plane crash." Apparently the Swiss had placed him on a "watch list" following his release, and they objected to his presence at the ceremony. However, following intervention from the Russian diplomatic corps, he was allowed to attend.

Eight Skyguide employees were also prosecuted for manslaughter. Three of the four managers convicted were given suspended prison terms and the fourth was ordered to pay a fine; four air traffic controllers were acquitted.

There were other far-reaching consequences of the Überlingen disaster. Aviation authorities began to advise that when a resolution advisory is in conflict with an ATC instruction, crews should follow the more immediate RA, and inform ATC accordingly – something which the Japanese authorities had been recommending following their own disaster eighteen months previously.

"JUST FLY THE AIRPLANE, DUDE."

The most recent major collision occurred in 2006 in Brazil and led to two very different sets of conclusions as to its cause – one from the Brazilian Centro de Investigação e Prevenção de Acidentes Aeronáuticos (CENIPA), the other from the American NTSB, who had been assisting with the investigations. While both air accident investigation branches agreed on the fundamentals of what happened, they disagreed on who was responsible; however, since the Brazilians take precedence in their own country's matters, the American pilots involved have become subject to court cases based on the Brazilian conclusions. After a lengthy legal process, they were found guilty. They were still more fortunate than their counterparts on the jet with which they collided: all 154 people aboard the Boeing 737 were killed.

Captain Joe Lepore and First Officer Jan Paladino's journey into the Brazilian legal system began when they took off from São José dos Campos, São Paulo State in Brazil, at 1751 UTC on 29 September 2006, heading for Eduardo Gomes Airport in Manaus and thence to Fort Lauderdale in Florida. They were carrying five passengers: two employees of Embraer, two ExcelAire executives, and *New York Times* columnist Joe Sharkey. The clearance which they were given for the flight in their Embraer EMB-135BJ Legacy aircraft specified three flight levels: flight level 370 on Airway UW2 to the Brasilia VOR, then flight level 360 from the VOR to an intersection on Airway UZ6, and flight level 380 from there to Manaus. However, when the ground controller passed on the clearance to the Legacy crew, he only included the initial flight level: "clearance to Eduardo Gomes, flight level three seven zero". Understandably, the Legacy crew took this to mean that they were cleared all the way through to Manaus at 37,000 feet, rather than moving between three different levels.

Responsibility for the flight was handed over from the Sector 5 controller of the Brasilia Area Control Centre (ACC) to the Sector

7 controller around 52 nautical miles south of the VOR, around an hour later. The Sector 5 controller failed to tell either the Sector 7 controller or the pilots that they had to descend from flight level 370 to flight level 360 when they reached the VOR: the beacon was within Sector 5 airspace, so the handover was "unusually early" (according to the NTSB's later reckoning). The Legacy crew reported in to the Sector 7 controller, confirming that they were maintaining flight level 370. They were instructed to contact the ACC when they were crossing the boundary into the next ACC area, and at 1851 they were told that they were under radar surveillance.

At 1902, the Legacy's transponder ceased registering simultaneously on five separate air traffic control radars; no altitude information was received from the small aircraft for the next fifty-eight minutes. However, no one either on the ground or within the cockpit noticed that this was the case, and the Legacy continued to fly at flight level 370. This might not have been a problem if everyone on the ground and in the air had been aware of their presence at that altitude – standard rules stated that aircraft flying in that direction on that airway should be at either flight level 360 or flight level 380 to ensure adequate separation between aircraft, but exceptions could be made – but no one bar the pilots knew where they were. The air traffic controllers assumed that the Legacy was at flight level 360, and the flight was handed over between controllers on that basis.

At 1916.35, the Legacy made a slight course deviation to avoid weather, although they did not inform the ATC of this. Unknown to them, from around 1926, ATC was trying to contact them without success; the seventh and final attempt was made at 1953.39, which did get through. By this point, First Officer Paladino had been trying to contact the ACC on various frequencies, but none of his dozen attempts had been successful. (Captain Lepore had left the cockpit for a toilet break and then remained away from the controls for some time, apparently to fix a problem with the toilets.) However, once the ACC did make contact, the co-pilot didn't hear all the decimals of the frequency which he had been told to tune to in order to contact the Amazonic ACC, so tried a further seven times to gain that information, just as the pilot returned to the cockpit. One second after the final call, at 1956.54, the Legacy collided with another aircraft.

Gol Transportes Aéreos Flight 1907 had departed from Manaus, heading for Rio de Janiero with a stop at Brasilia, at 1835. Captain Decio Chaves Jr headed the crew of six, and there were 148 passengers on board the 737. The scheduled flight was proceeding as normal – as the CENIPA report noted: "in the cockpit of the Boeing, moments before the collision, there was absolute tranquillity". They had just been handed over from Amazonic ACC to Brasilia, and had selected the correct frequency. The two pilots were mid-conversation when the collision occurred.

The two aircraft were coming towards each other at a speed of approximately 1600 kilometres per hour, with the 737 a little left of the Legacy and slightly above it. Neither aircraft's TCAS systems emitted any form of warning – unsurprisingly, since the transponder on the Legacy wasn't functioning – nor did either set of crew notice the other aircraft's approach. The left wing of each aircraft hit the other, tearing nearly seven metres away from the 737's wing, taking with it the entire left aileron. This left the aircraft immediately and irreversibly uncontrollable.

Not that that stopped Captain Chaves from trying his best to save the lives of his passengers and crew. Although the 737 was in a fast descending left spiral, and was about to break up, Chavez didn't panic or lose control. When his co-pilot Thiago Jordão Cruso asked what was happening, he told him he didn't know, but asked him to keep calm. As the cockpit voice recording (CVR) showed, Chaves was unaware that he had lost such a big chunk of the wing, and was trying to bring the aircraft back to straight and level flight. However, during the sixty-three seconds it took the 737 to spin to the ground, the aircraft broke up. It landed in the dense rainforest, about 200 kilometres east of the municipality of Peixoto de Azevedo.

Air force helicopter pilots found the wreckage near a cattle ranch, and it was clear that there was no hope of finding survivors. "We heard a loud explosion and some of our employees saw a plane flying low," the ranch manager, Milton Picalho, told reporters. "Judging from the direction the noise came from, I would say it crashed inside the [nearby Xingu Indian] reservation." Around 200 people, including members of the Kayapo people, helped with the search operation, and after confirmation of the devastation, three days of national mourning were declared.

Once the black boxes were found – the CVR memory module had become separated from the rest of the recorder and took nearly four weeks to locate – they were sent to the Transportation Safety Board in Canada for analysis.

On the Legacy, Captain Lepore was shocked by the collision, and First Officer Paladino told him to "just fly the airplane, dude" since the autopilot had disengaged. However, when he realized that Lepore was still shaken, Paladino took over the controls. Over the next couple of minutes, the captain tried to declare an emergency while the first officer flew the aircraft, and at 1959.13, Paladino noticed that the TCAS was off. This he hastily switched back on, with the co-pilot telling his captain to "just keep an eye for traffic" while they descended. At 1959.50, the transponder started to show up once more on the ground radar screens.

Passenger Joe Sharkey wrote an account of the collision for the *New York Times*, which he filed two days afterwards (1 October). In this he recalled that he "felt a terrific jolt and heard a loud bang, followed by an eerie silence, save for the hum of the engines." One of the other passengers confirmed they had been hit, and they could all see that there was now "a jagged ridge, perhaps a foot high, where the five-foot-tall winglet was supposed to be." The edge of the wing started to lose rivets and peel back as the pilots tried to bring the aircraft down. In addition to the left winglet, they had also lost the tips of the left horizontal stabilizer and elevator. "They were like infantrymen working together in a jam, just as they had been trained to do," Sharkey wrote. At that point none of them was aware that they had hit a 737, nor had any idea of its fate – they wouldn't learn that for a further three hours.

With radio relay help from a nearby 747, Polar Air Cargo Flight 71, the pilots were able to bring the Legacy into Cachimno Airport, part of the Brazilian Air Force Campo de Provas Brigadeiro Velloso. In a conversation with the Air Defence and Air Traffic Control Integrated Centre shortly after landing, Captain Lepore changed his response to a question about the TCAS on the Legacy: originally he admitted it wasn't switched on, but then changed his mind: "TCAS was off . . . The TCAS was on," he said at 2236, and when asked: "TCAS for sure was turned on. OK?" he replied, "OK!"

It was the start of his and Paladino's problems. They were detained by police, then confined to a Rio hotel for two months after their passports had been removed. Initially, although the pair were told that they were being treated as suspects in the deaths, Brazilian Federal Police spokesman Bruno Craesmeyer admitted: "The Federal Police believe that the American pilots are not as responsible as other people. There are more serious causes of the accident." However, as the blame game began, it became clear that the pilots were going to be portrayed as irresponsible amateurs who ignored controllers' orders, changed their flight plan without notifying the tower, switched off crucial equipment, and flew at the wrong altitude. When their passports were returned, they were quickly charged by the police with "endangering a vessel or aircraft" (a decision their lawyer called "premature, irresponsible and absurd" which was only made because the police were "looking for someone to blame for the crime") but allowed to return home to Long Island, New York. In the meantime, a major air crash occurred in Brazil on 26 July 2007, which put even more pressure on the government to improve the air traffic control system.

CENIPA's report took over two years to compile, partly because of the lack of participation of the Brasilia ACC controllers in the enquiry. Their investigations included considerable analysis of the ways in which the transponder could have been switched off, as well as the actions of the various air traffic controllers. As with so many incidents, one simple error wasn't the cause of the collision: the actions of the pilots and the air traffic controllers all contributed. CENIPA focused on the former; the NTSB's appendix to it noted that CENIPA's "interpretations, conclusions and understandings of the relationship between certain factual items and the demonstrated risk differ in a number of respects" from theirs, and that "the primary mission of ATC to separate aircraft within positive controlled airspace was unsuccessful". They pointed out three times that there was no evidence of regulatory violations by the Legacy crew, despite the CENIPA's reports frequent accusations of lack of "airmanship" on their part.

Lepore and Paladino's lawyer Joel Weiss commented: "The Cenipa report hides the real and obvious cause of this tragic accident. ATC placed these two competent flight crews on a collision course, traveling toward each other at the same altitude on the same airway. It also buries the fact that this was not only a result of major errors by individual air traffic controllers, but of institutional errors built into Brazil's ATC system." CENIPA's head, Brigadier Jorge Kersul, did comment about the transponder's non-functioning: "There is nothing that proves this was intentional . . . There is no reason for them to do that. The most probable hypothesis is that it was turned off inadvertently."

The pilots and four Brazilian ATC controllers were originally indicted for exposing an aircraft to danger and over the next five years charges would be brought, then dropped, then reinstated. The pilots were acquitted of negligence in December 2008 but charged with malpractice; however, that decision was overturned in January 2010. One of the air traffic controllers was sentenced to three years and four months' imprisonment for his part in failing to spot the transponder wasn't working; the pilots were sentenced to four years and four months' imprisonment for failure to observe cockpit warnings that the TCAS and transponder weren't working, which was commuted to community service in the United States – but that decision in its turn was altered by a federal court in October 2012 to a sentence of three years and one month under an "open" system. This was reduced still further in December 2013 by the Supreme Court, to two years and four months' imprisonment in an open prison (which, in Brazil, is a form of curfew). The pilots remained in America during these hearings, and further discussions regarding their futures, and any potential jail time, is still ongoing at the time of writing. Nothing, however, will remove the feeling that they shared with Joe Sharkey on the evening of the collision: "If anybody should have gone down it should have been us," Lepore kept repeating, while Paladino, "barely able to speak", added: "I'm just trying to settle in with the loss of all those people. It is really starting to hurt."

Part 2:
Ground Collisions and Near Misses

FOG IN THE WINDY CITY

A runway incursion is defined by the International Civil Aviation Organization (ICAO) as "Any occurrence at an aerodrome involving the incorrect presence of an aircraft vehicle or person on the protected area of a surface designated for the landing and take off of aircraft". While this includes incidents involving buffalo on the runway in the aftermath of the 2004 tsunami, and is used to cover all incidents where aircraft could potentially collide with another object or person (such as a snow plough, tractor or lawnmower on the runway as happened in Whitehorse, Canada, on 6 March 2009, at Pearson Airport, Toronto, on 23 October 2001, and at Dublin Airport on 29 May 2009, respectively), this section will look at incidents where aircraft were in the process of taking off or landing and they hit, or nearly hit, another aircraft.

On 20 December 1972, a North Central Airlines DC-9, Flight 575, was taking off from Chicago O'Hare Airport. It was quite a foggy night – visibility was only about a quarter of a mile. To the pilot's horror, as he began his take-off roll, he realized that there was another aircraft directly in his way: a Convair CV-880, Delta Air Lines Flight 954, which had recently arrived from Tampa, Florida, and was proceeding to the gate, its pilots unaware that the runway they were crossing was in active use for departures. Neither crew saw the other aircraft in time to prevent the collision, resulting in ten of the forty-one passengers on the DC-9 receiving fatal injuries as a result of the fire that followed.

"We had just started to climb and then there was a rumble and the plane came down and started swerving," one of the passengers on the DC-9 told reporters. "I don't know if we were completely taken off or whether the tail was still on the ground. We came down and flames burst out on the left wing." According to a radio report at the time, the pilot's compartment of the DC-9 was "completely gutted, the wings are on the ground, and the fuselage is twisted and broken."

Flight 954 was informed by the Automatic Terminal Information Service on arrival in the Chicago area that Runway 14R was being used for landings, and both Runways 14R and 14L for departures. Chicago Approach Control (CAC) informed flights at 1739 that they would now be landing on 14L and 14R, and O'Hare tower gave the CV-880 clearance to land on 14L at 1752. Runway Visual Range had decreased from 3,000 feet at 1739 to 1,800 feet in those thirteen minutes.

At 1755, the tower controller asked Flight 954 to report when they were clear of the runway, which they did at 1756. The tower control cleared the flight to ground control, as the ground controller tried unsuccessfully to contact them. Seventy seconds later, Flight 954's first officer, Harry Greenberg, contacted ground control, stating that "Delta 954 is with you inside the Bridge and we gotta go to the box" – in other words, head to the holding area. The controller told them, to "just pull over to 32 pad" and made a note that he had sent 954 to the 32R pad.

Unfortunately, that isn't where Delta 954 was heading. Since they had already gone onto the bridge route to the North-South taxiway, they believed that they were being directed to go to the 32L pad. This required them to cross the 27L runway – which in the normal course of events shouldn't have been a problem if it wasn't being used.

North Central Flight 575 was cleared to taxi to Runway 27L for departure at 1750, and at 1758.52, the local controller cleared the DC-9 into the take-off position. Visibility was one-fourth (a quarter) mile. Twenty-six seconds later, it was cleared for take-off; at 1759.24, Captain Nordseth reported he was starting the take-off roll, with the first officer, Gerald Adamson, at the controls. As the captain called, "Rotate," he saw the CV-880 in front of them. Exclaiming, "Pull 'er up!" the two men tried desperately to gain altitude so that they would miss the other aircraft. A second and a half later, the two aircraft collided.

On the CV-880, the pilots were not even aware of the DC-9 and the captain was dealing with an enquiry about connecting flights when they were hit, and the first officer shouted, "That guy crashed!" As he heard reports of a fire on board, Captain Robert

McDowell gave the order to "shut 'em down" and ordered an emergency evacuation. Large portions of the CV-880's left wing and vertical stabilizer were torn off by the collision; the DC-9's right main landing gear detached, and it also lost a flap from its right wing.

DC-9 Captain Nordseth quickly realized that his aircraft would not be able to maintain flight, so took control, and flew it back onto the runway. However, the two remaining landing gear collapsed rearward on touchdown, and the aircraft skidded on its belly off the runway, over a grassy area, and then onto Runway 32L where it stopped, and burst into flames.

Captain Nordseth pulled the fire extinguisher handles and ordered the evacuation. One of the stewardesses opened the main door, and tried to deploy the escape slide; it failed to inflate. She was pushed out of the aircraft by passengers trying to exit, so tried to coordinate efforts from the ground. The first officer slid out from the cockpit and came to help her. The captain went through the cockpit door into the cabin and encouraged passengers forward, then assisted both on the ground and in the aircraft. Four passengers succumbed to the smoke as they tried to reach the exits; five others died in their seats. One of the thirty-two who managed to escape died later.

On the CV-880, Captain McDowell oversaw an orderly evacuation of his aircraft. Because of the poor visibility, neither the Chicago Fire Department officers who had been sent to attend to the burning wreckage of the DC-9 nor the control tower personnel were aware of their involvement in the accident for nearly half an hour.

The accident investigation noted that Captain Nordseth did "all that could be reasonably expected of a pilot to avoid the collision", pointing out that there was only 5.3 seconds between when he said "rotate" to the impact. "The captain first had to see the CV-880, next evaluate the probability of a collision, then decide on a course of action, and finally initiate an action; the aircraft had to respond to the control inputs". They also noted that "the flight-crew's skill in maintaining control of the aircraft most likely averted more serious consequences".

Matters hinged on who heard what when. Nobody informed Captain Nordseth on the CV-880 that Runway 27L was in use.

The controller maintained that he hadn't heard the words "inside the Bridge", and so assumed that the aircraft was just clear of Runway 14L, near the 32R pad. This assumption was challenged by the Safety Board, who found that the controller should have confirmed the aircraft's position – but, since there were two pads designated 32, the aircrew should also have confirmed which of the pair the controller meant. The Board was also concerned about the ground control radar equipment in the O'Hare tower, and found that it "provided indistinct displays of airport ground traffic". The conclusion was that the probable cause was "the failure of the traffic control system to insure separation of aircraft during a period of restricted visibility".

"DID YOU HIT IT?"

The amount of air traffic using Luton Airport had already been brought up in the British House of Commons ten days previously when Court Line Aviation's BAC One-Eleven 518 G-AXMJ (Mike Juliet) Flight 95 was involved in a fatal incident with McAlpine Aviation's Piper PA-23 Aztec on 18 April 1974. Both aircraft were trying to use the same runway at the same time, and although the One-Eleven first officer and commander tried to take off to avoid the Aztec, they were unable to do so.

Flight 95 was heading from Luton to Munich-Riem, and received permission to taxi to Delta, one of the four holding points before it used runway 08 – the single runway at Luton was used in both directions, so was called runway 26 or 08. The Ground Movement Controller (GMC) held it there until airways clearance for the flight was received. At that point, Flight 95 was cleared to enter the runway, and backtrack (i.e. taxi down it in one direction then turn around and take off in the opposite direction) in preparation for take-off. At 1525.14, the aircraft was then told to contact the tower, and at 1525.25, Flight 95 was cleared by the tower to line up and hold.

Thirteen seconds later, at 1525.38, the McAlpine Aviation flight G-AYDE (Delta Echo), which was travelling to Manchester as a charter flight, contacted GMC asking for taxi clearance. GMC asked if the pilot wanted to use 26 or 08, and he chose 26. The Aztec was cleared to taxi to the intersection of the taxiways, and then GMC noted: "Delta Echo cleared to Alpha 26", allowing it to hold at Alpha point before entering the runway. The Aztec acknowledged, and at 1527 the pilot was asked to report ready for take-off. He replied he would be ready in thirty seconds – but then continued beyond Alpha, onto the runway. Inside the small aircraft, the passenger, who was an experienced pilot and in the right-hand front seat, asked the pilot on the intercom whether they had been cleared to taxi beyond Alpha, but by the time he realized that the pilot hadn't heard him, they were on the runway.

Seconds earlier, the tower had given the One-Eleven clearance to take off, and at 1527.31 Flight 95 acknowledged that instruction saying, "We're rolling, thank you." The first officer was handling the take-off, with the flight's commander carrying out the co-pilot duties from the left seat. The commander only looked up from the controls and out of the cockpit window when the One-Eleven reached approximately 100 knots, and both he and the first officer saw the Aztec entering the runway from the left. It was clear that its pilot hadn't seen the One-Eleven and was intending to continue onto the runway.

The commander instantly took over control of the One-Eleven and opened both throttles fully, steering the aircraft as far to the right as he could and trying to lift the left wing so that it would not hit the Aztec. It was too little, too late – although the passenger had seen the One-Eleven approaching from his right, and ducked down beneath the cockpit coaming, he didn't have time to alert the pilot.

"Mike Juliet, did you hit it?" the tower demanded. "I think so," came the reply. They had indeed. The outer six metres of port wing of the One-Eleven slammed into the Aztec, damaging its propellers, and slicing off the top of the plane to the level of the coaming. The pilot was killed instantly from a fractured skull; the passenger suffered injuries.

The danger wasn't over yet though; the damage to the One-Eleven's wing had released a large amount of fuel, and as soon as the commander had used full reverse thrust and maximum braking to halt the aircraft, he ordered an evacuation. This had its own problems – two of the forward exits seemed to have jammed, and the commander had to use considerable force to open them. As it later transpired, one of the doors had an incorrect part fitted, and the slides had not been stowed properly. However, all eighty-six passengers and five crew were able to deplane successfully.

The Accidents Investigation Branch of the Department of Trade submitted their report on 26 February 1975, and concluded that the "non-standard R/T (radio telephony) phraseology employed by the GMC Controller and the absence of any additional safeguards to ensure that aircraft comply with ATC instructions when approaching the holding point were considered to be contributory factors". The controller should have said, "Cleared to holding point alpha; runway 26", or "hold at Alpha" to remove any misunderstanding, and they recommended that there should be a runway control van near the holding points to avoid a repetition of the accident.

LOST IN THE FOG

The worst runway incursion and ground collision, which is still referred to as the benchmark against which all are judged, was the incident at Los Rodeos Airport, Tenerife on Sunday 27 March 1977. Five hundred and eighty-three people lost their lives when KLM Flight 4805 and Pan Am Flight 1736, both Boeing 747s, collided in the fog on the runway. Sixty-one of those on the Pan Am flight survived. It remains the deadliest accident in aviation history.

Although the tragedy unfolded over a mere eight and a half minutes, the seeds of disaster were sown when a bomb blast exploded at Las Palmas Airport, Gran Canaria, forcing aircraft that shouldn't have been using the Tenerife airport to land there. These included the KLM flight, whose pilot was the airline's chief flying instructor, Jacob Veldhuyzen van Zanten, and the Pan Am service helmed by Captain Victor Grubbs.

Neither captain wanted to be in Tenerife for any longer than they needed to. Van Zanten was concerned about the strict Dutch aviation regulations governing crew time; if they were on duty for longer than permitted, he would have to remain overnight in Tenerife, which would cause problems for his passengers and crew. After landing in Tenerife at 1340 GMT, and parking the 747 on the holding area apron, next to a Norwegian Boeing 737, he hoped to be back in the air quickly, but as other aircraft were directed to the same holding area he realized that the delay would be too long to keep his passengers on board, so allowed them to go into the terminal building. One of them, Miss Robina van Lanschot, a travel guide for the Holland International Travel Group, decided to stay overnight in Santa Cruz; she was the only person who arrived in Tenerife on the KLM 747 to survive.

Half an hour or so after the KLM flight landed, Captain Grubbs landed the Pan Am 747, and taxied across to the holding area. The captain had originally asked for permission to remain in a holding pattern over Las Palmas, waiting for it to reopen, since he had sufficient fuel reserve; this would save his passengers a further delay in their journey. Many of them were elderly people, heading for a cruise ship. However, his request was refused. Unlike his counterpart in the KLM flight, Captain Grubbs didn't allow his passengers to deplane, although he did open the main cabin doors to let in some fresh air.

At 1430 GMT, the control tower informed the pilots that Las Palmas Airport had been reopened. This meant that Captain van Zanten was going to be well within the permitted working-time limits – his company headquarters had confirmed that they were clear until 1800 GMT – so he decided that he would refuel his 747. Because of the way that the aircraft had been parked at the small airport filling the normal taxiway, this meant that Pan Am 1736 couldn't get to the runway to continue its flight to Las Palmas, despite being ready to do so. Captain Grubbs sent his first officer and flight engineer out to check the clearance, but they discovered that it would be impossible to get around the KLM aircraft. The three smaller aircraft had been able to manoeuvre around the 747s and leave, but Pan Am 1736 was forced to wait the thirty-five minutes it took KLM 4805 to refuel, and then extra time while its passengers were rounded up.

The weather was deteriorating as the afternoon progressed. Light rain and fog patches plagued the airport. Runway visibility had been ten kilometres in the mid-afternoon, but by the time the two 747s were ready to depart around 1650, visibility had reduced to two to three kilometres, and over the next quarter of an hour it closed in to just 300 metres. The difficulties in visibility played a major part in the catastrophe that followed.

Both aircraft were cleared and handed over to the aerodrome control frequency, which meant that they could hear the conversations going on between the tower and the other planes. Rather than use the taxiway to the holding area for runway 30, the KLM 747 was instructed to go to the end of the runway, and make a backtrack. At 1652, the Pan Am jet was told to taxi down the runway, and to "leave the runway third, third to your left". This meant that both 747s would be backtracking down the 3,400-metre runway; the KLM jet would go to the end, make a U-turn, and then report when it was ready to take off. The Pan Am flight would follow it initially, but then take the third taxiway off the runway to allow the KLM aircraft to depart. The alternative was for the Pan Am flight to wait until the KLM 747 had taken off before entering the runway, and with conditions getting worse – the control tower couldn't see where the planes were by this stage – it made sense to try to expedite matters as much as possible.

The quality of the transmission from the control tower wasn't clear – there was a lot of background noise, which may have come from a football match which was showing on television – and the Pan Am crew were not sure whether the controller had told them to take the "first" or "third" exit. They turned onto the runway, and were discussing what had happened in Las Palmas as the KLM crew confirmed to the tower that they had just passed the fourth taxiway. They were told once again to make a 180-degree turn at the end of the runway, and "report . . . ah . . . ready for ATC clearance".

On the Pan Am, First Officer Bragg was looking at the flip-chart diagram of the layout of the airport and saw that the first taxiway was "a 90-degree turn" so deduced that the controller must have meant the third one. Captain Grubbs thought that they probably could use the first one, but Bragg was insistent that it must be the third one, since that was a 45-degree turn. The radio officer asked for confirmation once again, and the tower was adamant: "The third one, sir; one, two, three, third, third one."

The Pan Am crew carried on with their pre-flight checks as Captain Grubbs peered through the fog trying to spot the taxiways. At 1704.26, they passed the "ninety degree" turn-off, and then the second one a minute later – but they then didn't realize that they were passing the third one. It meant that they were still rolling down the runway.

Eighteen seconds later, at 1705.44, the KLM 747 had reached the end of the runway, and radioed that they were waiting for the ATC clearance. "You are cleared to the Papa Beacon, climb to and maintain flight level nine zero, right turn after take-off, proceed with heading zero four zero until intercepting the three two five radial from Las Palmas VOR," came the reply. First Officer Meurs was repeating the instruction back to the tower as Captain van Zanten released the brakes and began to advance the throttles to take-off power. "We gaan," he told his crew ("We're going"). For whatever reason, this seasoned pilot had decided to take off before permission had been granted.

". . . we are now at take-off," Meurs concluded, six seconds after van Zanten had begun the take-off run. The tower assumed that this meant they were at the take-off position, rather than actually in the middle of the manoeuvre, and told them, "OK, standby for take-off, I will call you."

In the Pan Am cockpit, there was understandable consternation that the KLM jet might be given permission to take off before they were out of the way. "We are still taxiing down the runway," they urgently told the tower.

Fatally, the Pan Am message to the tower coincided with the tower telling the KLM jet to standby, resulting in an electronic squeal which meant that those on the KLM didn't hear the words "standby for take-off, I will call you". Nor did they hear the urgent message from the Pan Am. All they heard was the tower giving them an "OK".

However, the airwaves cleared in time for them to hear the tower tell the Pan Am to "report the runway clear", and the confirmation from the American aircraft that they "will report when we are clear". Captain van Zanten and First Officer Meurs were concentrating on the take-off, so only the flight engineer realized the problem. "Is hij er niet af dan?" ("Isn't he clear then?") he asked. "Is hij er niet af, die Pan American?" ("Is he not clear, that Pan American?") Captain van Zanten was emphatic: "Jawel." ("Oh yes".)

Five seconds later, Captain Grubbs saw the lights of the other Boeing 747 heading rapidly towards them. "He's coming!" he screamed. "Look – this son of a bitch is coming!" He pushed the throttles wide open, and tried to move his 747 out of the way onto the grass verge – but there was simply no time. The 27 degrees that he managed to swing the aircraft around saved some of the passengers' lives.

The KLM 747 was just starting rotation. On the Pan Am flight deck, First Officer Bragg was yelling frantically, "Get off! Get off! Get off!" At the same moment, Van Zanten saw the Pan Am in the way and, with an oath, he desperately hauled at the control column to try to lift his aircraft.

He managed to lift it sufficiently that the nose leg of the KLM 747 cleared the Pan Am fuselage, but, only 8.9 seconds after

Captain Grubbs had seen it approaching, the main undercarriage of the KLM 747 slammed into the other aircraft. The fuselage top was sliced off – "I have always thought that it looked as if someone with a giant knife had simply cut the entire top of the cabin off," Robert Bragg later wrote – and the distinctive "hump" of the 747 was demolished by the KLM's no. 4 engine. The left wing cut the vertical stabilizer at rudder level. Both planes burst into flames as the fuel ignited.

The KLM aircraft continued to ascend for a moment, but it was completely unflyable, and crashed 150 metres down the runway. No one inside had time even to reach for the doors before the fuel tanks exploded. There were no survivors.

Some on board the Pan Am 747 were luckier. Flight Officer Bragg reached for the engine fire extinguisher controls above his head, and found nothing there but empty sky. The floors of the flight deck and the upper deck collapsed, and the crew and the passengers were thrown to the lower level. The crew and many of those passengers were able to clamber through a hole in the port side of the fuselage and reach the ground ("Just to sink down in the green grass wet with rain was so heavenly," Captain Grubbs said later). Those who were seated on the starboard side by the impact zone were killed instantly; many of the others nearby were trapped in the wreckage and overcome by the fire. A few on the port side did manage to get onto the wing, and then jump the 20 feet to the ground, unheeding of the risk of broken limbs. One woman, among the first to jump, had broken legs and arms, as well as her back, since nearly everyone behind her had landed on top of her when they jumped.

"I was in shock, and I would have perished if it hadn't been for my husband," survivor Floy Olson recalled a decade later. "I heard a woman shout, 'We've been bombed!' That's what I thought, and I thought I was dying. I heard my husband shout, 'Floy, unfasten your seat belt. Let's get out!'"

As local people and taxicabs came to the aid of the survivors, fire crews battled the blaze on the Pan Am 747. The fog was so thick that the tower had not seen the accident, but heard the explosion and could see some light from the fires. The survivors were taken to hospital, where Bragg compiled a list and got in touch with Pan Am – alerting them before they were even aware the accident had happened, and by chance ensuring that Captain Grubbs' wife heard that he was alive and safe before the stories of the crash hit the television news.

The crash investigation began immediately with around seventy personnel coming from around the world – Spain, the Netherlands and the United States, as well as representatives of Boeing and engine builders Pratt & Whitney. KLM decided to send their best man to investigate on their behalf; they didn't realize at that stage that Captain van Zanten was one of those involved in the incident.

The eventual report prepared by the Spanish authorities didn't please KLM. The conclusions were blunt. After outlining the sequence of events, the report stated:

"From all of which it may be ascertained that the KLM 4805 Captain, as soon as he heard the ATC clearance, decided to take off.

The fundamental cause of this accident was the fact that the KLM Captain:

1. Took off without clearance.
2. Did not obey the 'standby for take-off' from the tower.
3. Did not interrupt take-off on learning that the PAN AM was still on the runway.
4. In reply to the Flight Engineer's query as to whether the PAN AM had already left the runway, replied emphatically in the affirmative."

They also commented on the "special weather conditions" in Tenerife – what looked like fog was actually "layers of low-lying clouds which are blown by the wind and therefore cause sudden and radical changes in visibility" – and the simultaneous transmissions between the tower and the Pan Am aircraft, which meant that the KLM crew didn't hear everything clearly.

Contributory factors were the use of the words "take-off", and the ambiguity that caused; the fact that the Pan Am crew didn't confirm which of the intersections it should have taken (although "this was not very relevant" as the crew were very clear to the tower that they were still on the runway); and the unusual traffic congestion as a result of the closure of Las Palmas.

The Spanish report was not unequivocally accepted. *Flight International*'s review of it noted its "superficiality and subjectivity", and it concluded: "By all means blame the pilot, alive or dead, if he was to blame; but to do so in this way is of poor service to air safety." The Dutch authorities were equally unconvinced, and felt that Captain van Zanten was being given too much of the blame. Their report suggested that "it can be established that the accident was not due to a single cause."

However, KLM did eventually accept responsibility, and paid compensation to the victims or their families. The tragedy led to other direct consequences within the industry, with clearer use of specific phrases ordered – notably that "take-off" is only used when the clearance is given, otherwise the word "departure" should be used – and was a factor in the introduction of the principles of Crew Resource Management, where those in the cockpit are encouraged to bring all their skills to bear on a problem.

DÉJÀ VU WORLDWIDE

The tragedy at Tenerife wasn't the last time that such collisions happened. Ninety-three people lost their lives in a similar incident at Madrid-Barajas Airport on 7 December 1983, when a Rome-bound Iberia Airways Boeing 727 collided in thick fog with a DC-9 belonging to the domestic airline Aviaco, which was taking thirty-seven passengers to Santander. One of the pilots from the 727 was found stumbling from the wreckage repeating, "It was my runway, it was my runway." It was the second fatal accident at Madrid in the space of two weeks – a 747 had crashed killing 183 people on 27 November.

Iberia's Flight 350 was authorized to push back from the gate at 0827 on 7 December, preparing to take off on Runway 01. The DC-9, Aviaco Flight 134, was running thirty-three minutes late thanks to the fog at Barajas, and at 0830, clearance was given to them to start up; at 0833 it began to taxi into position at the hold-ing point on Runway 01 through the outer taxiway, ready for its own departure. However, in the fog, the pilot of the Aviaco aircraft didn't see the centreline marking lights, and proceeded to go the wrong way up taxiway J-1, heading straight for the runway – at the other end of which the 727 had been cleared for take-off.

At 0838.45, the 727 began its take-off run. The DC-9 was on the runway, and at 0839.08, the control tower asked for its posi-tion. The pilot replied that they couldn't see the markings for Oscar Five, where they were meant to be heading – just as the 727 roared down the runway towards them. The 727 co-pilot had just called the V_1 speed (i.e. they had passed the point at which they could safely abort the take-off), and the pilot imme-diately tried to take evasive action, rotating early in an attempt to fly over the DC-9.

They didn't make it: the rear fuselage hit the DC-9. "It felt as though the plane split in two," an Egyptian lawyer travelling on the 727 recalled. "We felt the crash, the lights went out and the fire started immediately," Reverend Carlos Giamuzzi, another survivor added.

The DC-9's fuel tanks exploded and the aircraft was totally destroyed, with all five crew and thirty-seven passengers killed. According to contemporary reports: "Scraps of the Aviaco plane . . . were scattered on the runway about 300 metres from the charred hulk of the Iberia plane."

The 727 lost almost the entire left wing and the main gear on the same side. It slid down the runway for about 460 metres, spinning round so that when it stopped, it was facing the way it had come. Thirty-four of the passengers and eight crew were killed either due to the impact or the fire: five were killed instantly when the aircraft collided, the others were incapacitated by the fire and the violence of the 727's turn, so could not reach the exits. Nine died later. Among those killed was noted South African pianist Marc Raubenheimer.

Much the same sequence of events played out at Detroit Metropolitan Wayne County Airport on 3 December 1990, when another DC-9 taxied out onto the active runway, and was also hit by a 727, both belonging to Northwest Airlines. Luckily on this occasion, the fatality list was not so high.

Initial reports on the day suggested that the DC-9 had "got lost" and taxied onto the runway after the 727 had begun its take-off roll, and that the pilot tried to take off early to avoid the DC-9 but had hit its tail. The final report from the NTSB confirmed that this was indeed what had happened, and blamed a "virtual reversal of roles by the DC-9 pilots, which led to their failure to stop taxiing their airplane and alert the ground controller of their positional uncertainty in a timely manner before and after intruding onto the active runway." From the cockpit voice recorder, it was clear that the first officer was making the active decisions; during the conversations they were having, the first officer had "distorted his military flight experiences and career achievements" and the captain may well have thought that his number two knew what he was doing. The board found that "if the pilots had admitted to themselves that they were lost . . . they might have prompted the controllers to take appropriate action, which could have prevented the accident".

On the foggy December day, Northwest 1482, the DC-9, had been cleared to go from the gate towards Runway 03C ready for its flight to Pittsburgh, but they failed to turn onto taxiway Oscar 6. When the error was realized, they were told to turn right onto Taxiway Xray (sic), but instead they turned onto the active runway. Visibility had been deteriorating as they taxied ("Man, I can't see shit out here," was the first officer's helpful report as they tried to find their way around the airport), and it became clear that they appeared to be lost.

At precisely 1342, the DC-9 captain engaged the parking brake as he and the first officer looked round trying to work out where they were. At that exact moment, the crew members on the 727, Flight 299 for Memphis, were performing their take-off checklist, and were ninety-six seconds away from starting the take-off roll. For sixty-six of those seconds, there was silence in the DC-9 cockpit as the pair tried to decide if they were on a runway, and if so where they should go; the captain released the brake and taxied to the edge of the runway.

The 727 was twenty-four seconds away from beginning its roll as the DC-9 captain tried to contact ground control. Eleven seconds were lost due to an error on the frequency as he tried to report that they were stuck out there. Ground control came through asking them to "verify you are proceeding southbound on Xray now and you are across nine two seven". The captain was honest: "We're not sure: it's so foggy here we're completely stuck here." Ground control asked if they could confirm whether they were on a taxiway or runway, and they confirmed they were on a runway, "right by zero four". Control asked them to be specific that they were clear of Runway 3 Centre, and the captain said it looked as if they were on 21 Centre.

There was a ten-second pause, during which the 727 was rolling down the centreline of the runway, after its captain had decided that he did have adequate visibility for the take-off. Ground control asked if they were on 21 Centre, and there was a further five-second pause after their affirmative. Then Ground Control said urgently, "Northwest 1482, roger. If you are on 21 Centre exit that runway immediately sir."

Five seconds later, one of the DC-9 pilots gave an exclamation as the engine noise he had heard was suddenly revealed to be a

727, 422 feet away from them and approaching at 211 feet per second. Two seconds after that, the right wing tip of the 727 struck just below the first officer's middle window on the DC-9. As the 727 passed the DC-9, the latter's fuselage began to tear as the 727 wing tip started to disintegrate. The right main landing gear door of the 727 sheared off the right wing tip of the DC-9. The 727 wing in its turn sheared off when it reached the right engine of the DC-9, which separated from the pylon connecting it to the wing.

The cabin of the DC-9 burst into flames almost immediately – passengers reported "a tremendous explosion and a flash" and the oxygen masks dropped from the storage compartments. One of the flight attendants and a passenger tried to exit through the tailcone exit, but the release mechanism was "mechanically inoperable" and they succumbed to smoke inhalation. Six other passengers died, three from massive blunt force trauma from the 727 wing. The passengers who had not been directly in the line of impact escaped from the aircraft.

The 727 came to a halt, and the captain shut down the engines. After a deadheading fellow Northwest captain advised that there was no fire but there was a small fuel leak, the captain decided to sit tight and wait for the fire trucks to apply foam to the aircraft before allowing the passengers to deplane.

A couple of months earlier, on 2 October 1990, over 128 people died as the result of a hijacking that went wrong, and some very odd decisions made by those in charge on the ground at Guangzhou Baiyun Airport in China. Even though they were aware that a hijacker was likely to be forced to land at the airport, they continued with business as usual, and many of those aboard the China Southern Airlines Boeing 757 became innocent victims when the hijacked 737, Xiamen Airlines Flight 8301, skidded into them. At the time it was China's deadliest aviation disaster – or at least, that the People's Republic authorities had admitted to – although two further crashes have since had higher death tolls.

Xiamen Airlines Flight 8301 was hijacked by Jiang Xiaofeng, a twenty-one-year-old purchasing agent from Hunan Province, who claimed he was carrying explosives. (It was a bluff; none were found on him afterwards.) He ordered all the crew except the pilot to leave the cockpit, and told the pilot to fly him to Taiwan. However, for reasons that were never properly explained (but perhaps connected to the pilot's fear of punishment if he was seen to give in to a hijacker), the pilot failed to do so and continued to fly the aircraft towards Guangzhou.

The 737 circled above Baiyun Airport for around forty minutes, during which time the airport continued to operate as normal. On the runway, the pilot of a China Southwest Airways 707 was running through his pre-flight checks in the cockpit, and a China Southern Airlines Boeing 757, Flight 2812, was loading its passengers, and preparing to depart for Shanghai.

The pilot of the 737 declared a fuel emergency, and brought the aircraft in to land at Baiyun. However, as it taxied along the runway, the kidnapper tried to take control of the aircraft, and the 737 veered out of control. It sideswiped the 707, ripping open the cockpit, and then, still moving, slammed into the wing area of the stationary 757. The 737 flipped over and the rear of the 757 exploded into flames. The 737 also caught fire: "The plane was snapped in half like a matchstick," one eyewitness said. "All that was left of the fuselage was charred metal. It looked like a crematorium." Forty-six of the 110 passengers on the 757 died; seventy-five of the passengers and seven of the crew on the hijacked 737 were killed, including the hijacker. (Later figures suggested that the eventual death toll was 132, including the driver of a vehicle in the holding area into which the 737 swerved.)

A spokesman for the Civil Aviation Administration of China noted: "This serious incident has revealed existing problems in the management of the airport and airline company." No explanation was ever provided for why the runway wasn't cleared or the passengers evacuated during the forty minutes that the 737 was overhead, although they did finally agree that it was a mistake to allow an aircraft to taxi while another was attempting to land.

A CASE OF MISTAKEN IDENTITY

As with so many of the incidents described in this volume, the collision of USAir 1493 with SkyWest Flight 5569 (SKW5569) at Los Angeles International Airport (LAX) on the evening of Friday 1 February 1991 wasn't caused by one particular factor – although Robin Lee Wascher, the air traffic controller responsible for issuing the clearance to the USAir 737 to land, admitted to the NTSB enquiry that the accident happened as a result of "mistaken identity" on her part. She believed that Runway 24 left was empty – it wasn't. The display terminal for the ground radar system that might have warned her the SkyWest Metroliner was waiting on the runway at intersection 45, waiting for clearance to take off, was not working.

Thirty-four people died – including seventeen who had unbuckled their seat belts and were making their way to the exit on the 737 when they were overcome by smoke. "I can't think of a recent accident where this many people have been up and out of their seats and didn't make it out," James Burnett, the head of the National Transportation Safety Board investigation team, said a couple of weeks later.

The crash occurred at 1807 Pacific Standard Time, shortly after sunset, but while visibility was around 15 miles. The USAir flight from Syracuse to San Francisco, via Washington DC, Columbus, Ohio and LAX had been uneventful. At 1759, the pilot confirmed that he had visually acquired the airport and at 1803 he was instructed to contact Los Angeles tower.

Shortly before USAir 1493 saw LAX, SKW5569 had begun to taxi from Terminal 6 round to Runway 24 left. They reached taxiway Tango and waited there behind an Aero Mexico flight. At 1802 SKW5569 was cleared to taxi to the runway, and at 1803.38, they asked the tower for permission to proceed, and were told to "taxi up to and hold short of two four left". SKW5569 confirmed, "Roger, hold short."

At 1804.33, the captain of USAir 1493 contacted the tower as instructed, and informed them he was inside ROMEN, i.e. he was within 6.2 miles of the runway. The tower's controller did not acknowledge the message. However, ten seconds later, she told SKW5569 to "taxi into position and hold runway two four left; traffic will cross downfield." SKW5569 acknowledged this in its last transmission before the crash.

SKW5569 waited patiently while a Metroliner, Wings West 5006, was cleared to cross Runway 24 left at 1805.16. Thirteen seconds after that, USAir 1493 announced: "USAir fourteen ninety-three for the left side, two four left." After answering other transmissions, the tower came back to USAir at 1805.53. "USAir fourteen ninety-three cleared to land runway two four left." Two seconds later, the 737 confirmed. It was their last transmission.

According to the only surviving member of the flight crew, the USAir first officer David Kelly, the approach was normal, with thrust reverses applied after they had landed on the main landing gear about 1,500 feet from the approach end of the runway on the runway centreline. However, as he was lowering the nose of the 737 onto the runway, he saw another aircraft immediately in front of and below him – and the landing lights of the 737 were reflecting off its propellers.

There was no time to do more than desperately try to apply the brakes before the nose of the 737 hit the tail of the Metroliner, which the first officer believed occurred simultaneously with his airplane's nose wheel contacting the runway. There was a flash of light, the nose of the 737 dropped, and then an explosion and fire on impact. The 737 and the part of the Metroliner which was crushed beneath its left side continued down the runway for about 800 feet before veering left, and hitting an empty fire station about 1,200 feet away. The impact destroyed the cockpit, and damaged the left engine and an area of the left wing's leading edge of the 737.

Inside the 737, the flight attendants were repeatedly yelling at the passengers to "Get down, stay down" as the aircraft careered off the runway towards the fire station. As soon as it hit, they ordered the passengers to release their seat belts. They obeyed instantly: "When we hit the building there was a pretty big jolt, then we came to a very quick stop," passenger US Air Force

Captain Christina Voss recalled. "I remember one thing clearly: a very loud click of seatbelts being undone. It was amazing. Normally when you come to a stop, some people take them off right away, others wait a while – but this was everybody at once. One loud click."

The cabin started to heat up from the fire, and very thick black smoke started to emerge from the floor. Only three exits were usable, and many passengers began to escape through the right overwing emergency exit, although one woman in the exit row froze up and had to be pushed out. Unbelievably, the NTSB report noted, two male passengers "had an altercation at the open exit that lasted several seconds" – as other people tried to get out of the plane which was on fire! One woman was desperate to know if her violin had survived – it might not have been a Stradivarius, but it was as dear to her as if it were. She was lucky: when they were pulling wreckage from the site two days later, the violin was found. The case was burned on the outside, but the instrument within wasn't damaged.

The air accident investigators were already aware that Robin Wascher, the controller, held herself responsible. "I realized something went wrong," she told the enquiry. "I went to the supervisor and I said, 'I think this [the SkyWest plane] is what USAir hit.'" According to the report of her testimony in the *Los Angeles Times*, "she described her confusion before the accident". The report contained: "She said she directed the SkyWest metroliner onto the runway at a midpoint intersection, but she thought she was talking to the pilot of a Wings West metroliner that was on a taxiway near the end of the runway.

"This error positioned the SkyWest plane directly in the path of the landing jetliner. But Wascher said rooftop lights in her line of sight created glare on the control tower windows and made it difficult to see small planes at the intersection where the SkyWest plane was positioned.

"The controller also said that in the moments before the accident, she lost radio contact with the Wings West plane."

The board found that she had been distracted by the search for the flight progress strip (which contained constantly updated information about each departing aircraft) for a Wings West aircraft. In the confusion regarding that, and the problem with contacting Wings West 5006, she forgot about SKW5569, which meant that the SkyWest aircraft was left sitting at the intersection.

As a result of the accident, the NTSB recommended that LAX ceased to use the same runway for both arrivals and departures. This still hadn't been implemented by 19 August 2004, when an Asiana Airlines 747 had to initiate a go-around and overfly a South Western Airlines 737 which was entering the same runway. On this occasion, catastrophe was averted by the Asiana Airlines pilot realizing the danger.

CHANGING THE RULES

On 22 March 2000, Jim Hall, the Chairman of the National Transportation Safety Board (NTSB), appeared before the Committee on Appropriations Subcommittee on Transportation and Related Agencies House of Representatives to address them on the subject of aviation safety. He had prepared a detailed written statement on three areas – runway incursions, explosive mixtures in fuel tanks of transport category aircraft, and the need for updated flight recorders – but chose to talk to them about the one which he described as "one of the most significant safety issues facing us today": runway incursions. Hall recounted four separate incidents from the previous year, described below and these were also presented at a Public Hearing on the subject on 13 June 2000. In none of the incidents were any of the aircraft damaged, or any injuries reported.

On 1 April 1999, at 0210 Central Standard Time, a Boeing 747 operated by Air China as Flight 9018, and a Boeing 747 operated by Korean Air as Flight 036 were involved in a runway incursion on runway 14R at O'Hare International Airport in Chicago. The Air China 747 had just landed and was rolling out on runway 14R, when the local controller instructed the Korean Air flight to taxi into position and hold on runway 14R. After Air China cleared runway 14R at taxiway T-10 and the commander, Yeunan Yu, acknowledged the taxi instructions to get to their cargo ramp, the local controller cleared Korean Air for take-off for Seoul. However, the crew of the Air China cargo plane deviated from their assigned taxi route – the commander was receiving his instructions through an interpreter, who mistakenly moved his finger on the chart he was using – and inadvertently re-entered runway 14R at taxiway M.

As Korean Air Flight 036 approached rotation speed, the captain saw the Air China 747 crossing the runway ahead of him. The Korean Air captain had told Fuhe Tang, the first officer, who was the pilot flying, to slow down rather than stop, and its nose was over the centreline. Tang abruptly rotated the airplane, banking to the left as he did so to avoid the other 747. As he was doing so, the tower controller was bellowing "Stop!" at the Air China flight.

Korean Air Flight 036 reached 9 degrees of left bank shortly after take-off, passing directly over Air China Flight 9018 at a height of about 75 feet within three seconds. There was no controller runway incursion alerting system on the runway at the time – but even if there had been, it would have provided the alert only six seconds ahead of a collision, which would have been far too late. The Chinese authorities' reaction was simple: "The conclusion made is that Air China's crew takes full responsibility for the accident. No excuse."

On 27 June 1999, at 2149 Eastern Daylight Time, Icelandair Flight 614, a Boeing 757, and Air France Flight 6498, a 747, were involved in an incursion at JFK International Airport in New York. The Air France cargo flight landed on runway 22L, and the tower local controller instructed the flight crew to taxi via taxiway J and hold short of runway 22R. According to the air traffic control recording, the Air France flight crew responded, "Okay straight ahead on juliet and no hold short on 22 right," and crossed runway 22R as Icelandair flight 614 was departing for Keflavik. Icelandair flight 614 cleared Air France flight 6498 by about 100 feet vertically, and the Icelandair captain quickly reported the incident to the air traffic control.

The airline's general manager at the time, Gunnar Eklund, commented: "We are all extremely grateful that none of the 185 passengers and 7 crewmembers onboard was injured, thanks to the extraordinary split-second decision and immediate action taken by the captain." According to a report of the incident in *Newsday*, one JFK controller said: "This is the closest I ever saw two planes get together. I was hoping I didn't hear the sound of shearing metal," adding that the traffic tower became so quiet "you could hear a pin drop".

The third incident that Hall quoted took place on 22 November 1999 at 2236 Pacific Standard Time, when an MD-80 operating as Aeromexico Flight 432, and the 757 of United Airlines Flight

204 had an incursion on runway 25R at LAX. The local controller cleared Aeromexico flight 432 to land on runway 25L. After the flight landed, the controller instructed the flight crew to turn right on taxiway N and to hold short of runway 25R so that United Airlines 204 could depart. According to the air traffic control recording, the crew of Aeromexico Flight 432 read back: "November cross 25R." During an interview for the NTSB investigation, the controller said that she thought that the flight crew read back: "Short 25R." The controller explained that she saw Aeromexico Flight 432 slowing to turn on taxiway N but, after completing the turn, the airplane accelerated towards runway 25R. The controller restated the "hold short" instruction, but by the time she did, the United Airlines flight was on its way. United Airlines Flight 204 passed over Aeromexico Flight 432 by about 100 feet.

Two weeks later, on 6 December at around 2035 Eastern Standard Time, there was an incident at Theodore Francis Green State Airport at Providence, Rhode Island, that led to a controller announcing generally: "I have a United that doesn't know where the hell he is. Stop all traffic." As the FAA animation (which includes the actual transmissions from the tower and the aircraft involved) shows, United Airlines 1448 had just landed and when they radioed they were clear of the runway by point Bravo, they were instructed to "taxi to ramp, via taxiways November and Tango; report crossing runway 16". United 1448 repeated the instruction, and started to taxi. Unfortunately, in the foggy conditions, they took an incorrect left turn – making the manoeuvre too early – and started heading down the wrong taxiway, taking them towards runway 5R/23L, on which they had just landed.

At the foot of runway 5R two aircraft were waiting: USAir 2998, a Metrojet, was holding short behind a FedEx Boeing 727, Flight 1662. As the United 757 approached the end of the taxiway, bringing them onto the live runway, the controller – who had no idea that they had taken the wrong turning – gave FedEx 1662 clearance for take-off. The FedEx acknowledged the instruction, and began its take-off.

"1448 is on November by the runways here," came a rather hesitant message a second or so later from the United crew. "We don't see the ... uh ... Are we cleared across straight ahead on November?" Believing they were at a completely different inter-section, the controller replied, "United 1448, affirmative, cross Runway 16, join taxiway November, Tango on the other side."

The United crew acknowledged the instruction, but then added: "We're approaching Kilo here ... uh ..." This was at the intersection of the live runway with the taxiway – a point that was graphically made as the roar of an engine very close to them was heard. "Somebody just took off!" the United crew member said agitatedly. It was the FedEx 727.

The tower controller sounded puzzled. "United 1448, you shouldn't be anywhere near Kilo," she told them immediately. "Hold your position please. Just stop."

United replied, "We are currently on a runway; I am looking out to the right with a Kilo ... Ah, we need to go onto the Kilo taxiway."

This didn't tally with what the controller expected. "You were supposed to taxi November and Tango," she reminded them. "I need to know what runway you're on. I can't see anything from the tower."

"Uh, ma'am, we are on 23 Right, intersection of 16," came the reply – inaccurately. They were on 23 Left. "We did not connect with November. We are by Kilo to our right, and we just overshot Kilo, we did not see it." There was a pause, and then a correction. "Runway on 23, ah, Left here."

Telling the United aircraft to standby, the controller turned her attention back to the USAir Metroliner, giving them clearance for take-off. Before USAir could reply, the United pilot jumped in firmly. "Ma'am, I'm trying to advise you, we're on an active runway, United 1448."

The controller was equally firm: "23 Right is not an active runway. It's a taxiway when we're IFR or in the dark." She then asked everyone to standby and maintain radio silence until she spoke to them.

United 1448 repeated that they were on 23 Right and were looking at Kilo straight ahead. "If we can go straight we can get on Kilo and get off the runway."

The response wasn't perhaps as level as it should have been. "Don't talk – I have other things I need to do!" She once more gave USAir 2998 clearance for take-off. USAir 2998's pilot was very calm. "Till we figure out what's going on down there, we're just going to stay clear of all runways," he advised.

The controller replied, "Roger, hold short of Runway 5R. He [United 1448]'s not anywhere near the runway, but you can hold short." She then contacted the tower and told them that "2998 isn't going yet because 1448 doesn't know where the hell he is. We'll take him back and we'll flash you when we're ready."

She then tried to ascertain exactly where United 1448 was. "Ma'am, we're on 23 Left and 16," they replied. "I am facing into Kilo at this point. The nose is just over 23 Left." The controller still didn't seem to believe them, so one of the crew confirmed they were at a 300-degree heading, and said that when she looked out of the window, "I can see a sign that says '23 Left' to my right and a sign that says '16' to my left."

"Stop all traffic till advised please," the controller announced generally. "1448 has no idea where they are." This wasn't really true; 1448 knew – and were telling her – exactly where they were. It just didn't tally with what she expected. She told them to taxi straight ahead and to let her know what the next sign said. They crossed the runway and reached Kilo, and the controller gave them instructions to get them back where they should be. For the next two minutes, they were in constant communication, as 1448 slowly headed for the ramp.

Once they were nearly there, the controller contacted USAir 2998 again. They had been able to hear everything that had been going on, and when she advised them that "1448 is almost to the ramp; are you ready for departure?" they said that they'd "take the craft to the runway to hold" but they wanted confirmation that United 1448 was at the gate before they proceeded further. When that was received, the controller capped the entire affair by giving USAir 2998 the wrong runway heading!

As a result, the controller was "decertified, meaning you can't handle live traffic, underwent retraining for a period of time, was recertified and returned to duty," according to an FAA spokesman. The USAir pilot was commended by his airline for his actions that potentially saved the lives of hundreds of people.

ITALY'S WORST AIR DISASTER

By the start of the 1990s, various items of technology were available to assist controllers, but hadn't been installed at many airports. The NTSB had been making Safety Recommendations for some years, and the FAA had explained in August 1991 that it was acquiring the Airport Movement Area Safety System (AMASS). Many airports already had the Airport Surface Detection Equipment (ASDE) surface radar system working, and according to the FAA's project manager, AMASS was "designed to generate an aural and visual alert to local controllers at ASDE-3-equipped airports when an aircraft or vehicle is occupying the runway and an arriving aircraft is half to three-quarters of a mile (depending on the air traffic control facility involved) from the runway threshold or when a departing aircraft on the runway is moving at 44 knots or greater and is predicted to conflict with another aircraft occupying the runway." The AMASS system was meant to be operational by 2000, but by mid-2000, the date was already being pushed back to 2002 in some cases.

As a result of the publicity given to the congressional hearings in 2000, further Safety Recommendations were made, which included "that all runway crossings be authorized only by specific air traffic control clearance"; the installation of a "ground movement safety system that will prevent runway incursions; the system should provide a direct warning capability to flight crews"; "when aircraft need to cross multiple runways, air traffic controllers issue an explicit crossing instruction for each runway after the previous runway has been crossed"; to "discontinue the practice of allowing departing aircraft to hold on active runways at night time or at any time when ceiling and visibility conditions preclude arriving aircraft from seeing traffic on the runway in time to initiate a safe go-around maneuver"; and to ensure that everyone used the same phraseology "for airport surface operations, and periodically emphasize to controllers the need to use this phraseology and to speak at reasonable rates when communicating with all flight crews, especially those whose primary language is not English."

This last point was one that, had it been in global effect on 8 October 2001, might have been able to save the lives of 118 people, including four people on the ground, although it certainly appeared as if long-running fundamental problems with the state of Linate Airport in Milan, Italy were equally to blame. In the country's worst air disaster, Scandinavian Airways Flight 686, heading for Copenhagen, collided on take-off with a Cessna Citation CJ2 private business jet, with four people on board. All 110 people on the SAS McDonnell Douglas MD-87 died in the accident at the foggy airport, when the MD-87 pilot Joakim Gustafsson desperately tried to take off, despite only having one engine remaining on the aircraft. He was unable to halt the aircraft's momentum, and it smashed into a baggage hangar at the end of the runway at around 156 mph, killing four people within and injuring a further four. All of those on the Cessna also died – perhaps unnecessarily.

Given that the accident happened less than a month after the attacks by al-Qaeda on the World Trade Center and the Pentagon, there was some concern that this might have been a terrorist incident. "I thought a bomb in a suitcase had exploded, and I ran," one of the baggage handlers told reporters. However, within minutes, officials ruled out terrorism, and the blame was being put on a combination of "fog, pilot error and a non-functioning ground radar system". Two of those three would go on to form part of the cause as explained by the Italian authorities; one of the investigators sent by the SAS, though, was adamant that both pilots believed they were doing the right thing right up to the moment of impact. The problems lay elsewhere.

The Cessna was being taken on a test flight by Luca Fossati, president of the Italian food company Star, who was thinking of purchasing the plane. One of the Cessna Aircraft board members, Stefano Romanello, was the other passenger. The German pilots had flown in from Cologne, arriving a few seconds before 0500 GMT and had already filed a flight plan for the next stage of their journey – from Milan to Paris Le Bourget – to depart at 0545. As it transpired, the pilots were not fully qualified to fly in the conditions prevalent at the time, but this was not noticed by the authorities at Milan.

The MD-87 was scheduled to depart at 0535, but was running a little late; at 0541.39, the pilot requested Linate ground control for engine start clearance. This was granted, and he was told the slot time for take-off was at 0616. The MD-87 requested taxi clearance at 0554.23. The pilot was instructed to taxi to runway 36, number three holding position, and asked to advise when the aircraft entered the main taxiway.

The Cessna pilot asked for his start-up clearance at 0558.23, and was told that his slot time for take-off was 0619. At 0559.41, the SAS flight was told to contact the tower when taxiing past the fire station. The crew acknowledged and at 0601.24 changed frequency to speak to the tower. From now on, the two flights were on separate frequencies, and therefore could not hear each other.

At 0605.44, the Cessna pilot was told "to taxi north via Romeo 5" and to call the ground controller back "at the stop bar of the . . . main runway extension." The Cessna pilot acknowledged this instruction, confirming he had been told to go "via Romeo 5" and to "call back before reaching main runway". Although on the surface the order and acknowledgement appear to be saying the same thing, there was a critical difference – the Cessna pilots didn't confirm that they should be taxiing *north*. The route which they were being told to use took them around the top of the main runway, well out of the way of any potential runway incursion.

The Cessna taxied from the parking position, and followed the yellow taxi line in front of the ATA terminal building, until it reached a point where the line split into two – one larger path to the left (north), and a smaller one to the right (south-east). Instead of going on taxiway Romeo 5, they were now on Romeo 6. The Cessna continued down this, passing a side-stopping area, and crossing a runway-holding position, as well as a yellow marking indicating "S5", which was located before the intersection of Romeo 6 and the southern extension of Runway 18R. He continued on the same route, passing another side-stopping area, and another runway-holding position, and a yellow marking, this time showing "S4" – although that one was readable, but oriented opposite to the way he was travelling. At 0608.23, he informed ground control that he was "approaching Sierra 4". Ground control asked for confirmation of that position, and the pilot clarified: "Approaching the runway . . . Sierra 4." Four seconds later, he was ordered to "maintain the stop bar. I'll call you back." At 0608.40, the Cessna answered, "Roger, hold position."

After a brief discussion where he established the position of another aircraft, Air One 937, the controller, returned his attention to the Cessna, telling it to "continue your taxi on the main apron, follow the Alpha Line." The pilot confirmed this at 0609.28: "Roger, continue the taxi in main apron, Alpha Line the . . . Delta Victor Xray". At precisely the same moment, the tower controller was giving SAS 686 its take-off clearance, adding: "The wind is calm, report rolling, when airborne squawk ident." The SAS acknowledged. "Clear for take-off 36 at when . . . airborne squawk ident and we are rolling, Scandinavian 686."

During that conversation, the Cessna pilot confirmed that he would call ground control "on the main taxiway". He continued to taxi on Romeo 6, crossing over a STOP marking, painted in white on the back asphalt, and over another runway-holding marking (yellow on black), and then crossed a red lights bar, next to which was a lit sign with the inscription CAT III (white on a red background). Before entering the runway, the Cessna crossed yet another yellow-painted runway holding marking.

The Cessna was now on active runway 18L/36R, following the green lights present on taxiway Romeo 6, and heading for the runway centreline. The MD-87 was in its take-off run. At 0610.20, the cockpit voice recorder picked up an unintelligible exclamation from the SAS crew, which suggests that they maybe had a second's warning of the impact – certainly half a second before the collision, an additional large elevator nose-up command showed on the flight data recorder.

At 0610.21, with the nose of the MD-87 just off the ground – but with the main wheels still on terra firma – the two aircraft collided. Analysis of the black box data revealed that there were a number of contacts between the two, which resulted in the Cessna splitting into three major sections on the runway – two of which were destroyed by the impact fire.

The MD-87 right-hand main landing gear and its right-hand

engine separated from the fuselage, and in a heroic attempt to fly the aircraft with just the one engine, the pilot gradually advanced the throttles. The SAS flight was airborne for twelve seconds, reaching a height of approximately 35 feet. However, the ingestion of debris into the remaining engine meant that it couldn't sustain flight, despite speeding up to 166 knots (from the estimated 146 at collision). The MD-87 descended abruptly, hitting the runway with the left-hand main landing gear, the broken right-hand landing gear leg, and the tip of the right-hand wing. The pilot was still trying to do what he could, reducing engine thrust as the plane fell, and activating and deploying the engine reverse levers on the left-hand engine.

Despite maximum available reverse thrust, and the application of the brakes, it was to no avail. The aircraft skidded along the runway, its right-hand wing tip dragging the grass, and it smashed at 139 knots into the side of the airport baggage building, where it burst into flames.

Amazingly, no one in the control tower realized what was going on. The Cessna was on the runway in flames; the MD-87 had hit a building that was rapidly becoming a roaring inferno. Thirty-nine seconds after impact, someone in the Ufficio Controllo del Traffico (UCT) building, about 450 yards from the baggage building, contacted the tower, and said they had heard a number of bangs. The tower confirmed they'd heard them too, but they weren't sure what it was – the UCT thought it was like an engine increasing with some energy. In the tower, they thought it was as if someone had been "shaking the head of one of our supervisors against the window", according to the official translation of the tower recordings. "It was a similar sound, a hollow sound." Both parties agreed that they could see nothing abnormal, but that visibility was zero.

The first that anyone knew of the disaster was when one of the baggage handlers ran from the burning building, on fire. He was helped by a police officer and a customs officer on duty at the gate just north of the building, who immediately reported the blaze. At 0612, the fire control was warned that there was a fire at the building – but not initially that there was an aircraft involved. Two fire appliances were sent to the scene, and when they reported that an aircraft was involved, more vehicles were dispatched.

In the tower, the controller registered that he had not seen the SAS aircraft on the radar, and called the Area Control Centre for confirmation. They couldn't see any trace either. A few seconds later, another pilot, parked not far from the baggage-handling building, called ground control to pass on a message from the ramp agent. She had seen "a red streak of fire of something towards the localizer antenna". The tower activated the alarm.

However, it was another three minutes before they realized that the MD-87 was involved, and it wasn't until fourteen minutes after the collision that the ground controller revealed to anyone that the Cessna was missing. Thanks to a series of miscommunications between the tower and the fire services, the tower believed that the fire services had been using the runway to get to the scene of the blaze – which would mean that they would have spotted anything that was there – but then they started to receive messages that there was a fire on the runway, and wreckage in flames. One of the officers from the UCT volunteered to check the runway, and, twenty-six minutes after impact, confirmed that there was what remained of an aircraft on the runway. By this point, all aboard the Cessna had died. Three of them had been burned alive.

The official investigators soon realized that there were institutional failings at Linate Airport – many of the safety procedures that should have been in place were not followed. There was no ground radar – the old one had been out of use since 29 November 1999, and the new one hadn't been unpacked. The markings on the ground for the pilots to follow were not clear. The runway incursion system had been deactivated for several years. The charts of the airport weren't identical – to the extent that the SAS parking chart showed taxiway Romeo 6 in a completely different position to the official maps or the reality on the ground. Instead of following a clockwise logic, numbering from the north, the taxiways were designated R1, R2, R3, R4, R6, R5. When the Cessna informed the ground controller that he was at Sierra 4, this meant nothing to the man in the tower – they had no idea where those markings were.

The investigation wasn't helped by the rule in Italy that the police investigation into a potential crime took precedence, and by the time that the investigators were allowed access, part of the wreckage had been removed to a holding area, which prevented them from carrying out the on-site checks. It also slowed up the retrieval of the black boxes from the MD-87 (the Cessna wasn't equipped with either cockpit voice recorder or digital flight recorder).

Their findings were that the cause of the accident was "the runway incursion in the active runway by the Cessna". However, the "human factor-related action of the Cessna crew – during low visibility conditions – must be weighted against the scenario that allowed the course of events that led to the fatal collision; equally it can be stated that the system in place at Milano Linate Airport was not geared to trap misunderstandings, let alone inadequate procedures, blatant human errors and faulty airport layout."

Apart from the necessary changes in procedure at Linate, there were other major consequences of the disaster. Criminal charges were brought against tower controller Paolo Zacchetti, and Linate Airport director Vincenzo Fusco, who were found guilty in 2004 and sentenced to eight years' imprisonment; Francesco Federico, formerly responsible for Linate and Malpensa airports at Italy's National Agency for Civil Aviation, and Sandro Gualano, the former managing director of Italy's air traffic services provider. ENAV, both received six-and-a-half-year sentences. All appealed against conviction. At a further trial, which ended the following year, Fabio Marzocca, a high-ranking ENAV official, got four years and four months. Nazareno Patrizi, also with ENAV, and Raffaele Perrone, an airport official, were sentenced to three years and ten months. Santino Ciarniello, another ENAV official, was sentenced to three years and four months. Antonio Cavanna and Giovanni Grecchi, both employees of SEA, the company that operates Milan airports, and Sandro Gasparrini, an ENAV official, were given three years. Fusco and Federico were acquitted by the Court of Appeal, with Zacchetti's sentence reduced to three years. A final appeal to the Court of Cassation saw all the sentences confirmed.

There were some who saw Zacchetti as the 119th victim of the disaster – after all, if surface radar was deemed to be essential for the operation of his job, but was not available to him, how could he be convicted?

There is no question that runway safety has improved over the past decade, and lessons have been learned from the incidents around the world. In 2007, the American Airline Pilots Association warned that "the risk of a runway incursion event that could kill hundreds of people in a single accident is real and growing larger", and new measures have been brought in. Pilots now have to get explicit approval from the tower before crossing a runway – but as the pilot of Southwest Airlines Flight 844 from Minneapolis to Chicago Midway discovered on 1 December 2011, even that isn't foolproof. "I want you to acknowledge you cleared us on a runway while a plane was taking off," the Boeing 737 pilot told the tower a few moments after a catastrophe was avoided by the sharp eyes of his co-pilot, according to reports in the *New York Times*. "We had to hit the brakes and the thing went right over our head." The NTSB official report noted that they had to keep asking the tower for confirmation – the controller was convinced he had warned flight 844 to hold short; the tapes showed that he had indeed issued confirmation. Because the 737 had plenty of time to stop, it was classified as a category C incident; according to contemporary reports, the airport was busier that day because First Lady Michelle Obama was flying into Chicago.

The last fatal incursion in the United States involving a commercial aircraft was in 1996; however, the potential for disaster remains, no matter how much equipment is installed. As Jacqueline Yaft, Deputy Executive Director for Operations and Emergency Management at Los Angeles World Airports, told the *New York Times*: "It boils down to layers of safety. One system alone doesn't eliminate all risk or fix it all."

Part 3:
Death Comes on Swift Wings:
Bird Strikes

THE WRIGHT WAY

For thousands of years, the avian population had pretty much sole use of the skies; however, since the dawn of the ballooning era, mankind started to intrude on their territory, and the advent of powered flight meant that the birds' ingrained patterns have often conflicted with the needs of modern aviation. During the first century of manned flight, bird strikes were deemed responsible for the deaths of 231 people in forty-two fatal accidents, with eighty aircraft of various types destroyed.

As early as 1925, the British Director of Civil Aviation, Sir Sefton Brancker, wrote: "There is one form of collision which must not be altogether forgotten; the possibility of colliding with birds in flight. We have had one mysterious incident in which the pilot lost control of his aircraft flying over the sea at a low height, the pilot's opinion was that he had been struck on the head by a sea bird, several were flying nearby, but nothing was ever clearly proved. In the East, propellers of aircraft taking off have been broken by kites flying over the aerodrome. I have never heard of an aeroplane encountering a flock of ducks at night; such an eventuality might lead to danger of injury to the pilot, the propeller or wing structure. The best precaution to meet such a danger will be good screening for the pilot and robust metal construction."

Many different species of birds have been responsible for disasters – from starlings in Boston, Massachusetts, to vultures in Pakistan and bald eagles in Canada. However, where the species is given (and many reports simply stipulate that "birds" are involved) gulls and geese are the most regular culprits – notably in the most famous bird-strike incident, the ditching of US Airways Flight 1549 after take-off from LaGuardia Airport in New York, in 2009 described by state governor David Paterson as the "Miracle on the Hudson" (see page 144).

The first recorded bird strike came as early as 1905 when flying pioneer Orville Wright encountered a flock. According to the Wright Brothers' diaries, Orville "flew 4,751 meters in 4 minutes 45 seconds, four complete circles. Twice passed over fence into Beard's cornfield. Chased flock of birds for two rounds and killed one which fell on top of the upper surface and after a time fell off when swinging a sharp curve."

The first confirmed fatality was Orville Wright's student, Calbraith Perry Rodgers, who had made the first flight across the American continent in 1911. According to the wire report of the incident, on 4 April 1912, Rodgers "started from his usual place and soared out over the ocean, crossing the pier, and then returning, dipped close to a roller coaster in a beach amusement park.

"Seeing a flock of gulls disporting themselves among a great shoal of sardines, just over the breakers, Rodgers again turned and dived down into them, scattering the seafowl in all directions.

"Highly elated with the outcome of his dive, Rodgers then flew farther out to sea, all the time gradually rising until he had reached a height of about 200 feet. Making a short steep turn, he started at full speed for a pier, then suddenly dipped his planes and his machine began a frightful descent. Rodgers was seen by hundreds of persons on the pier to relax his hold on the levers and then, seemingly realizing that he was in danger, he made strenuous efforts to pull the nose of his machine into a level position.

"Failing in this, he managed to turn his craft further in shore and an instant later the craft crashed into the edge of the surf, not 500 feet from the spot where, on Dec. 10 last, he had finished his ocean-to-ocean flight. Many men rushed to his aid.

"Ernest Scott and James Godwin, life guards, were first to reach him. They said Rodgers head was hanging over one wing of the machine; the heavy engine was on his back, and the feet were drawn up, nearly doubling up over his shoulders."

Rodgers' rudder control had been fatally compromised. He died on the way to hospital, making him, according to the report, the 127th fatality – and the 22nd American – in the decade since aviation began.

STARLINGS IN BOSTON

Although there were various incidents over the half a century following Cal Rodgers' death in 1912 in which smaller aircraft fell prey to bird strikes resulting in the deaths of the pilot and the one or two passengers on board, the first major accident that was directly attributable to avian intervention occurred at Boston's Logan Airport on 4 October 1960. Sixty-two people died, and nine were seriously injured as a result of the ingestion of a flock of starlings into three of the Lockheed L1888 Electra's four engines.

At the time of the accident, there were already some serious questions being asked about the safety of the Electra: there had been four crashes involving the big four-engined turboprop airplanes since they were introduced into service at the start of 1959, resulting in 162 fatalities. Two of these could be put down to pilot error, but serious structural flaws had been revealed by mid-air disintegrations over Indiana and Texas, and there had been calls for the aircraft to be grounded while Lockheed worked on improving the strength of the wings, which had been affected by the intense flutter coming from weakened outboard engine nacelles when they vibrated at high speed in turbulent air. FAA Chief Pete Quesada had resisted the calls, insisting that the aircraft could remain in service, as long as they travelled no faster than 259 miles per hour.

The Electra had arrived in Boston at 1533 Eastern Daylight Time, and the aircraft was prepared to depart as Eastern Air Lines Flight 375 to Atlanta, Georgia, calling at Philadelphia, Pennsylvania; Charlotte, North Carolina; and Greenville, South Carolina. There were sixty-seven passengers on board and five crew, led by Captain Curtis W. Fitts. At 1735, Flight 375 departed from the ramp, and taxied to runway 9.

At 1739, Captain Fitts took off, but the Electra only got 30 to 40 feet into the air before witnesses noticed that it started to travel horizontally for several hundred feet before beginning to climb again. As it did so, a puff of grey smoke could be seen coming from engine no. 1, and a ball of fire from engine no. 2. The aircraft veered to the left, then returned to its original course – but it wasn't going at the right speed. After only reaching an altitude of 100 to 200 feet, the Electra made a flat left turn, then its nose pitched up and it rolled left into a spin, diving into Winthrop Bay almost vertically. From above the harbour, the pilot of an aircraft coming into Boston called to the tower, "An Electra just went into the drink!"

Passengers on board the Electra registered it making the turn, with one seeing a "dark smudge" that "passed through the propeller arc and over the engine nacelle". They were then fighting for their lives, as the aircraft broke up on impact with the cold water, the fuselage splitting into two pieces which soon sank into the mudflats, 600 feet from shore. Crowds quickly came to try to assist and human chains were created to cross the mud to retrieve the passengers, many of whose seats had separated from the fuselage on impact. Eleven survivors were found, one of whom died later in hospital; they had been in the rear section of the fuselage.

The presence of multiple bird corpses on the runway, at about the point where the Electra would have taken off, led Pete Quesada to make a very early diagnosis of the cause of the crash, particularly after Harvard ornithologist Dr Raymond Paynter confirmed that they were starlings, which could flock in their tens of thousands. "I knew people would laugh at me if I said birds could knock down an Electra," Quesada recalled after his retirement. "But I communed with myself and decided to announce that the Electra crash was caused by impact with thousands of starlings and that the massive ingestion resulted in multiple engine failure." He therefore said publicly that 60,000 to 84,000 starlings had struck the Electra on take-off.

However, given the well-documented problems that the Electras had been experiencing, the Civil Aeronautic Board's Arthur Neumann wasn't convinced by this theory. It was entirely possible that there had been multiple engine failure on take-off – even if mathematically the odds of three engines failing simultaneously were one in ten billion, according to one estimate. Neumann told the *Boston Globe* that "it seems highly unlikely that the birds could get by the propellers and into the intake – particularly in such a short period of time. But we are not discounting anything. Until we get the wreck up where we can inspect it, we can't say much." However, a jet engine expert was quoted in the same article saying that "a great flock of birds coming in contact with an airliner's engines at a distinct angle of flight can be extremely dangerous".

Time magazine's article twelve days after the crash suggested that "the birds could have plugged engine air intakes of one or more engines on the left side, and caused flameouts; they could even have fouled the mechanism controlling the Electra's great paddle-bladed props." They were pretty much spot on. The CAB carried out a large number of tests to see if the bird strike theory was correct, particularly after ornithologists confirmed that the birds had been killed during the late afternoon of 4 October. When the engines and propellers were recovered from the bay, feathers were found in the nacelle air scoops, at the bottom of the nacelles, and on engines nos 1 and 4, with a gull feather located in the cooling duct to the generator of engine no. 3. Propeller no. 1 was fully feathered (an unfortunate coincidence of technical term: it meant that the engine wasn't operating at the time of impact) and bird tissue and feathers were found in the gas paths of three of the four engines. General Motors, the engine manufacturer, conducted a number of tests introducing starlings into the engines in varying numbers and sequences, and the FAA oversaw further tests at the Lockheed's wind tunnel facility in Burbank, California. This revealed that anything over eight starlings ingested into the engine at take-off power produced an autofeather signal, and the engine failed to recover (start up again) two-thirds of the time – leading them to the conclusion that the probable cause of the accident was the "unique and critical sequence of the loss and recovery of engine power following bird ingestion, resulting in loss of airspeed and control during takeoff".

One key event also spurred the CAB into consideration of bird strike – two weeks after the loss of Flight 375, Captain W. H. Jenkins was piloting another Eastern Airlines Electra at Logan, and had to abort his take-off.

"We suddenly became cognizant of a large flock or cloud of starlings," he told the CAB's public hearing into the Flight 375 crash in January 1961. "These you cannot see from the end of the runway. Or we could not see them before we started out. They were just suddenly there. Starlings are very excitable birds: they wheel and turn in a flock so that one minute, when you are looking at them, you see nothing, and the next minute, as the cloud shifts, there is a big black cloud in front of you.

"They hit the front of the airplane, resembling machine-gun fire. Just brrrrrummm! There wasn't a square inch of my windshield that wasn't splattered with bird remains. I couldn't see a thing."

Jenkins was asked whether he had experienced a "period of distraction, a period of momentary hesitation before you made the decision to abort?" He reflected for a moment then explained that he'd be "remiss if I didn't say that I'd been looking for something like this to happen ever since the previous accident. We're all a little bit cautious about take-offs and landings here at Boston – LaGuardia and Idlewild too, for that matter. Naturally, we are aware of the bird situation; we do not want to become involved in it – sometimes you do. When this actually happens, to say what the time involved is when you reach up and follow through with the abortion, I'd say it was almost one instinctive motion so far as I was concerned." And there was a key difference between his flight and Flight 375: "Fortunately with me, I was still on the ground." By the time that Captain Fitts encountered the birds, he was airborne, and Jenkins was adamant that "if we're airborne, we have no choice. We have to continue."

As a result of the Electra crash, new safety standards for engines were introduced, and the problems of bird colonies near airports were examined further. However, the latter wouldn't help the passengers and crew on board United Air Lines Flight 297 from Newark to Washington on 23 November 1962. As a result of their deaths, the CAB was forced to note that changes in aircraft design had led to a higher risk of potentially lethal bird strikes. Aircraft were climbing and descending at considerably faster speeds than in previous years, when strikes were not considered to be more than simply a nuisance.

Flight 297 was operating at its assigned altitude of 6,000 feet at around 1219 Eastern Standard Time when Captain Milton Balog received information from Washington Air Route Traffic Control Centre: "Be advised there's been numerous reports of considerable amounts of ducks and geese around this area." The crew acknowledged receipt, and four minutes later were given their final approach instructions by Washington Approach Control. A minute later, at around 1224, the aircraft penetrated a flock of Whistling Swans, and two of the birds hit the aircraft. One of them collided with the right horizontal stabilizer, but only inflicted some superficial damage. The other, however, punctured the left horizontal stabilizer, travelled through the structure, and dented the elevator as it exited. Weakened by the impact, the structure failed, rendering the aircraft uncontrollable, and it descended from 6,000 feet in a matter of seconds, gathering speed as it went, crashing into a woodland area six miles from Ellicott City, Maryland. A farmer and his wife, on whose land the Viscount Vickers crashed, heard the engine's sputtering, "like a tractor motor choking", followed by three explosions as the aircraft crashed, and burst into flames. Wreckage was strewn over an area around 100 to 150 yards in diameter.

Bird strike wasn't immediately regarded as the cause: investigators initially wondered if multiple engine failure had occurred, as had happened in a previous crash involving a Viscount on 18 January 1960. That was blamed on an icing problem, which wasn't the case here. However, the presence of a partial carcass of a Whistling Swan at the crash site did set them pursuing the avian angle, and Washington National Airport had noted "birds" or "angels" (the term used for "contacts of unknown origin, not associated with precipitation, thought to be birds or insects" – no supernatural element was involved) on their screen throughout the day of the crash. Once bird debris was found within the wreckage itself, the true cause became clear. And, as a direct result, aircraft tail areas were required to withstand impact with a 3.7kg bird.

ATTRACTING THE BIRDS

Bird strikes weren't so common that airport and other authorities deemed it necessary to take every possible precaution against them happening. In the American city of Chamblee, Georgia, a new landfill site was allowed to open not far from Peachtree Airport, and, unsurprisingly, this became a place where birds congregated.

When DeKalb County took responsibility for Peachtree Airport from the military in 1960, they confirmed that they would "take action to restrict the use of land adjacent to or in the immediate vicinity of the airport to activities and purposes compatible with normal airport operations including landing and take-off of aircraft", but that didn't stop them from opening the landfill in the summer of 1962. In 1970, the FAA warned them there was a risk of bird strike as a result, and the county advised that they would shut the dump by August 1972. By the start of 1973, this still hadn't happened, and on the morning of 26 February, seven people paid the price for their slowness with their lives.

A Gates Learjet Model 24 owned by the Machinery Buyers Corp, was taking off from Peachtree at 1012 Eastern Standard Time. It was heading for Miami Florida, to pick up a customer, with two crew and five passengers on board. Take-off was normal, but by the time it crossed the airport boundary, smoke which was either blue-white or blue-grey (depending on the witness) was trailing from the left engine. The tower contacted the pilot, Captain Ernest Sellfors: "Lear 454RN it appeared the left engine laid a pretty good layer of smoke out of the left side there for approximately 300 or 400 feet." The response came back quickly: "We just hit some birds." When the tower asked if they were "returning to land", Sellfors was blunt. "Don't believe we're gonna make it."

The Learjet climbed to 250 to 300 feet before its nose began to rise. The aircraft wobbled, and then collided with the roof of a three-storey apartment building, two miles from the airport. Spewing burning fuel, it then crashed down into one of the few wooded areas near the airport, a ravine next to a busy highway, 165 feet from the damaged building. Captain Sellfors had managed to avoid hitting any other apartment complexes, the busy shopping centres and roads nearby, and an elementary school. The Learjet burst into flames and all aboard were killed. No one in the apartment block was killed, although one man was severely burned by the falling fuel.

There was no question that the flock of brown-headed cowbirds were the direct cause of this; another local pilot described the problems at the airport: "Just as we came across the runway, it was almost black with birds. They swarmed and parted as we went through them." The sanitary landfill was also regularly mentioned as a hazard.

The NTSB determined that the "probable cause of this accident was the loss of engine thrust during take-off due to ingestion of birds by the engines, resulting in loss of control of the airplane. The Federal Aviation Administration and the Airport Authority were aware of the bird hazard at the airport; however, contrary to previous commitments, the airport management did not take positive action to remove the bird hazard from the airport environment."

During legal action brought by Captain Sellfors' widow, claiming that the air traffic controllers at Peachtree should have warned him of the problem, it transpired that at approximately 9 a.m. on the day of the crash, birds were sighted in the grass adjacent to Runway 16. The manager, using a shotgun, managed to kill or frighten off these birds. While out on the airport perimeter he inspected the active runway 20 left and observed no birds near that runway. The judge ruled that the air traffic controllers were not negligent in failing to warn Captain Sellfors of the birds prior to take-off. The court found that there was no evidence presented that the controllers had sighted any birds immediately prior to the mishap. Mrs Sellfors was unsuccessful in her claim. However, another action was brought (Miree v DeKalb County/Miree v United States) which ended, after some years, with the determination that an airport manager could be held liable for failing to take the precautions possible at his level to end bird hazards. The FAA also developed guidelines regarding exactly which facilities could be permitted near an airport.

THIRD TIME UNLUCKY

Bird strikes weren't confined to the United States, of course. A few months after the incident at Peachtree, a potentially cata-strophic situation developed at Norwich Airport, in Norfolk, England, which thankfully resulted in no loss of life. According to Mr Justice Tudor Evans, the airport's "inadequate inspection system and haphazard and lax attitude to bird control were entirely to blame for the forced landing".

Captain Helge Mossin was in charge of the Fan Jet Falcon for the flight from Norwich to Gothenburg, Sweden for his Norwe-gian employers Fred Olsen Airtransport Ltd. He and co-pilot Captain Bjorn Pederen had flown in from Oslo on the morning of 12 December 1973 and picked up their six passengers. At 1520 they were cleared to taxi; Captain Pederen was handling the take-off, and neither he nor Captain Mossin spotted any flocks of birds as they taxied to the active runway.

They began their take-off at 1537, and just as they became airborne, just over halfway down the runway, they saw a flock of birds ahead flying just above the ground. Pederen increased the climb altitude slightly to ensure that the birds passed beneath them. A few seconds later, they spotted a second flock, who were flying higher, directly in the aircraft's flight path. Pederen therefore lowered the aircraft's nose, and this flock passed overhead.

It wasn't to be third-time lucky. After re-establishing the climb, they reached a height of between 100 and 200 feet – the data recorder was incorrectly mounted, so no precise figure could be ascertained later – when they saw a third flock. This one was right in front of them, and stretched from the ground to well above the aircraft. There was no way for Pederen to weave his way around them, and as soon as they made contact, they heard the sound of multiple bird strikes, which Captain Mossin later described as being "like a machine gun". Although Pederen maintained the climb, Mossin could see that the rpm on the engines was running down very rapidly, with both the pressure and exhaust gas temperature readings dropping. When Pederen heard a bang from the engines, which proceeded to make a rough and abnormal noise, he asked if the engines had failed. Mossin confirmed they had, and tried to move the thrust levers.

There was no response. They had been travelling at around 150 knots before hitting the birds; the speed had dropped to 135 knots. Easing the column forward to maintain speed, the Falcon began to lose height. Pederen spotted a field just ahead and slightly to the left, and once Mossin had given the okay, he lined the aircraft up for the approach. Managing to avoid some trees at the start of the field, they made a forced landing, tearing off the landing gear legs. Mossin received cuts to his forehead from the impact – the full seat belts in the cockpit were too restrictive during take-off and landing, so the crew usually just wore lapbelts – but despite blood streaming from cuts on his forehead, he made his way to the cabin door, and opened it so everyone could escape. The stewardess, who had gone back to help the passengers, also received some injuries.

A helicopter pilot, who had seen the forced landing, brought his machine in to land beside the wreckage and helped with the recovery; an ambulance happened to be passing and its driver went to their aid. By 1600, fire, police and ambulances were at the site.

Once again, it was clear that bird strikes were responsible, but the emphasis was on the protective measures that Norwich Airport had taken – or rather, that they had not. Usually, when bird flocks were seen from the tower, a crew was dispatched in a Land Rover to the appropriate area, and they tried to disperse the birds by driving up and down the active runway. The bird action coordinator at the airport had advised getting better equipment, but this hadn't been authorized.

Another problem was that the tower windows had become obscured both by recent rain and by condensation inside; the controllers couldn't necessarily have seen out – and there was a part of the runway which couldn't be seen from the tower anyway. The force of Mr Justice Tudor Evans' comments at the subsequent litigation was justified.

Another Falcon 20 was involved in an incident twenty-two years later, on 20 January 1995, at Le Bourget Airport in Paris, when lapwings were ingested into the left engine. All ten people aboard were killed; lengthy court proceedings followed, accusing the controllers of failing to carry out the agreed bird-scaring procedures at the right time.

LUCKY ESCAPES

The 129 passengers and ten crew on board an Overseas National Airways (ONA) DC-10 had a very lucky escape at JFK Airport in New York on 12 November 1975. The aircraft, piloted by Harold "Stinky" Davis and Ray Carrier, was taking ONA staff to Jidda, Saudi Arabia, via Frankfurt, and was about to take-off in a south-easterly direction when seagulls were sucked into the engine on the starboard wing. Carrier aborted the take-off, but as he tried to decelerate, the no. 3 engine exploded. Carrier jammed on the brakes, blowing out the tyres on the DC-10, and sending pieces of rubber all over the runway. The right landing gear collapsed, and the right wing was torn off, with the right engine falling off as the aircraft skidded for several hundred yards down a taxiway before finally coming to a halt in the soft mud near the end of the runway, about half a mile from the main buildings – but perilously close to a number of navigational buildings.

By chance, one of the ONA crew had been allowed to film the take-off from the cockpit using a Super 8mm camera, which produced clear evidence of the sequence of events. Davis had spotted the birds on the runway and told his co-pilot to watch the engine exhaust gas temperatures. A moment later came a loud sound "as if someone was hitting the nose of the airplane with a sledge hammer" and an explosion from the right wing, which then lifted up. According to the NTSB report, there had been at least six bird strikes.

Port Authority policeman Drew Johnson told the *New York Times*: "It looked to me like the plane became airborne several feet before the pilot aborted the takeoff. The plane caught fire as it hit the ground. The pilot got the chutes out before there was any severe fire." The fully fuelled aircraft burst into flames, producing a tower of thick black smoke that could be seen from more than 15 miles away. Although people approaching the aircraft couldn't believe it, everyone had got out safely, albeit that thirty of them had some injuries.

The NTSB report noted that the aircraft failed to decelerate properly after the bird strike because of the loss of the engine and the attendant hydraulic system. The wetness of the runway didn't help matters – but it particularly noted that "the bird-control programme at John F. Kennedy airport did not effectively control the bird hazard on the airport". This led to a complex legal battle between ONA and the Bank of America (who owned the aircraft) and the FAA, the Port Authority of New York and New Jersey, New York City, and several aerospace companies in both federal and state courts – the city was joined to the action because there were two landfills near the airport, which could have attracted birds. Settlements were finally reached in 1985.

JFK was also the scene of an incident involving an Air France Concorde which ingested Canada geese into its no. 3 engine when it was only 10 feet above the ground when coming in to land on 3 June 1995. The engine failed, and shrapnel from it then destroyed the no. 4 engine, as well as cutting several hydraulic lines and control cables. The supersonic transport landed safely but over $7 million worth of damage was caused, and the runway was shut for several hours. The French Aviation Authority sued the Port Authority of New York and New Jersey and eventually settled out of court for $5.3 million.

Bird strikes continued to be a problem, with the Bird Strike Committee USA claiming that at least 219 people had been killed since 1988 as a result of wildlife strikes on aircraft. An FAA study found that there were more than 82,000 wildlife strikes at over 1,600 American airports between 1990 and 2007. A US Air Force Boeing E-3 Sentry AWACS aircraft crashed soon after taking off from Elmendorf Air Force Base, after several Canada geese were ingested into both port engines – all twenty-four crew members on board were killed. Even the Space Shuttle *Discovery* wasn't immune to bird-strike damage: during launch on 26 July 2005, it hit one of the vultures that often circled around the launch pads at Cape Canaveral. More attention perhaps was being paid to that mission than most: it was *Discovery*'s first take-off since the loss of the Space Shuttle *Columbia* on 1 February 2003.

The best-known incident that occurred immediately prior to the Miracle on the Hudson was the emergency landing of Ryanair

Flight 4102 at Rome's Ciampino airport on 10 November 2008, which forced the closure of the airport for nearly 36 hours.

"We were on the final descent," one of the 166 passengers told BBC News, "and suddenly we saw smoke coming out of the engine. The airplane went a little bit up, then fell down rapidly on the ground. The masks came out, and people were crying. It was terrible."

The flight was heading to Italy from Frankfurt, and was on its final approach, fully established on the ILS, when it suffered an impact with a large flock of starlings, some of which were sucked into the engine. There was also extensive damage to the left wing, the left main landing gear and the belly of the fuselage. As it came in to land, the aircraft veered off the runway for a few moments after a tyre burst, but the crew were able to bring it back on to the runway, where they then brought it to a safe stop. The nose cone of the aircraft had multiple blood stains on it, and there were blood and feathers on some of the passenger windows. Although Ryanair's guidelines stated that the pilots should "go around" if the aircraft wasn't stabilized 500 feet from the ground, there was not sufficient time – or, with the damage to the engine, sufficient power – to risk aborting the landing and trying again.

Around twenty engineers from accident investigation units from the Italian Agenzia Nazionale per la Sicurezza del Volo (National Aviation Security Agency: ANSV), BEA (France), AAIU (Ireland), the NTSB, as well as civil aviation authorities EASA (Europe) and the FAA, plus representatives of Boeing and the engine manufacturer CFM, participated in an inspection of the engines under the lead of the ANSV, which was ordered in light of events on the Hudson river in New York the following January.

MIRACLE ON THE HUDSON

The first the outside world knew of the incident on 15 January 2009 was a wire report from US Airways which stated simply that "US Airways (NYSE: LCC) flight 1549, an Airbus A320 en route to Charlotte from LaGuardia, has been involved in an accident in New York at approximately 3:03 pm (sic) Eastern Time." No one could have guessed that one of the most dramatic air near-disasters of all time had just played out in the skies over New York – yet within a week the crew of US Air Flight 1549 was fêted by the British Guild of Air Pilots and Navigators with the prestigious Master's Medal. "The reactions of all members of the crew, the split-second decision making and the handling of this emergency and evacuation was 'text book' and an example to us all," read the commendation. "To have safely executed this emergency ditching and evacuation, with the loss of no lives, is a heroic and unique aviation achievement. It deserves the immediate recognition that has today been given by the Guild of Air Pilots and Air Navigators." Captain Chesley "Sulley" B. Sullenberger was heralded by everyone, from outgoing President George Bush to president-elect Barack Obama, and the NTSB's Kitty Higgins called it "the most successful ditching in aviation history".

The whole journey of US Airways Flight 1549 lasted a mere six minutes from take-off to ditching in the Hudson River. The Airbus A320-214 was heading from LaGuardia Airport in New York to Charlotte/Douglas International Airport in North Carolina, and from there to Seattle-Tacoma Airport in SeaTac, Washington. The crew, headed by Sullenberger, had brought the aircraft across from Charlotte earlier that day. Now, with 150 passengers and five crew aboard, it was given clearance to take off from runway 4 at LaGuardia at 1524.54. First Officer Jeffrey B. Skiles was flying the aircraft and everything seemed perfectly normal as the Airbus climbed through 700 feet, heading for 5,000 feet. At 1525.51, the departure controller instructed the flight to climb to and maintain 15,000 feet.

At 1527.10, Captain Sullenberger said one simple word: "Birds." Skiles had noticed birds on the right side "in a perfect line formation" as they took off, but at this point, large birds were filling the windscreen. A second later, the crew could hear various thumps and thuds, like a terrible thunderstorm, followed by a shuddering sound. Sullenberger then smelled something which he knew presaged serious trouble for the aircraft – "burning birds" coming from the engine into the air conditioning of the aircraft. It was the worst feeling he could ever have in his life, he told ABC's Katie Couric when he looked back a few weeks later: "I knew immediately it was very bad."

The engine sound began to decrease, and the captain immediately informed Skiles that "we got one roll . . . both of 'em rolling back". The Airbus ceased forward momentum, stopped climbing, and rapidly began to slow down. At 1527.19, Sullenberger tried "ignition, start", and then two seconds later told Skiles: "I'm starting the APU (auxiliary power unit)". Nothing happened, and instantly, Sullenberger took control of the aircraft. In less than fifteen seconds, the Airbus had gone from standard departure to being an aircraft in crisis. With no engines, Sullenberger knew that he had the world's biggest glider under his command – such forward momentum as they already had would provide airflow over the wings to provide sufficient lift.

Sullenberger had been flying for forty-two years prior to this, and knew that unlike every other time, this flight was not going to end with a normal landing on a runway, with his aircraft undamaged. As Skiles got hold of the QRH (the quick reference handbook, held in each aircraft cockpit to provide emergency help) to see if there was anything in there regarding loss of thrust on both engines, Sullenberger declared an emergency to ATC. "Mayday mayday mayday, this is Cactus fifteen thirty nine [sic] hit birds, we've lost thrust in both engines, we're turning back towards LaGuardia." Despite the content of the message, his voice was level and calm.

Controller Patrick Harten was equally measured. "OK, you need to return to LaGuardia, turn left heading about two two zero." As Sullenberger acknowledged the heading, the controller contacted the tower. "Stop your departures," he said simply. "We got an emergency returning."

Skiles hastily read through the QRH as the aircraft continued to lose momentum, and started to conduct Part 1 of the QRH Engine Dual Failure Checklist. "If fuel remaining, engine mode selector, ignition," Skiles said, and the captain confirmed, "Ignition." "Thrust levers confirm idle," and the captain again confirmed they were in the right position. About four seconds later, at 1528.01, Skiles realized that this wasn't going to be any use: "Airspeed optimum relight 300 knots. We don't have that." Sullenberger confirmed, "We don't" – in fact the maximum airspeed that the aircraft reached after the birds were ingested was 214 knots, not even three-quarters of the speed necessary to relight the engine using the procedure that the manual was suggesting.

The departure controller came through asking if Sullenberger wanted to try to land on runway 13 at LaGuardia, but while Skiles had been working through the manual, the captain had realized that they would not be able to return to LaGuardia. Given how far they had already travelled from the Queens airport, and the distance and altitude required to make the turn back, there would be problems with reaching the runway, with catastrophic consequences not just for everyone on board the Airbus, but those on the ground nearby. "We're unable," Sullenberger told the controller. "We may end up in the Hudson." Skiles continued to check the QRH, as Sullenberger noticed that he was getting a little bit of power from the left engine.

The captain confirmed to LaGuardia at 1528.31 that he would be "unable" to head back to LaGuardia, either to runway three one (sic), or runway four, which the controller then offered. "I'm not sure we can make any runway," Sullenberger replied. "What's over to our right – anything in New Jersey, maybe Teterboro?" The controller confirmed that "off your right side is Teterboro Airport. Do you want to try to go to Teterboro?" Sullenberger answered simply, "Yes."

However, that option was soon not going to be viable either, and Sullenberger made the "brace for impact" announcement in the cabin, and was reassured when he immediately heard the flight attendants shouting out their instructions to the passengers, getting them ready. "Heads down, stay down," they were chanting in unison.

At 1529.21, the controller told Flight 1549 to "turn right two eight zero, you can land runway one at Teterboro". Sullenberger's response was flat. "We can't do it." Despite their best efforts to relight the engines, it was clear that they were going to need to come down to earth very quickly – and the only smooth area that was sufficiently large to land the Airbus was the Hudson River.

In January, in freezing conditions, that was tantamount to suicide – or at least, that's what controller Patrick Harten considered when he received Sullenberger's final message, "We're gonna be in the Hudson." He told the public investigation into the near-disaster, "People don't survive landings on the Hudson River . . . I thought it was his own death sentence . . . I believed at that moment I was going to be the last person to talk to anyone on that plane alive." At the time, the temperature was minus 6 degrees Celsius (21 degrees Fahrenheit), with a light, 8-knot wind – which meant that the water in the Hudson was literally at freezing point, and exposure for any length of time was going to be deadly.

Sullenberger wanted to avoid any chance of the aircraft breaking up into pieces when it hit the water, in the way that a hijacked Ethiopian Airlines had done when it crashed in the Indian Ocean in 1996. To achieve this, the wings would need to be exactly level, the nose had to be slightly up, and the descent rate survivable. He needed to land just above the minimum flying speed, but not below it – but most importantly, all of these things needed to be simultaneous. He admitted later that he had to force himself to use all his training and concentrate on keeping calm, but he was certain that he would be able to do it.

If a pilot has to land an aircraft on water, then if possible, landing near boats to assist with rescue is ideal. Luckily, there were boats near where the Airbus was going to land – and, as it transpired, they were between two ferry terminals. At 1529.44, when it was clear that there was not going to be any last-minute relighting of the engine which would allow them to regain altitude, Sullenberger ordered, "OK, let's go, put the flaps out." Despite the main engines' lack of operation, the auxiliary power unit generated enough power to activate the flaps.

Nine seconds later, US Air Flight 1549 disappeared from the radar at LaGuardia; Patrick Harten carried on trying to contact the Airbus, suggesting Newark Airport as a further alternative, but he received no reply.

At 1530.03, less than three minutes after the birds had first hit the aircraft, Skiles confirmed that they were "two hundred fifty feet in the air . . . hundred and seventy knots . . ." The speed was down to 150 knots by 1530.16, and Skiles asked Sullenberger if he wanted the flaps to stay at position two. "Let's stay at two," Sullenberger replied, then asked, "Got any ideas?" The first officer simply said, "Actually, not."

The actual touchdown on the water was hard, with those in the back of the aircraft describing it as a violent, horrible impact. The Airbus scooted along the surface of the Hudson for a few seconds, then the nose came down as the speed decreased. Sullenberger and Skiles didn't have time for any self-congratulation – they still had a job to do, to get the passengers and their colleagues safely off the aircraft. There hadn't been time to notify the flight attendants that they were landing on water, so it came as something of a shock to them. Sullenberger came out of the cockpit and ordered everyone to evacuate.

The front door was opened, and the chute inflated automatically. By pure chance, unlike most of USAir's Airbus A320s, Flight 1549 was equipped with a slide at the front, ready for an extended overwater flight. People at the front started to file out in an orderly fashion. Unfortunately at the back, things weren't quite so serene: the aircraft had been holed beneath the tail. One of the passengers had pushed the flight attendant on duty at the back door out of the way and opened it – allowing the water to flood in. Despite the attendant's best efforts, she couldn't close it, and the water began to rise. She started to direct passengers towards the front, telling the more able-bodied ones to go over the seats to ensure that they could reach the door.

Some passengers were able to get into the life rafts; others waited on the wing. Sullenberger checked the cabin twice to ensure that everyone was out before he and Skiles jumped into the last life raft. By the time he exited the aircraft for the last time, rescue boats were already picking people up and taking them to the shore. Commercial vessels from the sightseeing cruise lines rushed to the scene, although one of the ferries had to be steered away after it came too close to the slides as the aircraft bobbed about in the ebb tide current.

All 155 people who had boarded the plane a few short minutes before were rescued. "We had a Miracle on 34th Street," Governor David Paterson said. "I believe now we have had a miracle on the Hudson." Five people, including flight attendant Doreen Welsh, were seriously injured; seventy-eight needed treatment for minor injuries or hypothermia.

Although it was pretty obvious from the sequence of events that the Airbus had suffered a bird strike, the NTSB still checked everything, particularly after it was revealed that there had been a compressor stall on the flight two days earlier; however, this had been caused by a faulty temperature sensor, which had been replaced. DNA testing on the organic remains found in the engines proved that a flock of Canada Geese had been responsible. The probable cause was stated as "the ingestion of large birds into each engine, which resulted in an almost total loss of thrust in both engines and the subsequent ditching on the Hudson River".

Sullenberger recalled that after the incident, he had recurrent dreams about finding a better way to deal with the situation. During their investigations, the NTSB ran a series of simulations; in them, seven out of fifteen attempts saw the pilots unable to reach either LaGuardia or Teterboro. In one final test, the pilot "crashed" trying to reach LaGuardia. In their final report, the NTSB noted that "the decision-making of the flight crew members and their crew resource management during the accident sequence" was one of the contributory factors to the survivability of the accident.

The NTSB provided a sheaf of recommendations for improving the situation regarding bird strikes, but one fundamental problem will always remain: birds don't read the recommendations, and despite people's best endeavours, they will not necessarily behave as aviators would wish them to. In 2012, there were 10,900 bird and other wildlife strikes reported for American civil aircraft; in the UK that same year, there were more than 2,200, with 167 of them causing damage to aircraft. With ever increasing numbers of aircraft in the sky, more and more pilots will need the quick reactions shown by Captain Sullenberger.

Part 4:
A Fatal Icy Touch

TOO COLD TO FLY

Snow, rain and fog can all contribute to air disasters – on 14 February 2014, while this book was being completed, a forty-three-year-old de Havilland Twin Otter belonging to Nepal Airlines slammed into a snow-covered mountain in Nepal and burst into flames, killing eighteen people, after apparently becoming affected by the weather. But the combination of snow and ice, particularly if it is allowed to accumulate, can be particularly lethal. The FAA rules may state that "no person may take off an aircraft when frost, snow or ice is adhering to the wings, control surfaces or propellers" but, as has been pointed out, in the sub-zero conditions that exist in many places in winter, the only way in which that would be feasible would be to fly the aircraft out of the hangar.

Ice is commonly a problem for pilots in two different ways – on the ground, and in the air. If precipitation (rain, sleet or snow) lands on an aircraft when it's on the ground in freezing conditions, it will freeze on the upper surfaces of the wing and on the tail. In theory, that is easy enough to deal with: aircraft are sprayed with a de-icer, such as propylene glycol, at the airport – it's similar to the antifreeze that is put in car radiators.

In-flight freezing is more difficult. It comes about when aircraft fly through clouds, which are made up of small droplets of liquid water. This water can still be liquid at temperatures below the normal freezing point (0 degrees Celsius/32 degrees Fahrenheit) if it is very pure, which the water in clouds is, since it has been condensed out of the atmosphere, and there's nothing for it to freeze on. In winter, the droplets' temperature can drop as low as minus 40 degrees (Fahrenheit or Celsius – it's the point at which the two scales are the same) and when the aircraft flies through the cloud, those droplets impact on its surfaces. The ice can then build up on the leading edge of the wings, the nose and the tail surfaces. There are two forms of this ice accretion: rime ice, which comes from smaller droplets, and clear (or glaze) ice, which is formed of larger droplets, which take longer to freeze, and allows the ice to spread more evenly over the surface area.

The effect of either type (or a combination of the two, known as cloudy or mixed ice) means that the surfaces of the aircraft are not the same shape as they are meant to be: the aerodynamics of the wing are altered, providing more drag and less lift. If the air cannot flow over the upper surface of the wing, it can create an aerodynamic stall, which leads to a temporary loss of control – and according to a report in the *Scientific American* in 2009, icing has been a contributing factor in 9.5 per cent of fatal air carrier accidents. Ice can also block the air inlet to the pitot-static system, which then produces errors in the pressure instruments, such as the altimeters, airspeed indicators and vertical speed indicators; and if it forms on an unheated aerial, it can seriously affect the performance of the radio.

There are various methods used to deal with the problem: ice can be removed with pneumatic de-icing boots, which inflate and deflate to break off any crust which forms on the wing during flight, or it can be prevented with an anti-icing system, which prevents the ice from forming in the first place, by blowing hot air from the engine compressor on to the wings.

One of the earliest accident reports to blame icing concerns the flight of American Airlines Flight 63, which crashed on the night of 15 October 1943. There is a great deal of speculation in the Civil Aeronautics Board report, which wasn't released until fifteen months after the incident, about what went on during the flight, and without instruments in the cockpit which could measure the external conditions, their conclusions are in many ways educated guesswork. They deduced the probable cause was "Inability of the aircraft to gain or maintain altitude due to carburettor ice or propeller ice or wing ice or some combination of these icing conditions while over terrain and in weather unsuitable for an emergency landing" and noted that had anyone been aware of what the true weather conditions were, the aircraft should not have been allowed to be dispatched without wing or propeller de-icing equipment.

The pilot, Captain Dale F. Dryer, had originally been cleared to fly at a height of 6,000 feet, but was told by his airline's meteorologist prior to leaving Nashville, the last stop on his flight from Cleveland to Memphis, that he would have a better wind at 4,000 feet, and it was assumed that he would follow that advice. However, on taking off from Nashville at 10.48 p.m. (Central War Time) he climbed to 6,000 feet, and reported reaching that altitude at 10.59 p.m. At 11.03, he was cleared to remain at that level. Three minutes later, he requested a change in flight plan, to cruise at 8,000 feet. This was agreed at 11.08 p.m. by both Nashville and Memphis.

Nothing further was heard from Flight 63 until 11.17 p.m. when Captain Dryer called Memphis. He identified the flight, but then shouted into the microphone so loud and fast that none of his short message was intelligible to those on the ground. He was asked to repeat the message more slowly – but that was the last that anyone heard from Dryer.

The inhabitants of the small town of Centerville, Tennessee, heard Dryer's aircraft in trouble, as he circled desperately trying to find a landing place for four to six minutes. According to witnesses, the DC-3 "suddenly zoomed high into the air and then plummeted to the bottom of a deep gulch" where it "just crumpled up like you'd take a paper bag and blow it up." All ten people on board were killed as the aircraft plummeted almost vertically into the ground.

American Airlines informed the CAB that the aircraft was not equipped with mechanical aids to assist with de-icing: these were removed during the summer months, and although it was mid-October, the DC-3 had not had its equipment replaced. It did however have carburettor de-icing equipment installed all year round, but this might not have been effective in the circumstances of the flight. The weather forecast was for icing above 8,000 feet, and although there was a cold air mass lower down, there should have been an area where temperatures were above freezing between the top of that cold air and 8,000 feet. However, the mass didn't behave according to the forecasters' prediction, and at 11.30 p.m. all altitudes above 2,200 feet were experiencing below freezing temperatures.

The CAB therefore believed that Captain Dryer tried to find the layer of above-freezing air, and when this wasn't apparent at 6,000 feet, he requested permission to go to 8,000 feet. However, he must have encountered considerable icing once he began the ascent from 6,000 feet, and therefore he needed to make a rapid descent to low altitudes, where the only above-freezing temperatures existed – which he achieved in between five to seven minutes. He put his landing lights on, which indicated to the investigators that he knew he could not climb or possibly even maintain altitude, but he had no option but to pull up in an attempt to avoid immediate collision with the trees on the hilly terrain over which he was flying. As he did so, the aircraft stalled; and, as the CAB noted: "It is not conceivable that a pilot of Dryer's experience would stall the airplane, or allow it to stall, unless conditions and circumstances existed over which he had no control."

THE MUNICH AIR DISASTER

One early incident which was blamed initially on the presence of ice took place fifteen years later, and is best remembered because of the identities of those who died – many of the Manchester United football team, the so-called Busby Babes. Returning from a match in Belgrade on 6 February 1958, their chartered British European Airways (BEA) Airspeed Ambassador 2 crashed on take-off at Munich Airport, killing twenty-three directly or through later injury.

The Ambassador was piloted by Captain James Thain and co-pilot Kenneth Rayment, and they had brought the team from Belgrade to Munich without incident. The footballers had been successful – although they'd drawn the match on the evening of 5 February, it was the second leg of the game with Red Star Belgrade, and they were through to the semi-finals of the European Cup. To ensure that the players were rested, Manchester United chartered a BEA flight to and from the game, which was set to depart the following morning.

Designated Flight 609, the BEA aircraft landed at Munich at 1315 GMT for refuelling – the Elizabethan class of Ambassador didn't have sufficient range to make the Belgrade–Manchester trip in one go. Conditions on the ground at Munich weren't good: it was snowing heavily, and there was slush building up across the runway.

The aircraft was refuelled, and the passengers prepared to continue their journey. At 1419, the Munich control tower gave Captain Thain clearance to take off between then and 1431. Kenneth Rayment was due to fly the second leg of the journey, and was in the captain's seat. As they started their take-off roll, Thain noticed that the engine was making an odd noise as they accelerated, and the port pressure gauge was fluctuating as the aircraft reached full power. Rayment aborted the take-off, and they prepared to start again.

That attempt was also aborted after forty seconds: the engines were over-accelerating, as they were running on an over-rich fuel mixture. This wasn't unusual in the Elizabethan, so while the pilots tried to work out what the best course of action was, the passengers deplaned, and returned to the airport lounge. The weather was closing in even more, and at least one of the passengers contacted the UK to say that they wouldn't be flying until the next day.

Over the next fifteen minutes, Thain discussed the situation with the Munich station engineer, who suggested that they would need to stay in Germany overnight. Thain didn't want to do this: he had tried opening the throttle more slowly during the last take-off, and thought that opening it even slower would work. The aircraft wouldn't reach rotation speed until further down the runway, but with a two-kilometre-long strip, this shouldn't cause a problem. Keen not to run behind schedule, he decided to give it a go.

Whether at this point Captain Thain should have checked the aircraft himself for ice remained a question that would be raised repeatedly over the next two decades, and would be held over his head until his early death in 1975. He brought everyone back on board, and the Ambassador got underway once more at 1456, reaching the holding point three minutes later. After making their final checks, they were given a brief window for take-off: they had to be gone by 1504 – and it was now 1502. Thain and Rayment held a brief discussion, and then decided to go for it. At 1503, they told the tower they were preparing to take off.

As radio officer Bill Rodgers informed the tower they were rolling, Rayment moved the throttle forward slowly and released the brakes. Thain notified Rayment of the increases in speed as they accelerated in 10-knot increments. V_1 – the point at which it was no longer safe to abort take-off – was set at 117 knots with rotation (lift-off) speed set for 119 knots.

At 85 knots, the port engine started to surge, so Rayment pulled back marginally on the throttle before pushing it forward. Thain called V_1 as they reached 117 knots, but instead of continuing to rise to rotation speed, the aircraft started to lose acceleration. It dropped to 112 knots, and then 105. "Christ, we won't make it," Rayment realized, as the aircraft skidded off the end of the runway.

It crashed into the airport perimeter fence and across the surrounding road before smashing into a house, tearing its left wing off. Part of the tail was torn off as the aircraft spun, and then the left side of the cockpit hit a tree, and the right side of the fuselage slammed into a wooden hut filled with tyres and fuel. The house and the hut both caught fire, and the fuel exploded. "There was a hellish noise. And then complete silence," Thain recalled twenty years later.

Rayment was trapped in his seat in the cockpit, and Thain ordered an evacuation of the aircraft. Those who were still alive struggled from their seats, some of them assisted by goalkeeper Harry Gregg. Thain rushed to get fire extinguishers to prevent the flames from reaching the fuel tanks in the wings. Eight of the Manchester United players died in the crash or shortly after in hospital; three staff and eight reporters were also killed, along with two other passengers.

Had there been ice on the wings? That's the conclusion that the West German Commission of Inquiry came to in April–June 1959 but they didn't take full notice of the evidence of Reinhardt Meyer, an experienced pilot and aircraft designer, who was one of the first people to reach the crashed Ambassador. He wrote a report on the accident on 16 April 1958, which stated clearly that he "saw no signs of icing either on the fuselage or on any part of the wings". Suspicions of a cover-up by the West German authorities were fuelled by the revelation by the British Air Line Pilots Association (BALPA) that the version of Meyer's statement which was read out to the Commission started immediately after that sentence in his statement. BALPA baldly alleged that "vital information about the absence of ice on the wings of the Ambassador was concealed by the German Chief Inspector of Accidents before the first German inquiry and subsequently".

Life would certainly have been easier for the West Germans if there had been ice on the wings: Rayment had died three weeks after the crash as a result of his injuries, so Thain was an easy target. Their Commission of Inquiry found that "ice accretion on the wings of the aircraft was the cause of its failure to become airborne" and didn't take into account the slush that was strewn across the runway. They turned down requests for a reopening of the inquiry maintaining that it appeared out of the question that any quantities of water or melted snow "worth mentioning" should have collected. They also noted that the marks of the emergency tail wheel in the snow demonstrated that the aircraft could have taken off. In the UK, an independent review was set up to consider "whether blame should be imparted to Captain Thain" under E. S. Fay, QC. It reported in 1960 that Thain should have inspected the wing "whether ice was present or not".

Thain wasn't prepared to accept responsibility. The accusations of ice had partly come from photographic evidence which seemed to show a sheen of ice on the wings shortly before the accident. In fact, the "ice" was the reflection of the sun on the wings. There was also, of course, ice accumulation after the accident, but that was not surprising, given the conditions. BALPA supported Thain's quest, and they were assisted by the Royal Aircraft Establishment (RAE), who carried out tests on Ambassadors, which showed that slush had a much larger effect on the aircraft's performance than had been thought.

This information was passed on to the West German Minister of Transport, and the Commission was reopened to take this into account. However, when this was reported in 1967, not much had changed. "The present commission," stated the report, "was no more able to gain an entirely clear picture of the course of the fatal take-off attempt than was the commission which conducted the initial inquiry. It was clear from eye-witness reports that the nosewheel had been raised half-way along the runway, lowered again after some 60 to 100 metres, and then, within the last third of the runway, raised again, high enough for the emergency tail wheel to touch the runway." They therefore believed that Thain should have been able to take-off – and the slush, which they considered was negligible, shouldn't have made a difference. "Even with these slush effects, however, the aircraft would have been bound to be able to unstick on attaining a speed of 117kt, if reduction in lift caused by wing icing had not resulted in an increase in the minimum unstick speed and thus, in the end, caused a failure of the unstick process."

The Germans were still fixated on ice, noting that an eyewitness may have said that the wings were free of snow, but he made the statement five years after the event, and it contradicted previous evidence given immediately after the event. They concluded that there was a layer about 5mm thick, and "arrived with adequate certainty" at the conclusion that at least 45 per cent of the wing's upper surface was covered, which explained the drop in speed after V_1. They did accept that "slush must be regarded as a further cause" but stuck to their guns about the ice.

In a very unusual move, the British Board of Trade published a translation of the Commission of Inquiry's findings, and added their own memorandum from the RAE, which stated that the slush, not ice, was the cause of the accident. BALPA pressed for the government to "dissociate itself from the [West German] report".

A second Fay Commission was therefore set up. They examined all the evidence and found: "(1) The cause of the accident was slush on the runway. (2) It is possible but unlikely that wing icing was a contributory cause. (3) Captain Thain was not at fault with regard to runway slush. (4) Captain Thain was at fault with regard to wing icing, but because wing icing is unlikely to have been a contributory cause of the accident, blame for the accident cannot in this respect be imputed to him. (5) Captain Thain was at fault in permitting Captain Rayment to occupy the captain's seat [on the left], but this played no part in causing the accident. In accordance with our terms of reference we therefore report that in our opinion blame for the accident is not to be imputed to Captain Thain."

While this may have cleared Thain in British eyes, he was never going to fly for BEA again. He wasn't impressed with them anyway: after the crash, they invoiced him for the cost of his lost airline cap and then they sacked him for letting Rayment fly from the pilot's seat. The Germans never changed their official viewpoint on the crash. "My father died aged just 54 believing that he was the victim of a great injustice," his daughter Sebuda said in 2008, shortly before the fiftieth anniversary of the crash. "He was bitter and who can blame him? He was an honest man and a fine pilot, and the crash was not his fault."

THE CAPITAL VISCOUNTS

Capital Airlines suffered two fatal accidents as a result of icing to their four-engined Vickers Viscounts, in April 1958 and January 1960. Flight 67 crashed on final approach to Tri-City Airport (now MBS International) at Freeland, Michigan, late on the evening of Easter Sunday, 6 April 1958; Flight 20 crashed into a farm in Charles City County, Virginia, while travelling between Washington National and Norfolk Regional airports twenty months later. Ninety-seven people lost their lives in the two incidents.

The CAB revised their report on the first crash in light of later accidents involving the Viscounts, and only the version from 1965 is now officially available. This states the probable cause of the accident "was an undetected accretion of ice on the horizontal stabilizer which, in conjunction with a specific airspeed and aircraft configuration, caused a loss of pitch control". However, the April 1959 report, quoted in contemporary papers, put the onus on Captain William J. Hull. It said that the aircraft probably stalled during a steep turn and fell to earth nose first. Its stall warning device was not working, and there were high gusty winds and the plane may have accumulated ice. The CAB added: "It is probable that the existing weather conditions contributed materially to this accident. The close-in approach, short radius of turn and the steep bank may well be attributable to an attempt by the pilot to keep the lighted runway in sight because of the restricted visibility occasioned by snow showers and freezing drizzle."

Flight 67 was meant to depart from LaGuardia Airport, but because of weather and field conditions in Queens, the inbound aircraft couldn't land there so it was diverted to Newark Airport in New Jersey. Passengers therefore had to be shipped to Newark, from where the flight departed one hour and sixteen minutes behind its 1800 scheduled time. It landed at Flint at 2237, and took off again at 2302. It was given clearance to approach Tri-City at 2310, and the crew spoke with Saginaw Air Traffic

Communication Station at Tri-City, when they were given the local weather observation, and the runway to use. The ceiling was 900 feet; there were light snow showers, which had started at 2225.

At 2316 Flight 67 reported that it was over the airport. Its lights were barely visible through the snow, as it made a turn onto the base leg for approach beneath the overcast, and was descending. As it turned on final approach, the aircraft flew a short distance beyond the centreline of the runway, so the pilots tried a steep turn to realign it. The Viscount levelled off, but then descended steeply and struck the ground. According to the *Midland Daily News*, "The four-engine plane slammed into a corn field of the farm of Warner Law, about 2,300 feet short of the 5,661-foot-long southwest-northeast runway of the airport . . . Bodies were scattered across a wide area. Charred and badly mangled, the victims were found not only in the shattered wreckage but also mired in the mud." One eyewitness described the aircraft landing almost square on its nose before it flipped over.

According to Tilda A. Norberg, who was waiting for her parents to arrive on the flight, "There was pandemonium at the airport. There was shrieking, alarms, the airport staff panicked . . . they were almost wringing their hands in helplessness. The crash was so close to the airport that everybody ran out onto the tarmac."

As the CAB discovered, the US Weather Bureau had issued a "flash advisory" at 1930 warning of occasional heavy icing in the clouds; this wasn't passed on to Captain Hull, or First Officer Earle Binckley. Nor were they told that two of their colleagues had experienced moderate turbulence and icing during their landing at Tri-City earlier that evening – and indeed that one captain had discovered an inch or more of ice on the wings of his Constellation on landing thirteen minutes prior to the accident.

On 29 January 1963, another Viscount was involved in an accident at Kansas City, Missouri, and the results of that investigation made the CAB reassess their opinion about Flight 67. That Continental Air Lines Viscount had operated for a short time – only about ten to twelve minutes – in icing conditions within clouds, and because the temperature was 37 degrees Celsius (98 degrees Fahrenheit, airframe anti-icing had not been used. However, when the pilot lowered the landing flaps to 40 degrees, it caused the nose to drop, and the pilot was unable to arrest the action with the elevator control; instead he had to retract the flaps by 8 degrees. When he landed, he discovered that while the wings were clear of ice, a build-up of ice between three-quarters inch and one and a half inches had occurred on the leading edges of the tail-plane and the vertical stabilizer. This, taken in conjunction with the tests that were carried out as a result of Capital Flight 20's accident on 18 January 1960, led the Board to produce their new probable cause for Flight 67.

Flight 20 crashed into swampland near Sandy Gut, a tributary of the Chickahominy River, about 30 miles south-east of Richmond, Virginia, at approximately 2219 Eastern Standard Time. Although the flight had begun at Chicago Midway, the actual aircraft which crashed wasn't used for the first leg of the journey, and only took over in Washington, D. C. Captain James B. Fornasero, First Officer Philip H. Cullom Jr, two flight attendants and forty-six passengers took off at 2140 with a standard flight clearance, travelling at 8,000 feet. They acknowledged a clearance to the Norfolk Outer Marker at 2205; they were not heard from again.

They had been travelling in the clouds for much of their climb to 8,000 feet and for around ten to fifteen minutes of their cruising time, and during this period and prior to their descent near the accident site, the aircraft would have been experiencing sub-zero temperatures, as well as light and occasionally moderate showers. CAB investigators estimated that in those conditions, a quarter to a half inch of airframe ice accumulation could have built up. However, all the evidence pointed to the crew failing to arm the ice-protection system in time: as a result, all four engines of the Viscount stopped delivering power as their propellers feathered. With no cockpit voice recorder or any communication between the crew and the ground, there was no way to tell whether Captain Fornasero had been unaware that he should have kept the ice-protection systems on at all times if the temperature was below 10 degrees Celsius (50 degrees Fahrenheit); or if he had waited until he had seen ice start to form before switching it on; or whether the system gave faulty readings. (The CAB failed to put the blame on the flight crew in their report.)

Whatever the reason for the lack of ice protection, it led to the engines flaming out. The crew would have gone through the normal emergency checklist, which at that point required them to either immediately relight, or descend to below the freezing level to allow the engine(s) to de-ice naturally. However, by doing so, they exacerbated their problem, since further ice could have been ingested during their descent. Circling over the land 50 miles north-west of Norfolk, they were able to get no. 4 engine to relight, and had just got no. 3 started when they simply ran out of time – they had not been able to slow down their descent sufficiently, so that by the time they had a chance to settle the aircraft with power from both engines, they were too close to the ground. In the foggy conditions, they had no chance of seeing where they were, so when they made contact with the trees, there were indications of an attempt to apply back elevator pressure on the control column. However, that simply led the aircraft to whip stall. It hit the ground with no forward velocity and burst into flames.

"Have you ever seen an old shed that's been set on fire and fallen down with the tin roof on top of it?" Richmond fire battalion chief John Finnegan Jr told reporters. "That's what it looked like. I would say absolutely there was no chance for anyone to get out of it." Sheared-off trees poked through the wings and what was left of the aircraft's fuselage. Only the tail section remained in one piece.

By the time that the CAB released their report into the accident, Capital Airlines was no longer a separate entity; in June 1961, it merged with its rival United Airlines in what was then the largest merger in aviation history. Long before that, though, they had dropped the phrase "descend to warmer climate for relight" from the emergency checklist for Viscounts, and ensured that, unlike Captain Fornasero, all their pilots had up-to-date operating information.

HITTING THE BRIDGE

Captain Fornasero and his crew may not have been held responsible for the crash of Capital Flight 20 in 1960, but twenty-two years later, the flight crew of Air Florida Flight 90 were deemed accountable for the crash of their Boeing 737 into the 14th Street Bridge over the Potomac River in Washington DC. Only five of the seventy-nine people on board survived – it would have been six, but one man, Arland Williams Jr, selflessly passed the safety preserver ring to others and succumbed before he could be rescued himself; like the Miracle on the Hudson nearly three decades later, it brought out heroism in people they didn't know they possessed.

At the State of the Union address a few days later, President Ronald Reagan commented on this bravery: "Two weeks ago, in the midst of a terrible tragedy on the Potomac, we saw again the spirit of American heroism at its finest. We saw the heroism of one of our young government employees, Lenny Skutnik, who, when he saw a woman lose her grip on the helicopter line, dived into the water and dragged her to safety." Four people on the ground were also killed. As the *New York Times* noted in a feature commemorating twenty years since the tragedy: "The Air Florida plane crashed because of a series of foolish mistakes – undo one and the plane soars over the bridge and everyone lives."

Photographs taken at the scene were flashed around the world while live coverage of the survivors' desperate plight was broadcast on the new CNN 24-hour news channel. They show clearly the thickness of the ice through which the aircraft had broken – and through which those who only a few moments before had been preparing for a relaxing flight to Fort Lauderdale in Florida, after an annoying delay stuck in their seats at the airport, had to navigate to have any chance of survival.

Washington National Airport had been closed for the morning of 13 January 1982, in common with most of the rest of the nation's capital. It takes a lot to shut Washington DC down but the severity of the blizzard had forced Congress to recess early, schools to shut down, and businesses to remain unopened or close their doors long before normal time. Thick wet snow fell from the skies, and clogged the sidewalks and roads. Those who had made their way from the suburbs into DC were released from work early, so that by 1600 Eastern Standard Time, the traffic on the roads out of the capital was much thicker than normal, and on the bridges over the Potomac, it was virtually at a standstill.

National Airport had reopened by noon, but by 1338, the runways needed clearing once more. The one runway which could be used for instrument landings and take-offs (Runway 18/36) was therefore closed to traffic once more, and it was ploughed. Although the earliest that the airport would come back on line was 1430, Air Florida ground staff decided to board their passengers on to the Boeing 737 which would form Flight 90 – the scheduled departure time was 1330. The crew, led by Captain Larry Wheaton and First Officer Roger Pettit, had brought the aircraft up from Miami, arriving at 1329, and they had requested an IFR clearance at 1359. Between 1400 and 1430, the seventy-four passengers boarded the aircraft at gate B12.

In the hope that the airport would be ready for them to depart at 1430, Captain Wheaton requested that the de-icing procedure should begin. The outside temperature was 24 degrees Fahrenheit (-4.5 degrees Celsius) and about a half-inch of wet snow had fallen on the aircraft while it was waiting at the gate. At about 1420, one of the maintenance personnel started to apply the appropriate de-icing and anti-icing fluid (heated Union Carbide Aircraft Deicing Fluid II PM 5178 containing 30 to 40 per cent glycol to 60 to 70 per cent water) to the left side of the fuselage. However, after the truck operator sprayed it onto an area about 10 feet in size, Captain Wheaton told him to stop – he'd just been told that the airport wasn't going to make 1430, and indeed, there were five or six aircraft ahead of them in the queue who had to leave before Flight 90 could push back from the gate.

At 1445, with Flight 90's departure more imminent, Wheaton asked the de-icer to continue. It was snowing heavily as he worked, and he dealt with the left side first, working backwards towards the tail, and ensuring that no ice or snow remained at the hinges or on the control areas. That operator was relieved by a mechanic, who proceeded to de-ice the right side of the 737, starting from the rear – although, because he believed the temperature was four degrees warmer, he changed the proportions of the mix, decreasing the amount of glycol. After checking the engine intakes and the landing gear for snow and ice, he completed the job around 1510.

Five minutes later, just before the doors were closed and the jetway was retracted, Wheaton checked with the Air Florida station manager how much snow was on the 737. The manager said there was a light dusting of snow on the left wing from the engine to the wing tip, but from the engine to the fuselage was clean – at least at the moment. Snow was continuing to fall heavily.

At 1516, "Palm 90", as it was designated by air traffic control, signalled that they were ready to go. They were given clearance to proceed at 1523, and a tug tried to push them back from the gate. However, because there was a combination of ice, snow and glycol on the ramp, the tug couldn't get traction on the slight incline, and it couldn't move the jet. When one of the crew suggested to the tug operator that they could use the 737's engine reverse thrust to push the aircraft back, he was firmly told that this wasn't the policy of American Airlines (who oversaw maintenance and other requirements for Air Florida at National). However, despite that advice, the engines were started, and the reversers were deployed, for between thirty and ninety seconds.

This didn't have the effect that Wheaton or Pettit wanted. The aircraft didn't go anywhere, although snow and slush were blown towards the front of the 737, and an area of snow melted around at least the left engine (no one noticed whether the same happened on the other side). They therefore shut the engines down, although the reversers remained deployed. The second man to work on de-icing the aircraft made a general examination of the engines, and couldn't see any ice or snow; no one else noticed water – in any form – on the wings.

The tug was disconnected, and a second one, with chains, was brought across. The snow carried on falling, and a light dusting started to form on the fuselage, the wings and the nose. The 737 pushed back successfully at 1535, and the engines were then restarted and the reversers stowed. As they prepared to take their position in the line for take-off, the pilots went through the after-start checklist, and when asked about the "anti-ice", Wheaton replied "off". This meant that the accuracy of their sensor readings would be diminished.

At 1540, Pettit noted that "it's been a while since we've been de-iced", although neither he nor Wheaton followed up on the captain's original comment about going "over to the hangar and get de-iced". Wheaton taxied his 737 closer behind the aircraft in front, in an attempt to use the heat and blast from the other airplane's exhaust gases to remove the snow and slush from the wings. Although in theory this might have seemed like a good idea – it apparently got rid of some of the excess weight – in reality, it was catastrophic: the heat turned some of the snow into a slushy mixture which proceeded to freeze on the wing leading edges and the engine inlet nose cone. Boeing even warned specifically about this in the operations manual, as did the FAA.

As these taxied down, Pettit noticed that there were unusual readings coming from the engines, which then seemed to rectify themselves. They should have been a warning to the pilots that ice was forming on the engine inlet probe, but neither Pettit nor Wheaton thought of this. And after their "de-icing" courtesy of the preceding DC-9, they didn't make any further visual checks of the exact amount of snow and slush they were carrying, which was clearly noticeable, since another pilot coming in to land at Washington commented on the "junk" on the Air Florida flight.

It wasn't as if they were unaware of the snow – Pettit referred to it as "probably the shittiest snow I've seen" as they taxied – but the aircraft in front of them seemed to be departing successfully. Neither pilot was overly experienced in flying in this sort of weather: Wheaton had only made eight take-offs and landings in snowy conditions; Pettit had only flown in snow twice before.

Once the aircraft immediately before them in the queue had reached the runway, Pettit and Wheaton carried out the take-off checklist. Pettit noted that it was a "slushy runway" and asked, "Do you want me to do anything special for this or just go for it?" His captain responded, "Unless you got anything special you'd like to do . . ."

At 1558.55, Flight 90 was cleared to taxi into position, and then cleared for take-off half a minute later – and asked not to delay the departure since there was landing traffic two and a half miles out from the runway. Wheaton handled control of the throttles to Pettit at 1559.45, although the responsibility for aborting the take-off remained with him.

As he advanced the throttles, Pettit noticed that the engine pressure ratio (EPR) reading wasn't what he was expecting, given the way that the aircraft was handling. They were being told by the EPR readings that they had throttled up to the correct EPR of 2.04, but because the anti-icing system hadn't been working, the readings were showing a false high: instead of 2.04, the real EPR was actually 1.70, and the aircraft simply didn't have as much power as it needed for take-off. "That's not right," Pettit said two seconds before 1600, but Wheaton believed they were okay, so didn't initiate an abort; despite being concerned, Pettit deferred to the captain's judgement. The aircraft accelerated to rotation speed, but as the captain called "V_2", and Pettit started to lift the aircraft from the ground, the stick shaker began to sound, warning the crew of an impending stall. It was 1600.31.

United Airlines Flight 90 stayed in the air for just over thirty seconds. Despite the captain urging the aircraft to go "forward forward . . . we only want five hundred", the 737 wouldn't climb. At 1601.00, Pettit said, "Larry, we're going down, Larry . . ." to which the captain could only say, "I know it . . ." Neither of them tried to go to full throttle; it might have saved the aircraft. But now, the nose had pitched up, and the aircraft came down – straight onto the 14th Street Bridge.

In the heavy snowfall, the 737 smashed into six occupied cars and a boom truck, killing four people, before tearing away a 41-foot section of the bridge wall and 97 feet of the bridge railings. It then plunged into the ice-covered Potomac River, a mere three-quarters of a nautical mile from the departure end of National's Runway 36.

One eyewitness, who was in a car on the bridge, told the NTSB: "I saw the tail of the plane tear across the top of the cars, smashing some tops and ripping off others . . . I saw it spin [a red car] around and then hit the guardrail. All the time it was going across the bridge it was sinking but the nose was pretty well up. I got the impression that the plane was swinging around a little and going in a straight direction into the river. The plane seemed to go across the bridge at a slight angle and the dragging tail seemed to straighten out. It levelled out a little.

"Once the tail was across the bridge the plane seemed to continue sinking very fast but I don't recall the nose pointing down. If it was, it wasn't pointing down much. The plane seemed to hit the water intact in a combination sinking/ploughing action. I saw the cockpit go under the ice. I got the impression it was skimming under the ice and water."

Most of the passengers died on impact, but five of them, as well as one of the flight attendants, managed to reach the surface and clung to the wreckage. The commuters on the bridge could only watch helplessly as they tried to stay afloat, before emergency services arrived and a helicopter hovered to pick the survivors up out of the water. One of the passengers, Priscilla Tirado, lost her grip on the life preserver which the helicopter crew were holding; without thinking, congressional aide Lenny Skutnik jumped into the water and dragged her to land. Arland Williams Jr kept passing the preserver ring to others, but when the helicopter returned to pick him up, he had disappeared beneath the icy water, and drowned. (The bridge was later renamed in his honour.) Divers were sent down into the wreckage, who reported that the majority of the passengers were still strapped in their seats.

By a terrible coincidence, half an hour after Flight 90 crashed, the Washington metro was shut down after a train on the Orange Line derailed, killing three people and injuring twenty-five. Emergency personnel were torn between the two incidents.

Once the cockpit voice recorder and the flight data recorder had been analysed, many of the NTSB's questions were answered. After multiple witness statements were taken, and the engine performance tested under similar conditions, they reported that "the probable cause of this accident was the flightcrew's failure to use engine anti-ice during ground operation and takeoff, their decision to take off with snow/ice on the airfoil surfaces of the aircraft, and the captain's failure to reject the takeoff during the early stage when his attention was called to anomalous engine instrument readings. Contributing to the accident were the prolonged ground delay between de-icing and the receipt of ATC takeoff clearance during which the airplane was exposed to continual precipitation, the known inherent pitch-up characteristics of the B-737 aircraft when the leading edge is contaminated with even small amounts of snow or ice, and the limited experience of the flightcrew in jet transport winter operations."

There were other consequences to the Flight 90 disaster. It marked the beginning of the end for Air Florida; even if it didn't directly trigger their bankruptcy in 1984, it sapped customer confidence. But more importantly, according to Robert L. Sumwalt III, vice chairman of the NTSB and a former airline pilot who took off from the same airport hours before the Air Florida crash, "This accident was pivotal because it helped draw attention to the fact that pilots need to communicate better. This accident was ingrained in the minds of the entire world, and we watched the recovery efforts as they happened. I don't know of any other accident that has had this amount of impact on aviation but also in other industries." Crew resource management became more important – as with the Tenerife disaster five years earlier (see page 98), the crew were not prepared to speak out when they saw there was a problem: from the CVR recording, it seems probable that Pettit wanted to abort the take-off, but deferred to his captain. The crash is now used as a teaching aid at Embry-Riddle Aeronautical University to highlight human error.

AN EXERCISE IN CONFUSION

The winter of 1981–82 produced other ice-related fatalities as well as the Air Florida disaster. On 23 January 1982, ten days after Flight 90's catastrophic plunge into the Potomac, World Airways Flight 30H skidded across a field and a taxiway at Logan Airport before hitting the below-freezing waters of Boston Harbour. Somehow, no one noticed that two of the passengers who had been on board had gone missing – it took three days before relatives of the missing pair were able to get confirmation that the computer check of the passenger list had been inaccurate. By that point, the bodies of Walter Metcalf and his son Leo had presumably been swept out into the harbour: they were never located. The incident was also controversial, since the NTSB responded to a petition regarding the probable cause, which altered its emphasis quite considerably.

The DC-10 flight was operating from Oakland, California to Boston, Massachusetts, with a stop en route at Newark, New Jersey. The bad weather which had in part caused Flight 90's problems was still taking hold, and so Captain Peter Langley was conscious that there could be problems on his approach into Logan, and even contemplated rerouting the flight to JFK in New York or Philadelphia. However, he decided to go into Logan, although aware that the runways there were slippery and that some of the taxiways had been closed because of the weather, as advised by the Automatic Terminal Information Services (ATIS) Field Condition Report 6. He was using the autothrottle/speed control system to control airspeed and manual flight control, although the computer didn't agree with his assessment of the necessary speed, and insisted that a higher airspeed be entered during approach.

Because of the higher airspeed, the aircraft touched down nearly 1,000 metres beyond the runway's displaced threshold – where it should have landed – and as soon as it did so, the captain realized that the runway was very slippery. The ground spoilers did not deploy properly, and even though Captain Langley applied full reverse thrust and fully depressed the brake pedals, the aircraft continued to slide inexorably forward. Thirty-four seconds after touchdown he could see that the aircraft was going to go off the end of the runway, and, as the first officer informed the tower that "we're going off the end", it went over the sea wall into the harbour. The wing-mounted engines of the DC-10 stopped running as soon as the aircraft entered the water; the centreline engine on the tail kept running at full reverse thrust, and did so for the next half-hour, causing problems for communication during the evacuation of the aircraft.

The nose section fractured from the rest of the fuselage, with the front row of seats – two banks of three and a double seat – thrown into the water, along with the flight attendant jump seats. Although no one registered it at the time, there had been three people in those seats; one of them climbed back into the main cabin, but the other two did not. Passenger evacuation began, with most people leaving from the exit over the right wing, and then wading through the 30-degree Fahrenheit (-1-degree Celsius) water to the shore. The captain swam to the fuselage and assisted with the evacuation, while the other flight crew swam to the shore. Within twelve minutes, they believed that everyone had been accounted for, and that there had been no fatalities.

According to the UPI report, that night was a "four-hour exercise in confusion, anger and frustration on the part of all parties – reporters, airport officials, airlines spokesmen and friends and relatives awaiting word about the fate of those aboard". There was definite confusion over the number on board: the Massachusetts Port Authority (Massport) said there were ninety-six passengers and twelve crew; World Airways and the NTSB said 196 passengers and twelve crew. In the end, the Massport spokesman agreed to use World's figures. There were also questions regarding whether Massport tried to keep reporters away from the scene of the crash to give them time to "properly treat the icy runway". (Massport denied this.) Only when the Metcalfs' relatives made a fuss to the police did the airline recheck the manual ticket stubs, and realize there had been two more people on the airliner. No trace of father or son's bodies was ever located, although their hand luggage was found.

The NTSB investigation initially found that the probable cause was that "the pilot landed the airplane without sufficient information as to runway conditions on a slippery, ice-covered runway, the condition of which exceeded the airplane's stopping capability". This lack of information came from failings within the FAA regulations, as well as the airport management's failure to assess and improve the conditions, and the tower controllers failing to transmit information they'd received from other pilots about the conditions to the pilot of Flight 30H.

However, after various new pieces of evidence came to light during various civil actions which followed the crash, particularly with regard to Captain Langley's willingness to disbelieve the condition reports which he had received, the NTSB were petitioned to reconsider the matter. Their revised report, issued in 1985, shared the blame between those on the ground and those in the air. "The probable cause of the accident was the minimal braking effectiveness on the ice-covered runway; the failure of the Boston-Logan International Airport management to exercise maximum efforts to assess the condition of the runway to assure continued safety of landing operations; the failure of air traffic control to transmit the most recent pilot reports of braking action to the pilot of Flight 30H; and the captain's decision to accept and maintain an excessive airspeed derived from the autothrottle speed control system during the landing approach which caused the airplane to land about 2,800 feet beyond the runway's displaced threshold." The inadequate system of reporting and the FAA failings became contributory factors – and these were addressed by the relevant authorities.

NOT LEARNING THE LESSONS

In their Aircraft Accident Reports, the NTSB, and other investigatory authorities worldwide, make a series of recommendations based on what they have learned from the incident under review. Often these lead to changes in aviation policy; however, there are times when the information is simply not passed on quickly enough between different organizations. Those involved with investigating the crash of Air Ontario Flight 1363 on 10 March 1989 were horrified to later discover that a similar accident occurred at LaGuardia Airport in New York involving USAir Flight 405 on 22 March 1992. Twenty-four people died in the Canadian crash, although forty-five survived; twenty-seven died and twenty-four survived the USAir crash.

"The aircraft was hitting trees, hitting trees, and at that point the aircraft I guess was decelerating and we were inside the blender effect," one of the passengers on board Air Ontario 1363 recalled. "You take a blender, throw in some metal, some trees, people and turn it on."

The Fokker F-28 was in the middle of a run between Thunder Bay and Winnipeg, and an extra stop had been required for refuelling at Dryden Regional Airport. Weather conditions were poor on the flight from Thunder Bay, and the aircraft was already around an hour behind schedule. It landed at Dryden, but there its problems really began: because the auxiliary power unit on the aircraft had not been functioning for some time, the engines would require an external power unit to restart. However, Dryden didn't possess this equipment. That meant that one of the engines would have to remain running for the entire time the aircraft was on the ground.

Flight 1363 landed at 1139 Central Standard Time, and was only on the ground for thirty minutes. During that time, Captain George Morwood and First Officer Keith Mills elected not to deplane the passengers, since that would simply add to the time that they were waiting, and carried out a "hot" refuel. This undoubtedly speeded things up, and kept the time on the ground to a minimum – time during which snow fell on the aircraft, leaving a layer between 0.6cm and 1.3cm thick on the wings.

In the ordinary course of events, the aircraft would be de-iced before take-off in those conditions, but because the engine was running, it was not permitted to use de-icing in case toxic fumes somehow got into the cabin. However, as became clear during the twenty-month inquiry that followed the accident, Captain Morwood wasn't as aware of the inherent dangers of ice on the wings as he should have been. Flight attendant Sonia Hartwick noticed the ice before they took off, but reasoned that since pilots didn't necessarily welcome operational information from the crew – and she already knew Morwood and Mills were annoyed over various incidents which had contributed to the aircraft running behind schedule – they knew what they were doing and she shouldn't worry about it.

At 1209, the aircraft began its take-off roll over the slush-covered runway 79. The first time the pilots tried to lift off, the Fokker settled back onto the runway, but they tried again, and achieved rotation for the second time at the 5,700 feet point of the runway – only 300 feet from the end. The aircraft failed to gain any altitude, and it mushed in a nose-high attitude, smashing into trees, and come to rest in a wooded area, about 3,000 feet from the end of the runway. It then caught fire. Forty-five people, including one of the flight attendants, were able to escape from the wreckage.

The accident investigation was taken over by a judicial inquiry led by Judge Virgil P. Moshansky, who insisted that he be allowed to conduct a wider-ranging investigation looking at all aspects of Canadian aviation. The interim report was completed in November 1990, and suggested that the new Type II de-icing fluid should be standard (since it was considerably more effective than Type I, the gylcol/water mix used up until then), and that there should be de-icing equipment on runways, rather than at the terminal gates.

Although he eventually noted that "Captain Morwood, as the pilot-in-command, must bear responsibility for the decision to land and take off in Dryden on the day in question", Justice Moshansky's final report was scathing about the state of air travel in Canada: "However, it is equally clear that the air transportation system failed him by allowing him to be placed in a situation where he did not have all the necessary tools that should have supported him in making the proper decision." Transport Canada had allowed Air Ontario to expand into too large an operation, and safety instructions simply were not being passed on to the pilots. As a result, a new set of Canadian Aviation Regulations were brought into operation "designed to enhance safety and the competitiveness of the Canadian aviation industry".

The same type of aircraft, the Fokker 28, was involved in the USAir Flight 405 crash at LaGuardia – an accident which occurred only a few days before the four-volume final Canadian report was released. When Justice Moshansky read about Flight 405, "My first reaction was, 'My God, it's Dryden all over again.'"

The similarities did seem very large. Although "contributing to the cause of the accident were the inappropriate procedures used by, and inadequate coordination between, the flight crew that led to a takeoff rotation at a lower than prescribed air speed" – rotation should have been called at 124 knots, but instead the captain rotated at 119 knots – the probable cause given for the American incident was "the failure of the airline industry and the Federal Aviation Administration to provide flight crews with procedures, requirements, and criteria compatible with departure delays in conditions conducive to airframe icing and the decision by the flight crew to take off without positive assurance that the airplane's wings were free of ice accumulation after 35 minutes of exposure to precipitation following de-icing. The ice contamination on the wings resulted in an aerodynamic stall and loss of control after lift-off."

USAir 405 had been delayed leaving Jacksonville on its inbound flight to LaGuardia, after reports of poor weather in the New York area, and a passenger choosing to deplane. It therefore arrived at Gate 1 at LaGuardia at 1949 Eastern Standard Time on 22 March 1992, sixty-six minutes behind schedule. They should have departed on the next leg to Cleveland nearly half an hour earlier. The two pilots, Captain Wallace J. Majure II and First Officer John J. Rachuba used the rest room after telling a USAir mechanic that the aircraft was "good to go". Neither of them walked round the aircraft to check everything was okay, but they weren't required to, even though it was snowing. It wasn't the sort of blizzard that can affect the Eastern seaboard – the snow was "not heavy, no large flakes" according to Rachuba. They had kept the windshield heat on low, and when Rachuba reached out of the cockpit window, there was a watery layer on the nose.

Type I de-icer was used to spray the aircraft, but that in itself caused a further delay, after the de-icing truck broke down behind the Fokker, which meant they were prevented yet further from pushing back. Given that twenty more minutes had elapsed, Captain Majure asked for a second de-icing, which was finished by 2100. Five minutes later, Rachuba requested taxi clearance, and was cleared to taxi to runway 13. During the taxi, the pre-flight checklist was completed, and the engine anti-ice was switched on.

Both pilots were well aware of the problem with ice, and Rachuba – who survived the accident – recalled that he checked the wings visually "maybe 10 times but at least 3". Rachuba suggested the possibility of using the aircraft in front to "keep our wings clear for us", but Majure, perhaps conscious of the errors made by the Air Florida pilots a decade earlier, noted that it could "cause us to re-freeze too".

Although the snow was still falling lightly, the pilots hoped that they would be on their way before there was any need to de-ice for a third time. As one of the NTSB investigators later explained, at LaGuardia, that wouldn't mean waiting for a de-icing truck to come out to them on the taxiway – they would have to delay their take-off yet further by going back to the gate. It could even have meant the flight being cancelled. But time kept passing – and it was 2134.51 before they were cleared for take-off. The aircraft had been out in the precipitation for over half an hour, and USAir guidance to flight crews was clear that "If the elapsed time since de-icing exceeds 20 minutes, careful examination of the surfaces should be conducted to detect the extent of accumulation [of ice] and to assure that the takeoff can be made safely and in compliance with existing [regulations]." Fokker suggested that the aircraft should be de-iced every 15 minutes in such conditions.

Rachuba made one last check before they proceeded to take-off: "Looks good from here," he said of the wings, and said that he couldn't see anything on the black stripe on the wing which was there to aid with such visual confirmation. A 727 that was behind them in the queue, and in front of which the Fokker passed during its taxi for take-off, said that Flight 405 was "a fairly clean airplane".

The take-off seemed normal until rotation – at least, that's how Rachuba remembered it – but in the cabin, some of the passengers seemed to think there was something wrong as the aircraft accelerated down the runway. The nose lifted from the ground, but it was quickly clear that something was in fact seriously wrong. The aircraft juddered from left to right and then back to the left. Majure tried to level the wings, as it felt as though the aircraft had lost lift, but they were heading towards the black waters of Flushing Bay. Both men knew that the aircraft wasn't going to fly, and their main concern now was to find somewhere safe to land, so they tried to hold the nose up.

Five seconds after the aircraft had briefly left the ground, the left wing scraped against the asphalt of the tarmac for 110 yards, and the landing gear bashed into a set of navigational lights along the side of the runway. It took off again, hitting a set of ILS antennas and a water pump house. The left wing tore off, and a fire broke out.

Flight 405 began to break apart as it careered over the edge of the embankment into Flushing Bay. What was left of the fuselage was "mangled pretty bad" according to Coast Guard lieutenant Chuck Jennings. "It's really hard to tell it's a plane at all." To some onlookers, it seemed as though the aircraft "catapulted" three or four times before it went into the water. The front part of the aircraft, from the nose to the fourth passenger window, ended up upside down, partially submerged in the bay. The rest of the fuselage split in two; one part floated on the bay, the other became submerged. The tail section remained on dry land.

Inside, some of the passengers had struck their heads and blacked out during the tumbling ride to the water; others found themselves upside down, strapped to their seats, submerged in water. Some were thrown from the wreckage out into the bay. Fifteen people drowned while others were able to swim to shore from the aircraft. Eleven others, including Captain Majure, were killed and one person with cervical spine injuries survived for a few hours. Thick black smoke billowed above the airport as emergency services quickly raced to the scene, with over 200 workers trying to get to the screaming survivors who were caught in the blustery snow and the powerful current in Flushing Bay.

Even before the NTSB had a chance to complete their investigations, an International Conference on Ground Deicing was called for 28–29 May 1992, which led to new rules regarding de-icing that came into effect the following November.

Not every icing incident leads to fatalities. Three months before USAir 405 went into Flushing Bay, Scandinavian Airlines Flight 751, a McDonnell Douglas MD-81, was able to crash land successfully, with only four people on board receiving severe injuries, leading to the incident becoming described as the Miracle at Gottröra. Captain Stefan G. Rasmussen and First Officer Ulf Cedermark believed that they had done everything necessary to check that the aircraft was de-iced before they departed from Stockholm on 27 December 1991, but they didn't realize that the very cold fuel which had sat in the tanks overnight had caused clear ice to form on the upper sides of the wings. The de-icer confirmed that there had been a lot of snow and ice under the wings but said, "It's perfect now". The lower side may well have been clear – but once the aircraft took off, the ice from the top got into the engines, slamming onto the fans with sufficient force to deform the fan blades, and disturb the airflow to the compressors. This meant that they stalled, which led to engine surges.

The first the crew knew of this was when they heard noises from the engine, as it surged – unknown to them, an automatic system had been installed which was increasing the throttle, even as the pilots were trying to throttle back to deal with the surge. By seventy-eight seconds after rotation, both engines had ceased providing thrust. Fellow SAS captain Per Holmberg, who was travelling in seat 2C, came straight to the cockpit to offer his assistance, and found himself helping the first officer deal with the emergency checklist while Captain Rasmussen tried to keep the aircraft flying. "Look straight ahead," Holmberg urged Rasmussen, as they tried a restart.

Once they were notified of the emergency, Stockholm ATC ordered the aircraft to make a right turn to bring it back to Arlanda Airport, but Rasmussen knew that there wasn't time. The MD-81 was descending too fast. While he concentrated on bringing the aircraft safely into one of the fields he could see in front of him (and made a quick course correction to avoid some nearby houses), Holmberg and Cedermark dealt with everything else – flaps and gear. As the gear locked, the aircraft hit the tops of the trees.

Flight 751 was coming down in the forest, near Vängsjöbergs Säteri in Gottröra, Uppland. Most of the right wing was torn off, and the aircraft began to bank to the right. A mere four minutes and seven seconds after it took off, Flight 751 hit sloping ground, first with its tail, and then slid for about 110 metres, breaking into three parts. There was no fire, and all 129 on board survived.

Although Rasmussen and the crew were praised for their actions during the flight, it became clear that Rasmussen had not followed a directive sent out by SAS: "It is the Pilot-in-Charge's responsibility to check the aircraft for any ice or snow that may affect performance." In particular, the section regarding clear ice made it plain: "Although the awareness within Line Maintenance is mostly good, the responsibility again rests with the Pilot-in-Charge that the aircraft is physically checked by means of a hands-on check on the upper side of the wing. A visual check from a ladder or when standing on the ground is *not* enough." The mechanic's failure to go out onto the wing to check it led him to wrongly conclude that there was no clear ice.

THE MYSTERIOUS CRASHES

Ice played a key role in two other crashes in 2008 and 2009, although in neither case was it immediately obvious. The crash landing of British Airways Flight 38 from Beijing to Heathrow led to the first ever Boeing 777 being written off, while the disappearance of Air France Flight 447 over the Atlantic Ocean was very hard to investigate until the black boxes were finally recovered in May 2011, nearly two years after the accident.

Some of the passengers involved in the British Airways crash weren't even aware that there had been any sort of emergency before they were told to leave the aircraft using the emergency chutes – Francis Charig wrote in the *Daily Telegraph* three weeks later that "the landing was so unsurprising that it was insufficient to stop me working on my Sudoku puzzle", while another passenger, Chloe Richards, told the BBC: "It felt like it had gone slightly sideways, but it didn't particularly feel like a crash. We thought it had just been a bumpy landing, until the oxygen masks and parts of panelling came down off the plane. It came to a very, very sudden stop. You're used to planes coming in quite slowly and having a bounce or two and gliding to a stop. But it was a very sharp stop and everyone jolted forwards and then the masks came down." Others, however, were injured, and an out-of-court settlement was reached on behalf of those who suffered what their lawyers described as "physical as well as serious psychological injuries, including developing a fear of flying and flashbacks".

The first time that any of the flight crew on British Airways 38 realized that there was a problem was when they were on the descent into London Heathrow, having brought the 777 nearly 5,000 miles around the world from Beijing. They had left China at 0209 GMT on the morning of 17 January 2008 with a route that took them initially up to 10,400 metres (flight level 341), then descending to 9,600 metres (flight level 315) for part of the way, because of the predicted "extreme cold" conditions along the border between China and Mongolia. For a flight of any duration, but particularly one with such hazards along the way, careful fuel calculations are required by the crew, and they agreed that 79,000 kilograms of fuel would be the correct total for the predicted conditions.

However, after they took off from Beijing, local air traffic control asked them to climb to a higher cruise altitude, 10,600 metres (flight level 348), and noted that they would closely monitor the fuel temperature during the flight because of the predicted low temperatures. When they were 350 nautical miles north of Moscow, they climbed to flight level 380, and then carried out another climb, to flight level 400, over Sweden. During all of these, the crew kept a weather eye on the Engine Indication and Crew Alerting System (EICAS); the minimum indicated temperature was -34 degrees Celsius (-29 degrees Fahrenheit), and no low fuel temperature warning was given.

Captain Peter Burkill was flying the aircraft as they descended into the stacking system around Heathrow, and it stayed holding for about five minutes, before being cleared for a radar-vectored Instrument Landing System approach onto runway 27L at Heathrow. Everything was set up exactly as normal, with landing gear down and the flaps set at 30 as the aircraft reached 1,000 feet above the ground.

At 800 feet, co-pilot Senior First Officer John Coward took control for the landing. He would bring it in under manual control, and he intended to disconnect the autopilot when they reached 600 feet. Shortly after he took over, the autothrottles ordered an increase in thrust, to which both engines initially responded. Fifty-seven seconds before touchdown, the thrust on the right engine suddenly reduced – and seven seconds after that, the same thing happened on the left. They hadn't shut down; they were simply not providing the power that the pilot needed.

Heathrow Tower gave the 777 a landing clearance as it passed 500 feet, and 70 feet later – thirty-four seconds before touchdown – Captain Burkill said that the approach was stable. Coward was clearly less sure: "Just" was his one-word comment. Seven seconds later, he saw that their airspeed was dropping lower than the 135 knots it needed to be for approach. The two pilots and First Officer Conor Magenis, who was also in the cockpit, immediately tried to work out what was causing the loss of thrust. The engines weren't responding either to the autothrottle or manual movement of the thrust levers, so the aircraft's speed was dropping all the time; Coward had his hands full just ensuring it kept on the correct glide slope. "Suddenly there was nothing from any of the engines, and the plane started to glide," he told the *Sunday Mirror* the following weekend.

When the airspeed dropped to 115 knots, a low airspeed warning sounded, and Captain Burkill retracted the flaps slightly to reduce drag and increase the length of the glide. By 200 feet, speed was down to 108 knots. With ten seconds to touchdown, the stick shaker operated, showing the aircraft was nearing a stall, so Coward pushed the control column forward, disconnecting the autopilot and reducing the aircraft's nose-high attitude, to avoid the stall. Burkill tried to start the auxiliary power unit, but it was clear to all three men in the cockpit that they weren't going to make the runway – instead they were only just going to clear the perimeter fence on Heathrow's Southern Perimeter Road. (A taxi driver on the perimeter road admitted that he ducked, genuinely believing that the aircraft was about to hit the roof of his cab.) Burkill transmitted a Mayday call as Coward pulled back on the column in one last desperate attempt to reach the runway. Three seconds later the aircraft hit the ground.

"I didn't think we'd clear the fence at first," Coward admitted. "As we landed I was bracing myself for an enormous thud. But instead of one thud, there was a series of thuds as it bounced along the grass." They had cleared the fence – just – and come down 110 metres inside the airport, 330 metres short of the runway. Both the nose and the main landing gears collapsed during the impact and the short roll forward. Within seconds the tower had issued the emergency call (the ATC recording is on YouTube), and emergency services were sent. Captain Burkill gave the evacuation command (inadvertently sending that to the tower rather than the cabin initially), and an orderly exodus from the aircraft began. Many passengers only began to understand what had happened when they saw that the undercarriage was damaged and the wheels were scattered around the area. One person suffered a broken leg, and there were minor injuries during the evacuation. For their actions in bringing the aircraft in safely, the crew received the BA Safety Medal, and the President's Award from the Royal Aeronautical Society.

Although Burkill and the crew were hailed as heroes by British Airways, the captain found that rumours spread that he had "frozen" in the cockpit during the emergency, and British Airways policy prevented him from speaking out. He told the BBC that cabin crew had been told various incorrect things about his actions, and wrote a book about the incident. Although he took voluntary redundancy from BA in August 2009, he returned to them in November 2010.

The Air Accident Investigations Branch results were confidently expected within thirty days of the incident, the BBC reported at the time. Instead, the final report came over two years later. Unlikely causes – such as radio interference from the Prime Minister's motorcade – were discounted, but a month after the accident, the AAIB released a special bulletin which suggested there was "no evidence of a mechanical defect or ingestion of birds or ice" or "of fuel contamination or unusual levels of water content" in the fuel. A second bulletin, in May 2008, noted: "There is no evidence of a wake vortex encounter, a bird strike or core engine icing. There is no evidence of any anomalous behaviour of any of the aircraft or engine systems that suggests electromagnetic interference." However by 4 September 2008, ice within the fuel feed system was believed to be the root cause.

By the time comprehensive tests had been carried out, the AAIB were able to state that there had been a restriction to the engine fuel flow at the Fuel/Oil Heat Exchanger (FOHE) on both engines, because ice had formed from the water that occurred naturally within the fuel while the aircraft was using low fuel flow for a long time in the very cold conditions. Their deductions had been aided by two further incidents – a Delta Air Lines flight in November 2008, whose engine had rollbacked while they were cruising at 39,000 feet, which had ahd been caused by ice clogging the FOHE; and an Airbus A330 which had had the same sort of problem with a similar engine. Rolls-Royce therefore redesigned the Trent 500, 700 and 800 engines to ensure this wouldn't happen again.

The cause of the disappearance of Air France Flight 447 remained a mystery for even longer. The aircraft crashed on

1 June 2009, but the wreckage wasn't located until 3 April 2011, and the black boxes not brought to the surface of the Atlantic Ocean until 1 and 2 May. Initial indications, from the few pieces of data that the French authorities had which had been automatically transmitted to the Air France maintenance centre, were that the pitot tubes had frozen over. These small forward-facing ducts use airflow to measure airspeed, and if they were giving inaccurate readings, the autopilot would have disengaged. For some reason thereafter, the crew had not maintained sufficient speed, and the Airbus A330 had crashed. Only when the CVR was examined did the truth emerge. Within four and a half minutes of the pitot tubes ceasing to function properly, Flight 447 fell from nearly 38,000 feet into the Atlantic Ocean. "This can't be happening," one of the co-pilots said four seconds before impact – and it shouldn't have done.

The Airbus A330 has fly-by-wire controls: the side sticks beside the pilots' seats send commands to computers, which then instruct the engines and hydraulics. It provides reliable automation: once an instruction is given, the aircraft gets on with doing what it's been told to do (say a twelve-degree turn to the right) while the pilot can then deal with other issues. There are various different modes for fly-by-wire depending on the conditions.

Because of the length of the journey from Galeão International Airport in Rio de Janeiro, Brazil to Charles de Gaulle International Airport in Paris, France, there were three pilots on the Airbus A330: Captain Marc Dubois, and two co-pilots, David Robert and Pierre-Cédric Bonin. The doubling up of co-pilots meant that everyone could take a break so they were working at maximum efficiency. The flight left Galeão at 2229 UTC on 31 May, and was expected to arrive in Paris just over 10.5 hours later.

Captain Dubois went off for his break at 0155, leaving Bonin at the controls. At 0206 Bonin warned the cabin crew they were heading into an area of turbulence, and a couple of minutes later, he turned the aircraft slightly to the left, and decreased speed, ensuring that the engine de-icing was switched on.

Two minutes after that, the serious problems began. The autopilot and auto-thrust disengaged, and the speed readings on the primary flight display and the integrated standby instrument system became unreliable, suggesting the aircraft was only flying at 60 knots rather than the 274 it really was. The lack of reliable input to the computer systems meant that the aircraft went into "alternate law" mode – which in practical terms meant that the autopilot could not be re-engaged, and the pilots needed to fly the aircraft.

With no auto-pilot, the aircraft reacted to the turbulence, and rolled to the right; Bonin overcorrected initially as he got used to the feel of the aircraft under the new conditions. However, he also made a nose-up input, which led to a brief stall warning, and while he was getting the aircraft's roll under control, it was starting to climb at 7,000 feet per minute. David Robert realized the aircraft was climbing, and asked Bonin to descend.

At 0210.34, the instruments started to register properly, indicating the aircraft was travelling at 223 knots, 51 knots slower than it had been before the autopilot disconnection. Bonin commented that he was "in TOGA" – increasing speed to the Take-Off, Go Around level, trying to increase speed and climb away from the danger. However, at 37,500 feet the effect of such a manoeuvre is very different to applying it at sea level: raising the nose produces a different angle of climb, and can actually result in descent – as was to happen here.

Flight 447 continued to rise, reaching just below 38,000 feet at 0211.10. And there it stalled. Over the next forty seconds, the aircraft fell 3,000 feet. Robert was confused: "But we've got the engines, what's happening? Do you understand what's happening or not?" At 0211.32, Bonin admitted, "I don't have control of the airplane any more now. I don't have control of the airplane at all." He was, however, still holding the stick back.

The Airbus was now falling at a rate of 10,000 feet per minute, as Captain Dubois re-entered the cabin, wondering what the hell the pilots were doing. Both men admitted that they'd lost control of the aircraft. Bonin tried operating the speedbrakes, but as the aircraft continued to fall, confusion reigned.

Robert tried to take the controls and push forward on his stick, but Bonin had not released his sidestick, so the computer announced "Dual input" and averaged out the two – one saying go down, one saying go up. It was only at this point that Bonin revealed that he had been trying to climb for the last couple of minutes. Robert took control but there was yet more confusion as Bonin was still trying to operate his stick even as his co-pilot desperately attempted to bring the descent under control. Knowing he had to pitch up, since by now they were at 4,000 feet, Robert received Captain Dubois' permission to do so (the captain had remained behind the two co-pilots, not taking control of the situation) – but then Bonin (perhaps inadvertently in panic) pushed the takeover button on his sidestick which was still pulled back. Bonin clearly didn't realize what had happened, as he desperately asked what was going on. Dubois ordered 10 degrees of pitch, which might have saved them from crashing, and Robert would have tried to implement it but his commands were frozen out from the system because Bonin's hand was on the takeover button.

At 0214.28, Air France Flight 447, with 228 people on board, hit the surface of the Atlantic and broke up. There was no chance of anyone surviving. An alarm was raised when it failed to make contact with either Senegal or Cape Verdean air traffic controls, with Brazilian, French, Spanish and US Navy reconnaissance aircraft sent to carry out an aerial search. There was no sign whatsoever, and that afternoon it was presumed that the aircraft had been lost with no survivors.

Wreckage and some jet fuel were spotted near the Saint Peter and Saint Paul Archipelago on 2 June, and five days after the aircraft vanished, the first bodies were found, along with some hand luggage which was definitely from Air France 447. The vertical stabilizer was located on 7 June and between then and 26 June, fifty bodies, including Captain Dubois', and 640 items of debris were retrieved.

Three underwater searches were unsuccessful, before a team from the Woods Hole Oceanographic Institution found a wreckage field from the aircraft on the bottom of the ocean, 12,500–13,100 feet beneath the surface on 3 April 2011. The black boxes were brought to the surface, and analysed, and a further 104 bodies recovered from the wreckage.

Preliminary reports were issued by the Bureau d'Enquêtes et d'Analyses pour la Sécurité de l'Aviation Civile (BEA), based on the failure reports and warnings which were automatically transmitted from the aircraft to Air France. One of these was a fault in the pitot-static system, which meant that the investigators knew that the pilots were flying without reliable speed data. However, with little more to go on, the BEA investigators could only say there was no sign of fire, and that it struck the sea in a normal flight attitude – i.e. it didn't plunge nose-first into the water. The information was enough for Airbus to alter the design of the pitot tubes. A third interim report incorporated some of the information from the black boxes, while the final report pieced together everything that had happened, and included many safety recommendations.

The ice crystals may only have obscured the pitot tubes for less than two minutes – but that was enough to create a situation in which human error and lack of training of the pilots to recognize the situation in which they found themselves played its part in creating a tragedy. As a BEA investigator said, "When it comes down to it, safety will always be based on the capacity of the pilots and the signals which they are given, which they have to understand and react to."

Part 5:
Explosive Decompression

COMETS FALL TO EARTH

It's a very common scene in a James Bond or other action film: the hero and the villain are fighting inside an aircraft. Eventually 007 or his equivalent gains the upper hand, and a window is broken, leading to everything including the bad guy being sucked out of the hole, to fall through the skies to his or her doom. Although many of these scenes couldn't happen exactly as seen on screen, explosive decompressions do happen, and can lead to fatalities.

An aircraft cabin is pressurized so that we don't all have to use oxygen masks the entire time to breathe. Usually the pressure is maintained at the same level that you'd find around 5,000-8,000 feet above sea level. Aircraft designers therefore have to find materials that have the necessary lightness combined with the desired strength from which to build the cabin.

This means that there could be a difference of over 30,000 feet in the pressure between the outside and the inside of the cabin – and if for some reason, such as mechanical failure, the pressurization inside fails, there's only a very short time (called the useful time of consciousness) before the effects of being at such a high altitude kick in. When something like that does happen, the pilots will bring the aircraft down to around 10,000 feet as quickly as possible. That's the level at which we can breathe without extra oxygen – since the tanks for the oxygen supply are not unlimited. This also keeps the aircraft at a high enough level that it's not burning too much fuel and putting everyone on board in danger for a different reason!

Some of the most dramatic images from air disasters have arisen from the effects of explosive decompression – the 747 in Hawaii, part of whose roof came off, for example – but it has also been responsible for some of the worst catastrophes, including the world's worst crash in Japan in 1985.

* * *

The investigation into the loss of not one but two Comet aircraft in unusual circumstances in the space of three months in 1954 would have a marked effect on future generations of flying. Not only were the effects of pressurization considerably better understood, but the distinctive shape of aircraft windows – with rounded rather than straight edges – was developed as a result.

Parts of the Comet which featured in the first crash, tail number G-ALYP, can still be seen at London's Science Museum. It was operating as British Overseas Airways Corporation (BOAC) Flight 781 on 10 January 1954, and had already travelled from Singapore to Beirut that day without any problems. It was the third ever Comet to be built, and the first to go into passenger service. Captain Alan Gibson was in charge of the flight, with William Bury as his first officer; there were four other crew aboard, as well as twenty-nine passengers, ten of them children. The flight landed at Rome's Ciampino Airport at 0830 GMT, and left at 0931. It was inspected by ground crew, who couldn't see any reason why it wouldn't be fit for flight.

The aircraft climbed rapidly, and at 0950, Gibson reported to Ciampino that he was at 26,500 feet over the beacon at Orbetello, and was continuing his planned climb to 36,000 feet. While in flight, Gibson was in contact with Captain Johnson on another BOAC aircraft, a slower Argonaut which had left Rome before them. Just after 0950, Johnson received a message which broke off suddenly: "GHJ from GYP: did you get my—" Around 1000, four people on the Mediterranean island of Elba saw the Comet plummet into the sea in flames.

Around 1150, the commander at Portoferraio harbour on Elba was informed that an aircraft had crashed into the sea south of Cape Calamita, and he quickly sent out boats, with a doctor and nurse on board. Over the next two days, fifteen bodies, various mail bags, and some aircraft wreckage and personal effects were recovered from the site. The bodies were autopsied, and it was clear that death had resulted from impact against parts of the aircraft, and that the bodies had serious lesions as a result of explosive decompression and deceleration. Although the Comet had been burning up, those on board were already dead.

BOAC immediately suspended all Comets from flying. It wasn't the first accident that had happened to the pioneering

British aircraft: on 3 March 1953, a Canadian Pacific Airlines Comet had crashed during take-off from Karachi, India, although pilot error was blamed for this. Exactly two months later, on 3 May, a Comet had crashed near Calcutta, India, killing all forty-three people aboard. However, this had been during a tempest and a dust storm, and it seemed that that had been responsible.

A committee headed by BOAC's Deputy Operations Director of Engineering was immediately set up to probe the causes of the G-ALYP accident, which suggested a modification to the aircraft manufacture and two special inspections. The chairman of the Air Safety Board wrote to the Minister of Transport and Civil Aviation, noting: "The Board has considered all the available information resulting from recent investigations and has noted the nature and extent of the modifications planned as a result. It realizes that no cause has yet been found that would satisfactorily account for the Elba disaster, and whilst the Calcutta disaster is completely accounted for if the aircraft is supposed to have encountered a gust of very great severity (which would have broken any other aircraft) we cannot eliminate that the accident might have been due to some other cause which was possibly common to both disasters." However, they recognized that BOAC was doing everything possible, and recommended that Comet flights be allowed to continue. The salvage operation on G-ALYP was still continuing, but nobody realistically expected them to find much more than they already had.

On 23 March 1954, regular services resumed. On 8 April 1954, just over two weeks later, Comet G-ALYY, which was chartered to South African Airways, crashed near Naples while on a flight from Rome to Cairo, on the second stage of its flight from London to Johannesburg. The aircraft had been flying for approximately the same length of time after take-off as G-ALYP, and was at roughly the same altitude, nearing the top of its climb. BOAC suspended all Comets once more, and on 12 April, the Ministry of Transport removed the UK Certificate of Airworthiness from all Comets. The *New York Times* called it "a stunning blow to [Britain's] proudest pioneer industry" while BOAC chairman Sir Miles Thomas described the new crash as "a very great tragedy and a major setback for British civil aviation".

South Africa Airways Flight 201 had been delayed leaving Ciampino for Johannesburg on 7 April, after an inspection discovered a faulty fuel gauge and thirty loose bolts on the left wing. It therefore departed Rome at 1832 on 8 April, twenty-five hours late. The crew reported at 1837 while passing through 7,000 feet, and then again at 11,600 feet at 1849. Eight minutes later, the Comet was passing Naples, and at 1907, Captain William Mostert contacted Cairo to confirm an arrival time of 2102. Soon after, the aircraft disintegrated. At dawn the next day, air-sea rescue services started a search, and later on that day, a British European Airlines aircraft saw oil 70 miles east of Naples, and bodies and wreckage in the water 30 miles south-east of Stromboli – a part of the Mediterranean which in those days was too deep to allow anything to be salvageable.

However, the chances of two aircraft meeting the same fate for different reasons were simply not feasible, so Comet maker de Havilland and the Royal Aircraft Establishment at Farnborough joined forces to investigate the causes of the crashes, with the manufacturer providing use of another Comet for test purposes. This aircraft, G-ALYU, was put through the equivalent of over 3,000 test pressurized flights – and when it reached 3,060 "flights", the cabin structure started to fail.

Many more experiments followed – including making a light wood scale model of the Comet which broke up in exactly the same way that the wreckage recovered from the seabed indicated that G-ALYP had disintegrated near Elba. It became clear that the area near the corner of a window was, contrary to all expectations, not able to cope with the pressure. When a large piece of the cabin skin was discovered in a later examination of the sunken wreckage site, it contained the two windows at the top of the fuselage – and from that, the investigators were able to deduce that the first fracture in the skin had begun near one of those windows, and the cabin had split from there.

The report into the accidents quoted a version of Sherlock Holmes' famous maxim when eliminating other theories: "If in the process of eliminating possible causes you become completely confident that you have eliminated every other possible cause, then you are driven to say that the possible fatigue rises to the most probable cause." Lord Cohen's report noted that metal fatigue had caused the explosive decompression on the first aircraft, and it seemed logical that the same cause could be ascribed to the second ("the explanation offered for the first accident appeared to be applicable to the second") and that neither accident was due to wrongful act, default or negligence – in particular, there was no way that anyone could have foreseen when they allowed Comet services to resume, that there would be such a catastrophic repetition.

DC-10 DECOMPRESSION

Workers preparing the Karl G. Jansky Very Large Array telescope in 1975 were horrified when while building the tracks north of US Route 60 they found human remains in the ground. These were sent to Albuquerque for identification and cause of death, and after a year they were identified as being those of G. F. Gardner of Beaumont, Texas. The discovery of Mr Gardner's body brought to an end the saga of National Airlines Flight 27.

On 3 November 1973, the DC-10 was flying from Miami to San Francisco, via New Orleans, Houston and Las Vegas. It left Houston at 1440 Mountain Standard Time (which is one ahead of Pacific Standard Time, and seven hours behind GMT), with Captain William Broocke and First Officer Eddie Saunders at the controls. There were 116 passengers and twelve crew members on board as they flew over Carlsbad, Socorro and the Plains of San Agustin.

Around 1640, they were near Socorro, New Mexico, flying at 39,000 feet with the autothrottle disengaged. Captain Broocke and Flight Engineer Golden Hanks were discussing various aspects of the autothrottle system, and they decided to check certain functions of the system to see exactly how they worked ("You want to try it and see?" Hanks asked, and Broocke replied, "Yeah.") Their experiment involved re-engaging the autothrottle, and then trying to find out where it got its various inputs from by pulling circuit breakers on the engines. When the captain activated the autothrottle then reset the airspeed indicator for a slightly slower speed, the autothrottle started to slow the aircraft down. Satisfied with what he had established, Broocke disengaged it.

As he did so, there was an explosion. The no. 3 engine fan assembly had disintegrated, and its fragments were penetrating the no. 1 and 2 engine nacelles and the right wing area. However, most critically, fragments of the fan blades started to strike the fuselage, causing the cabin to depressurize rapidly. The air filled with a grey-blue smoke, and people grappled for the oxygen masks, assisted by the crew – or at least, they reached for those oxygen masks which did drop. According to the flight attendants later, the mid-section masks dropped, but elsewhere it took up to three minutes before they deployed, and on the rear left side of the cabin, they never dropped at all.

Amidst the confusion, some of the fragments from the blade struck the window by Mr Gardner's seat, 17H. Although Gardner was wearing his seat belt, there was sufficient slack in it that when the window blew out, he was pulled towards the gap. He was partially forced through the window, but held in place by his belt for a moment – enough time for the person next to him to desperately try to stop him from being sucked through the hole. However, the efforts were in vain: Gardner was pulled through by the pressure, and despite extensive searches by the New Mexico state police and other local organizations, no trace was found of his body – until the work began on the Major Array two years later.

On the flight deck, Broocke tried to control the aircraft, after electrical power to the cockpit went down and he had to switch on emergency power. He started an emergency descent, and the aircraft landed safety at Albuquerque nineteen minutes after the engine had failed. At that point, no one among the crew was aware of Mr Gardner's involuntary exit from the aircraft; this only came to light on landing. Twenty-four people needed hospital treatment for smoke inhalation, barotrauma and minor abrasions.

The NTSB report discovered that there were problems with the design of the fan but they were not impressed with the crew's decision to run an in-flight experiment. "Regardless of the cause of the high fan speed at the time of the fan failure, the Safety Board is concerned that the flight crew was, in effect, performing an untested failure analysis on this system. This type of experimentation, without the benefit of training or specific guidelines, should never be performed during passenger flight operations," Chairman John H. Reed wrote within the report, and emphasized it by repeating the thrust of the comment at the end.

Exactly four months later, another DC-10 was involved in an accident concerning explosive decompression, which led to one of the highest aviation death tolls ever, as 346 people lost their lives. It was the worst in aviation history, until the Tenerife ground collision (see page 98) three years later. The most tragic part about it was that it was a preventable disaster. The cargo hatches on DC-10s could not be relied on to latch properly, and needed to be checked carefully. And unfortunately the last person to latch them on Turkish Airlines Flight 981 on 3 March 1974, was someone who couldn't read the languages in which the advisory notices were written.

Flight 981 had flown into Paris' Orly Airport from Istanbul that morning, arriving at 1002 GMT, and should only have been on the ground for an hour. However, because of a strike by BEA staff, there were far more people needing a flight back to London Heathrow, so it took ninety minutes to load the aircraft. It therefore took off at 1130, and at 1136.10 it was cleared to climb to flight level 230. At 1138, Captain Nejat Berköz had reached flight level 90, and was travelling at 300 knots.

A few seconds before 1140, as the aircraft was flying over the town of Meaux, the flight crew could hear the noise of decompression, and First Officer Oral Ulusman announced that "the fuselage has burst". In the confusion someone pressed the radio button, so at 1140.13, the air traffic controller at North Area Control Centre heard a garbled transmission from the DC-10 – described as "a heavy background noise mingled with words in the Turkish language and the pressurization warning and then the overspeed warning" in the official report. At the same time, Flight 981 disappeared from the secondary radar scope – and on the primary scope, the track split in two. One part remained stationary for two to three minutes; the other curved on a 280 degree heading. The radio transmission ceased after nearly thirty seconds, then picked up again two seconds later for a further seven seconds before cutting off.

As soon as the decompression started, Berköz and Ulusman tried to regain control of the aircraft, which had quickly assumed a 20-degree, nose-down attitude, and started to speed up. The increased speed started to lift the nose and Berköz made one last attempt to level off. It was too late: seventy seconds after decompression, most of Flight 981 hit the ground in the forest of Ermenonville, cutting a swath through the trees in the forest, killing all aboard instantly. The aircraft had been unflyable – all the control cables that ran beneath the section of floor which had been sucked out of the aircraft had been severed.

The radar trace had been accurate: the aircraft had actually been in two pieces in the air. The rear cargo hold hatch had failed, which had led to the cargo area decompressing. That caused a section of the cabin floor above the now-open hatch to fail, and blow out through the hatch, taking with it six passengers, still strapped in their seats. They were ejected about 15 kilometres from the main point of impact, and landed in a turnip field.

Although preliminary newspaper reports suggested that "the possibility of an explosion" was "supported by an important number of aviation specialists" – particularly given that the same day, a British Airways jet had been hijacked in Beirut – it soon became obvious that the hatch decompression hadn't come about because of any sort of bomb blast. The hatches on a DC-10 had failed on American Airlines Flight 96 when it was flying over Windsor, Ontario, on 12 June 1972. On that occasion, the hydraulic system didn't rupture, so the pilots had some degree of control over the aircraft, and were able to bring the DC-10 in to land with only minor injuries. The recommendations made by the NTSB in the light of this incident were not fully followed through by manufacturers McDonnell Douglas.

Examination of the wreckage showed that the locking pins on the hatch had been interfered with, which made it easier for the hatches to be closed, but equally made them considerably less resistant to pressure. A small viewing port had been added to ensure that the baggage handlers could confirm that the locking pins were in the right place – but the notices explaining what handlers should do were in Turkish and English. The Algerian-born baggage handler hadn't been told what the window was for, and although he could read and write in three languages, English and Turkish weren't among them. The error was compounded when neither the Turkish Airlines ground engineer nor the DC-10's flight engineer checked the door.

The French Secretariat for Transport's report was scathing. It ascribed the cause to the circumstances of the door closure at Orly, and the lack of changes which had been made as a result of the earlier accident. "All these risks had already become evident, nineteen months earlier, at the time of the Windsor accident, but no efficacious corrective action had followed." The investigators did not believe that the baggage handler should face charges though.

This time, action was taken. The latches were completely redesigned, and vents were cut into the cabin floor of a number of aircraft with outward-opening doors to ensure that the pressure would equalize if there was a blow-out.

THE WORST SINGLE-AIRCRAFT DISASTER

Even without the events of 12 August, 1985 would have been a very bad year for aviation. In May, an Aeroflot Tupolev Tu-134 collided with a Soviet Air Forces Antonov An-26, killing ninety-four people. In June, TWA Flight 847 was hijacked and flown repeatedly around the Mediterranean (see page 311), and Air India Flight 182 was blown up off the Irish coast (see page 374). At the start of August, a Delta Air Lines Lockheed crashed and exploded within inches of the runway at Dallas-Forth Worth, killing 137 people on board and on the ground. In November, the hijacking of EgyptAir Flight 648 led to a massacre in Malta (see page 316), and the following month, Arrow Air Flight 1285 crashed shortly after take-off from Gander in Newfoundland, killing 256 US service personnel and their families.

But it became the worst year ever, with the crash of Japan Airlines Flight 123, a Boeing 747 which was flying from Tokyo to Osaka and crashed into the side of Mount Takamagahara in Japan on 12 August. Incredibly, despite the severity of the incident, four of the 524 people on board survived, but its total of 520 dead made it the highest total of fatalities from a single-aircraft incident.

Although many accidents related in this volume involve a chain of events, few of these stretch for as long as that relating to JAL 123, whose problems really began on 2 June 1978, seven years before its impact on Mount Takamagahara. That is when aircraft number JA8119 was involved in an incident at Osaka Airport. JA8119 was a Boeing 747SR – the SR standing for "short range". These were special variants of the 747 Series 100 which were specially configured for use for domestic flights with a higher than normal density seating arrangement. A standard Boeing 747-100 could take 366 passengers in three classes, or 452 if divided in two; the 747SR had more compact fuel tanks and an extended passenger space, so could seat up to 550 passengers.

During a routine flight into Osaka, JA8119 "floated" before landing (i.e. it remained just above the surface of the runway as a result of the effect of the air pressure from the ground on the wings), and on touchdown, the tail struck the runway, which caused substantial damage to the rear underside of the fuselage. It also meant that the rear pressure bulkhead was cracked. This had to be replaced – or at least, part of its lower half had to be. This work was carried out by Boeing, and the aircraft returned to active service.

On 12 August 1985, that "repaired" bulkhead ruptured. If it had been on the ground at the time, it would have been annoying, and required work, but not been the greatest problem. Unfortunately, at the time, the aircraft was climbing through 23,900 feet, at a speed of 300 knots. It had arrived at Tokyo International Airport at 1712 Japanese local time as Flight 366, and was then inspected and prepared for its operation as Flight 123. The flight plan indicated it was going to cruise at 24,000 feet at 467 knots for the fifty-four-minute journey to Osaka. Captain Masami Takahama was in charge of the 747, although the flight was going to be handled by First Officer Yutaka Sasaki as part of his training for the position of captain.

Flight 123 took off at 1812, twelve minutes behind schedule, packed with passengers heading home to celebrate the holiday season of Bon, which began the next morning. It followed the prescribed route, heading south and climbing towards 24,000 feet, then banking toward the west as it passed by the island of Oshima, south of Haneda. It was approaching the east coast of South Izu Peninsula at 1824.35 when, in the words of the official Japanese report, "the aircraft was brought into an abnormal situation which greatly affected continuation of the flight". That was something of an understatement: the bulkhead door had blown off – taking with it the vertical stabilizer, a large portion of the tail fin, the rudder assembly, and tubing and valves attached to the auxiliary power unit. The damage from this led to the hydraulic pressure dropping, and the aircraft's ailerons, elevators and yaw damper becoming inoperative. The blown-off parts crashed to the sea into Sagami Bay, and were found the next day by the crew of a Japanese destroyer.

In the cabin of Flight 123, off-duty flight attendant Yumi Ochiai heard a loud noise overhead in the rear. Instantly, the interior of the cabin turned white as the cold outside air rushed inside as a result of the explosive decompression. Ochiai claimed she saw the vent hole at the cabin crew seat open – the vents which had been put in as a response to the DC-10 disaster in Paris in 1974, and which were meant to equalize the pressure if there was a similar decompression – although some experts doubted she could have seen this from where she was seated. The ceiling above the rear toilet came off, and the oxygen masks dropped.

Captain Takahama ordered a 7700 squawk – sending the emergency code signal on their transponder – then radioed back to Tokyo ATC that there was "immediate, ah, trouble". At this point he was using the international aviation language of English; later as the situation worsened, controllers would suggest that they used Japanese for ease of communication. He requested clearance to "turn back to Haneda. Descend and maintain [flight level] 220." Fifteen seconds later, they asked for a radar vector to Oshima, and Tokyo ATC gave clearance to fly on a course of 90 degrees after making a right turn.

Takahama acknowledged the instruction, but the controllers at Tokyo ATC saw on their radar at 1828 that the aircraft wasn't turning east on a 90-degree heading – it was still heading northwest, and holding an altitude of 24,500 feet. That was when the pilots realized just how bad their situation was: they had no control of the aircraft (they had no idea that they had lost the stabilizer). The 747 was veering violently from side to side (yawing), had its nose down one moment, and up the next (pitching) and its wings were tipping up and down alternately (rolling). It also started to develop a phugoid motion – the aircraft pitched up with its nose above the horizon, and the speed decreased; but as that decayed, the nose dropped below the horizon, so speed started to pick up again. Put all of those movements together and you have a roller-coaster in three dimensions – and that's what continued happening to JAL 123 until shortly before it crashed. Each cycle took about a minute and a half to complete.

Tokyo Control ordered the aircraft to take the course for Oshima, and was simply told "now uncontrollable". Japan Airlines operation centre contacted them on the company frequency, but all the crew could tell them was that they thought a rear cabin door was broken and that they were going to descend.

Flight 123 passed over Suruga Bay, and north of Yaizu City, then started to head towards the mountainous area near Mount Fuji. Tokyo ATC kept passing on instructions but watched helplessly as the aircraft descended from 21,000 feet to 17,000, and carried out a full 360-degree circle at one point. The only control that Captain Takahama had at all was with engine thrust. However, each of the aircraft's phugoid motions was bringing it lower; at 1848, it was at 7,000 feet over Oku-Tama, but then climbed to 13,000 feet five minutes later. At 1854.19 they started talking to Tokyo Approach Control, and confirmed that they were 55 nautical miles north-west of the airport. At 1855.05, Tokyo Approach confirmed that either Haneda airport or the US air base at Yokota was available to them. The last words heard from the cockpit were an acknowledgement of this.

In the cabin, the oxygen supply for the masks had run out at 1835, but the passengers had little trouble breathing given the altitude they were now at. Many of them began to write messages to their loved ones on their boarding cards. They watched in surprise as the aircraft did a full circle near Mount Fuji.

From his home in the remote mountain village of Nippara, Keiichi Yamazaki heard the sound of the 747 approaching. "All of a sudden a big airplane appeared from between mountains, just like out of nowhere," he told *Time*. "Four times it leaned to the left, and each time it tried to recover its balance to the right. It was flying just like a staggering drunk." The crew managed to make an abrupt right turn just short of Mount Sanpei, then flew towards Mount Mikuni.

For a moment, it seemed as if the aircraft might miss the mountain, but it suddenly plunged into a dive, banking to the left. It started to drop at a sharp angle, almost vertically, then sliced through the trees of Mount Takamagahara, clipping a ridge, then plunging down, crashing into a second ridge, and flipping onto its back, breaking into pieces, before the fuel tanks exploded.

Nobody should have been able to survive the impact. Members of Japan's Self-Defence Force (their air force) made passes over the site, but it was clear that there was nowhere for helicopters to land safely in the dark. From the look of the wreckage, it seemed no one was left alive. Looking down on the site from a helicopter the next morning, *Time*'s Edwin Reingold noted: "There was no sign of life. No bodies were visible. But this was deceptive. The plane had broken apart, and major parts of it, as well as its human cargo, had been flung into the ravines and gullies on either side of the narrow ridge. The air was filled with a vile stench from the burning plane, in grim contrast to the cool, clear, bracing air of the cloud-shrouded mountaintop."

But at least four people had survived. In fact, one doctor who arrived on the scene the next day told *Time*: "If the discovery had come ten hours earlier, we could have found more survivors." The first people to reach the aircraft arrived at 0900 the next day; to their amazement, they found Yumi Ochiai pinned between seats. She had heard the helicopters the previous night and tried to wave, but hadn't been seen. She recalled that there were other voices during the night which had gradually stopped.

Twelve-year-old Keiko Kawakami was the next to be found, caught in a tree; amazingly, she had only suffered some cuts and torn muscles. Mother and daughter Hiroko and Mikiko Yoshizaki were the last located, and their discovery prompted hopes from the relatives of others that there might be yet more survivors. Sadly, that was not to be.

The report by Captain Takahama that there was a problem with a rear door captured the attention of the NTSB who helped with the investigation, alongside experts from Boeing. However, attention quickly focused on the rear bulkhead, particularly after details of the previous accident and repair came to light, and by 26 August, when the *Time* report was published, the work that was carried out was being scrutinized.

It transpired that the repair had not been carried out properly: a single plate should have been used, but instead it had been cut in two so that it could "fit" the space required. That meant that its resistance to metal fatigue was drastically reduced, and Boeing's experiments showed that it was likely to fail after around 10,000 pressurizations. JA8119 had undergone 12,318 successful flights before it failed.

The official causes were given as "deterioration of flying quality and loss of primary flight control functions due to rupture of the aft pressure bulkhead of the aircraft, and the subsequent ruptures of a part of the fuselage tail, vertical fin and hydraulical flight control systems.

"The reason why the aft pressure bulkhead was ruptured in flight is estimated to be that the strength of the said bulkhead was reduced due to fatigue cracks propagating at the spliced portion of the bulkhead's webs to the extent that it became unable to endure the cabin pressure in flight at that time.

"The initiation and propagation of the fatigue cracks are attributable to the improper repairs of the said bulkhead conducted in 1978, and it is estimated that the fatigue cracks having not been found in the later maintenance inspection is contributive to their propagation leading to the rupture of the said bulkhead."

Boeing may have been responsible for the bungled repairs, but it was JAL's reputation which suffered as a result of the crash and subsequent enquiry. According to the *New York Times*, although the airline "followed an elaborate protocol to atone for the 520 people killed, providing everything from personal apologies by the company's president to memorial services for the dead to financial reparations", it suffered a drop in income, both from passenger services and cargo trade. The airline's president, Yasumoto Takagi, resigned, and two years later, the company was privatized.

UNZIPPING AN AIRCRAFT

The paradise islands of the fiftieth American state, Hawaii, were the setting for two major incidents resulting from explosive decompression in the space of ten months. In the first, incredibly, only one person was killed when the top of the fuselage was blown off, leaving the passengers and crew exposed to the bitter winds; in the second, nine passengers died when their seats were blown out of a hole in the side of the aircraft.

The death of flight attendant Clarabelle "C. B." Lansing on 28 April 1988 when explosive decompression seriously damaged Aloha Airlines Flight 243, led to a major reorganization of the way in which old aircraft were treated, and how the FAA oversaw their maintenance and repair. Engineer Matt Austin – who was to spend over $45,000 of his own money trying to prove an alternate theory to the NTSB's conclusions regarding the fate of the flight – travelled on the nineteen-year-old Boeing 737, *Queen Lili'uokalani*, a week before the fatal incident, and noticed that the luggage racks were rattling and swaying when the thrust reversers were deployed – but it didn't particularly surprise him, given that this was common across older Aloha jets.

When the roof came off Flight 243, *Queen Lili'uokalani* was on its ninth flight of the day hopping between the islands that make up Hawaii – Captain Robert Schornstheimer had taken the aircraft on round trips from Honolulu to Hilo, Maui and Kauai, and then First Officer Madeline "Mimi" Tompkins had joined him at 1100 Hawaiian Standard Time for the flight from Honolulu to Maui and onto Hilo. There seemed to be nothing wrong with the aircraft: the previous first officer had carried out the required visual inspections at the start of the day's runs, and the maintenance log didn't suggest that there was anything out of the ordinary.

Flight 243 left Hilo Airport heading back to Honolulu with Tompkins at the controls. The pilots were joined in the cockpit by an FAA air traffic controller, and the three flight attendants were dealing with the eighty-nine passengers. Gayle Yamamoto had almost certainly stopped thinking about the crack that she thought she'd seen on the aircraft as she boarded the 737 at Hilo. Surely the flight personnel wouldn't have taken off if the crack in the upper row of rivets along the joint had been potentially danger-ous? It was a clear day, and the passengers had a good view of the islands as the aircraft climbed out of Hilo and levelled out at 24,000 feet.

At 1345.43, there was a "whoosh", and a sound of wind came from behind the pilots. Tompkins' head was jerked backwards and she saw debris, including pieces of grey insulation, floating in the cockpit. Schornstheimer turned, and was horrified to see that "there was blue sky where the first-class ceiling had been". The captain took control of the flight, which was starting to roll from left to right.

The trio in the cockpit all donned their oxygen masks, and Schornstheimer followed standard decompression procedure, starting to bring the aircraft down to a level where the passengers could breathe without the aid of oxygen. The noise in the cockpit was incredibly loud, and the only way the two pilots could communicate was by hand signals. Schornstheimer believed he had switched on the passengers' oxygen supply, but, unknown to him, it didn't work.

Thankfully for the passengers in the first-class cabin, the seat belt sign was still illuminated, and they were strapped into their seats. Flight attendant C. B. Lansing wasn't so lucky. When the decompression occurred, she was swept off her feet, and out through a hole in the left side of the fuselage directly above the cabin. (Her body was never found.) One of the passengers, Stan-ford Samson, recalled that books, paper and money were all flying around. One of the other flight attendants was being pulled towards the hole, but the passengers grabbed her and held onto her. She had been hit by debris, and was suffering from concussion and severe head lacerations. Another flight attendant, who had been further back in the aircraft, crawled along the aisle, trying to keep the passengers calm. Some of them began to sing hymns.

In the cockpit, Tompkins tried to contact Honolulu ARTCC to warn them that they were diverting to Maui, but she couldn't hear any reply over the howling wind that was still making communication nigh on impossible. In fact, the ARTCC hadn't got her first message, but they did see the emergency 7700 squawk, and controllers were trying to get hold of her.

Schornstheimer brought the aircraft down to 14,000 feet, as pieces of the fuselage continued to stream from the hole. "The plane was disintegrating so pieces were falling off it, moulding was coming down, and the wind was catching it," passenger Eric Becklin recalled. "The hole up front got bigger and bigger, and I knew it was just a matter of time before the plane came apart."

The flight crew weren't aware of the entire problem: they weren't able to communicate with the flight attendants, but they tried to make it clear to the tower control at Maui that they had a serious situation on their hands ("They still don't understand," Tompkins can be heard saying to the captain at one point on the CVR). Schornstheimer started to slow as the aircraft reached 10,000 feet, and when they had decreased speed to 210 knots, the wind had gone down correspondingly, so the pilots could finally talk to each other properly again. This was extremely useful as they needed to calculate the correct landing speed in their condition.

Just to add to their problems as they began the approach to Maui, the left engine failed, and refused to restart. They were coming in fast so that Schornstheimer could retain some control. To those on the ground, it looked like a "cargo plane with the big cargo door open" that had gone into a nosedive. The nose wheel hit the ground first, then the main wheels – and then *Queen Lili'uokalani* settled on the ground for the last time, a mere thirteen minutes after the hole had first appeared. The passengers were then evacuated from the aircraft, with sixty-one of them needing treatment for injuries.

Investigators quickly dismissed the possibility of sabotage or a bomb aboard the aircraft; what worried them far more was that this incident was similar to the crash of a 737 owned by Far Eastern Air Transport in 1981. Everyone on that aircraft died when the fuselage floor as well as the roof peeled back at around the same altitude as the Aloha flight. Both aircraft operated over the Pacific Ocean, where the warm salty air can be highly corrosive, and the constant pressurizations – particularly on an aircraft being used for short-haul journeys like *Queen Lili'uokalani*

– would eventually lead to cracks appearing. The FAA had already recommended a close inspection of the upper-fuselage skin of 737s because of potential cracks, but there was a big difference between the government saying that and it being carried out by small airlines like Aloha – particularly when it wasn't made a requirement by the FAA.

What didn't help the investigators was the inability to find the section of the fuselage which had broken off. What they were trying to establish was why there had been such a large peeling back on the 737: Boeing maintained that the 737 should decompress safely with as much as a 40-inch crack in the skin – the hole should release the pressure in a controlled way. But on the *Queen Lili'uokalani*, a huge section had instead come away.

Extensive tests on what did remain revealed that the problem came from the lap joints, which join large panels of the aircraft's skin together, and run longitudinally along the fuselage. As long as those panels were bonded strongly together, fatigue cracking wasn't expected to be an issue, but it became clear that there were deficiencies in the bonding. The NTSB found evidence of fatigue damage in multiple sites on the *Queen Lili'uokalani*, with rivets being forced to carry the loads which the joints should have been bearing – with cracks inevitably starting to form as the rivets ceased being able to take the weight. When numerous such cracks linked up along a lap joint, it failed completely, and led to the decompression.

The NTSB's conclusion wasn't unanimous. The probable cause was given as "the failure of the Aloha Airlines maintenance program to detect the presence of significant disbanding and fatigue damage which ultimately led to the failure of the lap joint at S-10l and the separation of the fuselage upper lobe". The contributory factors were a lack of proper supervision of the Aloha maintenance force; the FAA's failure to monitor Aloha effectively; the FAA's failure to make the lap joint inspection mandatory; and Boeing and the FAA's failure to deal with the manufacturer's discovery that some of the lap joints on the 737s might be liable to low durability, corrosion and premature cracking.

Board member Joseph T. Hall felt that this was too narrowly focused, bearing in mind that no one had predicted the nature of this sort of cracking, and felt that it was not right to say that the

Aloha maintenance programme was the probable cause. "Undetected disbanding and fatigue cracking" was his preferred version.

A more radical suggestion came from engineer Matt Austin, who thought that the cause of the decompression was what was known as a fluid hammer, something that boiler engineers had become aware of over half a century earlier. On a boiler, if a lap joint fails, a hole opens in the shell; the water inside instantly turns to steam, and the resulting increased pressure causes an explosion – a fluid hammer. Austin's theory was that a 10-inch by 10-inch hole opened in the roof of the cabin, and the powerful stream of air caught flight attendant Lansing and sent her towards the hole. Her head and right arm went through the hole, but for a moment, her body plugged it, blocking the escaping air. That created a jolt of pressure that ripped the aging jet apart. "Slamming the door on a 700 mph jet stream creates a localized, short-duration high-pressure spike, up to several orders of magnitude (greater than) the allowable design pressure," Austin explained in 1998. "This is a fluid hammer." According to Austin, one of the NTSB's own photos shows where Lansing's skull hit the exterior of the aircraft, which would fit with where he believed the original hole occurred.

The NTSB didn't disagree that a fluid hammer could have such an effect, but they didn't agree with his "conjecture involving the role the flight attendant's body played," chairman James Hall noted. "The roof of the Aloha airplane came off as a result of multiple site damage – mainly, small fatigue cracks. These cracks joined together, resulting in the catastrophic separation of the skin." The main NTSB investigator, Brian Richardson, did agree that the fluid hammer phenomenon needed investigating.

HOLE OVER HAWAII

The disaster on the *Queen Lili'uokalani* could have been much worse: the fuselage could easily have given way at any point during the aircraft's descent or during landing – an eyewitness said that the 737 "settled and just sort of buckled". If the passengers hadn't been wearing their safety belts, they could well have been victims. It's been suggested that the fatality rate on the second tragedy to hit Hawaii within a year was higher because one of those killed wasn't wearing his belt despite the seat-belt sign still being illuminated owing to turbulence.

The NTSB reached two differing conclusions on the incident involving United Airlines Flight 811 on 24 February 1989, but for a rather different reason: believing that the missing cargo door would never be found in the depths of the Pacific Ocean, the Board went ahead with a final report based on the available evidence. That was released on 16 April 1990; five months later the door was recovered in two pieces, which forced them to discount their conclusions and start afresh.

According to one of the passengers on board, commercially licensed pilot Mike Rutherford, Captain David Cronin was told after the accident that an attempt to duplicate the scenario which unfolded aboard his aircraft in the simulator had resulted in the conclusion that it was impossible to bring the aircraft back in one piece. Luckily, as with so many pilots involved in the incidents in this book, Captain Cronin was not aware that he was doing the impossible. And, as his first officer pointed out to him, "What a **** of a thing to happen on your second-to-last month." ("No shit," was Cronin's response, unsurprisingly.)

The 747 had taken off from Honolulu for Auckland, New Zealand at 0152 Hawaiian Standard Time, with three flight crew – Captain Cronin, First Officer Al Slader and Flight Engineer Randal Thomas – fifteen flight attendants and 337 passengers on board. Since the crew could see thunderstorms both on the radar and through the cockpit windows, they requested permission to deviate course slightly, and Captain Cronin decided to leave the seat-belt sign illuminated longer than normal.

They were still climbing, passing between 22,000 and 23,000 feet at 300 knots, when there was a thump which shook the aircraft. "What the hell was that?" asked Captain Cronin. Then a few seconds later, the cockpit door blew open as what sounded like a huge explosion took place. The cabin filled with flying debris and the fog which signifies explosive decompression. The temperature dropped like a stone. Ceiling panels fell, door panels and side panels blew off. Most of those aboard were convinced that somehow they were in the middle of "another Lockerbie" – Pan Am 103 had exploded over the Scottish village only a couple of months previously.

Flight 811 was no longer intact. In the right-hand side there was a huge gaping hole, and an empty space where the seats in and around row 9 had been. Nine passengers, who were seated in seats 8H, 9F, G and H, 10G and H, 11G and H and 12H, were ejected from the aircraft. "All of a sudden, the man seated next to [my wife] just disappeared," one of the passengers recalled. Some of them fell for four minutes down to the ocean, possibly conscious for a minute or so as they went; at least one was sucked into the engine. The flight attendant who had been serving drinks was knocked down and bleeding profusely, and was anchored by the passengers to make sure she wasn't blown out.

Captain Cronin decided to make a 180-degree turn and return to Honolulu, dumping fuel as they went, and bringing the aircraft down to a lower altitude to help with breathing. In such circumstances – as happened with the Aloha flight the previous year – the crew's standard operating procedure is to don their oxygen masks, so that they can perform the necessary physical exertions. This Cronin and his crew tried, only to discover that there were no oxygen bottles: they had been by the cabin door, and had gone in the explosion.

They could have been the debris that caused damage to both engines on the right side of the aircraft. No. 3 engine had to be shut down almost immediately, and no. 4 followed suit shortly afterwards. Flight Engineer Thomas went to see what the situation was, and returned to the cockpit ashen-faced – according to passenger Rutherford, Thomas was mouthing to himself, "F***!" when he saw the damage. "For some bizarre reason that scared me more than the hole in the aircraft!" Rutherford commented later. Thomas returned to the cockpit and told his colleagues, "The right side is gone from about the . . . one right back. It's just open. You're just lookin' outside . . . Looks like a bomb, fuselage it's just open . . . Some people are probably gone."

In the cabin, everyone was strapped in, many of them – crew included – convinced that they were going to come down in the ocean. "'I was resigned to the fact that I was going to die," Australian Roger White told reporters. "All I could think about were shark bites. I just put my head down and waited." One woman succumbed to hysteria, and lunged for the door to the aircraft, trying to get out, but she was quickly subdued. The aircraft was almost eerily quiet, particularly after the noise of the wind at the higher altitudes. Suddenly a chorus of voices started to yell, "City lights! City lights!"

Cronin brought the aircraft down steadily with no engines operative on the right-hand side. The 747 was carrying 220,000 pounds of fuel, but they could only dump 5,000 pounds a minute – and on two engines, they couldn't stay up for much longer.

"I don't know if we're gonna make this," Cronin admitted at one point, "I can't hold altitude." Thomas was blunt: "You're gonna make it." Al Slader added, "Make sure we don't hit any ****ing hills on the way". As the crew prepared for the emergency touchdown, the control tower asked if they knew how many "souls on board if you have it". "I don't have the paperwork in front of me right now," Randal Thomas pointed out. "We're too busy right now," Al Slader told the tower.

The aircraft was coming in fast – around 200 knots – but Cronin was able to bring it in safely. The flaps weren't working properly, and the landing gear was held until the last minute since they didn't need their drag – they needed as much power as possible to reach the airport. But, twenty minutes or so after the hole opened in the side of the aircraft, they were on the ground. Once the passengers were deplaned by the chutes, the investigation began in earnest.

Once explosives were ruled out, the NTSB focused on the cargo door, but with no idea where it had ended up within the

Pacific Ocean, they had to work off probabilities as to why the door failed.

When the 747 was designed there were two options for the cargo doors: they could open in or outwards. A "plug" door – one which opens inwards and wedges into the passageway as the plane pressurizes – would need wide inside clearances, and would not allow full use of the cargo space. Therefore, the cargo door on that 747 opened outwards. This required some precision engineering to ensure that it remained fast against the enormous pressurization forces which would be exerted on it during every flight. Boeing devised complex mechanisms to ensure the door remained shut, but there were various glitches, and each time one arose, they would deal with solving that specific problem, rather than consider reworking the entire mechanism.

On United 811, the door was secured with a toggle, which sent 28 volts of electricity down a set of relays and switches which activated three 115-volt actuator motors. The first lowered the door until the bottom edge reached the fuselage; then two U-shaped hooks, one either side of the door, engaged pins on the doorway, and the second actuator wrapped the hooks around the pins, pulling the door in tightly. Finally 8 C-shaped latches engaged eight pins attached to the door sill, with the third actuator rotating the latches around the pins. Once that was done, the door was finally locked with eight J-shaped aluminium bars on top of the latches, activated by a handle in the middle of the door. That in its turn switched off the power to the toggle, as well as turning off a warning light in the cockpit.

However, electrics don't always work, and there were occasions when the doors had to be locked manually – using a wrench! When Pan Am inspected their fleet of 747s following a cargo door opening incorrectly on 10 March 1987, they found that many of the locks had been damaged, and Boeing advised that special steel braces should be fitted on the locks. However, not every airline carried out the changes quickly; the change might only have cost $2,000 per door, but they asked for – and received – time to carry it out from the FAA. On 28 November 1988, the jet that formed Flight 811 was having a major service, but the work wasn't done.

Unfortunately, there were other electrical issues with the locking mechanism: the toggle switch could have remained live after the final locks were activated, thanks to a faulty sensor, and there was a possibility that a stray signal from other electrics in the vicinity could have sent a signal which opened the latches. These were theories which were promoted by relatives of one of the deceased passengers.

The NTSB considered all of these but decided that "the probable cause of this accident was the sudden opening of the improperly latched forward lower lobe cargo door in flight and the subsequent explosive decompression. Contributing to the cause of the accident was a deficiency in the design of the cargo door locking mechanisms, which made them susceptible to inservice damage, and which allowed the door to be unlatched yet to show a properly latched and locked position. Also contributing to the accident was the lack of proper maintenance and inspection of the cargo door by United Airlines, and a lack of timely corrective actions by Boeing and the FAA following the 1987 cargo door opening incident on a Pan Am B-747."

The discovery of the cargo door five months after the report was issued, and an incident at JFK on 13 June 1991, prompted them to change their minds. The cargo door on another United Boeing 747 opened, caused by electrical short circuits in the cargo door wiring. The damage from that was similar to that found on the cargo door of Flight 811. The NTSB therefore reissued their report, determining that "the probable cause of this accident was the sudden opening of the forward lower lobe cargo door in flight and the subsequent explosive decompression. The door opening was attributed to a faulty switch or wiring in the door control system which permitted electrical actuation of the door latches toward the unlatched position after initial door closure and before takeoff. Contributing to the cause of the accident was a deficiency in the design of the cargo door locking mechanisms, which made them susceptible to deformation, allowing the door to become unlatched after being properly latched and locked. Also contributing to the accident was a lack of timely corrective actions by Boeing and the FAA following a 1987 cargo door opening incident on a Pan Am B-747."

Captain Cronin and his flight crew received the Secretary of Transportation's Award for Heroism. "What could have been a tragedy of massive proportions was averted by the crew's heroic

conduct during that terrifying emergency," the House of Representatives was told. "Even with the threat of personal injury or
death, the crew acted with the courage and skill of true well-
trained professionals.

"The flight attendants have shown that beneath their smile
and kind words are even greater qualities: courage, commitment, and concern for the safety of airline passengers. Now
more than ever, these are the virtues that stand out when people
think of flight attendants.

"The pilots maneuvered the impaired plane back to safety
with skill and adroitness. Calm, cool, and collected, they are the
embodiment of the fearless aviators in the sky."

LOSING THE CAPTAIN

The *Sydney Morning Herald* headlined its story on Captain Tim Lancaster's feat of survival following an explosive decompression with the words, "This is your captain screaming". Lancaster only survived thanks to the efforts of his entire crew, as co-pilot Alistair Atcheson brought the aircraft in to land at Southampton Airport.

On Sunday 10 June 1990, British Airways Flight 5390 was being flown from Birmingham airport in the UK to Malaga in Spain, with eighty-one passengers and four cabin crew in addition to pilots Lancaster and Atcheson. Although departure had been delayed for an hour, the take-off was uneventful. Co-pilot Atcheson handled the BAC One-Eleven, known as the "jeep of the skies" as it was such a reliable aircraft, for the first part before handing over to Lancaster for the climb to flight level 230 (23,000 feet). As normal, both pilots had released their shoulder harnesses, and Lancaster had loosened his lapstrap.

Thirteen minutes into the flight, at 0733 GMT, as Flight 5390 was over Didcot in Oxfordshire, all hell broke loose. Steward Nigel Ogden had just popped on to the flight deck to see if the crew would like a cup of tea, since the flight attendants were starting the drinks service for the passengers. His hand was on the door handle to leave when there was an enormous explosion, and the door was blown out of his hands. He jumped to the obvious conclusion that there had been an explosion.

The entire fuselage filled with the blue-grey mist that follows explosive decompression, and the aircraft started to plummet towards the ground from the 17,300 feet it had reached. The door had been blown onto the flight deck, and was lying across the radio and navigation console. Worse, though, was the sight that greeted Ogden at the front of the aircraft: the windscreen in front of Captain Lancaster had blown out, and he had been sucked into the gap. The captain was half in, half out of the aircraft, his shirt pulled off his back, and his body bent up, doubled over the top of the aircraft. Worst still was the position of Lancaster's legs: as he had been pulled forward, he had disconnected the autopilot.

Atcheson hadn't loosened his lapstrap, so was safe. As Ogden desperately jumped over the control column and grabbed Lancaster round the waist to stop him going out completely, Atcheson contemplated donning his oxygen mask but decided not to, since he wanted to be able to shout instructions to the crew. As the pressure started to equalize, the wind began to rush in, but it sent all the papers on the flight deck and the cabin spiralling around. Passengers were understandably frightened, particularly as they could see through the gap where the door had been, and were greeted with the sight of the captain being held back by the flight crew – one of the other stewards, John Heward, had run in and was holding Ogden's belt to stop him from slipping further, then put the captain's shoulder strap around him to give him some more traction. The third steward, Simon Rogers, came through and helped to remove the remains of the doors from the controls, then Rogers and Heward unwrapped the captain's legs from the autopilot so Atcheson could regain control.

Atcheson started to bring the aircraft down to flight level 110, and reduced its speed. He tried to make a distress call, but the sound of the rushing wind on the flight deck prevented him from being able to make himself understood – which meant that all of the many emergency procedures weren't activated as quickly as they could have been.

Ogden and Rogers were trying to pull Lancaster back inside the aircraft, but the effect of the slipstream going past the aircraft's nose stopped them. Ogden's arms were beginning to tire – with the effect of the pressure, Lancaster was weighing more like 500 pounds – and for a moment, Lancaster slipped. It was imperative not to let the captain go: although the crew weren't at all sure whether he was alive or dead (his eyes were open, and blood was coming from his nose and the side of his head as he constantly butted the direct vision window on the left of the aircraft), if they had released him, there was a chance that the body might have became jammed in a wing or, worse, one of the engines, making Atcheson's already difficult job bringing the aircraft in tantamount to impossible. Ogden was now exhausted, so Simon

Rogers strapped himself into the third pilot's seat and hooked Lancaster's feet over the back of the captain's seat, holding on to his ankles.

Atcheson brought the One-Eleven down to flight level 100, and slowed to 150 knots, in preparation for landing at Southampton. He wanted a 2,500-metre runway, because of concerns over the weight of the aircraft with all the fuel for the run to Malaga still on board, but the best they had was 1,800 metres. Having to do all the necessary calculations alone and without the aid of the books, which had been sucked out of the aircraft, Atcheson told the passengers that the windscreen had blown out, and warned them to prepare for an emergency landing. Ogden and the other flight attendants ensured all the passengers knew what they had to do, and reassured them that they were going to be fine.

And they were – Atcheson landed successfully eighteen minutes after the explosive decompression, and there wasn't even a need to use the emergency chutes: the passengers were able to disembark down the stairs as normal. None of them had been injured in the incident. Bloodstains and pieces of clothing from the captain, though, could be seen flapping from the aircraft.

Lancaster was taken to Southampton General Hospital, suffering from bone fractures in his right arm and wrist, a broken left thumb, bruising, frostbite and shock. Ogden had a dislocated shoulder, and frostbite to his face and left eye. Lancaster was flying again within five months. The crew were commended by the Air Accident Investigation Branch (AAIB): "The combined actions of the co-pilot and cabin crew successfully averted what could have been a major catastrophe. The fact that all those on board the aircraft survived is a tribute to their quick thinking and perseverance in the face of a shocking experience."

The windscreen had come out for an equally shocking reason: it had been secured by the wrong sort of bolts! The AAIB was scathing: "The windscreen fitting process was characterised by a series of poor work practices, poor judgements and perceptual errors, each one of which eroded the factors of safety built into the method of operation promulgated by British Airways." They noted that the windscreen was probably the only critical item on the aircraft that could have failed owing to the various errors committed – and it failed dramatically. It had been replaced twenty-seven hours before the flight, and the aircraft had not been flown since. The Shift Maintenance Manager was directly blamed for "inadequate care, poor trade practices, [and] failure to adhere to company standards and use of unsuitable equipment". BA were also criticised for not monitoring those practices.

THE GHOST PLANE

Although the final incident in this section wasn't due to explosive decompression, it demonstrates the problems that occur when an aircraft is not pressurized properly. On 14 August 2005, Helios Airways Flight 522 crashed into the side of a mountain after a lack of oxygen incapacitated the crew, and the aircraft ran out of fuel. From the data retrieved from the black boxes, and subsequent investigation, it appears that numerous warning signals were simply ignored. Most tragically, flight attendant Andreas Prodromou, who held a UK commercial pilot's licence, tried at the last moment to take control of the aircraft, but within minutes of his taking the captain's seat, both engines flamed out.

Flight 522, a Boeing 737-31S, was due to leave Larnaca International Airport on Cyprus for Prague, with a stopover at Athens, at 0600 GMT. There were 115 passengers and six crew on board, under Captain Hans-Jürgen Merten and first officer Pampos Charalambous, and the first leg of the flight should only have taken 105 minutes. The flight took off at 0607; the last contact with its crew came thirteen minutes later.

The aircraft had been flown in from London Heathrow the night before, arriving at Larnaca at 0125; the cabin crew had noted that there was a problem with the right aft service door: "seal around door freezes & hard bangs are heard during flt" was the entry in the Cabin Defect Log. The flight crew added this to the Aircraft Technical Log as "Aft service door requires full inspection". The ground engineer at Larnaca checked the door visually, and carried out a cabin pressurization leak check. "Door and local area inspected. NIL defects. Pressure run carried out to max diff. Safety valve operates at 8.25 psi [the reading for the differential pressure]. No leaks or abnormal noises," he wrote in his log, and released the aircraft for its next flight at 0315.

The climb-out from Larnaca started normally, with Captain Merten requesting cruising level at flight level 340 (34,000 feet). Clearance was given by Nicosia Area Control Centre (ACC) at 0611. At 0612.38, a warning horn began to sound in the cockpit, as the aircraft went through 12,040 feet. A minute and a half later, the captain called Helios Airways' Operations Centre, and reported that the "take-off configuration warning" was on, and that the "cooling equipment normal and alternate off-line". The dispatcher arranged for the on-duty engineer to speak to the captain.

At this point, testimonies differ. Immediately after the accident, the engineer said that the captain reported that "the ventilation cooling fan lights were off", which the engineer didn't hear clearly, and the captain repeated. Merten then asked where the cooling fan circuit breakers were, and the ground engineer said they were behind his seat.

However, the engineer had to give a statement to the police five days after the accident, and his account was more detailed. Merten had said, "Both my equipment cooling lights are off." This was normal, so the ground engineer asked him what the problem was, since the lights should have been off if the system was working normally. The captain then replied that "they are not switched off". The engineer then said that "given the close proximity of the pressure control panel and the fact that he [the Ground Engineer] had used the pressure panel prior to the flight and the pressure panel has four lights", he asked the captain to confirm that the pressurization panel was selected to AUTO. The captain didn't respond to this, but asked where the equipment cooling circuit breakers were, and the engineer said they were behind his seat.

While this conversation was going on, the aircraft passed through 18,000 feet and the passenger oxygen masks deployed in the cabin. This was designed to happen when the cabin altitude exceeded 14,000 feet. For some reason, the cabin wasn't receiving any oxygen. The conversation ended as the flight passed through 28,900 feet, but when the dispatcher tried to call the aircraft again, there was no reply.

At 0623, the aircraft levelled off at flight level 340. Six minutes later, the dispatcher, concerned at the lack of reply, contacted Nicosia ACC and asked them to call the crew. For four minutes, Nicosia tried in vain, and then asked another aircraft to try to get in touch; this was equally unsuccessful.

They asked the flight to squawk stand-by, but there was no change in the transponder signal.

The aircraft crossed from Nicosia into Athiniai (Athens) airspace at 0636, with Nicosia ACC informing their counterparts at Athens of the lack of response, and asking them to let the Cypriots know if they received a response. The flight meanwhile continued to follow its planned trajectory, turning at a beacon, and entering the flight lane.

Thirty-six minutes later, at 0712, Athens Radar Control contacted the flight to issue a descent clearance, but there was no reply from Flight 522, either to their calls or from other aircraft. At 0716, the radar controller informed the ACC supervisor about the radio failure, and in turn the supervisor contacted Athens Approach Control, Athens Tower and the Hellenic Air Force (HAF).

Four minutes after that, the aircraft seemed to be making a standard instrument approach procedure for landing at Athens – but it wasn't descending from flight level 340. It flew over the airport at 0729, and eight minutes later, it went into the holding pattern. At 0753, the alert was sounded.

Half an hour later, two HAF F-16s approached the 737, which was still in the holding pattern at flight level 340. They tried to get hold of the crew using as many frequencies as they could think of, and using the prescribed interception signals, but there was no reply. One of the F-16s took a closer view, and couldn't see any sign of structural damage or fire.

At 0832, the F-16 pilot filed a full report. The captain's seat was empty, and there was someone in the first officer's seat, slumped over the controls. In the cabin, he could see three passengers seated motionless, with oxygen masks on their faces, two on one side of the aircraft, one on the other. There were no lights on in the cabin, but as the daylight shone through, he could see oxygen masks dangling from the overhead units. Athens ACC declared that the aircraft was in distress.

The cockpit voice recorder on the aircraft was one of the old types; it had half an hour of tape on it on a loop, so only the last thirty minutes would be retained. It therefore wasn't much help in discerning what happened in the early part of the flight, but at 0848, it registered chimes, and then the emergency override being used. These were followed by the cockpit door opening, someone entering, adjusting a seat, removing an oxygen mask from its box, and the oxygen flow starting.

According to the F-16 pilot, someone came into the cockpit at 0849, and sat down in the captain's seat, donning a set of head-phones, but apparently not an oxygen mask (although since this was transparent, the F-16 pilot might not have been able to see it). He put his hands on the panel in front of him. (From his clothing, investigators deduced that he was the only male flight attendant on board.) Fifty seconds later, the left engine flamed out, and the aircraft turned steeply to the left, heading north. The F-16 pilot tried to get the attention of whoever was in the captain's seat, but he didn't respond, just bending forwards from time to time.

Flight 522 began to make its final descent and the F-16s had to pull back because of the erratic movement of the 737. When they approached again, the man in the captain's chair was motionless. At 0854.18, the CVR picked up a very faint distress call, made by someone speaking weakly.

As the 737 went through 7,000 feet, the man in the captain's chair seemed to notice the F-16s, and made a hand motion. In the hope that whoever he was would be able to follow commands, the pilot made a hand signal indicating that he should follow the F-16 down to the airport. The man on the 737 pointed downwards. He didn't follow the F-16.

The 737 started to head south-west at 0859.20 as it continued to descend, and twenty-seven seconds later, the right engine flamed out. The end came quickly after that. Although the man at the controls tried to level the aircraft out, it fell from the sky rapidly, and hit the hills near Grammatiko village, 33 kilometres north-west of Athens Airport at 0903.32. It burst into flames as it broke up and rolled down a hill into a ravine. There were no survivors – the captain and the first officer's bodies were autop-sied, and both had succumbed to hypoxic hypoxia (lack of oxygenated arterial blood caused by reduced oxygen pressure).

How could this have happened? The pressure in the aircraft had not been correct, and the pilots had succumbed after their time of useful consciousness had expired. Somehow, one flight attendant had managed to stay alive. A re-enactment of the flight showed that the cabin had never been pressurized.

The Greek investigation showed that there had been a rapid decompression on the aircraft on a previous flight when an aft service door hadn't been closed properly, and it had also had equipment cooling problems. Incidents on other 737s showed that the warning horns could sometimes be misunderstood, as appeared to have happened here – and indeed the take-off configuration warning horn was the same as the pressurization horn.

Their investigations led them to the conclusion that somehow the crew had missed the fact that the pressurization mode was in manual, rather than automatic. It was missed during two sets of pre-flight checks. (The first officer had a record for checklist discipline and procedural difficulties.) Neither pilot spotted a warning light on the panel. It was missed during the after take-off checks. The pilots then misunderstood the meaning of the horn – which was odd (or indeed, as the official report called it, "irrational"), since the take-off configuration horn could only have sounded while the aircraft was on the ground. By the time they might have realized there was a problem, it was too late: hypoxia was affecting their decision-making and stress levels. From that moment on, everyone on the aircraft was doomed.

Helios Airways didn't survive much longer; it closed down in late 2006. Its lawyers had criticized the report, claiming that the pilots couldn't have made such mistakes – but the evidence from the wreckage was incontrovertible. The pressurization was set to manual. Helios former chief pilot Ianko Stoimenov, chairman of the board Andreas Drakos, chief executive officer Demetris Pantazis, and operations manager Giorgos Kikidis, were accused of manslaughter and causing death through negligence by the Cypriot courts, but were acquitted. Pantazis, Kikidis, Stoimenov and chief engineer Alan Irwin were tried in Athens and sentenced to ten years' imprisonment, although they were given the option to "buy out" their sentences for €75,000 each.

As a direct result of this crash, the FAA ordered 737s to be equipped with two extra cockpit warning lights, which had to be fitted by 14 March 2014. They should prevent a further tragic loss of life.

Part 6:
Fire!

BRITISH BLAZES

There are very few people who won't admit to a touch of arson-phobia when they're flying – that's not a fear of someone committing arson (although no doubt that's pretty high on the list), but of fire itself. In any enclosed space, fire is a danger; when you're 37,000 feet in the air it's even worse. There have been many incidents of fires aboard aircraft over the past decades, but as the accounts in this section demonstrate, they don't always have to be fatal.

The first recorded in-flight fire – on a civilian aircraft anyway; there had been plenty of aircraft fires during the Great War – came on 2 October 1926, when a Blériot 155 belonging to French company Air Union came to grief over Leigh in Kent. The aircraft had left Le Bourget in Paris at 1230 GMT, with a mechanic, five passengers and a large amount of cargo, including some furs. At 1524 the pilot had passed over Tonbridge on his way to Croydon Airport when observers on the ground noticed that flames were coming from the rear of the aircraft. The pilot turned as if to land at nearby Penshurst Airport, but the flames spread rapidly. After only a few minutes, the aircraft slowly turned over and then crashed to the ground. The resulting fire was too strong for anyone to have a chance of rescuing any of the seven people aboard.

It was the second accident involving a Blériot in two months; the only other model 155 had crashed due to engine failure on 18 August, killing a crew member and two of the thirteen passengers. No more Blériot 155s were built.

The fire on a BOAC 707 at London Heathrow could easily have cost more than the lives of four passengers had it not been for the sterling efforts of the crew – and one flight attendant in particular, who went back inside the burning aircraft to help an elderly disabled passenger (and possibly another person who was travelling with a child), and paid with her own life.

BOAC Flight 712 was heading for Sydney, Australia, via Zurich and Singapore on 8 April 1968. In addition to Captain Charles Taylor, First Officer Francis Kirkland and Flight Engineer Thomas Hicks, there were two extra people in the cockpit: Acting First Officer John Hutchinson and Check Captain Geoffrey Moss, who was meant to be evaluating Taylor's performance. Twenty seconds after the aircraft had taken off at 1527, the crew felt a shock and a bang. In normal circumstances, Taylor and his crew would probably have reacted more efficiently, but the extra personnel on board created confusion.

The thrust lever for the no. 2 engine "kicked" towards the closed position, and the instruments showed that it was running down. With the fire bell running, Captain Taylor therefore ordered his crew to carry out the engine failure drill, which included fully retarding the throttle. The undercarriage was still retracted, so a warning horn sounded when Engineer Hicks retarded the throttle. Both he and Captain Moss reached for the horn cancel switch simultaneously, while First Officer Kirkland instinctively – but mistakenly – hit the fire bell cancel button to switch off the horn. When the bell stopped sounding, Hicks stopped reaching for the engine fire shut-off handle, and didn't pull it. As the later investigation noted, he should have done so.

Check Captain Moss then looked round and saw that the engine was on fire. He wasn't the only one to spot it. In the tower, controller John Davis saw the blaze, and told the 707 to make a left turn to bring it back in to land. He also alerted the emergency services.

On the 707, Hicks switched from the engine failure drill to the engine fire drill but about ninety seconds after the start of the fire, no. 2 engine, along with part of its pylon, detached itself from the rest of the aircraft and fell into a gravel pit, luckily not injuring the children who were playing there. Captain Taylor lowered the undercarriage and selected full flaps, although they didn't open fully.

In the cabin, the passengers were understandably panicked, particularly as the windows on the side near the fire were starting to melt. The crew kept repeating the emergency landing drill, even though they weren't sure that the aircraft was going to make it that far.

The same thought was probably going through Captain Taylor's head. He declared a Mayday emergency and was cleared to land immediately – other aircraft were kept holding. He was able to bring the aircraft for a perfect emergency landing 212 seconds after it had taken off.

Before the crew could start the fire drill and evacuation could even begin, the left wing exploded, with fragments reaching the right side. Taylor immediately ordered his crew to get out of the aircraft, before the engine fire shut-off handles were pulled, or the fuel booster pumps and main electrical supply shut off.

There were five usable doors for evacuating the cabin, but the over right wing exit quickly became unusable. The Chief Steward, Neville Davis-Gordon, had to go out on to the right wing to get one of the passengers who had become stranded there because of the spread of the fire; he brought her back on board and directed her to a safer exit. Most of the passengers got out from the right-hand galley door, as three of the crew used the cockpit rope.

Two of the flight crew manned the rear right door: the escape slide had twisted when it was activated, so one of the stewards had to climb down to straighten it before it could be used. He then couldn't get back into the aircraft, leaving his colleague Barbara Jane Harrison alone at the door, shepherding the passengers out. Some she encouraged to jump; others needed less verbal assistance, and she pushed them out onto the slide.

There were continuing explosions from outside, and the slide became punctured and deflated. Harrison was about to jump when she realized that there were still some people on board. She went to the help of an elderly disabled woman but the smoke and flames were too much; their bodies were found beside each other. One hundred and twenty-two people escaped alive. Barbara Jane Harrison was awarded the George Cross, the highest award for civilian bravery; Davis-Gordon received the British Empire Medal.

A COSTLY CUP OF TEA

In 1980, a fire broke out on a Saudi Airlines flight which was possibly caused when a pilgrim travelling to Mecca ignited a gas stove to make a cup of tea. Even if that wasn't the direct cause of the blaze, the fact that having an open flame inside the cabin was even possible seems unbelievable to us today (in much the same way as smoking on aircraft does). The situation on Saudi Flight 163 was worsened by problems when people panicked, blocking the emergency exits and jamming the doors. The Lockheed L-1011 Tristar became a flaming tomb for all aboard. None of the 301 passengers or crew survived, making it at the time the third worst aviation disaster in history.

Flight 163 was on its way from Karachi to Jeddah, with a stop-over at Riyadh. It took off from there on the last leg of its journey at 1808 GMT on 19 August 1980. On board were many Muslim pilgrims, some of whom, it was pointed out by the Saudi Civil Aviation Directorate, "traditionally carry with them – secretly – such flammable equipment" as gas stoves. According to contemporary newspaper reports, the pilot, Captain Mohammed Ali Khoyter, had reported that one of the pilgrims sitting in the rear economy section had ignited the stove but the fire quickly spread from the back to the front of the aircraft, going through the economy section through to first class "while the plane was still in the air". Searchers certainly found two damaged butane stoves in the back of the aircraft wreckage, along with a fire extinguisher that had been used, presumably, in a vain attempt to douse the flames.

The black box recordings bear these reports out to an extent, although there is no mention on the cockpit voice recorder of a pilgrim, or the potential cause of the fire. The crew didn't have time for such speculation.

Seven minutes into the flight, alerts went off in the cockpit indicating smoke in the cargo hold, so after the captain and First

Officer Sami Abdullah M. Hasanain had confirmed that the alarms weren't malfunctioning, the flight engineer, Bradley Curtis, went out into the cabin to check on the situation. When he returned, he said that there definitely was a fire back there. The captain decided to turn back for Riyadh.

The fire and smoke got worse in the cabin and the passengers began to panic, refusing to listen to the flight attendants' instructions. People were fighting in the aisles, and the cabin crew couldn't even get to the fire extinguishers to try to tackle the blaze. To add to the problems, the no. 2 engine malfunctioned after the fire burned through its operating cable.

Passengers were ordered to sit down and assume the brace position. "Nothing will happen to aircraft, ladies and gentlemen," came one announcement. "Fasten your seatbelt, don't stand like this. Sit on your seats." The smoke filled the back of the aircraft as the passengers ignored the imprecations of the crew and continued to stand as the jet came in to land. "Give me your attention please," the flight attendant said desperately. "Be seated ladies and gentlemen, we are about to land; there's no reason to panic." The last sound on the CVR was the attendants reminding them about the brace position, and the aircraft coming down to earth.

The CVR tape stopped at that point, but the captain was still in contact with the tower. He asked if there was any fire in the aircraft tail, but none could be seen. He brought the aircraft to a stop at the end of the taxiway two minutes and forty seconds after touchdown – rather than at the landing position where fire crews were lined up and ready. The last message from the cockpit stated: "Okay, we are shutting down the engines now and evacuating."

Since the engines weren't switched off, the fire crew couldn't get near enough to try to open the doors, and for reasons that will never be known, they weren't opened from the inside. The engines weren't shut down for a further three minutes, but the fire crews were only able to force a door open to gain access to the aircraft nearly twenty-five minutes after it had touched down, during which time the fire had spread uncontrollably inside. Firefighting helicopters did their best to douse the flames but with no success.

It's possible that the crew had not depressurized the cabin; if that were the case, then the doors wouldn't function. (Certainly the pressurization doors were still shut.) That might have happened because the crew had become overcome by the fumes themselves. Equally, the passengers might have been asphyxiated. At the time, the Saudis theorized that since most of the bodies were jammed against the exit doors, "it was clear that the passengers were pushing each other and gathered at the main exit doors where most burned corpses were found – a fact which may have hindered the crew from carrying out their duties".

Safety recommendations following the tragedy included a change to the insulation used for the aircraft. Since Captain Khoyter's crew resource management was criticized, Saudi Airlines instituted better training and emergency procedures. It also sealed off the cargo compartments so that no fire could occur within them (even if that meant they couldn't transport live animals). The NTSB, who saw the Saudi report, also recommended that better hand-held extinguishers be fitted on all aircraft.

BLOWING INTO THE WIND

Flammable materials within the cabin were reduced yet further as a result of the fire aboard British Airtours Flight 28M on 22 August 1985, and the layout of aircraft – with spaces around the emergency exits – was also reconsidered. The 737 was packed with passengers for the charter flight to Corfu, and as one of the survivors of the incident pointed out at the time, "Many did not stand a chance. The aisles of those planes are so small. People were just on top of each other trying to get out."

Captain Peter Terrington and First Officer Brian Love had four cabin crew with them for the flight, which was due to leave at 0600 GMT. There had been a small problem with the no. 1 engine on the 737 the previous day – it had been accelerating slowly – but this had been fixed, and there had been two uneventful flights subsequently. Love would be flying the aircraft for the first part of the flight, and once the 131 passengers were on board, engines were started up as normal.

Clearance to taxi was granted at 0608, as the cabin crew carried out the safety demonstration. The purser Arthur Bradbury and flight attendant Joanna Toff strapped themselves in at the front of the aircraft; their colleagues Sharon Ford and Jacqui Urbanski were at the rear. Captain Terrington lined the aircraft up on the runway (full nose-wheel steering could only be controlled by a tiller on his side of the flight deck), and Love then took control. They were cleared for take-off at 0612.

Terrington advanced the throttles, noting that the no. 1 engine acceleration was acceptable – Love agreed, having been on the problematic flight the previous day – and autothrottle was selected. Love began to accelerate the aircraft for take-off; Terrington sounded off at 80 knots (the agreed V_1 speed, beyond which the take-off couldn't be aborted, was 140 knots), but then twelve seconds later, (thirty-six seconds after the take-off run had begun) both men heard a thump.

Terrington assumed that either a tyre had burst or they'd had a bird strike. Either way the course was simple. "Stop," he instantly ordered, closing the throttle, applying reverse thrust to both engines, and checking that the speed brakes were extended. Love applied maximum wheel braking, but Terrington was conscious that this could be tyre failure and advised him not to hammer the brakes.

As Terrington then started to tell ATC that they were abandoning take-off, the fire bell began to ring, so he advised that they had a fire on no. 1 engine. The ATC could see that was the case from their vantage point and told them, "Right – there's a lot of fire. They're on their way." When Terrington asked if he needed to evacuate the passengers, the controller told him, "I would do via the starboard side."

The aircraft was still decelerating, and Terrington warned the cabin that they would need to evacuate on the right-hand side. Purser Bradbury stuck his head round the flight-deck door and confirmed the order.

The passengers needed no encouragement. Those in the front three rows couldn't see the fire on the left-hand side of the aircraft; everyone behind them could see clearly that there was an intense blaze raging. The windows were starting to crack and melt, and smoke was already getting into the cabin even before the aircraft came to a halt. Some of the passengers started to get out of their seats even before the aircraft stopped, with others telling them to sit down and stay calm – but some people couldn't wait, and started to block the aisles.

Before the evacuation order was given, Bradbury had seen the fire coming up over the leading edge of the left wing, and flowing back over the wing's surface, and even as the aircraft was slowing to its final halt on the taxiway, he went to the right front door to release the slide. To his horror, although the door unlocked normally, the slide container lid jammed on the doorframe, keeping it shut. Could he send passengers safely out through the left front door, he wondered, and cracked the door open a small amount to have a check. Confident that the fire wasn't spreading forwards fast enough to cause problems, he opened the door fully, and checked the slide had opened. This was about twenty-five seconds after the aircraft had stopped, and Joanna Toff started to direct passengers out of that door – although she had to pull free some of them who had become jammed together between the forward galley bulkheads and were forming a bottleneck. One young girl was lying on the floor, so Toff pushed another youth back, and yanked the girl forward by her collar, and pushed her down the slide.

Bradbury moved across to the right door, and cleared the obstruction; seventy seconds after the aircraft had stopped, he was able to start funnelling passengers off the 737 through that door, until the thick black smoke coming from the cabin became so dense and acrid that both he and Toff had to use the slides at their doors before they succumbed. Toff had been about to get her smoke hood to look for other passengers, but a fireman at the bottom of the slide told her to jump. Seventeen passengers had escaped via the left front door, thirty-four through the right.

As the aircraft had come to a halt, the woman sitting next to the right overwing exit tried to pull it open, using her armrest which was mounted on the hatch. Not surprisingly, this didn't work so her friend sitting next to her leaned over and yanked at the "Emergency Pull" handle. The hatch fell into the aircraft, and was quickly put on one of the few vacant seats. Forty-five seconds after the 737 had stopped, the two women in the emergency row quickly got out onto the wing, followed by others, even though the smoke from the cabin was obscuring the gap. The area around the exit quickly became a mass of bodies pushing forward towards the exit, with people all around falling to the floor. Many of the twenty-seven people in total, including a child and a baby, who escaped that way, collapsed temporarily either within the exit or next to it, and eventually the exit became blocked with people's bodies half in and half out of the aircraft.

Those on the left side near the fire didn't have a chance. Huge tongues of flame were shooting into the cabin through the windows, lapping up the ceiling, and engulfing those sitting there in flames. Twenty seconds after the aircraft stopped, the fire had penetrated the fuselage through the cargo hold and started to enter the cabin through the floor air-conditioning grills.

At the back of the aircraft, things were even worse. Flight attendants Sharon Ford and Jacqui Urbanski had opened the rear right-hand door even before the 737 had turned onto the taxiway, and had deployed the slide ready to send passengers out the moment the aircraft came to a halt. However, the moment it did so, thick black smoke started to billow from the exit, obscuring one of the women who could briefly be seen standing at the door. One of the survivors recalled seeing the other flight attendant trying to direct passengers towards the door, but no one made it off the aircraft that way – including the two cabin crew. Many of the passengers had panicked on seeing the smoke, and had stumbled and collapsed in the aisle, which meant others had needed to scramble over the seatbacks towards the centre cabin area. According to one survivor, "people were howling and screaming". Only five of the thirty-four people in the rear rows survived.

On the flight deck, Terrington had turned right off the runway, and brought the aircraft to a halt on the taxiway. (With hindsight, this made matters worse: the wind direction simply fanned the flames.) He ordered Love to carry out the engine fire drill on the left engine, and shut down the right engine, since that was the side he had ordered the evacuation. The two pilots started to go through the passenger evacuation drill but Terrington could see that fuel and fire were starting to spread forward from the left side of the 737. He opened the sliding window on the right side of the flight deck and ordered Love to get out. He then followed his colleague down to the ground using the fabric escape strap.

The fire service had been notified by the tower of the emergency but some of them had already heard and seen the disaster unfurling in front of them, and were on their way even before the alarm siren sounded. A British Airways crew coach got to the scene four minutes later and helped to evacuate the survivors from the scene.

A third fire appliance had to be taken from the paint shop to use to fight the blaze, and didn't get to the taxiway until four to five minutes after the 737 had stopped. The driver looked up, and saw a small hand waving above a man who was trapped in the right overwing exit. He jumped out of his cab, climbed onto the wing, and pulled a young boy clear, over the body of the man who had been trapped there. The lad was the last person brought off the 737 to survive.

The firefighters tried to get on board wearing breathing equipment to search for any more survivors, but as they did so, there was another explosion, and one of them was blown out onto the tarmac. The officer in charge refused to allow any more attempts until they had a better water supply – they were running out on the vehicles. Worse, a number of the hydrants on the airfield were dry when they tried to replenish there.

After thirteen minutes, the Greater Manchester Fire Service arrived, and with their help, a two-man team went onto the aircraft. They reported there were a number of bodies, but they did find one man, alive but unconscious, lying in the aisle near the front of the 737. Unfortunately, he died six days later in hospital.

The Air Accidents Investigation Branch were able to find the cause of the problem with the engine very quickly: a blade had broken from its cowling and severed the main fuel line; they were far more concerned with the loss of life after the 737 had stopped. They didn't criticise Captain Terrington for his actions in the circumstances, but they made multiple recommendations – notably that in similar situations, "all abandoned take-offs and emergency landings should end with a full stop on the runway" without worrying about the resulting disturbance to aircraft movements. Operators should also ensure that aircraft are not stopped with a fire upwind of the fuselage, if possible.

As their report noted, "all the 'basic ingredients' of the fire at Manchester were typical of those which could apply to any other aircraft involved in such an incident", and as a result they also recommended that aerosol cans with butane and flammable gases shouldn't be carried. They also wanted aircraft configuration to be examined to ensure that people can get to the emergency exits more efficiently – something which quickly became mandated.

All four of the cabin crew were awarded the Queen's Gallantry Medal for their actions, as were two of the firefighters, on 6 August 1987. The crew also received the Flight Safety Foundation Heroism Award, which operated between 1968 and 2011 to "recognise civil aircraft crew members and ground personnel whose heroic actions exceeded the requirements of their jobs and, as a result, saved lives or property".

HAZARDOUS CARGO

Low-cost airline ValuJet didn't have the strongest safety record even before the crash of Flight 592 into the Florida Everglades on 11 May 1996. From its start-up in October 1993 to the week of the incident, it experienced more than 284 "service difficulties" – the FAA's description for things that could be as serious as an aircraft rolling off the runway because of worn tyres – and had four more serious "incidents" in the first five weeks of 1996: a hard landing and tail strike; a nose wheel that strayed off the runway when the crew could not see taxi lights; an aircraft that skidded on ice at low speed; and a flight attendant injured in turbulence. The FAA insisted that the airline undergo a 120-day "Special Emphasis Review" which led to more training for pilots and an agreement by company president Lewis Jordan to slow down his company's growth. The company was praised by some for its rapid response to regulators' concerns, but others were less convinced: Department of Transport Inspector General Mary Schiavo announced publicly that she would not fly with the airline, who had the second worst accident rate in the United States. The FAA review was still underway when Flight 592 disappeared.

According to ValuJet's records, there were 104 passengers aboard the Douglas DC-9, alongside Captain Candalyn Kubeck, First Officer Richard Hazen and three flight attendants. In fact there were 105: four-year-old Daniel Darbor wasn't included in the list. Delmarie Walker, who Atlanta police believed was responsible for the murder of her friend Catherine Holmes, was on board. Flight 592 should have left Miami International heading for Atlanta, Georgia, at 1300 Eastern Daylight Time, with a flight time of just over an hour and a half, but, perhaps not too surprisingly given ValuJet's record, there was a delay because the right auxiliary hydraulic pump circuit breaker needed unexpected maintenance.

As well as the passengers, the aircraft had 4,109 pounds of cargo – baggage, mail and what was deemed COMAT (company-owned material). This consisted of two main tyres and wheels, a nose tyre and wheel, and five boxes that were described on the manifests as "Oxy Cannisters [sic]-'Empty'". The COMAT was placed in the forward cargo compartment.

Flight 592 pushed back from the gate just before 1340, and started its taxi four minutes late. It was cleared for take-off at 1403.24, and at 1404.32, it was climbing to 5,000 feet, and cleared to climb and maintain 7,000 feet. The flight's eventual cruising level was flight level 350 (35,000 feet). They never reached it.

At 1410.03, as the DC-9 was climbing through 10,634 feet at 260 knots, there was an odd sound from behind the cockpit. Captain Kubeck wondered what it was, but twelve seconds later, realized that "we've lost everything". The departure controller was trying to hand over responsibility for the flight to Miami ATC, but Kubeck said to First Officer Hazen, "We need, we need to go back to Miami."

From behind Kubeck there were shouts in the background of "Fire!" repeated over and over, and attendant Mandy Summers put her head onto the flight deck to announce that they were on fire. Hazen radioed that they needed to return to Miami immediately, and was given a bearing and permission to descend.

The shouting subsided (at least as far as the cockpit voice recorder was concerned) at 1410.36, and the controller asked what the problem was. "Fire," Kubeck said briefly, with Hazen adding, "Uh, smoke in the cockp . . . smoke in the cabin." The controller gave further instructions which Kubeck started to comply with.

At 1411.12, just over a minute after the odd sound had been heard, Summers told the crew that they were "completely on fire". As Kubeck flew the aircraft, Hazen said they needed to land at the closest available airport, and the controller supplied further headings. Hazen acknowledged this. It was the last proper transmission from the DC-9. As the data recorder showed, the systems on board the DC-9 were rapidly failing as the fire spread.

At 1413.42, ValuJet 592 disappeared from the radar screens. The CVR had ceased functioning at 1411.45 for seventy-two seconds, and then clicked back in for a few seconds before the DC-9 finally crashed, at a 72-degree angle, nose first into the Francis S. Taylor Wildlife Management Area in the Florida

Everglades. Two fishermen nearby saw the aircraft strike the ground nearly vertically, followed by a great explosion and a 100-foot spume of water and smoke. "Aside from the engine smoke," one of them told investigators, "no signs of fire were visible." "The wreckage was like if you take your garbage and just throw it on the ground," pilot Daniel Muelhaupt, who flew over the site radioing for help, told CNN. There were no survivors.

The investigators were seriously hampered by the terrain in which the aircraft had come down. The oil slick from the aircraft fuel caused major problems. Miami Fire Lieutenant Luis Fernandez explained: "We've had to pull the airboats out of the water. It's not like the ocean; there's no water circulating, so there's no way for the fuel to dissipate. What we're having to do is land on high ground and then have our rescuers slush through four feet of water." And that was before they encountered the alligators and snakes! In the end, around two-thirds of the 110 people on board were identified from fragments that were found, but no autopsies could be carried out to find out whether they had died from smoke inhalation, the fire or the crash itself.

The NTSB investigation focused on the so-called "COMAT" in the cargo hold. Far from being innocuous oxygen cylinders, the "Oxy Cannisters – 'Empty'" were in fact unexpended chemical oxygen generators, which had not been made safe adequately and not been packed properly. They were in cardboard tubes, with no indications of hazardous material on them. There was considerable disagreement whether ValuJet should have allowed them on board, and why their maintenance contractor, SabreTech, had just put duct tape around the canisters, rather than covering the firing pins with the proper plastic caps.

The NTSB found that because the pins weren't correctly covered, one or more of the generators had been activated before take-off – possibly during the loading, but even as late as the take-off roll – and that had started the fire in the hold. The sound that first heralded the emergency to the crew was one of the tyres exploding; the oxygen from the cylinders was feeding the fire, which both removed the amount of smoke the blaze would produce, and made it develop very rapidly. This would have meant that unlike in many fires, where smoke is the first indication of trouble, the fire itself was the first sign of danger – as indicated by the shouts from the passengers. There were no smoke detectors or fire suppression devices in the hold – nor were there required to be – so earlier detection was unlikely. If there had been, then chances are Captain Kubeck would have had time to turn the aircraft around. Suggestions of an electrical fire on the aircraft were dismissed.

The NTSB said that the probable causes were SabreTech and ValuJet's handling of the material, although they were not as critical as some of the families of the victims would have liked. They pointed to various comments made in the immediate aftermath of the crash which indicated that ValuJet were well aware of what they were carrying. (The NTSB did point out that "Contrary to its authority, ValuJet's practices before the accident might have included the shipment of hazardous aircraft equipment items aboard company airplanes".) They felt that it was ValuJet who should carry the can: "Our loved ones bought tickets on ValuJet Airlines, not SabreTech," they noted. "In this situation, authority can be delegated, responsibility cannot. In simple terms, the person that hires the hit man is responsible for the murder."

SabreTech was found guilty by a federal grand jury of mishandling hazardous materials and improper training, fined $2 million and ordered to pay $9 million in restitution. One of the mechanics held responsible, Mauro Valenzuela, went on the run and was indicted for contempt of court; two other mechanics were acquitted. The verdict against SabreTech was reversed in part in 2001 by the Court of Appeals, although the improper training conviction was upheld; the fine was reduced to $500,000, three years' probation and no restitution. The company was also indicted by a Florida state grand jury on 110 counts of manslaughter, and 110 counts of third-degree murder; they settled these by pleading no contest to a charge of mishandling hazardous waste and made $500,000 donations to charity.

ValuJet was grounded on 17 June 1996 by the FAA, five days after families of three of the victims claimed the airlines posed a threat to passengers. They started operations again on 30 September that year, and in 1997 bought AirTran, merging the operations and flying under that name; AirTran was acquired by Southwest Airlines in 2010.

As a result of the ValuJet crash, all chemical oxygen generators and oxidizers were banned as cargo on passenger aircraft from

23 May 1996; fire detection and suppression systems were required for Class D cargo holds in all US commercial passenger airliners as of 19 March 2001; and all cargo aircraft are now required to have fire detection systems and a way to shut off air flow to the cargo compartment. This led to a large number of aircraft being retired, and over $300 million spent by airlines. The FAA also keeps a much closer eye on new airlines during their initial start-up period.

HIDDEN DANGER

The crash into the Atlantic Ocean of Swissair Flight 111 also led to multiple changes in aircraft operation, notably in the materials that are used on board aircraft, and the way in which wiring is installed. One tiny spark from an entertainment console probably set fire to the metallized polyethylene terephthalate (MPET) covered insulation blankets, and from the moment that the pilots first thought they smelled something odd, the MD-11 with 229 people aboard was doomed. As the Canadian Transportation Safety Board concluded: "From any point along the Swissair Flight 111 flight path after the initial odour in the cockpit, the time required to complete an approach and landing to the Halifax International Airport would have exceeded the time available before the fire-related conditions in the aircraft cockpit would have precluded a safe landing."

The MD-11 with Captain Urs Zimmermann and First Officer Stephan Löw at the controls took off from JFK in New York heading for Cointrin Airport in Geneva, Switzerland at 0018 GMT on 2 September 1998. Forty minutes later they had reached flight level 330, and were in contact with Moncton Air Traffic Services Area Control Centre – earlier there had been a short period during the flight when they appeared to be out of contact, but it seems as if that was purely down to mis-selection of radio frequency.

Löw was flying the aircraft at around 0110 when the pilots detected some form of odd odour in the cockpit. When Löw got up to investigate, he discovered that there had been some smoke in the cockpit, but it wasn't there now, and nor was there any in the passenger cabin, as the flight attendant in the first-class section confirmed. (She too could smell the strange odour in the cockpit when she was called in.) Believing that this was simply a problem with the air conditioning, they dismissed it – but four minutes later, at 0114, they made a "pan pan" call to Moncton ACC. This is an expression, spoken three times in succession, used in the case of an urgency: a condition concerning the safety of an aircraft or other vehicle, or of some person on board or within sight, but that does not require immediate assistance. They were about 66 nautical miles south-west of Halifax Airport in Nova Scotia, and had smoke in the cockpit. They therefore needed to land as soon as possible. They'd spotted the smoke again a minute or so before they called Moncton, and started looking at potential landing spots; at this point, Löw took over flying the aircraft once more. Although Captain Zimmerman initially suggested returning to Boston, about 300 nm behind them, he quickly accepted Moncton ACC's suggestion of Halifax, which was now only 56 miles away. Both pilots donned their oxygen masks.

At 0116.34, they were cleared to fly directly to Halifax, and to descend to 10,000 feet. He then briefed the master of the cabin (the chief flight attendant) that there was smoke in the cockpit, and that the crew should prepare the cabin for landing at Halifax in about twenty minutes to half an hour.

When they transferred to a different controller for the approach, they were cleared to 3,000 feet although Löw stated they wanted to stay at 8,000 feet until the cabin was ready for landing. At 0119.28, they were given a landing approach, since they were only 30 miles away, but at this stage they were still at flight level 210 and descending, so needed more time. They were told to turn to a heading of 360 to give them the space to lose altitude. One of the flight attendants came up to the cockpit, and moved the bag with the approach charts for Halifax nearer to the captain so he could access it quickly without leaving the controls. They also realized they would need to dump fuel before they landed. It was now 0121.20.

Zimmerman and Löw agreed to descend to 10,000 feet and head south to dump the fuel, and they inadvertently triggered the radio to the controller rather than the internal communications for a moment as they checked the Air Conditioning Smoke checklist – switching off the power supply in the cabin. That caused the recirculating fans in the ceiling to shut off. They reached 10,000 feet by 0123.30 and were told that they would be off the coast in about 15 miles. They asked for notification of when they could start dumping fuel.

Starting from 0124.09, things clearly started to go badly wrong; unknown to the two pilots, because the fans were no longer recirculating the air, the fire had now spread into the space above them. At 0124.09, the autopilot disconnected and Löw notified the controller that they were now flying manually, and asked for clearance for anything between 9,000 and 11,000 feet – he told them they were cleared at any altitude between 5,000 and 12,000 feet.

At 0124.42, less than thirty seconds later, both Zimmerman and Löw virtually simultaneously declared an emergency, almost certainly caused by the ceiling of the cockpit crashing in on top of them. That declaration was repeated a few seconds later by Captain Zimmerman, who also said that they were starting to dump fuel, and they had to land immediately. It was the last that anyone definitely heard from Swissair Flight 111.

At 0125.16, Löw told the captain that he was now concentrating on flying, not doing anything else. Four seconds later, Zimmerman referred to something that was burning already, and Löw indicated that his side was completely dark – all of his displays had shut down, and he was working off the standby instruments.

The flight data recorder stopped working at 0125.40; the CVR followed suit a second later. The aircraft was spotted on radar screens from 0125.50 to 0126.40 at a level of 9,700 feet. Captain Zimmerman left his seat to fight the fire; he never returned to it. Löw continued trying to fly the aircraft, but the cockpit was filled with smoke. He certainly shut down engine no. 2 after receiving an engine fire warning.

Swissair Flight 111 crashed into the Atlantic Ocean near the fishing community of Peggy's Cove, at the entrance to St Margaret's Bay in Nova Scotia at 0131.18. There was no hope of any survivors, although rescuers were quickly on the scene, going slowly through the water just in case some had by a miracle made it through the inferno and subsequent crash.

The investigation into what caused the fire in the first place was severely hampered by the discovery that the two black boxes had ceased working six minutes before the crash. The Canadian Transportation Safety Board took the lead on the enquiry, with assistance from their counterparts in Great Britain and the USA. Nearly two million pieces of wreckage from the aircraft were brought up and taken for examination. Heat tests showed that there were higher temperatures at the front of the aircraft, and by examining the ducts, they were able to quickly rule out a bomb, explosion, or fire in the cargo hold, passenger compartment or anywhere in the lower half of the aircraft. (Some have claimed that there were sufficient grounds to suspect a bomb, but the evidence was dismissed as "bad science".) Melted plastic drip marks on portions of the carpet from near the co-pilot's seat helped to identify which parts of the ceiling were hot.

The wiring therefore became the most likely culprit with arcing possible between portions of wire exposed by cracks in the insulation. Air-test flows on a duplicate MD-11 allowed them to pinpoint the origin of the fire to a two-square-foot area above the cockpit, and they were able to show that the MPET on the blankets would have easily caught fire. But they still weren't sure exactly which wire had been responsible – the finger of suspicion pointed at the in-flight entertainment network but they couldn't find a wire that fit the parameters. However, nearly three and a half years after Swissair Flight 111 crashed, they located at least one wire that did, exactly where they suspected it had to be.

The board's findings were summarized: "It was determined that the fire most likely started from an electrical arcing event that occurred above the ceiling on the right side of the cockpit near the cockpit rear wall. The arcing event ignited the flammable cover material on nearby metallized polyethylene terephthalate (MPET) covering on the thermal acoustic insulation blankets. As the fire spread across the surface of the insulation blankets, other flammable materials became involved, including silicone elastomeric end caps, hook-and-loop fasteners, foams, adhesives, thermal acoustic insulation splicing tapes, and metallized polyvinyl fluoride (MPVF) insulation blanket cover material. The fire progression was rapid, and involved a combination of these materials that together sustained and propagated the fire." The Canadian TSB made many recommendations, which the FAA issued as "airworthiness directives" regarding the wiring on the MD-11 and elsewhere, but as the FAA noted in 2007: "We have concluded that we are unlikely to identify and eradicate all possible sources of ignition."

Between 1990 and 2010, there were eighteen major accidents involving in-flight fire, which resulted in 423 fatalities. As a safety report prepared by the Royal Aeronautical Society issued in 2013 noted: "While the number of fatalities caused by aviation accidents has decreased, the risk of future fire related incidents or accidents has increased due to the proliferation of lithium batteries and other risks ... The aviation industry and regulators acknowledge that there will be ignition sources and fuel sources for fires within aeroplanes. Only through multiple layers of mitigation can the risk be kept to an acceptable level." Those tests may mean that there are yet more things we can't take on board an aircraft when we fly. Better that than the alternative.

DEATH OF A DREAM: GOING SUPERSONIC

It was a symbol of the "white heat of the technological revolution", an example of Anglo-French cooperation, a glorious reminder of the days when aviation was about beauty – Concorde was all these things, as well as a money pit, and regarded by some as an environmental hazard. Schoolchildren would make sure they were looking out of the windows as it flew over, with its distinctive shape and dropped nose. But one crash and fire was enough to bring its days to a close – and it followed in the less than illustrious footsteps of its Soviet rival, the "Concordski", the Tupolev Tu-144.

The Tu-144 was actually the first to fly of the two rival supersonic transports (SSTs), with the prototype taking off on 31 December 1968, going supersonic for the first time on 5 June 1969, and exceeding Mach 2 (twice the speed of sound) on 26 May the following year – the first commercial transport to do so. Although there were many similarities between the Tu-144 and Concorde, the often-repeated myth that the Soviets "stole" the technology from the West is simply not true: because of restrictions on sales of equipment to Communist countries which could be used for military purposes, many of the control mechanisms couldn't be purchased by the Soviet designers, and they had to find their own work-arounds. Aeroflot's representative in Paris was arrested in 1965 with plans for the Anglo-French Concorde, but these were early designs, and certainly the Soviets benefited from industrial espionage, but the two aircraft grew further apart the more they were developed.

In 1973, both the Tu-144 and Concorde were going to be demonstrated at the Paris Air Show – a place with an unfortunate reputation for crashes. The Concorde went first on 3 June, with its pilot Jean Franchi demonstrating exactly what the Western aircraft could do. In what was described as a "seemingly effortless show", Franchi performed a high-speed fly-by, and then concluded by pulling up steeply and climbing to approximately 10,000 feet before levelling off.

Tu-144 pilot Mikhail Koslov had been boasting about the power and capabilities of his aircraft throughout the air show, and in front of the 350,000 spectators, he proceeded to show that anything the Concorde could do, he could do better. After his fly-by, he also started to pull up steeply, the afterburners streaking yellow flame and his turbofans thundering. As the audience watched in horror, the aircraft apparently stalled at around 2,000 feet, and then began a sharp dive towards the ground. Koslov tried to pull it out and climb, but as he did so, his aircraft began to break up. The left wing detached, the aircraft rolled sharply, and the tail, nose and right wing had separated before the Tu-144 thundered into the village of Goussainville, killing all six crew members as well as eight people on the ground and destroying twenty homes.

A year after the crash, the French and the Soviet governments claimed that it was impossible to determine the cause of the crash, and no report was issued. However, many years later, it was revealed that there had been a French Air Force Mirage fighter in the vicinity, possibly trying to carry out a bit of espionage of its own, perhaps related to the Tu-144's own unique design – and it's possible that Koslov was surprised to see the Mirage there and that's why he began the sharp dive from which he eventually could not pull out. The theory is that the two governments agreed not to embarrass each other with the results of the crash – the Soviets disclosing the Mirage's presence, and the French highlighting the technical problems of the Tu-144. A Russian documentary aired in 2005 claimed that there were some experimental controls on board the Tu-144 being used for the first time at the air show, and that the captain had told his crew the night before, "If we are going to die, then at least we will die all together".

The Tu-144 never became the success that the Soviets had hoped for. It went into service as a freight carrier on 26 December 1975, and started to carry passengers on 1 November 1977, the sixtieth anniversary of the October Revolution. However, one of the Tu-144D variants crashed during a pre-delivery test flight on 23 May 1978 thanks to a problem with the fuel pump, killing two members of the crew; there had been multiple problems with the design of the aircraft causing fatigue cracks. The passenger service was cancelled a few days later, and production of the whole line was brought to a halt on 7 January 1982, with the aircraft taken out of service in July 1983.

Concorde, meanwhile, continued to operate. Air France and British Airways each had seven of the SSTs, but restrictions over their usage made them not as profitable as had been anticipated. Scheduled flights began to Rio and Bahrain in January 1976, and both airlines began to service Dulles Airport in Washington in May 1976 and JFK in New York in November 1977.

As with any aircraft, there were some problems. The NTSB contacted their counterparts in France, the BEA, with some safety recommendations following assorted incidents where tyres had blown out during take-off. And it was a tyre blow-out that led to the crash of Air France Flight 4590 at Charles de Gaulle Airport on 25 July 2000.

By coincidence, the crash occurred the day after British Airways had announced that it had discovered hairline cracks in the wings of all seven of its Concordes, but the Air France Concorde had been inspected four days prior, and no problems were noted then. Captain Christian Marty was flying the aircraft, with eight other crew and 100 passengers on board, on a charter flight heading for New York, where the passengers would embark on the cruise ship *MS Deutschland* for a sixteen-day cruise to Manta, Ecuador.

At 1358.27 GMT, they requested use of the whole of runway 26 right for a 1430 take-off; clearance was given at 1407.22. At 1434.38, the ground controller cleared the Concorde to taxi to the runway, and at 1442.17 it was given take-off clearance.

Captain Marty began the take-off roll fourteen seconds after clearance, and the aircraft reached 100 knots in thirteen seconds, and its V_1 speed – 150 knots – nine seconds after that. However, before it could reach rotation speed (198 knots), the right front tyre on the left main landing gear was destroyed. A piece of metal had come off the aircraft that had preceded Concorde on the runway – a DC-10 belonging to Continental Airlines – and when the SST rolled over it, the tyre exploded, sending large pieces of rubber against the underside of the left wing, and into part of fuel tank no. 5, sending the Concorde towards the left edge of the runway, and causing it to clip one of the steel landing lights.

A severe fire broke out under the left wing, just as both engines nos. 1 and 2 surged and started to lose thrust, more severely in the case of the latter. The tower controller told the crew that there were flames behind the aircraft, as the fuel from the tank caught fire. Marty began rotation, as the engineer, Gilles Jardinaud, announced that engine no. 2 had failed (although he said nothing about the loss on engine no. 1). At 1443:22 the Concorde took off at 205 knots, as the engine fire alarm began to sound. Jardinaud announced, "Shut down engine two," and the captain called for the engine fire procedure. The fire handle for that engine was pulled, stopping the alarm. (No one in the cockpit had time to notice another Air France aircraft, a 747 which was waiting to cross the runway; on board was French president Jacques Chirac.)

Concorde was now flying at 200 knots, 20 below the speed it needed to be travelling. Marty called for landing gear retraction, but it didn't work – the left main landing gear door wasn't opening. The engine fire alarm began to blare again, and First Officer Jean Marcot kept the captain informed of the speed, but without thrust, and with the landing gear still out, there was no chance that the Concorde could climb or gain speed.

For a moment, the crew thought they might just be able to make Le Bourget Airport, but that soon proved impossible. Engine no. 1 gave up completely, and with the left wing melting from the temperature from the fire, the right wing lifted, banking the aircraft to over 100 degrees. Marty reduced the power on engines nos. 3 and 4, but it was far too late. Concorde stalled, and crashed into an annex of the Hôtelissimo hotel in the suburb of Gonesse, near Charles De Gaulle. It was consumed by a violent fire, and four people on the ground, as well as all 109 aboard, were killed.

The official investigation by the BEA found that the sequence of events was caused by the metal strip left on the runway. Continental Airways was placed under investigation by the French authorities in March 2005, as were Henri Perrier of Aérospatiale, the Concorde manufacturers, and Concorde chief engineer Jacques Herubel, the following September. Charges were brought against them, as well as two Contintenal employees and Claude Frantzen, a French airline regulator employee. Continental claimed that the Concorde was on fire when it passed over the strip, but this defence was not successful. They were found criminally responsible for the crash. Continental mechanic John Taylor received a fifteen-month suspended sentence; the others were acquitted. On appeal, Continental was cleared of criminal but not civil responsibility.

All Concordes were grounded in the aftermath of the crash; although they resumed flying in late 2001, they never recovered properly. The last Air France Concorde flew in May 2003; British Airways ended its services in October the same year. As the *Observer* noted when reporting the crash, it was the "death of a dream".

Part 7:
Hijackings

THE FIRST HIJACKS

While many of the situations that can lead to air disasters and near misses can be controlled by the efforts of the crew in the cockpit, there are others which are completely out of their hands – in particular, when one or more of the passengers decide that they want to be in control. Throughout the history of air travel, there have been instances of hijackings: contrary to popular opinion, it's not a phenomenon that was started by the Palestine Liberation Organization (PLO) and their ilk in the 1960s and 1970s; and neither did it come to an end following the tragic events of September 11, 2001 when four hijacked aircraft were used as weapons by forces controlled by Osama bin Laden. True, many additional safety features were incorporated as a result of 9/11, but hijacks continue to this day (and with the advent of 3D printers, which can create weapons that are currently undetectable by security forces, some fear that there may be a resurgence).

If you choose to believe the list of historical hijackings on Wikipedia, the earliest hijacking in the world took place in Brazil in September 1932, nearly three decades after the Wright Brothers first took to the air. Yet there are many reports of earlier events which qualify.

There was an incident a year earlier in Peru: commercial pilot Byron Rickards flew from the capital, Lima, to the southern city of Arequipa on 21 February 1931, and when he arrived, his Panagra Ford Tri-motor was surrounded by soldiers. Rickards was told that his plane was now in the service of the revolution and that he would fly revolutionaries wherever he was ordered. Rickards wasn't going to go along with this, and point blank refused – and continued refusing until 2 March, when, apparently, the revolution had succeeded in its aims and Rickard was free to go, provided he took one of the Junta with him.

Walter William Crothers was charged with stealing an airplane in September 1930, the property of the Aero Club of New South

Wales, Australia. According to contemporary reports, "it was alleged that Crothers obtained the plane from the caretaker of the Hargrave Park Aerodrome, and had intended flying it to Katoomba, where he had arranged with a number of public men to give an exhibition of flying". Crothers had form for aeroplane-related crime: a year earlier, he was "the first man in Australia to be fined for flying without a licence". (Crothers decided on more sedate forms of transport for his next crimes: a 1933 court report indicates he had switched to stealing cars.)

J. Howard "Doc" DeCelles claimed in a newspaper article in 1970 that it was he who had been the world's first hijacking victim, over forty years previously. He was working as a flying postman for the Mexican company Transportes Aeras Transcontinentales on a route between San Luis Potosí, Toreon and Guadalajara in December 1929, when he was approached by one of the last remaining lieutenants of Mexican rebel Pancho Villa, General Saturnino Cedillo. The general informed him that he was taking over DeCelles' aircraft, and the pilot was to take Cedillo and his men to a secret destination – no maps were provided, but the men knew where they were going, and were able to guide him over the Mexican mountains. He was forced to put down on a road, and then kept prisoner for a few hours, before being released and allowed to fly home. Although DeCelles claimed he had kept his flight log, he didn't file a report with any authorities, nor was it covered by any contemporary newspapers or journals, so it is hard to ascertain the truth of his story.

However, a trawl through the newspapers between 1903 and 1929 reveals that plenty of other such crimes took place. In mid-August 1911, E. E. Lessard, an aviator from St Louis, "telephoned the police that someone had stolen his monoplane. So far as known, that is the first time anyone ever complained of the theft of a flying machine." Lessard had filed a patent for his particular model of monoplane four months earlier, so one can understand his fury at its theft – although details of the incident are no longer known (and the story only received coverage outside St Louis because of the apparent uniqueness of the crime).

Ransom H. Merritt would certainly seem to have the strongest claim to be the first hijacker, since, during the course of his crime, he took control of an aircraft which wasn't his, and was responsible for the death of someone on board – in this case, Anthony Spileno, a fellow young airfield mechanic.

However, the situation wasn't totally clear cut: certainly, Merritt had every intention when he took the airplane up of returning it safely. The hijacking took place in June 1917, shortly after the United States had entered the First World War. Merritt hadn't waited for the formal declaration of hostilities between America and Germany: a former scholarship student at Cornell University and a newspaper reporter, he had been keen to serve in the fight against the Kaiser and had travelled to Canada, where he joined the army, and was sent to the Western Front. Thanks to the intervention of his father, he had been sent home from Europe, and was now serving as an enlisted mechanic at the government aviation school near Mineola, Long Island.

The first-class private in the Aviation Section of the Signal Corps wasn't one of the "student aviators" who were being given a quick course in flying at the base before being shipped out to serve in France; his role was strictly on the ground. As the *New York World* reported, his duties "were to keep engines of flying machines in order and to tune them up." He and Spileno were "not permitted to fly".

This wasn't going to stop Merritt. Serving on the Western Front, he would have seen the exploits of the fliers who went into battle against the Red Baron and his colleagues, and he obviously wanted to experience the thrill himself. The reports don't indicate whether Spileno was an active participant in the theft of "LWF tractor No. 113", but since he was in the passenger seat, chances are that he was. Later investigations, however, did reveal that "Merritt had often boasted he was 'going up alone some day'".

For thirty-five minutes – the last thirty-five minutes of his life – Merritt achieved his aim of flying: he "drove the machine with a recklessness that took away the breath of Captain Walter G. Kilmer, in charge of the post, and the entire personnel of the school . . . who stood gazing at the flight. Merritt sprinted, dipped, dived, looped, turned, twisted, and did everything except loop-the-loop".

There was only one problem – Merritt didn't know how to land the aircraft. He tried something logical – he aimed the airplane for the ground from 3,000 feet up, and then, once he had descended 2,000 feet "he pulled abruptly on the elevating levers". This was, literally, his fatal mistake.

"The right wing of the biplane crumpled like paper," recounted the *New York World*'s reporter. "The machine stopped a second, and then dropped straight to earth. The crash that came to the watchers' ears an instant later meant that pilot and passenger and a $3,000 tractor were no more. Spileno's body was so badly mangled that it could not be sent home for burial."

Aircraft thefts occurred across the 1920s in the United States: in December 1921, Frank Strand, a "jobless aviator" in Chicago committed a crime described as "the first time probably in the whole history of aviation when a civilian aircraft was stolen from its hangar". Like Merritt before him, Strand wasn't as competent at flying as he should have been – although he did have "eight hours' flying experience" – and crashed the plane. Unlike Merritt, Strand was able to walk away from his crash, and was assisted by the farmer in whose field he had "landed" – although once the theft was discovered, his bandaged head was a bit of a giveaway to the police searching for him!

Six years later, an airplane was stolen so it could be used to "get to a party in a hurry," according to the *Pittsburgh Gazette*. In 1929, "[t]he first airplane known to have been stolen was recovered here today, but the two young pilots who 'borrowed' it at the point of pistols in Kansas City escaped," the *Painesville Telegraph* reported.

The Brazil incident in 1932 also led to the deaths of both hijackers and hostage. A Sikorsky S-38 registration P-BDAD belonging to Brazilian airline Panair do Brasil (although apparently still painted as if it were part of Panair's predecessor NYRBA do Brasil) was stolen on 25 September from the company's hangar by three men who took a fourth man hostage. It seems as if none of them had received training in flying an aircraft, but they were able to get the machine to leave the ground. They didn't manage to stay up for long though – they soon crashed to earth near the town of São João de Meriti in the Baixada Fluminense region. According to Brazilian historians, they were connected to the uprising taking place in the state of São Paulo against the federal government which had begun in July that year; the Constitutionalist Revolution only lasted a further week following the hijacking – as described in the book *Brazilian Adventure* by Peter Fleming, brother of 007 creator Ian Fleming.

KILLING TEACHER

One of the first confirmed hijackings during which an innocent man was killed in the United States took place in October 1939. Earnest P. "Larry" Pletch was twenty-nine at the time, and obsessed with two things – women and flying ("I would rather fly than eat," he told the deputies who arrested him). Brought up in Frankfort, Indiana, he was a high-school dropout who was an expert with machinery, happier tinkering with an engine than helping on his family farm. In the summer of 1938, despite never having received any form of training, Pletch was able to steal an airplane at 3 a.m., and fly it 250 or so miles north-west to Danville, Illinois, where he landed it in a seven-acre field before heading south-west to the town of Vernon, not far from St. Louis, where he gave flying exhibitions, and even, after only two weeks' flying, started to give lessons!

Pletch's passions for women and flying led to his arrest after he wooed seventeen-year-old Goldie Gerkin, then abandoned her after five days when she refused to marry him. He was still out on bail for this in September 1939 when he married his third wife, Francis Bales of Palmyra, Missouri, whom he had met while he was working for a carnival. (Pletch already had a four-year-old daughter who lived with her mother in Frankfort). The marriage lasted only a few days, and Pletch returned to Indiana; however, in late October, Pletch decided he needed to find her, so borrowed a car and returned to Missouri. While searching, he met Carl Bivens, a thirty-nine-year-old flight instructor who was giving lessons in a yellow Taylor Club monoplane, which was fitted with dual controls; Pletch asked for advanced flying lessons, which Bivens was happy to provide.

The first two lessons on Friday 27 October went perfectly normally: Pletch clearly had an innate aptitude for flying, and Bivens was impressed by his new pupil. They took off to begin a third lesson at 4 p.m., and around forty minutes later were cruising at 5,000 feet. Pletch decided that he wanted the mono-plane for himself – or, at least, that's as good a theory as any which has been proposed. Pletch told prosecutors: "I just don't know why I killed him, but I did" – a comment which formed the banner headline for the local paper, the *Bloomington Evening News* a few days later

"Carl was telling me I had a natural ability and I should follow that line," Pletch later confessed. "I had a revolver in my pocket and without saying a word to him, I took it out of my overalls and I fired a bullet into the back of his head. He never knew what struck him.

"The ship began to pitch and then to dive. It went crazy and I remembered reading about a dying man 'stiffening' at the controls, and then I fired another shot into the back of his head."

Pletch was able to pull the aircraft out of its potentially cata-strophic dive at 1,500 feet, and landed it near Cherry Box, Missouri, where he buried Bivens' body. He then took off once more, heading for Frankfort. Not making it home before dark, he landed and slept in a farmer's barn, before resuming the flight the next day. He overflew his parents' home, apparently "with the intention of smashing the plane into the side of my father's barn" but "lost my nerve". He flew north-west, and when it grew dark, he brought the Taylor Club down in a cow pasture near Blooming-ton, Indiana. There he was the object of great excitement among the local youngsters – and interest from the local police. He had been spotted flying over Brown County State Park, east of Bloom-ington, and the local telephone switchboard operator, Bertha Maner, called the police after numerous residents told her that the aircraft had landed at the Dillman farm. Once they had confirmed that the licence number of the airplane matched the stolen aircraft, the police got in touch with the owner of the local store, where Pletch had gone in search of food. While Pletch waited patiently for his hamburger to be cooked, the police surrounded the store, then went in and arrested him; Pletch didn't resist.

Initially Pletch claimed that Bivens' death had followed a fight between them, and Pletch had acted in self-defence. Supposedly the two men had agreed to steal the aircraft (which belonged to a friend of Bivens'), and were going to use it to fly to Mexico to test out some "extremely high-efficiency aviation fuel" which Pletch said he had invented. When Bivens tried to back out of the plan, a fight ensued. The Missouri state police quickly discounted this, and Pletch confessed.

Although his trial and conviction for the "fantistic [sic] airplane slaying" (as the Associated Press described it) followed very speedily – within five days of the murder, Pletch was starting his life sentence without possibility of pardon or parole – it raised legal questions regarding in whose jurisdiction his crime took place, and indeed, if there were no witnesses to say exactly where it happened, would the perpetrator somehow manage to get away with the crime?

Pletch didn't face the death penalty at the request of his victim's widow, to the great relief of Pletch's mother, who had advised him to make his peace with God when she saw him in the cells before his trial. He remained incarcerated until his death in 2001, during which time he applied for a patent for a "Traction increasing device for dual wheel vehicles".

AERIAL PIRACY

The first hijacking (as opposed to theft) of a commercial aircraft took place shortly after the end of the Second World War when *Miss Macao* was taken over by a group of pirates. This *Miss Macao* wasn't the winner of a beauty pageant, but a Catalina seaplane that belonged to a subsidiary of Cathay Pacific.

Because Macao, as a province of Portugal, hadn't signed up to the International Monetary Fund and the Bretton Woods restrictions on gold trading, which had been designed to get the world's economy back on its feet following the depredations of the war, it quickly became an important trading centre with Hong Kong and Saigon. In 1946, MATCO, the Macau Aerial Transport Co., was established, using "amphibious carriers" (i.e. seaplanes) since it had proved impossible to build a landing strip within Macao. The waters of Porto Exterior were therefore used to take off and land.

In June 1948, a group of three local farmers decided that they would get rich considerably quicker if they took over one of these seaplanes, plundering its contents, and perhaps even ransoming some of the rich people aboard. They had around $3,000 for expenses, according to a contemporary report in *Time* magazine, and one of them, the Mexican-born Chiu Tok, had learned to fly aircraft in Manila. They involved Wong Fu (aka Huang Yu), who knew the area where they planned to bring the seaplane.

On 16 July, therefore, the quartet bought tickets for Hong Kong and boarded the aircraft, with Tok heading for the front near the pilots, and Wong Fu strapping himself into a seat at the back – he was to take no active part in the hijack. There were twenty other passengers on board, including four Chinese millionaires and other prominent Macanese businessmen, one of whom was indeed carrying large quantities of gold in his luggage. Former US Navy pilot Captain Dale Cramer was in charge, with twenty-three-year-old Australian Ken McDuff acting as co-pilot, and a young Macanese stewardess, Delca da Costa.

Once the seaplane had taken off and was on course for Hong Kong, the hijackers swung into action. As McDuff came back into the cabin to retract the wing floats, Tok moved forward, and ordered Cramer to hand over control of the aircraft at gunpoint. McDuff and some of the other passengers tried to interfere, and one of the passengers was shot. McDuff grabbed an iron flag bar to attack Tok and the panicked farmer shot out wildly, his bullets hitting both the pilots. Cramer slumped over the controls, killed instantly – and forcing the seaplane into a spiral dive. As the passengers were thrown into the aisles, *Miss Macao* hit the water. Everyone bar Wong Fu was killed: he had managed to jump from a rear emergency exit.

Wong Fu refused to say anything to the authorities initially, but once one of the bodies was found with a bullet wound, the pressure on him intensified. Police officers were placed near him in the hospital, and a recording device was put by his bed. Eventually Wong Fu confessed.

Since the Catalina was flying the British flag, it was expected that Wong Fu would be tried in Hong Kong, and since air piracy wasn't covered under the piracy laws in force at the time, it was likely he would be charged with murder. However, it seems that there was insufficient evidence to bring him to trial in Hong Kong, and there was a question of jurisdiction, since the crime occurred over Chinese waters. After Wong Fu was held in Macao prison for three years, he was released on 11 June 1951. Sources differ as to his fate, although most agree that he was subjected to some form of summary judgement, either unofficially by the Chinese, or from the relatives of the Macanese who died in the crash. Some say he was returned to his village first; one more lurid account suggests that he was "murdered at the door of the prison".

According to one of the pilots' forums, it was following this incident that the idea of using metal detectors to screen passengers was first mooted, but, like the idea of keeping the cockpit door locked during flight, was deemed impractical. The former wouldn't arrive until the early 1970s; the latter only really came into force following 9/11.

THE ASYLUM SEEKERS

With the imposition of major restrictions on travel between East and West following the division of Europe after the Second World War, there were a number of hijackers whose motive was to escape from Communism.

One of the first took place on 25 July 1947, when three Romanian army officers hijacked an aircraft which was meant to be on an internal flight from Bucharest to Craiova, with Lieutenant Aurel Dobre forcing pilot Vasily Ciobanu at gunpoint to fly them to Turkey. During the scuffle that followed, the flight mechanic, Mitrofan Bescioti, tried to take the gun from Dobre, but it went off, leaving Bescioti dead. The aircraft was flown to Çanakkale in Turkey, where the officers were captured. The two juniors, Romeo Ştefănescu and Zefir Bălteanu, were paroled; Dobre was imprisoned.

The three officers were part of a group trying to escape from the Communist rule, and the always paranoid security apparatus automatically assumed that Ciobanu was also a member. According to his granddaughter, after being declared an accomplice, and thus an enemy of the state, Ciobanu was accused of espionage and treason, and sentenced to death in July 1950. However, the sentence was not carried out and instead he spent sixteen years in prison for political reasons, of which five were endured in the lead mines in the northern part of the country. Ciobanu died in 1982 in a tram accident, having officially never been allowed to fly again following the hijacking.

The most spectacular asylum hijacking took place on 24 March 1950, four months before Ciobanu was sentenced. The triple hijacking hit the headlines around the world, as eight former RAF officers took control of three separate Dakota DC-3 passenger aircraft operated by Československé Státní Aerolinie (CSA), the Czech state airline, and flew them to the US airbase at Erding, east of Munich, in the American zone of Germany. In a book and film about the incident, the Communists tried valiantly in the months that followed to portray the pilots as gangsters who had traitorously kidnapped virtuous Czechoslovak citizens, whose adherence to the Communist ideals was the only thing that gave them the necessary strength to survive their ordeal.

This wasn't perhaps the whole picture. A number of Czech pilots, who had served with the RAF during the Second World War, were employed by the CSA in the period following hostilities, and they were aware that this might provide them with an opportunity to escape to the West. By spring 1950, quite a few had already tried to do so, leading to a situation where the ex-RAF crew were only allowed to fly on domestic routes within the Communist bloc, and no longer possessed their passports. In addition, family members were barred from travelling on the same flights, on the assumption that the pilots would not be prepared to escape without their wives and children. The situation for the pilots worsened when they realized that the CSA was starting to train new pilots who would be deemed "politically trustworthy" – and once they were in place, the older generation would be disposable, which could lead to their arrest, interrogation and possible imprisonment at the hands of the secret police, the Státní bezpečnost (StB).

As with many reports of escapes from Communist states, contemporary reports in the West were misleading – sometimes deliberately, because the escapees would not want to jeopardize the positions of those left behind. In this case, reading the stories in the *New York Times* might make you think that this was a spur of the moment decision, planned over a cup of coffee at Prague's Ruzyně Airport on 23 March, and carried out the next day! It was anything but that.

The only way to ensure that the wives and families of the escaping officers were also able to reach the West was to hijack more than one aircraft, so that the families of one officer would be on an airplane piloted by one of their colleagues. In the end, the leaders decided that it would be best to take three aircraft on early morning routes: the security guards at the airports would hopefully be less alert, and there would be less people travelling on the airplanes who might object to the revised routing into Germany.

Each flight should have been bound for Ruzyně Airport in Prague, and Erding was chosen as the alternate destination, since the flight times were similar, and one pilot, Doležal, had visited there once before, when in May 1948 another ex-RAF officer had hijacked his plane and forced him to fly there.

Friday 24 March 1950 was chosen as the date for the escape, and the various passengers in the group bought their tickets for one of three flights: the 0635 from Brno; the 0630 from Ostrava; and the 0700 from Bratislava. The day before, all of the prospective escaping passengers headed for their respective airports, waiting for the final confirmation from the group leaders. The three pilots who would be responsible for the hijacks – Vit Anget- ter, Ladislav Světlík and Oldřich Doležal – met at Ruzyně, and agreed the fine details of the plan. They then piloted their sched- uled flights to the three airports, exactly as normal.

Only one of the passengers failed to turn up the next morning: Antonín Vendl had a run-in with someone dressed in a leather overcoat whom he believed was an StB officer on the night of the 23rd, and, fearing that the plan had been discovered, decided not to go to Ostrava Airport. Everyone else, however, checked in for their flights.

Vit Angetter was co-pilot on the Brno flight, accompanied by fellow conspirators Kamil Mráz, the radio operator and naviga- tor, and air hostess Lída Škorpíková. The pilot, Captain Josef Klesnil, and flight engineer Jan Tuček were not part of the plan. The DC-3 was full, with twenty-six passengers on board, eight of whom were hoping not to return to Czechoslovakia, including Angetter's wife Eve, who had booked using her maiden name, and a CSA employee, Miroslav Hanzlíček, who had helped to ensure that everyone was able to book on the right flights.

Once Klesnil had flown the aircraft for take-off, Škorpíková entered the cockpit to divert his attention while Mráz and Anget- ter dealt with Tuček, binding and gagging him at gunpoint then hiding him in the small luggage area at the rear of the cockpit. Angetter then returned to his co-pilot's seat, and took over flying the airplane at the appointed time. However, when Angetter unexpectedly switched on the autopilot, Klesnil asked what was happening, and was not happy to learn that Angetter was serious about flying to the West – partly because he was in the middle of arranging an escape for himself and his family, and any perceived involvement in this escapade would seriously jeopardize that. He therefore asked Angetter to make sure that it would be clear to the authorities that he was a completely unwilling participant, and allowed himself to be tied up.

Although both Klesnil and Tuček had now been dealt with, Angetter, Mráz and Škorpíková knew that there were potential problems among the passengers who were not part of the escape attempt – notably from the CSA president, Leopold Thurner, who habitually carried a gun. Luck, though, was with this group: Angetter changed course to fly 240 degrees towards Erding, and maintained radio silence while they flew over the Russian Zone – they were conscious that the Russians might very well try to bring them down if they became aware of the hijack. Once they were over the American Zone, Angetter contacted Erding, requesting asylum, and landed there at 0818. As soon as they had done so, Angetter warned the base commander, Colonel Park Holland, that two more aircraft were on their way and would use the password "Way of Freedom".

When Thurner realized that they were not in Prague, and indeed not even within the Communist sphere of influence, he drew his gun, crying out that this was "Treason!" However, as he tried to get through the cockpit door, which Angetter had wisely locked, American military police were entering the aircraft through the rear door, which Škorpíková had opened as soon as she could. They disarmed Thurner, and removed him from the DC-3, before the other passengers followed.

Nearly two hours earlier, the Ostrava flight had taken off, five minutes later than scheduled. Only one of the aircrew was part of the plan – pilot Ladislav Světlík – with co-pilot Mečislav Kozák, radio operator and navigator Cestmír Brož and flight engineer Gejza Holoda completely in the dark, although all three had also served with the RAF. Brož was likely to be a problem, since he was a committed Communist; Světlík was on his own in the cockpit, although he did have help from fellow pilot and escaper Viktor Popelka, who was travelling as a passenger. (There were three other escapers among the twenty-three passengers – Popelka's wife, travelling under her maiden name, and Oldřich Doležal's wife and young son.)

Half an hour after take-off, once they had reached a height of 1900 metres, Světlík activated the autopilot and headed back into the passenger cabin to use the toilet. Popelka entered the cabin to chat with his friend Kozák, seating himself in Světlík's captain's chair. When Světlík returned from the toilet, he locked the cockpit door, then went to stand behind Brož, who was in his work compartment in the area between the pilots and the door. Brož was talking to the control tower at Prague and refused to stop the conversation when Světlík politely asked him to; however, once the captain displayed his Luger pistol and advised the radio operator not to be a hero, Brož saw sense, and allowed himself to be taken to the luggage compartment at the rear, and put in there with his hands tied. Světlík then repeated the procedure with Holoda, as Popelka kept Kozák's attention firmly on himself.

Světlík now moved forward and stood behind Kozák, jabbing him with the gun, and requesting that he vacate his chair. Quickly realizing what was happening, Kozák asked Světlík to make it clear that he was not a willing participant – much as he might have wanted to escape, he had a wife and three children, with a fourth on the way, so he had to return – so he suggested that Světlík hit him on the head to make it look as if he was trying to prevent the hijack. Světlík did so with a convenient piece of metal. All of this could be witnessed by Brož, who would hopefully confirm that the other crew members were not party to the hijack.

Two hundred kilometres west of Ostrava, Světlík changed course for Linz in Austria, climbing to 3,000 metres and flying just above cloud level. Like Angetter, he maintained radio silence during the aircraft's passage over the Russian Zone, only breaking it once they reached Linz, which straddled the river Danube, the border between the Russian and the American Zones, and contacting Erding control tower, giving the agreed password. At 0850, they touched down in the USAF base. Despite the presence of a deputation of Communist Party officials on board, no one screamed that this was treason when they realized where they had landed; instead, they meekly followed the instructions from the American military police to disembark from the aircraft.

It would be another forty minutes before the final DC-3 arrived in Erding, an anxious time for everyone involved. The Bratislava flight was beset with more problems than the other two, even if, unusually, all of the aircrew – pilot Oldřich Doležal, co-pilot Bořivoj Šmíd, radio operator and navigator Stansislav Šácha, flight engineer Jan Královansky, and air hostess Eva Vysloužilová – were involved in the escape.

The trouble began with some of the passengers involved in the escape not following the instructions regarding keeping their luggage inconspicuous – if there was one thing guaranteed to raise suspicion, it was the sight of a simple daytime flight suddenly looking as if everyone was heading off for a long break! This meant that the aircraft would be 750kg overweight if a normal fuel load (1,800 litres) was used; Doležal therefore had to drop the fuel to 1,200 litres – which made the flight to Erding more hazardous. It was impossible not to lessen the fuel load: 1,200 litres was sufficient for the flight to Prague that the DC-3 was ostensibly making, and all manner of alarms would have been raised if Doležal had failed to act normally.

The security at Bratislava was also tighter than normal: in February 1950, Czech world figure skating champion Alena 'Áji' Vrzáňová had defected to the West. When airport security spotted the name Vrzáňová on the passenger manifest, they started to carry out extra checks; the Vrzáňová in question was Aji's mother Anna, who was, indeed, one of the escapees. Eventually all twenty-five passengers were allowed on board – but the aircraft's departure was delayed to 0730, and then, as it was taxiing to the runway, Šácha received a message from the control tower ordering the plane to return to the terminal. Knowing that they were now committed to the escape, Šácha claimed that there were interference problems on the radio and he couldn't hear the message. He switched the radio off and Doležal took off straightaway to ensure that there was no attempt to block their departure.

The DC-3 was supposed to stop at Brno before heading on to Prague, but as they approached Břeclav, about 80 kilometres into their journey, Doležal radioed Brno to say they wouldn't be able to land, owing to an undercarriage fault. He then set course for Linz, taking them over the Russian Zone for what Doležal later described as a "nerve-racking" hour. Given their suspicious behaviour – ignoring the request to return, and then failing to make the scheduled stop – Doležal expected that the Czechoslovak authorities would call in help from their Russian comrades, and even though Colonel Holland had ordered fighters to be on station at Linz to help the escapers if they hit problems, there were no guarantees that the DC-3 wouldn't come under attack. However, they reached Linz safely, and proceeded to Erding, arriving there at 0930.

As with the first plane, there were those on board the Bratislava flight who were not at all happy about arriving in the West. One of the passengers was an armed StB agent, Karel Nejepinský, who, yelling about treason, tried to get into the locked cockpit as three Americans boarded from the rear. Nejepinský wasn't impressed by the American officer's claim that one of the pilots didn't like Czechoslovakia, and he implored the other passengers not to leave the sovereign Czechoslovak territory on board the aircraft. They ignored him, and Nejepinský was disarmed and removed from the airplane.

Of the eighty-five people aboard the three DC-3s, twenty-seven elected to remain in the West – the original twenty-six escapers plus one man who took advantage of the situation, and an American working for the US Information Service in Prague who was allowed to go about her business immediately. The other fifty-seven people were kept together and questioned before being allowed to return – the level and nature of the questioning was a matter of some debate in the days and weeks that followed, with the Americans understandably downplaying any hints of coercion on their part. The escape ratcheted up tensions in the Cold War, particularly after America refused to return the twenty-seven defectors – who were tried in their absence by the District Court in Prague 2 District in July 1950. The aircrew were sentenced to death; the passengers to twenty-five years' imprisonment. Angmetter, Mráz, Popelka and Šmíd later flew missions for the CIA over the Soviet Union.

The aircrew who were not part of the plot also suffered: Josef Klesnil, Mečislav Kozák and Gejza Holoda were fired from the CSA. Klesnil managed to escape across the border in April 1951; Holoda's attempt resulted in his capture and a thirteen-year prison term. The Czechoslovak authorities tightened security, placing StB agents on every flight, including one in the cockpit, and removing virtually all former RAF aircrew from active duty. No one else was going to escape that way.

THE ROAD TO LEGISLATION

Before the advent of terrorist organizations, such as the PLO or al-Qaeda, hijacks were normally carried out by groups of people with a personal rather than political agenda. These tended to be private individuals, bound by some common cause. However, in December 1954, a hijacking was carried out on behalf of a sovereign state: Israel had only been brought into existence six years earlier, and it's fair to say that many of those in charge had not yet fully transitioned into using the more common diplomatic and peaceful methods of achieving their aims. As Israeli Foreign Minister Moshe Sharett wrote in his diary at the time: "What shocks and worries me is the narrow-mindedness and the short-sightedness of our military leaders. They seem to presume that the state of Israel may – or even must – behave in the realm of international relations according to the laws of the jungle."

On 11 December 1954, five Israeli soldiers were captured by the Syrians, while engaged in trying to place wiretaps on the Syrian phone network. This wasn't something that the Israeli Chief of Staff Moshe Dayan was going to allow; the soldiers were to be returned as quickly as possible, and if necessary force would be used against the Syrians. The next day, a Syrian Airways Dakota – a civilian flight with four passengers and five crew – was forced down by Israeli jets and made to land at Lydda Airport (now Ben-Gurion, the scene of the terrorist attack by the Japanese Red Army in 1972). Those on board were interrogated for two days by Israeli authorities, before the country finally gave in to international protests and released them. (There are suggestions by some historians that the Syrians did indeed release the captured soldiers in return.)

Sharett was furious, telling Pinhas Lavon, the defence minister, in a formal letter: "I have no reason to doubt the truth of the factual affirmation of the U.S. State Department that our action was without precedent in the history of international practice."

Sharett believed that Lavon was responsible for a press campaign that tried to persuade Israelis that the aircraft had been a danger to national security; this backfired when the passengers were released, because it seemed as if the government had backed down in the face of international pressure, despite a threat to their borders.

Hijacking an airplane wasn't a crime in the United States at this point. Even the Federal Aviation Act of 1958 failed to criminalize the activity, since, presumably, no one could believe that anyone would try. There weren't many places that an American would have to force passage to, and if someone tried to force an aircraft to land somewhere within the North American continent, the authorities would have the airplane surrounded within moments of touchdown.

However, they were overlooking at least one incident that had taken place shortly before noon on 6 July 1954. Fifteen-year-old Raymond Kuchenmeister tried to use a .38 calibre revolver to force the pilot of an American Airlines aircraft to fly him to Mexico – unsuccessfully. Kunchenmeister wanted to be "treated like a man" rather than a boy, and at 260 lbs (18 stone), he certainly looked the part. Accompanied by his twelve-year-old brother, he was originally planning on hitchhiking from Cleveland to Montana to look for a job, but then thought he would "pirate" an airplane. His brother Donald wisely decided at the last minute he wanted no part of the scheme, leaving Raymond to run out to the ramp where American Airlines flight 153 from New York to Mexico City was taking on passengers.

"This is my ticket," Raymond told the gate employee, waving the gun around, before boarding the aircraft. After telling the stewardess to leave the door open for his brother, Kunchenmeister asked her where the captain was, and then barged into the cockpit. He pointed the gun at Captain William F. Bonnell and demanded that he fly him to Mexico. Bonnell originally thought this was a practical joke by the cargo handlers, but once he realized that the boy was serious, Bonnell waited for his co-pilot to distract Kunchenmeister then grabbed a revolver from his flight kit and fired. The shot hit the boy in the hip, but Bonnell didn't think that it had "slowed him up much . . . He still pointed the gun and he looked like he meant business. Then I decided to fire a little higher." The second shot hit Kunchenmeister in the groin, and he died of his wounds shortly after.

Bonnell explained that he didn't know what else he could have done. "I had a maniac on my plane. We had women and children," he told reporters. What he could not have known was that Kunchenmeister's gun was unloaded. "I shot to protect myself and them," he added. "I feared he would kill the crew in flight."

HIGHWAY TO HAVANA

It did seem as if Kunchenmeister's attempted hijack was an isolated incident; however, after it became largely illegal for American citizens to travel to Cuba in January 1961, as part of incoming president John F. Kennedy's campaign against the country that would escalate with the disastrous Bay of Pigs incident and the Cuban Missile Crisis the following year, there were those who saw aircraft as the obvious way of reaching the country, even if the pilots weren't meant to be heading there.

On 1 May 1961, Antulio Ramirez Ortiz, a Miami electrician, boarded National Airlines Flight 337 that was meant to be going to Key West, using a ticket in the name of "Elpir Cofresi". As soon as the airplane was in flight, Ortiz entered the cockpit and held a steak knife to the throat of Captain Francis X. Riley and ordered him to fly to Cuba. This wasn't purely because he wanted to visit the country; according to Ortiz, he had been offered $100,000 to assassinate the country's leader, Fidel Castro, by the Dominican strongman Rafael Trujillo. He wasn't intending to carry out the mission: Ortiz was one of Castro's most fervent supporters (at least at that point), and wanted to warn him of the plot. "If I don't see Havana in thirty minutes," he told Riley, "we all die."

Riley, quite naturally, agreed to take Ortiz to Cuba, and, once they had realized that the aircraft wasn't the start of some form of American invasion (the idea of a hijack still being an alien concept), the Cuban air traffic controllers diverted the flight to a military base south of Havana, where Ortiz was taken off the airplane, along with his luggage, and the aircraft allowed to resume its normal course. It arrived in Key West only three hours late. Ortiz tired of life under Castro quite quickly, and tried to return to the United States; when he did manage to enter the US via Jamaica in 1975, he was arrested, and tried. Rejecting his call for leniency, US District Judge William O. Mehrtens said it was his crime and "the hijackings perpetrated by those who followed your example that caused Congress to pass the skyjacking statute", and passed the same sentence of twenty years' imprisonment which he gave to all skyjackers.

Another aircraft was hijacked and sent to Cuba two months later, on 24 July 1961. Wilfredo Roman Oquendo, a former member of the Cuban secret police under the regime of ex-President Carlos Prio Socarras, wanted to return to the land of his birth, and seized control of the Eastern Air Lines airplane, which was en route from Miami to Tampa, forcing the pilot, Captain William E. Buchanan, at gunpoint to change course to heading 210 degrees. They landed at Havana just ahead of an expected guest – the first Soviet cosmonaut, Yuri Gagarin. The thirty-two other passengers and the five crew on Flight 202 were released by Castro's government the following day, but Oquendo was detained. (According to the contemporary report in *Time* magazine, the New York Police Department and the FBI investigated a report that there were plans to hijack five airplanes and fly them to Cuba, with two gunmen on each flight; nothing further was heard of this.) Castro tried to negotiate for the release of the airplane, saying he would return it if the US similarly returned ten Cuban aircraft which had been used to bring people across to the States. The Secretary of State refused to discuss the matter, claiming it was a civil matter since those particular airplanes were being held against an unpaid bill – another fourteen aircraft had been returned – but in the end the Eastern Air Lines machine was exchanged for a gunboat used by three Cubans to emigrate to the States at the end of July.

This was the start of what became an unofficial policy between the countries that operated for the next decade, despite the laws against air piracy that would shortly be passed by the United States. In most cases during the 1960s, when aircraft were hijacked and taken to Cuba, the Cubans would put the passengers and crew in hotel accommodation overnight while another airplane was flown down to collect them. The hijacker would be permitted to stay in Cuba, and the crew would then fly the empty aircraft back to the US. The Cuban government in turn billed the airline involved for the costs. It reached a stage where aircrews were given route maps to Cuba, a plan of the airport at Havana and other useful items to help ensure that the hijackings went smoothly, with no loss of life or injury, and *Time* magazine published a tongue-in-cheek guide entitled "What to Do When The Hijacker Comes" in its December 1968 issue. During the first eleven months of the year, seventeen aircraft had been diverted to Cuba, and "a record of sorts was set last week when three jets carrying 238 people made forced landings in Havana within eight days", the article said.

A SURFEIT OF HIJACKINGS

Setting aside Raymond Kuchenmeister's fatal attempt to travel to Mexico, Bruce Britt Senior's actions on 31 July 1961 are usually referred to as the first hijacking of an aircraft on actual US soil. Britt was an engineer who had been working for some time on a gas-line project in Corning, California, and was angry because he believed he was owed a considerable sum in back wages. He planned to get the 1920 Pacific Airlines flight from Chico Airport to San Francisco, and from there somehow find a way to get back to Smackover, Arkansas, where his wife and son were waiting for him. Breaking speed restrictions as he drove to the airport – he was clocked at 120 mph at one point – Britt made the flight by the skin of his teeth.

However, he didn't have a ticket. Abandoning his car near the boarding gate, Britt rushed on to the DC-3, and sat down in a seat behind the cockpit. When ticketing agent William Hicks told Britt he needed a ticket, the engineer ignored him, but after Hicks repeated his comment and then began to walk away, Britt acted. Withdrawing a .38 calibre pistol from his overnight bag, he shot Hicks in the back, telling him, "This is my ticket." Hicks fell to the floor, and Britt's second bullet missed him, embedding itself in a bulkhead. (Britt later claimed he fired a third time, at one of the air hostesses, but this wasn't confirmed.) He then announced that he would shoot the passengers one at a time, beginning with San Francisco attorney J. Albert Hutchinson, whom he frightened with a shot fired over his head.

Britt then demanded access to the cockpit, which he was eventually given, and once within, he proceeded to threaten Captain Oscar Cleal, demanding to be taken to Arkansas. "Take off, or I'll take over," he said bluntly. Cleal did as requested, but when he told Britt that the cabin door had to be closed before take-off, the hijacker shot him in the head, leaving Cleal blinded for life.

In the ensuing confusion, co-pilot Alan Wheeler tackled Britt, and managed to get the gun from him. At this point, Britt pulled a knife, but three passengers, including attorney Hutchinson, helped to subdue him. As this was going on, Hicks was able to exit the plane, and crawl to call for help from the Butte County sheriff's office. Cleal and Hicks both survived; Cleal had to retire from flying, but spent many years advising on counter-measures against such terrorism. Britt pleaded guilty to three counts of attempted murder; he became eligible for parole in 1973. The incident was reported in the *Ohio County Times*, with its columnist Paul Harvey – a personal friend of Captain Cleal – coining the term "skyjacking".

Less than two days after Britt's foiled attempt came the skyjacking that started the process which led to the passing of the air piracy bill, as father and son Leon and Cody Bearden tried to head for Cuba. Continental Airlines Flight 54 was supposed to run from Los Angeles to Houston, with stops at Phoenix, El Paso and San Antonio, but on 3 August 1961, the Beardens had different plans – they were going to take the state of the art Boeing 707 to Cuba and present it to Fidel Castro as a gift in exchange for citizenship. (This came as news to Bearden's wife back home in Arizona, who told reporters that "her husband never mentioned Cuba, expressed no interest in airplanes, jet or otherwise, and didn't have any guns around the house".)

Twenty minutes before the plane was due to land at El Paso, the Beardens entered the cockpit behind two stewardesses, and Leon told Captain B. D. Rickards to alter course for Cuba, suggesting that there were two other gunmen besides himself and his son still within the passenger cabin. Rickards used a code word to warn El Paso air traffic control that they had been hijacked, then managed to persuade the older Bearden that there wasn't sufficient fuel on the 707 to make the trip to Havana non-stop. It made sense to refuel at El Paso, since they were so near.

As the 707 came in to El Paso, Leon Bearden made the stewardesses call for four volunteers to remain on board, as well as the six air crew: he maintained that the authorities might take chances with the lives of the sextet of airline workers, but would be less likely to risk civilians. One of the four who volunteered was Border Patrol agent Leonard Gilman; he was joined by Private First Class Truman H. Cleveland, Continental employee Jack Casey, and private citizen Luis L. Erives.

Once the other passengers were off, the ground staff began

refuelling the aircraft, but took their time over it. Leon Bearden abandoned his idea of handing over the 707, simply wanting to get to Cuba and begin a new life. He started to try to negotiate with Continental for a better aircraft – a DC-6; in conjunction with the FBI, the company offered a DC-7.

What the Beardens didn't realize was that President John F. Kennedy himself had taken an interest in events in El Paso, and had given a direct order that no deals were to be made with the hijackers. After some eight hours had passed, Cody Bearden – who Gilman later noted looked as if he was "itching to kill someone" – snapped suddenly and accused everyone of stalling. His father agreed and ordered Captain Rickards to take off. Rickards tried to do as he was ordered, but the Border Patrol officers who followed the 707 onto the runway had other ideas – a hail of rifle and submachine-gun bullets greeted the airplane, which came to a halt, with its landing gear and engine damaged, and with punctures to the pressurized cabin. Flight 54 was not going any further.

Shortly before 1 p.m., the rear door to the 707 opened, and the two stewardesses were released, followed a few minutes later by the four members of the crew. FBI agent in charge Francis Crosby entered the plane, and started trying to bring things to a peaceful conclusion with the two Beardens. Crosby and Leonard Gilman were able to communicate silently with their eyes, and the moment that Leon Bearden's eyes were off him, Gilman smashed him with a right cross, breaking his own hand in the process. Leon fell to the deck, blood spurting from his cheek. Cody looked at the commotion, allowing Crosby to overpower him. There was minor confusion when it wasn't clear initially that there had been only two hijackers, and not the four that Bearden had indicated – two innocent people were roughed up in the belief that they were part of the "pirates".

Interestingly, the FBI allowed some of their plans to be publicized in the immediate aftermath of the case, as some senators were calling for pilots and crews to be allowed to carry guns to help prevent hijacks. If the 707 had taken off, the Air Force would have been ordered to "shoot the nose off the plane".

Less than a week later, on 10 August, the president decreed that armed plainclothes border patrol officers would start flying on various flights, and that the cockpit doors on many would be kept bolted shut. The last straw was the attempt on 9 August by

Albert Charles Cadon to hijack Pan Am Flight 501 from Houston to Panama, via Mexico City and Guatemala City, and force the pilot to take it to Havana. All that the authorities could charge him with was crime on the high seas, assault with a dangerous weapon, and assault with intent to commit a felony.

The young Frenchman had boarded the plane during its stop-over in Mexico City and then once it had taken off, according to the contemporary reports, "Cadon – his pistol cocked and ready – rushed down the aisle from the back of the cabin, kicked open the door to the pilot's compartment, and went inside, closing the door behind him." There he claimed that he was an "extremist and a revolutionist" and claimed to crew members that he was hijacking the plane to protest United States policy in Algeria. (Tortured artist Cadon had a history of mental problems, and although he had joked about hijacking an airplane, no one, not even his wife, had believed that he might go ahead with it.) The crew managed to get a brief message out alerting the authorities to the hijacking, and American fighters made a vain attempt to intercept the flight before it reached Havana.

Once the aircraft was on the ground in Cuba, Cadon was removed, and the other passengers were speedily allowed to continue their journey – some prominent politicians were apparently on board, and it was in Castro's interests to keep them friendly – although it couldn't be quick enough for some. "There was no reason for Castro and his dirty-maned pirates to detain us those 8½ hours in Havana. The plane had fuel. The crew was ready and able to fly. But they put us all in a room – an air-conditioned room – and once in a while they would bring us some bum sandwiches," complained Richmond lawyer Hector Vioni.

Cuba refused America's requests to extradite Cadon; Mexico also applied for extradition, which was eventually granted three months later, and he was given a sentence of eight years, nine months there (considerably less than the thirty years he could have received, and much less than a US court would have given). The value of some paintings Cadon left behind in the States increased dramatically as a result of the publicity given to the skyjacking and in April 1963, Cadon wrote to some of his American contacts pleading for "the difference between what you paid for my paintings and what they are worth now"!

TERROR IN THE SKIES

At the end of the 1960s, the skyjacking phenomenon started to take on a nastier edge. Although there were still people who hankered after the delights of Havana – one used-car dealer from Baltimore was already wearing his Bermuda shorts and sandals when he hijacked an Eastern Airlines flight in 1969, so he could hit the beaches as soon as he arrived – skyjackings were being used to promote political causes.

One of the most publicized of these was the hijacking of El Al Flight 426 on Tuesday 23 July 1968 by members of the Popular Front for the Liberation of Palestine (PFLP) – the one and only time that the Israeli national airline was subject to a successful attempt. (Anyone who travelled with El Al prior to 9/11 will recall that their security measures were then regarded as highly restrictive but, equally, highly effective.) As *Time* magazine pointed out a couple of years later: "The blackmail precedent [was] set" by these events which led to skyjacking becoming "a Front specialty" ever since.

The PFLP was founded in 1967, an offshoot of the Arab Nationalist Movement, founded in 1953 by Dr George Habash, a Palestinian Christian who had been uprooted from his home of Lydda during the establishment of the Israeli state. Their goal was to "create a people's democratic Palestine, where Arabs and Jews would live without discrimination, a state without classes and national oppression, a state which allows Arabs and Jews to develop their national culture." This of course meant that Israel was their primary target – the state, rather than the people themselves, the PFLP maintained. However, according to Habash, looking back in 2006: "What happened in the 1967 War destroyed our dreams. We said that the world does not understand or know about the Palestinian problem. This is how the idea of hijacking planes came about. Let the whole world know about the crisis that happened to us."

The three well-dressed Arab passengers didn't attract any particular attention when they boarded the London Heathrow to Lod Airport flight via Rome. However, an hour after the aircraft had completed its Italian stopover, Ali Shafik Ahmed Taha, described as a "swarthy man who evidently had flying experience", entered the unlocked flight deck and hit the co-pilot, Maoz Poraz, with his pistol then ordered Captain Oded Abarbanel to change course and fly to Algiers. Meanwhile, in the cabin, the passengers were kept cowed by the sight of Yousef Khatib and the other unnamed hijacker waving pistols and hand grenades around. These weren't businessmen at all: they were highly trained Palestinian Arab commandos, working for the PFLP, who had been issued with Iranian and Indian passports to get them on board.

The aircraft was impounded as soon as it touched down at Dar-el-Beida Airport (now Houari Boumediene Airport). However, unlike previous hijackings, during which all the passengers were released bar the hijacker(s) who wanted to remain in the destination country (i.e. Cuba), this time those in charge only let some of the passengers go free. The non-Israelis were released, and were given a free sightseeing tour around Algiers by their reluctant hosts, and then sent to France on board Air Algérie Caravelle jets.

The other twelve passengers, along with the ten crew, were held, along with the aircraft. It was a game-changing move by the PFLP; they demanded the release of various terrorists held prisoner by the Israelis in exchange for the hostages. In a show of good faith, the ten women and children still on board were let go at the end of the week, and negotiations continued for five weeks, complicated by the political situation between Algeria and Israel – the Arab country had declared war on Israel in 1967, and had rejected the ceasefire agreement which brought the Six-Day War to a close; it also regarded El Al as a paramilitary organization rather than a civilian airline. Finally, sixteen convicted Arab terrorists were handed over "in gratitude" – not in exchange, it was emphasized – for the release of the hostages.

Hostage-taking wasn't the priority in the PFLP's next attack on El Al though: on 26 December 1968, Naheb H. Suleiman and Mahmoud Mohammed Issa Mohamad raced out of the transit lounge at Athens Airport, claiming to an El Al ground official that they had forgotten something on an Olympic Airlines aircraft nearby. However, they were armed with a submachine gun and hand grenades – as well as leaflets about their cause, which they threw in the air – and one of them opened fire at El Al Flight 253, a 707 which was taxiing in preparation for take-off for Paris and New York, killing marine engineer Leon Shirdan, and injuring two women as the bullets tore through the fuselage. The other terrorist threw two hand grenades at the engine on the right wing, which created panic among the passengers on board, as well as others on the ground. The captain ordered the passengers to get down and cover their heads as the bullets flew. The men were arrested, and apparently confessed that they had intended to destroy the jet and kill all the Israeli passengers. Mohammad was sentenced to seventeen years and five months' imprisonment.

However, skyjacking became the PFLP's standard way of operating, with the terrorist organization even going so far as releasing a fundraising stamp in the spring of 1970 to celebrate its successful skyjackings. This culminated in the events of September that year when the PFLP tried to stage a major coup with multiple simultaneous hijackings. As they pointed out: "The headlines have shown that our cause is now clearly publicized".

One of the key players was Leila Khaled, then twenty-six years old. She had come to prominence when she was responsible for the hijacking of TWA Flight 840 on 29 August 1969 along with Salim Issawi. The armed pair made their move as the flight from Rome to Israel overflew Brindisi, and by the time it was passing over the Corinth Canal, the captain had informed the passengers that there was an emergency but there was "no need to worry".

According to one of the passengers, Thomas D. Boyatt, who cabled an account of the incident to the Foreign Service Journal two days after the hijacking, Khaled then announced the aircraft had been seized by the "Che Guevara Brigade of the Palestinian Liberation Movement because a Zionist assassin was on board." (This was interpreted later as a reference to Israeli general Yitzhak Rabin; Khaled claimed that she was unaware that he was their target – as events transpired, Rabin had changed planes in Rome onto an El Al flight.) Both hijackers assured the passengers that they were not the enemy and that they were in no danger; the aircraft, meanwhile, flew to the newly completed Damascus International Airport in Syria, after first circling Tel Aviv, where fighters ensured it didn't try to land – although Khaled had only asked the pilot to head for there so she could see what used to be Palestine for the first time since she had been forced to leave as a small child.

Once the 707 was on the ground, the passengers used the emergency evacuation procedure, with a few sustaining slight injuries as they tried to get away from the aircraft – Khaled had warned them that the aircraft would explode shortly after touch-down. Issawi tried to make the fuel supply ignite by firing his pistol at the 707, with Boyatt commenting: "Had he been success-ful, he would have blown himself up, I think. This was a prospect which many of us viewed with less than normal concern." But then the front of the aircraft "disintegrated in a puff of smoke followed by a large explosion." According to the Aviation Safety Network report: "One hijacker threw hand grenades and another explosive device into the cockpit, destroying the front of the plane." It was later rebuilt. Khaled later recalled that the fuse on the dynamite they used failed to go off, so Issawi went back in to reignite it.

The majority of the passengers were released by the Syrians the next day. Six Israeli passengers were detained by the Syrians; the four women were released on 1 September, the two men a few months later after some tense negotiations between Israel and Syria (who, it seems, simply took advantage of the situation to gain some concessions from the Israeli government). Israel released thirteen prisoners to Syria and fifty detainees to the UAR, in exchange for two Israeli pilots and the hostages.

The hijackers were imprisoned by the Syrians for forty-five days, and released in October. Khaled was photographed in Jordan that month, smiling broadly as she brandished her weapon – as a result, she needed to have extensive plastic surgery, since the image was distributed worldwide. "The surgeon just made a few differences to my nose and my chin," she recalled. "But it worked. No one recognized me." She also wrote to a number of the passengers from Flight 840, explaining to them that the PFLP were striking at America's Middle East policy and that the hijack "was not meant against them personally".

Over the coming months the PFLP carried out various attacks on aircraft, for some reason focusing particularly on Athens Airport. On 21 December 1969, Maha Abu Khalil, Sami Aboud and Isam Doumidi intended to hijack a TWA Boeing 707 bound for Paris and New York, fly it to Tunis, and then blow it up as a protest against America's support for Israel. Unfortunately for them, they were caught with two guns and three hand grenades in their hand luggage, and they were arrested. Doumidi made a full confession to the authorities.

The PFLP were held responsible for the bombing of Swissair Flight 330 (see page 363) on 21 February 1970, and this was followed by a third incident involving Athens Airport on 22 July 1970. Six commandos from the PFLP held forty-seven people hostage on an Olympic Airways jet bound there from Beirut (where cleaners had smuggled the weapons on board for the hijackers), demanding the release of seven people being held by the Greek government including the three prospective hijackers from the previous December, and others who had been responsible for attacks on the El Al office in Athens during which two people died. The passengers were freed once the seven prisoners were released.

HOSTAGE SUNDAY

Although they had caused considerable international unrest, the previous hijackings and attacks on aircraft were simply the appetizers for the PFLP's main event, which took place on what came to be known as "Hostage Sunday", 6 September 1970. Three decades later, many commentators were amazed that Osama bin Laden could come up with the idea of simultaneously hijacking planes for the 9/11 plot; in fact, if they had chosen to look back at the history of the Middle East, it was nothing new. PFLP leader Dr Habash and his top lieutenant, Dr Wadi Haddad, devised a similar plan in July 1970 – although, unlike bin Laden, they did not intend to use the airplanes as mobile weapons of mass destruction. The main goal of their operation, as their spokesman Bassam Abu Sharif later explained, was "to gain the release of all of our political prisoners jailed in Israel in exchange for the hostages".

All the flights were bound for New York, from as far afield as Amsterdam, Zurich and Frankfurt. However, much as they had worked out the complexities of the hijack itself, it became increasingly clear that the PFLP didn't really know exactly what to do next – they were willing to hold hostages, but, at that stage, it seemed as if they lacked the will to kill people to get their way. A threat, after all, can only work if both the person making the threat and the person threatened are sure that it will be carried out.

Problems arose for the hijackers right from the start. Leila Khaled was one of a team of four assigned to take over El Al Flight 219 from Amsterdam; she and Nicaraguan-American Patrick Arguello were allowed to board the flight. The two others, travelling on Senegalese passports under the names Diop and Gueye, were not permitted to travel by El Al security: their passports had consecutive serial numbers, and while they had booked seats in first class, they had come in at the last minute to pick them up. El Al were suspicious of Khaled and Arguello, and Khaled recalled that they underwent extensive questioning before

they were given the okay to fly. Although they were officially transit passengers, having flown in from Germany, their bags were
removed from the aircraft and searched – but no one thought to
ask the pair to empty their pockets. "I had two grenades and
Patrick had a pistol and a grenade," Khaled explained.

Perhaps as compensation for the inconvenience, the two
hijackers were given good seats near the front of the economy
section. Half an hour after take-off, as the 707 was almost at
cruising height, they made their move, showing everyone in
economy their grenades, and removing the pins from the bombs
with their teeth to show that they were armed. The purser sent
one of the flight attendants, Michal Adar, to investigate the
screams that ensued, and as he entered first class, he saw Khaled
and Arguello running towards them. Shots were being fired at
the hijackers by undercover Israeli security officers, but Khaled
ignored them, and told the flight attendants to get the door to
the cockpit open.

Captain Uri Bar Lev had no intention of letting the hijackers
in. When the purser told him over the intercom that the hijackers
were threatening to blow the jet up if they weren't allowed to enter
the cockpit, he instantly came up with a plan. "The security guy
was sitting here ready to jump," he later recalled. "I told him that
I was going to put the plane into negative-G mode. Everyone
would fall. When you put the plane into negative, it's like being in
a falling elevator. Instead of the plane flying this way, it dives and
everyone who is standing falls down."

As the pilot began the manoeuvre, Khaled was thrown off
balance, and several of the passengers pounced on her, bringing
her to the ground, and used neckties to tie her up. Arguello threw
his grenade down the aisle, but it failed to detonate. He was hit
over the head with a bottle of whisky by one of the passengers,
and then one of the stewards, Shlomo Vider, and an Israeli security agent in the first-class cabin tried to get possession of his gun.
Arguello was able to shoot Vider in the stomach before witnesses
to the increasingly desperate struggle heard a soft popping sound
– the security agent's own weapon discharging. Arguello was
mortally wounded. (Khaled's version of events is rather different:
according to her, the armed guards began shooting at them,
hitting Arguello four times in the back before he was hit with the

whisky bottle. She was knocked unconscious and came round to find herself being tied up and kicked.)

Captain Lev brought the aircraft in for an emergency landing at London Heathrow, and the two shot men were taken to Hillingdon hospital by ambulance; Vider recovered from his wounds after surgery, Arguello died on the way. Khaled was arrested, and after being treated in hospital, was taken to West Drayton police station before being transferred to Ealing police station.

The first part of the plan was a spectacular failure, but the PFLP had more than one objective that day. The hijackers who were charged with taking control of TWA Flight 741, carrying 149 passengers and ten crew, were considerably more successful. The flight from Frankfurt had taken off as scheduled at 11.45 a.m., and shortly after Captain Carroll D. Woods had announced that they were passing over Brussels, there was a commotion in the economy (coach) cabin. A man and a woman were running through the cabin, the man holding a hand grenade in his left hand, a revolver in his right; the woman had two hand grenades. Stewardess Bettie McCarthy came out of the galley, to face the pair, who were in their late twenties or early thirties, according to eyewitnesses. Purser Rudi Swinkels was behind them, but when they noticed him, the man waved his gun at him and told him to get back. Swinkels dived behind the bulkhead separating first class from economy.

McCarthy was ordered to let the hijackers into the cockpit, and knocked on the door. Flight engineer Al Kiburis opened it – and as McCarthy tried to warn him it was a hijacking, the two PFLP terrorists forced their way past her. The man told co-pilot Jim Majer to turn the airplane around. The rest of the crew put their hands up, as the captain explained that they would need to change altitude and advise Brussels air traffic control of their plans. The hijacker agreed, insisting that from now on the 707 was referred to as "Gaza Strip" (or "Gaza 1"). The new heading – Jordan. As they flew across West Germany, US Air Force fighter craft accompanied them, but were powerless to intervene.

At the same time, the PFLP took control of a third aircraft, Swissair Flight 100, a DC-8 with a similar number of passengers and crew under Captain Fritz Schreiber on board. The flight was on its way from Zurich when French air traffic controllers received the surprising announcement from a female voice that "Swissair Flight 100 is in our complete control. Our call sign is Haifa 1. We will not answer to any other code."

As news of the skyjackings spread around the world, US President Richard M. Nixon cut short his Labor Day weekend in California to return to Washington DC to take control of the situation. There were many considerations for the Americans: they were allied with Israel, but the Soviet Union was supporting their Arab enemies. This was also at the height of the Vietnam conflict, and Nixon and his National Security Advisor, Henry Kissinger, were determined that the Middle East would not become another proxy battleground between the superpowers. And, of course, because the aircraft that had been hijacked were heading for New York, there was a rather larger domestic problem: there was a large number of Americans were directly involved.

As far as the PFLP were concerned, the hijackings themselves had certainly brought the situation in Palestine to the attention of many people who would not otherwise have heard about the conflict in the Middle East.

Even before the hijacked aircraft arrived in Jordan, there was a further twist to the situation. The two hijackers who had not been allowed on board the El Al flight decided to use their initiative, so purchased tickets for the Pan Am 747 flight from Brussels to New York via Amsterdam. They were nearly foiled again – a message reached the 747 shortly before take-off, warning the captain about the two suspicious passengers. Captain Jack Priddy got flight director John Ferruggio to locate the pair, and then he came down to the cabin, and personally searched them. "They seemed like nice fellas," Priddy said a few days later. "I'm no professional, but I went over their bodies and hand luggage fairly closely." However, Diop and Gueye had guessed that they might be searched, and before Priddy or Ferruggio approached them, they had secreted their weapons under their seats; one of them also had a Styrofoam pouch around his groin in which he apparently kept the grenades.

As soon as Pan Am 93 reached 28,000 feet, the two men got to their feet, headed for the cockpit, and instructed Priddy to head for Beirut – whose airport at that time wasn't rated for 747s.

Despite pleas from the air traffic controllers for the hijackers to reconsider, they refused, and forced Priddy to make what turned out to be a successful landing. However, once they got there, no one in the PFLP knew quite what to do: Diop and Gueye hadn't realized that a 747 would be unable to land at the makeshift airport in the desert which awaited the other aircraft, and so, a new plan was devised.

Guerrilla demolition experts came on board the 747; one of them remained after refuelling was completed to wire up explosive charges in the cabin and in the toilets as the flight headed for its new destination, Cairo. The PFLP were not impressed with President Nasser's involvement with the ongoing Middle East negotiations, and decided to blow the jet up in his country's capital to make their displeasure abundantly clear.

As the 747 started its final descent into Cairo, after circling to allow the hijackers to confirm visually that this was indeed Egypt, the bomber asked the stewardess for some matches, which she provided, although she cautioned him that smoking wasn't permitted during final approach. He waited until the 747 was a hundred feet above the ground – then lit the fuse to the explosives. Smelling this, John Ferruggio promptly informed the attendants to prepare to evacuate the aircraft the moment it came to a complete stop. This they did, activating the emergency slides so passengers could slide down. Unaware of the imminent destruction of the aircraft, Captain Priddy moved the 747 forward a few yards, which caused injuries to some of the passengers caught on the slides. While the jet was hastily being evacuated, one of the hijackers politely informed Priddy that he had two minutes to get out. As it was, everyone escaped from the aircraft in less than ninety seconds – the fastest time Ferruggio had ever heard of, as he admitted at a news conference later that day.

"We were probably no more than forty or fifty, sixty feet away from the airplane and the entire cockpit blew off," co-pilot Pat Lavix recalled. "When I looked up at the nose of the airplane, it was gone, and I could see the captain's seat was sitting on the floor all by itself." As stewardess Nellie Beckhans recalled: "It was a happy moment when we heard everyone got off the airplane. We lost our possessions and our shoes but we were alive and safe."

Egyptian authorities arrested the two hijackers, although there was some delay in bringing charges against them.

The two hijacked airplanes, the TWA and Swissair flights now renamed Gaza 1 and Haifa 1, were heading for Jordan as instructed – specifically, to Revolution Airport, the name the PFLP had given to a former RAF airstrip in the middle of the desert (originally known during the British occupation as Dawson's Field). It was so new that not even the PFLP's spokesman knew about it and had to be told that it wasn't actually an airport, but an area in the desert. According to PFLP member Abu Samir, the leadership had been told that the strip could support anything that landed on it – even the Devil. They filled 200 barrels with sand and soaked rags with diesel so they could mark the land for the pilots – and those, plus headlights from the Jeep, were all that Captain Wood had to bring the TWA jet in, since of course there were no ground navigational aids or air traffic control to assist. Slightly to his surprise – and everyone's relief – the ground held, and the captain switched off the engines for the final time, as the 707 was surrounded by dozens of heavily armed PFLP fighters.

Less than an hour later, Haifa 1 was also on the ground, barely 50 yards from the TWA aircraft – Captain Schreiber had to hit the brakes hard when he landed, applying full reverse thrust on the engines to avoid hitting the other airplane. This sent a cloud of dust and sand into his plane's ventilation system, and many passengers desperately tried to escape from the aircraft, believing that it was on fire. They were herded back to the aircraft, and as the temperature dropped, the PFLP started to wire detonators to large lumps of plastic explosives under the seats of the airplanes.

The next morning, yet a further complication arose. Although the PFLP guerrillas were surrounding the aircraft and guarding their hostages, they discovered they were in their turn surrounded by tanks from the Royal Jordanian Army. The political situation within Jordan was precarious: King Hussein was still nominally in charge of the country, but the Palestinians increasingly were in control – diplomat William Quandt recalled that at that time, he needed a Palestinian escort if he wanted to travel around the capital Amman, since the Palestine Liberation Organization (PLO) had roadblocks everywhere. This added an extra wrinkle to the situation for the Americans – Hussein's pro-American government was on the verge of collapse, and the hostage situation at Revolution Airport was exacerbating the situation.

The PFLP made their first demands that morning, after calling a press conference and bringing journalists in from Amman. They would blow up the airplanes with the passengers on board, unless Leila Khaled and a host of other Palestinian militants imprisoned in Israel and around Europe were freed within seventy-two hours. The passengers' passports were checked, and the PFLP bussed 127 women, children and old people to Amman. No Jews or Israelis were allowed to leave, though, which for many brought back memories of the holocaust, particularly when they heard they were being kept back for "interrogation". Six Jewish men – including three US government employees and two rabbis – were also taken to a safe location 100 miles away from Revolution Airport; this meant the PFLP would still have hostages in case the Israelis mounted a rescue operation. Those sent to Amman unfortunately arrived at a time when street fighting between the Palestinians and the Jordanian Army was having one of its sporadic high points, leaving some believing that they would almost have been safer waiting at the "airport".

The following day, 8 September, negotiations began, under the auspices of the Red Cross, who most of the countries involved authorized to act on their behalf; the major sticking point, though, was that the Israelis categorically refused to have any part in the discussions. They did not negotiate with terrorists. "We wanted to fight them, and thought that we were winning," Israeli Minister of Police Shlomo Hillel explained later. "We knew that giving in to terrorists only encourages them. There is nothing easier than to capture an unprotected non-Israeli plane, hijack it to a remote place and then demand that Israel release its prisoners."

In Washington, President Nixon mooted the idea of bombing the airport but Secretary of Defence Melvin Laird, not wanting to drag America into yet another war, played for time, claiming that the weather conditions weren't favourable. Nixon dropped the idea. American forces were put on alert for a possible strike, with the 82nd Airborne Division and the Sixth Fleet both brought to operational readiness. On the ground, conditions were worsening, as the sanitation tanks filled to overflowing, and the kitchens the PFLP had set up became unable to cope with the demands.

The situation developed dramatically on 9 September. As the Red Cross managed to get an extension to the deadline (partly because their negotiator was trapped in his hotel in Amman and unable to get out to the airport to do his job!), the PFLP brought a third aircraft into the equation. A London-bound BOAC Vickers VC-10, Flight 775 from Bombay, was hijacked and brought to Revolution Airport, adding a further 105 passengers and ten crew to the hostages.

This put increasing pressure on the British, in particular, to capitulate – they were holding Khaled, and refusing to let her go. At a cabinet meeting that day, the pros and cons were discussed:

"Advantages: We should get her out of our area of responsibility and should be seen to have fulfilled the PFLP demands thereby saving the lives of the United Kingdom Nationals.

"Disadvantages: The pilots and the airlines share the view that there should be no capitulation to blackmail.

"We should also be throwing overboard our previously declared attitude on hijacking and should lose all credibility in international civil aviation circles. We should also be in breach of the Tokyo Convention of 1963."

Peter Tripp of the British Foreign Office's Near-East Department at the time spoke to a BBC documentary thirty years later, when the papers quoted above were revealed: "There was a price to be paid in letting [Khaled] go, we would have to abandon or at least compromise our own principles. But when the chips are down, do you sacrifice the lives of forty or fifty passengers in an aircraft for one terrorist woman? The answer in our book was, no you don't."

Negotiations were not helped by the absence of the PFLP leader Dr Habash – in North Korea on a "shopping trip" – and the consequent mixed messages coming from the Palestinians. There were attempts to barter the release of the non-Jewish hostages separately on Thursday 10 September, but these discussions came to nothing.

The next day, rumours started spreading among the PFLP guerrillas that either the Americans or the Israelis were planning military action – something that was indeed under consideration. The PFLP panicked, starting to wire the wings of the airplanes with explosives, and turning back Red Cross convoys that for the previous couple of days had been bringing in supplies that had made the hostages' lives marginally more bearable. The PLFP demanded that Red Cross negotiators confirm that there were no plans underway by any of the five nations whose hostages remained on site – the UK, USA, West Germany, Switzerland and Israel – to make a pre-emptive strike. They did so, although Israeli Deputy Premier Yigal Allon said, "I would not suggest speaking about military measures at this moment. We must wait and see what will happen."

Other players in the Palestinian power struggle wanted involvement – the PLO felt that the PFLP were out of their depth, and that they were starting to cause more harm to the Palestinian cause than good with their actions. The PLO intervention had a positive effect for a lot of the hijack victims – those being held in Amman were released, and bussed out of the country, and it was agreed that many of the others, still at the airport, would also be set free if the prisoners held in Europe were released. The PLO, controlled by Yasser Arafat, also felt that only Israelis with "military capability" would be kept, in an attempt to force a deal with Israel over Arab prisoners held there.

In the early evening of 12 September, the airplanes were completely evacuated, and once everyone was clear, all three were blown up. This wasn't the end of the hostages' ordeal; as per the PLO plan, they were then separated, with the Jewish passengers and the male crew members taken one way, and the other passengers heading to Amman. Those being kept for further "interrogation" were now being deemed political prisoners; the others awaited the results of the negotiations with the Western countries. These were getting increasingly tense, with the British ambassador warning on 13 September: "Some of the more irresponsible and violent PFLP have got the idea that we are not going to release Leila Khaled. They have told us through an intermediary that if we do not within a few hours at least give an assurance that we are prepared to do so, something very serious will happen. These people are quite capable of killing hostages."

British Prime Minister Edward Heath – who had only come

into office three months earlier – felt there was no option but to make a unilateral agreement with the PFLP, particularly since the Americans weren't prepared to put pressure on their "obdurate" allies, the Israelis, to negotiate. At 7 p.m. on 13 September, the British government announced on the BBC World Service that they would swap Khaled for the hostages. While this delighted the PFLP, it infuriated the Americans. "It was a good step for us that we saw governments could be negotiated with. We could impose our demands," Khaled later recalled. "The success in the tactics of the hijacking and imposing our demands and succeeding in having our demands implemented gave us the courage and the confidence to go ahead with our struggle."

Once the British had given in, it was only a matter of time before the other European nations did similarly, with both Switzerland and West Germany reaching deals over the next ten days. The hostages, meanwhile, were caught up in the increasingly open warfare between the Jordanians and the Palestinians, which was escalated by King Hussein's decision to declare martial law. The troops' activities against the Palestinians earned the period the description "Black September", the catalyst for the creation of the terrorist group by that name which was responsible for the massacre at the Munich Olympics in 1972.

Israel continued to hold firm, despite the deals made by the other nations, and eventually, the Palestinians released all the hostages in return for Khaled and six other terrorists held in European prisons. None of the hijackers was caught. By 28 September, the crisis was over.

OPERATION THUNDERBOLT

Although many of the PFLP felt that hijacking had served its purpose, including its founder Dr George Habash, it was still one of the weapons in their arsenal, as the PFLP's Special Action Group (PFLP-SOG) proved six years after the events at Dawson's Field when they took control of Air France Flight 139 – once again thanks to the lax security at Athens Airport.

The Airbus A300, staffed by twelve crew members headed by Captain Michel Bacos, was heading from Tel Aviv to Paris on Sunday 27 June 1976 and had just stopped over at Athens where fifty-eight additional passengers joined, making a total of 246 on board. These included Fayez Abdul-Rahim Jaber and Jayel Naji al-Arjam, two senior members of the PFLP-SOG, and two West Germans, Wilfried Bose and Brigitte Kuhlmann, both members of the terrorist group *Revolutionäre Zellen*. No one had been staffing the metal detector at Athens Airport, and the hand baggage X-ray machine might as well have been unmanned for all the attention its operator was paying to it. These lapses allowed the four terrorists to bring guns and hand grenades on board.

Captain Bacos received the distinction of being the first Air France pilot to have to submit to the demands of terrorists when the four made their move, about seven minutes after take-off, as soon as the passengers were allowed to remove their seat belts. Kuhlmann stood up, clutching two hand grenades, and took control of the first-class cabin, while Jaber and al-Arjam threatened the passengers in economy, whose screaming alerted the crew to the situation. When flight engineer Jacques Le Moine opened the cockpit door, he was faced by Bose carrying a pistol and a hand grenade. Pointing his gun at Bacos' head, he ordered the pilot to head for Benghazi in Libya.

Kuhlmann then made an announcement on the Airbus's intercom, informing passengers that the flight was under the control of the Che Guevara Group and Gaza Unit of the PFLP, and that henceforward it would be known as Haifa 1. The passengers were then treated brutally if they showed any signs of resistance as the hijackers took their identity papers for checking. One French oil executive was heard to moan: "My God! This is my second skyjacking. I can't survive another one." At least one member of the Israeli reserve armed forces destroyed his military ID before the hijackers could take it.

The flight landed in Benghazi shortly before 1500, and the PFLP negotiated for refuelling. During the seven hours spent in the blazing heat, one of the passengers, Patricia Martel pretended to be pregnant, and cut herself severely, claiming that she had just suffered a miscarriage. Her ploy was successful: after she was examined by a Libyan doctor, she was allowed to leave the aircraft. The information which she was able to pass on after she was questioned by Scotland Yard detectives on her arrival back in Britain was invaluable, particularly for the Israelis. They had been made aware of the hijack almost immediately, and were anxious to find out what they could. They had initially believed the Airbus would be brought back to Tel Aviv, but when it became clear that it was heading south into the heart of the African continent, they began to make alternate plans.

Haifa 1 landed at Entebbe Airport in Uganda at 0315 on 28 June, with just 20 minutes of fuel remaining in the tanks. At the time, the central African country was ruled by the pro-Palestinian and anti-Israel despot Idi Amin. After he expelled the Israelis from his country for refusing to sell him Phantom jets, Amin offered their embassy building to the PLO to use as a headquarters. He welcomed the PFLP-SOG hijackers, and his army effectively acted as a back-up force for the terrorists. After nine hours on the tarmac, the Airbus was moved to the Old Terminal at the airport, and the passengers and crew were allowed to disembark.

At this point, the hijackers were joined by four further comrades, who helped them to separate the Jews and the Israelis from the others – one young Jew, Jean-Jacques Maimoni, had a French passport, and could easily have joined the Gentile group, but he was definite about being "an Israeli and a Jew". Had he not done so, chances are he would have seen his twentieth birthday rather than becoming one of the four victims of the crisis.

The hijackers then made their demands known on Radio Uganda. Forty Palestinians held in Israel and thirteen others, held in Kenya, France, Switzerland and West Germany, were to be freed by Thursday 1 July at 2 p.m. These included a Melchite Catholic Archbishop who had been gunrunning for the Palestinians; Kozo Okamoto, the only survivor of the three Japanese Red Army members who massacred twenty-seven people in 1972 at Tel Aviv's Lod Airport; and six members of the Baader-Meinhof gang. If this didn't happen, they would start to kill the hostages. International condemnation followed – some of it from surprising sources, including the PFLP's own headquarters in Beirut, and the Arab League in Cairo.

Idi Amin happily showed his support for the hijackers and their desire for a free Palestine, visiting the Old Terminal and addressing the hostages. Shortly after that, the hijackers agreed that the non-Jews and non-Israelis could be freed; an Air France aircraft was sent to collect them. Captain Bacos and his crew were released by the hijackers, but Bacos refused to leave. He made it clear that as far as he was concerned, all the passengers were his responsibility, and he would not leave them "no matter what happens", and his crew followed his example. A French nun who tried to offer her place to one of the Jewish hostages was not allowed to do so and was forced to go on the aircraft.

The freed hostages were flown back to Europe, where they were closely questioned by members of the Israeli special forces, who were preparing to carry out a military strike on Entebbe Airport. One of the released passengers was a Jewish French officer, who had a very detailed memory, and was able to provide accurate descriptions of the disposition of the hostages and the hijackers. By pure chance, the terminal in which the hostages were being held had been designed by an Israeli contractor, who still retained the blueprints. From everything that they learned, the Israelis realized that the only way to free the hostages was a full assault – more stealthy options had been considered but in the light of this information, were clearly not going to be viable. Lieutenant-Colonel Yonatan Netanyahu, Major Muki Betzer, Major General Dan Shomron and Intelligence Officer Colonel Ehud Barak of the Israeli Defence Force (IDF) continued to pull together a plan – which some of the soldiers would later joke sounded more like a script for the popular TV series *Mission: Impossible* than a sane and sensible plan of campaign.

The Israeli government had been in constant discussions about the situation at the highest level with Amin, and stroking his ego in an effort to get him on side, but it became clear that he would not intervene on the Israelis' behalf with the hostages, and that the PFLP-SOG were serious about their threat: indeed, it appeared that if their demands weren't met in full, all the hostages would be killed. Therefore, with the deadline rapidly approaching, the Israeli cabinet very reluctantly agreed to open negotiations with the PFLP-SOG.

Although the hijackers had called for the release of the hostages by their deadline, the surprising news that the Israelis were changing their stance encouraged Amin to tell them to extend the deadline by a further seventy-two hours, to 2 p.m. on Sunday 4 July. According to the Israelis, Amin also took the opportunity to try to line his own pockets, adding to the Israelis' concerns that even if they went ahead with the release of the terrorists from prison, the hostages wouldn't be freed. Israeli Defence Minister Shimon Peres told *Time* magazine: "Amin not only took the terrorists' side and allowed local Palestinians into Entebbe to help the skyjackers, he also sent a special plane to Somalia to bring in more terrorists to guard the hostages. We had more than a feeling that even if we decided to accept all the demands of the terrorists we would have no insurance that our people would be allowed to return home. From the military point of view, it was the greatest risk we ever took."

Dry runs of the planned military option, originally known as Operation Stanley, but later changed to Operation Thunderbolt, were carried out on 2 July, and negotiations made for the four Hercules aircraft carrying the Israeli troops to refuel in Kenya on the journey back. The plan was for the Israelis to masquerade as a convoy of soldiers travelling behind President Amin – in his trademark black Mercedes – which would allow them to get into the airport without arousing suspicion. There, they could overwhelm the terrorists, despite the presence of the Ugandan army forces. A Mercedes had been found – and repainted black – and was going to be started a few minutes before the Hercules it was on touched down: its starter was too unreliable otherwise, and without it there would be no plan.

The aircraft took off on the afternoon of 3 July, before the final go-ahead had been given by the cabinet: only once the soldiers were in the air were full details given to the politicians, and the assent provided. Three Hercules were filled with troops, one was ready to transport the hostages back. Two 707s followed behind, one a mobile command post, the other a mobile hospital. They flew mere metres above the Red Sea to ensure that they weren't detected by Egyptian or Saudi radar and arrived in Entebbe at 11 p.m.

They say that no battle plan survives contact with the enemy, and it was true of Operation Thunderbolt – perhaps because Amin had not been using his Mercedes to visit the airport, Ugandan guards stopped the convoy and had to be shot, destroying the element of surprise. Yonatan Netanyahu was mortally wounded during the assault, and three of the hostages died – Jean-Jacques Maimoni, because he stood up and the IDF soldiers instinctively assumed he was a hijacker, and Pasco Cohen and Ida Borochovitch were killed in the crossfire. According to one of the hostages, Wilfied Bose had the opportunity to kill his prisoners when the raid began, but didn't do so, and in fact told them to take shelter in the rest room. Bose and the other hijackers were all killed.

After a firefight with Ugandan soldiers as they transported the hostages to the Hercules ("I think I'm the only soldier in the history of the IDF who carried a half-naked beauty in red underwear over his shoulder while running from bullets," Sergeant-Major Amir Ofer later commented), the Israelis withdrew, shooting at the Ugandan Air Force's MiG fighters to ensure they weren't used to follow them. All bar four of the hostages were returned to Israel the next day.

One hostage had been removed to hospital in Kampala; a day after the raid, seventy-five-year-old Dora Bloch was dragged from her bed and shot on President Amin's orders. The Ugandan president tried to get the United Nations to censure Israel's actions (the *Voice of Uganda* official paper ran a banner headline: "Israelis invade Entebbe"); although there was a debate about the issue, there was no official condemnation. As Israeli Foreign Minister Yigal Allon pointed out: "The terror is not directed only against Israel. Each country can find itself in a position where a minority group starts terror operations. If we do not unite against this kind of violence, we could lose our chance to survive as human beings."

As a result of his actions, Captain Bacos was awarded the Legion of Honour; the rest of the crew received the Order of Merit from a grateful French government. (Bacos was, however, not so popular with his Air France employers.)

The Greek government were stung by the criticisms of Athens Airport security: "We have strengthened security measures, which were already very strict," he claimed. "Now we have covered all our weak points. It is not true that transiting travellers were not being checked on entering the transit lounge, but in any case we are now checking everyone." As events would prove, this wasn't necessarily the case.

INVADING MOGADISHU

A year after the Entebbe raid, another commando force released hostages held by the PFLP, this time at the Somali airport of Mogadishu. The West German counterterrorism group, GSG9, had been set up following the disastrous events at the Munich Olympics in 1972, and sprang into action once Lufthansa Flight 181 reached its final destination. Unlike the Israeli raid at Entebbe, all the hostages were retrieved alive – although Captain Jurgen Schumann had been shot and killed.

The hijack of Flight 181 was linked to another terrorist operation underway at the same time – the kidnapping and ransom of Dr Hanns-Martin Schleyer, who was simultaneously president of both the Confederation of German Employers' Associations and the Federation of German Industries. Schleyer was captured on 5 September 1977 by members of the Red Army Faction who wanted to negotiate the release of eleven members of the Baader-Meinhof Gang (its predecessor). The Red Army had strong links with the PFLP – their members were trained by PFLP leader Wadi Hadad at a camp in South Yemen – as well as many other terrorist organizations around the world. However, negotiations were not going as speedily as the Red Army wanted; the West German government refused to knuckle under and release the terrorists, or provide them with the large sums of money that they demanded.

The Red Army leadership realized that more pressure would need to be applied to the West German government, so they took advantage of the lax security at Palma de Mallorca Airport. Four members of the PFLP – who had more experience with hijacking, despite the, for them, bad outcome of the Entebbe mission – were assigned to the hijack: Zohair Youssif Akache, who used the alias Captain Martyr (or Walter) Mahmud throughout the operation; his fiancée Hind Alameh (aka Shanaz Gholoun); Suhaila Sayeh (aka Soraya Ansari); and Wabil Harb (alias Riza Abbasi), all in their early twenties. Akache was believed responsible for three murders in London earlier in 1977, and had learned to fly a Cessna aircraft – meaning that the aircrew would probably not be able to fool him as easily if they tried any tricks regarding the 737's capacities.

On 13 October 1977, five weeks after Schleyer's kidnapping, the hijackers boarded the Boeing 737 heading for Frankfurt, using fake Iranian and Dutch passports. The quartet waited until the flight was half an hour or so out of Palma before moving into action. Stating that they were part of Commando Martyr Halime, they took over the aircraft, sending the co-pilot Jürgen Vietor to join the passengers, and ordering Captain Schumann to fly to Nicosia. The 737 didn't have sufficient fuel to reach the Cyprus airport, so permission was given to refuel in Rome. Although the West Germans hoped to persuade the Italian government to intervene, and prevent the jet from leaving, the Italians were happier for it to go, and they didn't object when it took off without clearance, heading for Cyprus.

While the 737 was being refuelled, the hijackers released their demands, which were copied to *The Times* in London (although they didn't receive it until after the hijack was over). The ultimatum specifically linked the hijack to the kidnapping of Hanns-Martin Schleyer, and repeated many of the same demands – including the release of eleven Red Army prisoners, with each given DM100,000 – but also demanded the release of two PFLP prisoners held in Istanbul, and a ransom of $15m. The prisoners were to be sent to Vietnam, Somalia or Yemen and the ransom paid by 17 October at 8 a.m. GMT, or the eighty-six passengers and crew on Flight 181 and Schleyer would be killed immediately.

The refuelled aircraft took off for Cyprus, but was warned not to approach Nicosia; instead, it landed at Larnaca. Mahmud again demanded that the authorities refuel the 737 or he would blow it up. Mahmud refused to enter into any discussions with either the Cypriot foreign minister, who asked them to release the women, children and the sick, or the local PLO representative, who gave up after being abused by Mahmud.

The West German government put GSG9 on standby, and thirty commandos headed for Cyprus, ironically landing at Larnaca just as Flight 181 was taking off; while the German border protection force group flew to Ankara to await instructions, Flight 181 began a tour of the Mediterranean. Mahmud wanted to go to Beirut, but the airport was closed to them; the same happened at Damascus, Baghdad and Kuwait, so Schumann was ordered to fly to Bahrain, despite information that the airport was closed.

Troops surrounded the 737 when it eventually landed at Bahrain but backed off after Mahmud threatened to shoot the co-pilot. Flight 181 was refuelled once more and took off for Dubai. Despite attempts by the authorities there to block the runway and prevent the airplane from landing, Schumann made it clear that they were out of fuel – they were going to be coming to earth there, come what may. The obstructions were moved. Shortly before 6 a.m. on 14 October, Flight 181 took up residence in Dubai.

During the negotiations for essentials – food, water, and medicine – Captain Schumann was able to pass on a coded message about the make-up of the hijackers (Schumann: "Could you get us four cartons with cigarettes?"; Tower: "OK, any type?"; Schumann: "Mixed. Different ones. Two of these and two of these maybe."; Tower: "Roger, OK. Mixed"). Unfortunately, this information reached the hijackers when the Dubai Minister of Defence gave a press conference, leading to the first direct threat to Captain Schumann's life. The Dubai authorities procrastinated, as West German GSG9 troops flew in; other Western powers offered their support, with the British sending two members of the Special Air Service (SAS) to help. The commandos were preparing their assault – for which the Dubai authorities had reluctantly given permission, on the proviso that their own troops could take part – and had been able to scout the aircraft by pretending to be mechanics. They had even been able to take a birthday cake aboard for stewardess Annemarrie Staringer – which in an odd moment of mutual cooperation was shared between the hijackers and the hostages!

A mere forty minutes before Mahumud's deadline expired at 1 a.m. on 17 October, Flight 181 took off again. The GSG9 troops were nearly ready to make their move, but the hijackers caught them by surprise. Schumann piloted the 737 first to Oman and then to Yemen, where once again they had no option but to land on a sand strip. Schumann and co-pilot Victor were not certain what state the aircraft was now in, and Schumann went to examine the wheel. For reasons that have never been fully explained, he was outside for some time – some reports suggest that he was in contact with the Yemeni authorities trying to persuade them to stop the aircraft from taking off again – and when he returned to the 737, he was summarily executed by Mahmud, in front of the passengers. As one passenger later explained, once they saw that, "We didn't have any hope left."

The next morning, co-pilot Jurgen Victor was at the controls as Flight 181 took off for Mogadishu in Somalia. The West German commandos had not been allowed to enter southern Yemen, despite their government offering major financial assistance to the country if they helped, so headed for Jidda in Saudi Arabia. Hans-Jürgen Wischnewski, described as Chancellor Helmut Schmidt's chief troubleshooter, was now with them, and was given a free hand in all negotiations.

Captain Schumann's body was unceremoniously dumped from the aircraft once it landed in Somalia. Victor was told by Mahmud that he was free to leave the plane, since they were not intending to go anywhere else. Victor refused to leave without the other passengers and crew. Mahmud set a fresh deadline of 4 p.m. local time for the release of the hostages (they had landed around 6.30 a.m.), and started to pour duty-free alcohol over the passengers and crew, explaining to them that it would make them burn better when the aircraft was set on fire.

To buy time for the commandos to arrive, a West German diplomat told Mahmud that the eleven prisoners were on their way, but it would take seven hours for them to arrive from Germany. (A video from the Somali Archive uploaded to YouTube contains portions of the negotiations between Mahmud and the authorities in Mogadishu, and shows the plane on the tarmac.) The deadline was therefore pushed back to 2.30 a.m. Tuesday 18 October. Mahmud told the tower not to try any tricks. "This will not be another Entebbe," he warned.

The West Germans thought otherwise. The GSG9 commandos were flown into Mogadishu on a 707 that landed with its lights out; a news report of their arrival at 8 p.m. was supressed. For the next six hours, the commandos planned their raid, with assistance from the Somali authorities.

Shortly before 2 a.m., twenty-eight commandos in full stealth gear approached the rear of the 737. Mahmud's attention was diverted by conversations with the tower, which were designed to make him believe that the Red Army prisoners were on the way, and then Somali forces set off an explosion on the runway. As Mahmud and two of the hijackers ran to the cockpit to check what was happening, the GSG9 team boarded the 737, coming through the emergency doors and shouting at the passengers to lie down. Perhaps remembering the fate of some of the hostages at Entebbe, the passengers and crew did so. All four hijackers were shot – Harb and Alameh fatally; Mahmud died of his wounds later, and his fiancée, who had been hiding in the toilet, was wounded. The hijackers' grenades luckily failed to explode properly. The hostages were quickly deplaned, and picked up by waiting cars. The assault lasted a mere five minutes; only one passenger received slight wounds.

A few hours later, the hostages and commandos were flown to Cologne-Bonn Airport. Three of the Red Army members whose release was demanded committed suicide in their cells; the Red Army executed Hanns-Martin Schleyer, and dumped his body in the boot of a car.

UPPING THE STAKES

Two hijackings in 1985 demonstrated, like so many disasters in this volume, how a combination of circumstances can lead to success or failure – and with so many lives at risk if errors are made, the stakes are frighteningly high.

On Friday 14 June, TWA Flight 847 was supposed to travel from Cairo to London, stopping off at Athens and Rome en route. Once again, terrorists took advantage of lax security at Athens to board the Boeing 727, although, to be fair to the Greek authorities, they were able to prevent Ali Atwa, one of the three Lebanese hijackers, from boarding the aircraft, taking him into custody. A decade on from the activities of the PFLP, these terrorists were members of Islamic Jihad and their aim was to secure the release of some 700 Shi'ite Muslims who were being detained in Israel. Islamic Jihad had recently started to make its name known for suicide missions, and were regarded as one of the most dangerous of the groups in the Middle East.

The two terrorists, using the aliases Ahmed Gharbiyeh and Ali Youness, bided their time until the flight was twenty minutes into the leg to Rome Leonardo da Vinci Airport; they then took control of the 727, waving their guns and hand grenades around, and generally trying to cow the passengers into submission. Captain John Testrake was ordered to fly the aircraft to Beirut, and although the Lebanese tried to prevent it from landing, they had little option when Testlake informed them: "He has pulled a hand-grenade pin and is ready to blow up the aircraft if he has to. We must, I repeat, we must land at Beirut. We must land at Beirut. No alternative."

Once there, the demands began afresh. "They are beating the passengers. They are threatening to kill the passengers. We want fuel now. Immediately. Five minutes at most, or he is going to kill the passengers," came the message from the crew followed a few moments later by the voice of the hijacker. "The plane is booby-trapped. If anyone approaches, we will blow it up. Either refuelling the plane or blowing it up. No alternative."

While the refuelling was carried out, the hijackers listed their demands, and also asked to speak to a representative of the mainstream Shi'ite force, Amal. Their leaders were not willing to get involved. Unlike many hijackers, this pair released twenty women and children almost immediately, sending them out on one of the yellow escape chutes. Once the 727 was refuelled, Captain Testlake was ordered to fly to Algeria, whose authorities also tried to prevent it from landing, only backing down after a direct request from US President Ronald Reagan to Algerian President Chadli Bendjedid. Twenty-one more passengers were released by the hijackers during the five hours that Flight 847 was in Algiers, before the engines were fired up once more, and Testlake was told to return to Beirut.

Officials there were even less keen on TWA 847 than they had been the previous day. In the end they only relented when the hijacker announced that they were "suicide terrorists!" adding: "If you don't let us land, we will crash the plane into your control tower, or fly it to Baabda and crash into the Presidential Palace"! However, when the hijackers demanded once more to speak to someone from Amal, and were once again refused, they took direct action. They first tried to find any Israelis on board, and then, when they couldn't locate any, vented their anger against US Navy Diver Robert Dean Stethem, who, they claimed, was someone who had taken part in "security blow-ups in Lebanon". Beating him with an arm rest, they then shot him, and threw his body onto the tarmac. Testlake's horrified call to the tower: "He just killed a passenger! He just killed a passenger!" was followed by the hijacker's warning that another would follow in five minutes.

These terrorists were determined to show that they meant exactly what they said and were not afraid to be violent towards their charges. As released passengers would relate, one of the original pair had been brutal, thumping passengers on the head as he strutted up and down the aisle. It didn't help that according to some witnesses, one of the hijackers didn't speak much English and told people to "stand up" when he meant "sit down". "You only had to be hit in the head with a gun once to know what they wanted you to do," hostage Robert Peel Jr explained later. Only stewardess Uli Derickson had the temerity to stand up to them: she spoke German, as did the hijacker, and was able to communicate with him. She also saved the lives of all the passengers when she offered to use her Shell Credit Card to pay for the refuelling at Algiers Airport, an action which led to some ill-informed people accusing her of aiding and abetting the hijack, and leading to her decision to leave TWA.

An Amal official and his bodyguard went on board Flight 847 very soon after, preventing another death, and began discussions with the hijackers. One of their demands was that all the airport lights were turned off – apparently because they feared that the Israelis or one of the countries whose nationals were threatened might try to mount an Entebbe/Mogadishu-style raid. In fact, their motives were very different: the darkness provided cover for them to bring another half-dozen terrorists on board to support the hijackers, and to remove seven passengers who had Jewish or Israeli-sounding names. These were taken to safe hiding places in Beirut to be used as hostages in negotiations with the Israelis.

After stocking up with sandwiches, apples and bananas, and arranging for the refuelling of the aircraft, the hijackers told the pilot to prepare to depart at dawn. They had demanded that their erstwhile colleague Ali Atwa be freed from custody and sent to Algiers by the Greeks, or they would kill the eight Greek citizens on board, which included singer Demis Roussos.

The 727 once more travelled from Beirut to Algiers, where three passengers were immediately released, and after discussions with two high-ranking Algerian officials who boarded the jet soon after touchdown, a further fifty-eight joined them (all having their cash and other valuables removed from their hand luggage before they were freed). However, once the hijackers started to run out of patience with a lack of movement on their key demands, they threatened to fly away, and then destroy the aircraft, perhaps with its remaining passengers still on board.

The next morning, 16 June, they flew back to Beirut for the third and final time, demanding food and fuel, and stating that their next communique would be their last. They produced a letter, apparently signed by thirty-two of the hostages (which was reprinted in papers around the world), addressed to President

Reagan, begging him not to launch military action. In fact, there were only twenty-nine signatures on the document, which was supposedly written "freely and not under duress". It went on to implore Reagan to "Please negotiate quickly our immediate release by convincing the Israelis to release the 800 Lebanese prisoners as requested NOW." (The word "NOW" was capitalised and underlined.) The terrorists also wanted a meeting with the Amal leader (and Lebanese minister of justice) Nabih Berri, as well as representatives of the United Nations and the Red Cross, and the ambassadors of Britain, France and Spain.

Berri effectively took charge of the situation; the 200 Lebanese soldiers who were guarding the plane were removed, leaving Amal in charge. The runways at the airport were mined to prevent any prospective rescuers from landing there. And, most critically, the hostages were removed from Flight 847, and sent in groups to various locations around Beirut. The American government recognized Berri's key role: Robert C. McFarlane, President Reagan's national security adviser, noted that Berri "has in his hands the ability to end the hijacking".

Although it took a further two weeks to resolve the crisis, Berri's actions did bring about a peaceful resolution, the politician much better able to negotiate than the maddened, tired hijackers. Hostages were released in trickles as discussions continued – a sick man one day, three more the next. Both passengers and crew urged President Reagan not to try to rescue them, but to try and put pressure on Israel to meet the demands. In the usual sort of face-saving that characterizes such manoeuvres, the release of thirty-one prisoners the following week by the Israelis was, of course, a pure coincidence and wasn't linked to the hijackers' demands – but of course, US Secretary of State George P. Shultz would be delighted if some hostages were freed.

Two days before they were finally freed, the remaining hostages were treated to a luxury meal by their "hosts", and on 30 June – after final hurdles involving the US promising not to carry out retaliation, and indeed "reaffirm[ing] its longstanding support for the preservation of Lebanon, its government, its stability and its security for the mitigation of the suffering of its people" – the thirty-six passengers and three crew were transported in Red Cross buses to Damascus from where they were flown to

Frankfurt, West Germany, to be greeted by US Vice President George H. W. Bush.

Robert Stethem's sacrifice didn't go unheralded; he was buried in Arlington Cemetery, and a US Navy destroyer was commissioned in his honour in 1995. As for the hijackers – Hasan Izz-al-Din, Imad Mughniyah, Ali Atwa and Mohammed Ali Hamadi – most of them managed to evade justice for a long time. Hamadi was arrested in 1987 and convicted in May 1989 in West Germany; he was freed in December 2005, and returned to Lebanon. The other three featured on the FBI Most Wanted Terrorists list which was compiled in the wake of the 9/11 attacks; Hamadi joined them in February 2006. Imad Mughniyah was apparently killed in a car bomb in 2008, and there were rumours that Hamadi was killed by a CIA drone attack in Pakistan in June 2010.

MASSACRE IN MALTA

The passengers on EgyptAir Flight 648 might reasonably have hoped that their ordeal might end in a similarly negotiated way. As accounts written decades later show, no one who has been part of a hijacking as a hostage ever forgets what happened, or the constant fear, but many such incidents were passing off without major loss of life. Unfortunately for fifty-eight of the eighty-nine passengers, mismanagement, miscommunication and sheer folly resulted in their deaths.

Once again the departure airport for the ill-fated flight was Athens, with the Boeing 737 bound for Cairo on the evening of 23 November 1985. The US State Department had issued an advisory notice warning Americans not to use Athens in the wake of the TWA 847 hijacking, but this was lifted in July 1985 after both the International Air Transport Association and the Federal Aviation Administration inspected it and judged it one of the world's "best guarded" terminals. However, as hostage Jackie Pflug recalled, this wasn't really the case – the security officers were careless in their inspections. It was claimed that the Libyans were responsible for the hijacking (the terrorists simply described themselves as "Egypt's Revolutionaries"), and that members of the Libyan embassy in Athens were able to bring the weaponry into the airport using diplomatic immunity, and passed guns and hand grenades to Omar Mohammed Ali Rezaq (who used the alias Nibal during the hijacking) and his fellow hijackers in the transit area of the airport.

The familiar pattern began, with the hijackers waiting for the "fasten seat belts" sign to be switched off before taking over the aircraft. The 737 under the control of Captain Hani Galal was just overflying the Greek island of Milos when a well-dressed young man rose from his seat in first class and started to wave a gun around, while a colleague did the same in the economy section, and a third entered the cockpit and put a gun to the captain's head. The passengers were ordered to hand over their passports, and any Israelis were immediately badly treated.

However, this was where the passengers' luck really began to run out, even if they didn't fully realize it at the time. Egyptian security agent Medhat Mustafa Kamal drew his weapon and shot one of the hijackers, killing him. In the firefight that followed between him and the remaining hijackers, Kamal and two stewardesses were injured. But more importantly, the fuselage of the jet was punctured, leading to a loss in cabin pressure.

As the oxygen masks automatically fell from the ceiling, adding to the chaos already present inside the cabin, Captain Galal took emergency action, and descended from 35,000 feet to 14,000 feet, and categorically refused to obey the hijackers' demands to fly to Libya. With the damage to the aircraft, and limited fuel, there was no chance of reaching it safely. The only place to set down was Malta.

Understandably, the Maltese authorities tried their hardest to dissuade the captain from bringing the 737 – and its attendant problems – in to land, but when he explained that he was very short of fuel, they reluctantly agreed. Despite that, they didn't provide landing lights, and Galal had to use all his training and fifteen years of experience to bring the aircraft in safely. He was told to taxi to a remote area, and the runway was then blocked off by police buses. Captain Galal later explained that he carried out some "technical" steps at that point to ensure that the 737 couldn't take off again – this was not going to be a repetition of TWA 847's tour of the Eastern Mediterranean.

By this point, the hijackers had rearranged the passengers into national groups: Palestinians were seated at the left rear, Greek passengers at the right rear, with the only two Israelis on board, twenty-four-year-old Tamar Artzi and her travelling companion, twenty-three-year-old Nitzan Mendelson, placed at the right front, with American and Australian passengers beside them. Once they landed, the two injured crew members and eleven female passengers were released.

The 737 landed at Malta at 2115 on 25 November, and the hijackers started to demand to be refuelled. The Maltese authorities, under the direct supervision of the prime minister, Dr Carmelo Mifsud Bonnici, refused. After the third time they asked, and had not been answered, Rezaq announced that a passenger would be killed every few minutes unless their demands for fuel and safe passage to Libya were met. Oddly, they made no other demands or political statements – it was speculated at the time that they were waiting for further instructions regarding these that never came.

The Maltese refused. Fifteen minutes after making his demand, Rezaq therefore called passenger Artzi to the door. Believing she was about to be released like the other women earlier, the girl went to the door willingly – and was shot at point-blank range in the head. By chance, she turned her head at exactly the right moment and the bullet grazed her right cheek and ear lobe. Believing that she had been killed or at the very least been mortally wounded, the hijackers threw her out of the plane to the tarmac, where she lay.

"He's killing her now," Captain Galal told the tower. "Do something he's killing her now. He's outside shooting her now . . . I am the Captain . . . you are wasting lives . . . you are wasting lives . . . He's killing her . . . He has killed her already . . . And in fifteen minutes he will kill another one."

And he did. When Nitzan Mendelson's name was called, she cowered into her seat, desperate not to be found. In the cockpit, Captain Galal told the tower they were preparing another passenger for execution, and told the people listening that he held them responsible for the killings.

One of the hijackers tried to pry Mendelson from her seat – reluctantly assisted, according to some contemporary eyewitness reports, by one of the EgyptAir crew – but Mendelson clung to it, digging her fingernails into the cloth covering. Screaming, "Save me, spare me" to the other passengers and the hijackers, she tried to hold onto the aisle carpet as she was dragged by her feet to the doorway. Her screams were silenced by a bullet in the back of the head. Mendelson wasn't dead, and Artzi tried to crawl to her side. However when one of the hijackers spotted Artzi moving, he shot her in the hip. "They shot us as a sport," she told reporters later, "as though they were shooting dogs." (Mendelson later died of her injuries.)

The next victim was the first of the Americans on board. Fisherman biologist Patrick Scott Baker was summoned to the door, but, like Artzi, he turned his head at the correct time, and only received a graze – although he didn't let on to his "murderers" that they had failed, tumbling to the ground, and waiting for them to move away from the doorway before rising to his feet, and racing for the control tower.

Inevitably, overseeing the executions meant that Rezaq had to leave the cockpit for a few minutes, and Captain Galal used the time to give the control tower as much information as possible about where everyone was, to aid any potential rescue plan – Rezaq was the only one of the terrorists who spoke English. When Rezaq returned, Galal recalled: "I was prepared to do anything to prevent more killing, especially killings like this in cold blood" – he had no way of knowing that none of the victims had died. According to Galal, Rezaq was making small jokes among his repeated insistence on fuel.

The fourth target, Scarlett Marie Rogenkamp, wasn't so lucky. She was shot in the back of the head, and died instantly. There was nearly a three-hour gap before Jackie Pflug was summoned, around 10 a.m. on Sunday. Like all the victims after Mendelson, her hands had been tied behind her back with neckties that the hijackers took from the passengers before she had been placed on "death row". She too was shot in the head and thrown off (although she survived her injuries). Australian Tony Lyons could see that his passport was the next one on the top of the pile and became "resigned to the fact that I was going to be shot". When Rezaq left the cockpit to use the toilet, Galal made a desperate plea to the control tower. "Please do something. They're going to kill us all."

Help was already there. Egyptian President Hosni Mubarak had been attacked for his slow reaction earlier in the year when terrorists took control of the Italian cruise liner *Achille Lauro*, and as soon as he was aware of the hijacking, he sent a team of eighty commandos to Malta – the Maltese didn't have anyone with the sort of training which would be required to storm an aircraft successfully. A C-130 with the troops on board arrived in Malta on Sunday morning, around the time that Jackie Pflug was shot, but Mubarak only gave the go-ahead for the operation after Galal's message showed that time was running out.

The Egyptian plan was for three two-man teams to take the 737. One pair would come into the cabin through the baggage compartment while the others entered through front and rear doors to dispose of the hijackers. Some reports suggest that they intended to do this at suppertime – the Maltese were negotiating with the hijackers to release the nine children still on board in exchange for food – but in the end they went in early.

It was an unmitigated disaster. The grenades the Egyptians used to get through from the baggage compartment to the cabin began to burn the plastic of the airplane, creating a dense poisonous fog. One of the hijackers hurled a grenade at incoming Captain Ibrahim Dahroug and the explosion took the commando's leg off. The hijackers threw their grenades, adding to the carnage. As Tony Lyons recalled: "All of a sudden there were grenades, a lot of shooting, then fire in the fuselage – thick, acrid smoke that choked you when you tried to breathe. I stumbled over people, fell out the door and down the stairs onto the tarmac."

Captain Galal had tried to distract Rezaq from noticing the light that indicated that the cargo door had been opened and the raid was underway, but once the Egyptians started firing, Rezaq went to the door of the cockpit and threw a grenade out into the cabin. He then turned and fired at Galal, grazing the captain, who wasn't where he expected him to be. Galal was reaching for the emergency fire axe, and in the confusion, Rezaq didn't see the axe descending towards him in time. It knocked him out.

But by then it was too late. "I have never seen or heard anything like it," the captain later told a news conference. "Three grenades, three high intensive grenades were thrown on passengers inside a place like a 737. It was hell." One of the two hijackers and fifty-seven passengers died, including all nine children. But Galal was adamant, even in the immediate aftermath of the devastation, that there was no other option. "Our only hope was storming the airplane. The hijackers were very desperate and bloodthirsty people. I think with such people we need to take no chances."

Rezaq, however, tried to flee the 737 with the passengers and was shot in the chest. He was captured by Egyptian commandos at St Luke's General Hospital. He was imprisoned on Malta, but only served seven of his twenty-five-year sentence. He travelled to Africa, but was captured in Nigeria and sent to the United States for trial. In October 1996, he was sentenced to life imprisonment with a no-parole recommendation, despite defences of insanity and obedience to military orders. Tamar Artzi, Patrick Baker and Jackie Pflug all testified at his American trial. "I think people need to be responsible for what they do," Pflug told the trial. "I think it's important to make sure that this doesn't happen again."

She was overly optimistic. Just under five years later, on September 11, 2001, something much worse occurred.

THE DAY EVERYTHING CHANGED:
SEPTEMBER 11, 2001

Hijacking may have been part of aviation history stretching back almost as far as the first flight by the Wright brothers, but the start of the twenty-first century saw a horrific new development. Al-Qaeda leader Osama bin Laden wasn't content to hijack airplanes in order to ransom the hostages, or use them as pawns to gain some political advantage. He wasn't interested in the contents of the airplanes – the passengers or the people. He was interested in the potential devastating power of a large metal cylinder travelling at speed – using an ordinary jet airliner as a weapon of mass destruction.

The idea wasn't totally new, of course. Kamikaze pilots were a fundamental part of the Japanese Air Force during the Second World War, but those were honourable men who saw it as their duty to kill themselves in the service of their emperor and use their planes to take as many of the enemy with them as they could. In fiction, the idea of using a jet as a guided missile had been seen in many places, including in *The Running Man*, a short science fiction novel by Richard Bachman, the penname of Stephen King; and in horror novel *The Fog* by British writer James Herbert. Rather bizarrely, the first episode of *The X-Files* spin-off, *The Lone Gunmen*, featured a plot about a government conspiracy to fly a commercial aircraft into the Twin Towers in New York to boost US arms sales. That aired on 4 March 2001, and inevitably sparked suggestions that someone had taken it seriously. (For the purposes of this chapter, the events of 9/11 are accepted as having taken place as officially described, rather than the arcane theories of conspiracy theorists.)

Al-Qaeda had been an increasing threat to America and other Western countries during the last decade of the twentieth century, responsible for many terrorist attacks. In December 1998, US intelligence was aware that bin Laden's men were looking into hijacking planes, but no one thought that they were doing so for anything other than "standard" hijack reasons – forcing the release of prisoners from jail. However, evidence from al-Qaeda mastermind Khalid Sheikh Mohammed (KSM) after his arrest in 2003 indicated that bin Laden had begun plotting the 9/11 attacks as early as 1996. The "planes operation", as KSM dubbed it, was designed with ten aircraft in mind, attacking targets on both coasts of the United States. (This was an extension of the failed Opan Bojinka plot – see page 402.) Bin Laden, originally thought of as one of the financiers of al-Qaeda, but by this point now one of its operational leaders, felt that this was overcomplicated, and thought that four would be more achievable. KSM found recruits for the operation, including four from Hamburg, Germany – among them Mohammed Atta, who became the operational commander once they were all in the US.

By the summer of 2000, three of these four – Atta, Marwan al-Shehhi and Ziad Jarrah – were in Florida and had started learning how to fly. The fourth hijacker, Hani Hanjour, already had a commercial pilot's licence so didn't enter the US until early 2001, when he took refresher lessons in Arizona. The four pilots didn't simply go on a flight simulator at an airport for a couple of hours and decide that such training would be sufficient to enable them to fly Boeing jets. They may not have been the world's greatest pilots – none of them received particular praise for their skills from their flying schools – but they trained and prepared for what they needed to do. They all earned their basic private flying licences and carried out the training for their commercial FAA pilot's licences. By the end of 2000, Jarrah, Atta and Shehhi were simulating flights on large jets. Both Jarrah and Hanjour requested and received training flights down the Hudson Corridor, the low-altitude flight path that goes past buildings like the World Trade Center. Hanjour practised flying near Washington, DC. A back-up pilot, Zacarias Moussaoui, carried out training in Minnesota, in case one of the selected quartet had second thoughts; he attracted suspicion when he sought fast-track training on large jet airliners, and was arrested on 16 August.

A group of fifteen other terrorists began arriving in spring 2001; these men would act as "muscle" during the hijack. In July, bin Laden gave the go-ahead. During the days leading up to what Khalid Mohammed described as the "Holy Tuesday operation", bin Laden warned close associates to return to Afghanistan before 10 September.

Four planes were targeted: American Airlines Flight 11, flying from Boston to Los Angeles; United Airlines Flight 175, on the same route; American Airlines Flight 77 from Washington DC, also heading for Los Angeles; and United Airlines Flight 93, scheduled to go from Newark International Airport to San Francisco. Atta was in charge on Flight 11, along with Abdul Aziz al-Omari, Satam al-Suqami, Wail al-Shehri and Waleed al-Shehri; Atta and Omari flew in from Portland, Maine; the others drove to Logan Airport. Marwan al-Shehhi was running the Flight 175 operation, with Fayez Banihammad, and three Saudis: Mohand al-Shehri, and brothers Ahmed al-Ghamdi and Hamza al-Ghamdi. None of them was stopped by security as they proceeded to their flights. All boarded the flights and took their seats, with Flight 11 pushing back from the gate at 7.40 p.m., and Flight 175 following suit just before 8 a.m.

Around the same time, the hijackers of Flight 77 were checking in: Hani Hanjour was joined by Khalid al-Mihdhar, Majed Moqed, Nawaf al-Hazmi and his brother Salem al-Hazmi. Although two of them set off the security alarms, they weren't properly checked by the staff, and were allowed to proceed onto the plane. In Newark, pilot Ziad Jarrah was met by Saeed al-Ghamdi, Ahmed al-Nami and Ahmad al-Haznawi, and the four men were able to board Flight 93 unimpeded, taking their seats in the first-class section – the other hijackers divided their numbers between coach (economy) and first class.

Flight 11 was the first to come under al-Qaeda control. Around 8.14 a.m., two of the hijackers stabbed two of the flight attendants, and then were able to gain access to the flight deck – whether by threatening the flight attendants or using their key is unknown. One of the attendants was seriously hurt, and needed medical help; one of the first-class passengers had his throat slashed.

Mohammad Atta then headed for the cockpit, as former Israeli army officer Daniel Lewin tried to take action against the hijackers; he was stabbed by one of them. Claiming they had a bomb, the hijackers used some form of irritant spray to force everyone out of the first-class compartment. Around 8.20 a.m. stewardess Betty Ong used an airphone to contact the American Airlines office, and for the next twenty-five minutes was able to keep the authorities posted on activity on the aircraft. One of the other stewardesses, Amy Sweeney, also got through to the ground, speaking to the American Flight Services Office in Boston, passing on crucial information about the identity of the hijackers from their seat numbers.

Atta's training didn't include all the diverse controls in the cockpit, and he hit the wrong key when he tried to reassure the passengers that this was a normal hijacking. Instead of his message reaching the cabin, it was heard by air traffic control at Boston Centre: "Nobody move," he said. "Everything will be okay. If you try to make any moves, you'll endanger yourself and the airplane. Just stay quiet."

By 8.38, it was clear to the two women in contact with the ground, as well as the other passengers, that the aircraft was being flown erratically, and was in a steep descent. Three minutes later, air traffic control seemed to believe that Flight 11 was heading for Kennedy Airport.

At 8.44, Betty Ong's call to the American Airlines office cut out. Amy Sweeney was asked if she could identify exactly where they were. "We are flying low," she replied. "We are flying very, very low. We are flying way too low . . . Oh my God, we are way too low."

At 8.46, Flight 11 crashed into the North Tower of the World Trade Center in New York City. There were no survivors.

At 8.14, pretty much the exact time that Flight 11 was hijacked, United Airlines Flight 175 departed from Boston. Approximately thirty minutes later, the hijackers went into action. According to the information provided by passengers as the hijack elapsed, knives, Mace and a bomb threat were used; the flight crew were stabbed; and the pilots were killed. Once again, passengers were moved to the back of the aircraft, and it is a reasonable assumption that Shehhi and his team used the same game plan as Atta on the earlier flight.

At 8.51, Flight 11 began to descend, and refused to answer calls from New York air traffic control. A minute later, two phone calls were received on the ground: Peter Hanson was able to tell his father that he thought "they've taken over the cockpit" and that the aircraft was making strange moves. He asked his father to call the airline, but his father contacted the local police instead. One of the flight attendants was able to make a brief call to United's San Francisco office, giving much the same information.

At 8.58, Shehhi changed course, and started to head for New York City. The passengers were restless, and talking about trying to take control of the airplane, according to passenger Brian David Sweeney's last conversation with his mother. Peter Hanson called his father again at 9 a.m. telling him that "it's getting very bad on the plane" as it was making "jerky movements". Hanson had guessed the hijackers' intentions: "I think we are going down . . . I think they intend to go to Chicago or someplace and fly into a building . . ."

The intention was right; the location wasn't. At 9.03 a.m., United Flight 175 hit the South Tower of the World Trade Center. There were no survivors.

American 77 departed from Washington Dulles Airport at 8.20 a.m.; once again, there was approximately thirty minutes before the hijackers struck. This time they used box cutters and knives, although there were no reports of Mace or the threat of a bomb. The passengers, as before, were moved to the back of the aircraft, but the captain, at least, wasn't killed by the hijackers. At 8.54, Hani Hanjour, now in control, turned the 757 south, and switched off the aircraft's transponder.

By the time that Renee May, one of the passengers, called her mother in Las Vegas at 9.12 a.m. from Flight 77, both towers of the World Trade Center had been hit. A few minutes later Barbara Olson contacted her husband Ted, who was the solicitor general of the United States. She told him that the pilot had told them they had been hijacked, and was able to let him know that they were flying over houses in a north-easterly direction. Olson told his wife about the two other hijackings and crashes, but when he was asked about it later, he didn't think that she thought Flight 77 was about to crash. However, their call was cut off.

At 9.29 a.m., the autopilot was disengaged with the plane at 7,000 feet, approximately 38 miles west of the Pentagon. Three minutes later Dulles Radar Approach Control tracked an aircraft heading eastbound "at a high rate of speed". Air traffic control at Washington's other airport, Ronald Reagan Washington National, told the Secret Service that an unknown aircraft was heading towards the White House. In fact, it was at that point five miles west-south-west of the Pentagon and turning to face the US Army headquarters.

Hanjour pushed the 757's throttles to maximum power and dived towards the Pentagon, hitting it at approximately 530 miles per hour. It was 9.37 a.m. Everyone on board was killed.

When multiple aircraft are hijacked, the aim has usually been to try to carry out the actual takeover as near simultaneously as possible – as the Czech Air Force and PFLP tried to do in earlier incidents. The al-Qaeda terrorists had the same idea: all four of the aircraft they targeted on September 11 were due to take off between 7.45 a.m. and 8.10 a.m. Owing to heavy air traffic, however, United Flight 93 was more than twenty-five minutes late when it took off. This meant that by the time the hijack took place, news of the other events was just starting to spread.

United 93's pilots should have been warned of the danger earlier: the 9/11 Commission Report is scathing about the slow response time of the FAA. Four minutes after the second jet hit the Twin Towers, controllers at Boston asked the Command Center to "get messages to airborne aircraft to increase security for the cockpit". They didn't do so, and the only alert that United 93's Captain Jason Dahl received came from one of the flight dispatchers, Ed Ballinger, who used his own initiative to send a warning to his sixteen transcontinental flights to "beware any cockpit intrusion".

Dahl received the message at 9.24 a.m.; two minutes later, he asked for confirmation from Ballinger. He got it from the hijackers instead at 9.28 a.m., with a transmission from Flight 93 on the ground relaying a struggle and a declaration of Mayday from one of the crew before Arabic voices were heard reassuring each other that everything was fine. Jarrah tried to announce to the passengers: "Ladies and Gentlemen: here the captain, please sit down keep remaining sitting. We have a bomb on board. So, sit." Like his second message, telling them that they were returning to the airport, this was in fact received by ground control. At some point around now, a woman, believed to be flight attendant Debbie Welsh, struggled with the hijackers, but then begged for her life before being silenced, probably permanently. (The last thirty-one minutes of United Airlines 93's flight were preserved on the cockpit recorder; only Flight 93's recorder survived the impacts.) Two bodies were seen by the passengers outside the cockpit, which were probably the pilot and co-pilot.

Around 9.30 a.m., Tom Burnett called his wife to tell her that his plane had been hijacked, and that the hijackers had knifed one of the passengers (probably Mark Rothenberg – the only first-class passenger who didn't make a call during the flight). The plane changed course – with the hijackers trying to allay suspicion by contacting the FAA for a new flight plan which would take them to Washington. Other flights were moved out of Flight 93's erratic flight path, which saw it climb from 35,000 feet to 41,000 feet and reverse course.

Burnett spoke to his wife again around 9.34 a.m., and learned about the attacks on the World Trade Center. This tallied with what Burnett had already surmised, from the hijackers' talk about crashing the aircraft, and he realized they were on a suicide mission. Flight attendant Sandy Bradshaw called United Airlines in San Francisco about the same time, and in her six-minute call, she explained that the hijackers were in the cabin behind the first-class curtain, and the rest of the passengers were at the back. The plane was now heading towards Washington DC once more.

The passengers on board Flight 93 sounded almost unnaturally calm. Lyz Glick recalled that when she spoke with her husband Jeremy, "I didn't hear any screaming. I didn't hear any noises. I didn't hear any commotion." This was the same impression that Lauren Grandcolas's husband Jack received from the message she left for him.

By this point, the passengers were starting to consider taking matters into their own hands. While Mark Bingham made a call to his mother, discussions were going on in the background, and sounded "like a calm boardroom meeting". Passengers were passing phones around so that everyone had a chance to speak to their loved ones.

The hijackers were also acting unnaturally – at least compared with their comrades on the other aircraft. Flight 93 began descending much earlier than the other jets had – when they crossed below 5,000 feet, they were less than a dozen miles from their target. Yet Flight 93 was at that level while still 150 miles from Washington. It seems logical that either the White House or the Capitol Building were the terrorists' targets – the White House was evacuated at a run from 9.45 a.m., after the initial order to leave was given at 9.20 a.m.

At 9.40 a.m., the transponder signal was switched off, but the 757 was still tracked as it headed for Washington, even if air traffic controllers couldn't tell its altitude. At 9.45 a.m., Tom Burnett called his wife for the third time, and told her that a group of them were working on a plan; at 9.47 a.m., Jeremy Glick told his wife that the passengers had voted to try to take the plane back. Three minutes later Sandy Bradshaw told her husband that passengers were in the rear galley, filling pitchers with hot water to use against the hijackers.

The hijackers realized that something was up – at 9.53 a.m., the cockpit recording shows that they were concerned about possible passenger retaliation. A minute later, Burnett made his fourth and last call to his wife, who believed that he thought he was going to survive the incident – he told her to tell their three daughters he'd speak to them later. "We're waiting until we're over a rural area. We're going to take back the airplane," he explained, adding: "If they're going to crash this plane into the ground, we're going to have to do something . . . We can't wait for the authorities. I don't know what they could do anyway. It's up to us. I think we can do it."

At 9.55 a.m., Jarrah reprogrammed Flight 93's navigational system to head for Reagan National Airport, four miles from the White House, with an expected arrival time of 10.28 a.m. They never made it that far. At 9.57 a.m., the passengers on United Flight 93 began their attack, with Todd Beamer announcing, "Are you ready guys? Let's roll" – possibly using a food cart as a battering ram and a shield. As the passengers shouted defiance at the hijackers, the terrorists prayed "Allah o akbar" (God is great). They also suggested shutting off the oxygen supply, a pointless move given the altitude of the 757 at this stage.

From this point, events are not totally clear. The autopilot was disconnected, and the cockpit recording suggests that the hijackers aimed the jet for the ground, rather than let the passengers take over. Some accounts suggest that the passengers – two of whom were pilots – tried to prevent the crash, with the words "roll it up" or "lift it up" heard just before the recording ends. Ground witness Terry Butler suggested it was trying to make a sharp right-hand turn before it hit the ground. Others have claimed that the 757 was shot down and that there was a smaller jet near the scene.

The exact time of Flight 93's crash into the ground is also disputed. A seismic study suggested it was 10.05 a.m.; the FAA said 10.07 a.m.; the 9/11 Commission stated it was 10.03 a.m. Whatever the time, Flight 93 hit an empty field just north of the Somerset County Airport in Pennsylvania and disintegrated. The black boxes were found 15 and 25 feet inside the crater created by the impact. Everyone on board died.

The death toll was huge, and of course, those on board the aircraft were not the only ones to die in the attacks on September 11. Five minutes before Flight 93 crashed, the South Tower of the World Trade Center collapsed to the ground, followed half an hour later by the North Tower. A third building, 7 World Trade Center, collapsed at 5.20 p.m. that afternoon. There were 2,753 victims at the World Trade Center, including 411 emergency workers; 184 died at the Pentagon, and 40 were killed aboard United 93.

The purpose of terrorism is to terrorize. Even if Osama bin Laden failed to achieve all his aims on that September morning, thanks to the actions of the passengers on United Flight 93, he changed the face of flying for ever. Passengers from the UK travelling to America the month after 9/11 were greeted with astonishment by customs officials and airline workers – but if everyone were to stop flying, then the terrorists' victory would have been total.

Part 8:
An Explosive Situation:
Bombings on Board

STEPPING OUT

The first hijacking may have taken place less than a decade after the Wright brothers initially took flight, but it took considerably longer before anyone tried to destroy an aircraft mid-journey – excepting, of course, those that were engaged in combat. The motives of those who carried out the early bombings weren't always known, but the effects of their actions certainly received widespread publicity.

Although the incident near Chesterton, Indiana on 10 October 1933, described in the next chapter, is often accepted as the first confirmed bombing of a commercial aircraft, there is good reason to believe that the crash of the Imperial Airways plane *City of Liverpool* on 28 March that year was as a result of such sabotage – and that the person responsible did so, knowing that he was condemning his own sixteen-year-old niece to a fiery death.

The *City of Liverpool* was the plane assigned to Imperial Airways' regular run between London, Brussels and Cologne, and on 28 March, it was heading back on the two hour flight from Belgium to the aerodrome at Croydon, South London. Fifteen people were on board, including Dr Albert Voss, his niece Lottie, and his business partner, Mr L. O. Dearden. Voss had emigrated from Germany to the UK, and was working as a dentist in Manchester, making regular trips to the continent.

As the *City of Liverpool* flew over fields near Essen, it suddenly burst into flames and crashed like a meteor into a field, instantly killing all aboard. Or at least, that's what everyone assumed to begin with – until they found the body of Dr Voss some distance away from the wreckage. How did this sixty-nine-year-old dentist's corpse end up two miles away, with unusual burn marks on him and his overcoat rolled under his arm? The Salford coroner decided to postpone Dr Voss's funeral on police advice after an investigation was carried out by Imperial Airways which revealed some unsettling information.

"The fire on the air liner broke out near where Mr Voss sat, and he must have flung himself from the aeroplane immediately," the coroner stated. "The pilot must have then been unaware of the fire, or he would have immediately tried to land. The fingers of Mr Voss's left hand were badly burned, but the right hand was only slightly burned. There is some question as to whether this is consistent with the possibility that he held some flammable or explosive material in his hands. There is a suggestion that he committed suicide, and tried to make his death look like an accident, sacrificing the air liner and all aboard. It is a terrible thought, especially as his own niece was one of the passengers."

Voss had a £500 insurance policy cover for the flight – a considerable sum in those days – as well as other policies. The coroner also revealed that he was "undoubtedly financially embarrassed, and was wanted by the police for alleged embezzlement in Germany". The idea that he was committing suicide was backed up by claims that he had tried to take his life with a large quantity of aspirin the previous October.

Examination of the wreckage showed that the fire began either in the lavatory, aft of the passenger cabin, or in the luggage compartment behind that. There was no sign of fire originating in either the engine or the petrol tanks. Coupling that with the clear indications that Voss "stepped out of the aeroplane voluntarily" and it seemed to many likely that he was responsible.

However, was there another reason than suicide? According to Voss's son, Albert Jr, the trips his father used to make to Europe were not simply taken for pleasure. At the coroner's inquest into the deaths of his father and the others, held a week after the coroner had stopped the funeral, Voss Jr alleged that Voss and Dearden were drug smugglers, and that "working with a former Air Force Officer named Pleass they would take frequent trips from the continent by air, drop packages of dope attached to tiny silk parachutes from the plane windows at pre-arranged spots". According to the *Time* magazine reporter, this story set "every neck a-crane in the little courtroom". Voss claimed that his father and Dearden knew they were about to be arrested when the *City of Liverpool* landed, so his father set fire to the airplane, jumping on the "1000-to-1 chance" that he might survive.

Albert Voss Jnr was estranged from his father at the time of the latter's death, so his story has to be treated with some scepticism, particularly as his brother Hugo testified that their father never used matches, and was "convinced he was incapable of doing such a dastardly thing" as to "deliberately or accidentally set fire to the liner, by which fourteen people were roasted to death". The coroner seemed more taken with the latter version, particularly after expert testimony that it was impossible to say whether he had been blown out of or had jumped out of the *City of Liverpool*, and instructed the jury that "although Mr Voss's reputation was an unenviable one, there was no positive evidence that he had been responsible for the fire". An open verdict was returned.

In an equally odd postscript to the story, Dr Voss's widow Jessie, his second wife, was found dead in the Rochdale Canal in Manchester six months later.

A MOB HIT?

There was no question in the minds of the investigators that there had been an explosion aboard United Air Lines Flight 23, which spiralled out of the sky and hit the ground near Chesterton, Indiana – some fifty miles south of Chicago – on 10 October 1933, falling, according to witnesses, "like a blazing comet". All seven people on board perished, but those within did not all die on impact – some of the farmers who tried to approach the crash site to render assistance told reporters they "saw the victims milling around on the inside of the cabin unable to save themselves. Some said they even heard the screams." What no one ever was able to determine was who planted it, or why.

The new Boeing 247 aircraft, registration NC13304, was on a routine flight from Newark, New Jersey to Oakland, California, and was en route between Cleveland and Chicago when the explosion took place. The airplane had been Boeing's showcase exhibit at the Chicago World's Fair earlier in the year, and could carry ten passengers – although there were only four on board this leg of the journey – with a cruise speed of 188 mph (explained as "more than three miles a minute" to the readers of the Associated Press). There didn't seem to be anything particularly unusual about the passengers: a young woman off to visit her sister, who was getting married the next day; a retired grocer who was carrying a smallbore rifle and cartridges, and made a fuss about taking a brown paper parcel into the cabin with him (it was found intact after the crash, so wasn't suspicious); a fridge salesman; and a radio serviceman, whose wife was afraid of airplanes, so didn't know her husband was travelling on one. The crew were equally above suspicion.

The pilot, Harold R. Tarrant, was in charge of the aircraft for the trip from Cleveland to Chicago. The 247 left Cleveland at 6.57 p.m., and was due at its destination around 10 p.m. It was raining, and Tarrant kept in touch with the local weather bureaus. About 9 p.m., there was a huge explosion, which people over an area of four square miles could hear, and Flight 23 plummeted to the ground. Some witnesses claimed that they could "hear the throbbing of the motor as it fell" which led officials to believe that a motor or gasoline tank had exploded, and that "Pilot Tarrant was attempting desperately to make a landing." (Investigators were later able to establish that Tarrant cut the throttles, but there was little more that he could do.) The tail broke off, and the 247's radio operator, along with one of the passengers, were swept from the aircraft; their bodies were eventually found some distance from the wreckage.

Coroner Carl Davis of Porter County took charge of the scene, as United Air Lines began to carry out its own investigation. This was, they explained, "the first fatal crash to a multi-motor ship in seven years of flying over 60,000,000 miles". It didn't help that souvenir hunters removed some of the evidence from the scene – the local tavern owner, Donald Slont, took one of the propellers, leading the investigators to believe at one point that its loss was responsible for the crash, and there were portions of the aircraft around the town for some time to come, despite the efforts of the investigators to collect them all. What the Crime Detection Laboratory of Northwestern University, as well as Chicago-based Underwriter's Laboratories, did discover was that a piece of blanket, part of the 247's equipment, and several pieces of the metal surface of the airplane had been pierced many times by small bits of metal. This seemed to suggest some other agency involved.

The American Bureau of Investigation (the forerunner of the FBI) were called in, and interrogated the relatives of the crew and passengers, as well as the pilot who had flown the airplane from Newark to Cleveland, and thus was the only person who had been aboard it that night to survive. Melvin Purvis, the G-man responsible for the manhunt for many of the notorious Chicago gangsters, was in charge, telling the *New York Times*: "Our investigation convinced me that the tragedy resulted from an explosion somewhere in the region of the baggage compartment in the rear of the plane. Everything in front of the compartment was blown forward, everything behind blown backward, and things at the side outward." Traces of nitroglycerine and other chemicals were found, but nothing more to indicate exactly what explosives, or whether there was any timing mechanism connected.

What Purvis also couldn't produce was any motive: there had been a dispute between United and its pilots, but that had been settled; convicted kidnappers had been flown to prison in a chartered United airplane the previous weekend – had their friends taken some bizarre revenge? Other airline manufacturers were pursuing their own designs, so they wouldn't need to take such drastic action to rid themselves of competition. Could the bombing be gang-related, given that the airplane was going to Chicago? There were suggestions in the *Chicago Tribune* that a gangster was on the verge of being arrested and charged in November 1933, but this wasn't followed through.

In January of 1934, Attorney General Homer S. Cummings officially declared that the cause was "willful or careless placing of a bomb" – the theory being that the explosive might have been left inside the toilet on a pile of blankets during an earlier journey by someone who thought he was going to be searched at journey's end, and then wasn't able to collect it. The bomb then finally became displaced from its cushion by an air bump and was set off when it struck the metal side of the compartment, or dislodged when someone went to collect a blanket on the cool autumn evening. However, no evidence regarding the careless bomber's identity ever materialized, and in September 1935, the case was officially closed, and remains a mystery to this day.

Witness Howard Johnson, who revealed Donald Slont's kleptomaniac tendencies at the crash site, was interviewed for an oral history project at the turn of the millennium by the Westchester Public Library. He recalled: "I guess it had something to do with some labor racketeer because they said that . . . It was all rather vague but they said that someone got on the plane in Cleveland and had a suitcase and then they got off and no one saw them take the suitcase off. So that's no doubt what happened. They just left the bomb on the plane."

Flight 23 bears one unhappy distinction: Alice Scribner's death marked the first time that a United Airlines' flight attendant died in the course of duty.

COPYCAT EXPLOSIONS

After two incidents in such a short space of time, it's rather surprising that the next confirmed bombings of aircraft didn't come until sixteen years after United Flight 23, with many contemporary reports linking the destruction of a Philippine Airlines DC-3 on 7 May 1949 with the atrocity carried out by Albert Guay in Canada on 9 September the same year.

The Philippine Airlines flight from Daet to Manila was carrying thirteen people (ten passengers and three crew – although early reports suggested there were only nine passengers) when it disappeared over the Sibuyan Sea. The DC-3 was last heard from around 3 p.m. local time on 7 May, and was scheduled to arrive in Manila an hour and a half later. When there was no sign, search airplanes were dispatched, but were unable to find any indication of wreckage. A further eleven aircraft were sent out the next day. What they found led to a detailed police investigation, and on 2 June, it was revealed that "a woman and her lover killed thirteen persons" using a time bomb, which exploded as the DC-3 flew over Lamon Bay. "The bomb was placed aboard the plane because the woman's husband was a passenger on it. At least four suspects, including the woman, were being held." The detectives had found a mystery package in the wreckage, bearing a non-existent destination, which led them to Crispin Verso, whose lover's husband was on the aircraft. She denied all knowledge of Verso – but then offered to pay his trial expenses. It transpired that she and her lover had hired two ex-convicts to carry out the bombing, which was carried out with TNT. All four were sentenced to death.

This story received publicity worldwide (the extant version of the report of the arrest was published in a Perth, Australia, paper), and was almost certainly read by Canadian jeweller, Albert Guay, described by a reporter at his trial as a "ferret-like man with [a] pencil moustache who coupled lust for a 19-year-old waitress with a consuming greed for money". Guay wanted to be rid of his troublesome wife, and was certain that he could ensure that he wasn't connected to the crime.

Around 10.25 a.m. on 9 September 1949, Quebecois North Shore eel fisherman Patrick Simard heard an explosion coming from a DC-3 plane travelling 500 feet over his head; as debris rained down around him, he watched the airplane bank to the left, straighten out again – and then fall from the sky onto Cap Tourmente, near the tiny fishing village of Sault au Cochon, close to Saint-Joachim in the Charlevoix region of Quebec province. Simard was first on the scene, and realized that no one could possibly have survived the impact – the back end was intact, but the cockpit and the main part of the fuselage had been ripped apart. Canadian Pacific Airlines Flight 108 had only left Quebec's Ancienne Lorette Airport a few minutes earlier bound for Baie-Comeau. Twenty-three people were on board; all died.

A thorough investigation was soon underway, and it quickly became apparent that this could not be explained by crew incompetency, the condition of the aircraft or its loading. There were no indications of faults with the fuel tanks, the hydraulics, the electrical system, or the de-icing and fire-extinguishing systems. When the National Research Council scientists at Ottawa carried out a controlled explosion on a duplicate DC-3 compartment using dynamite, the resulting wreckage bore the same marks as that from Flight 108. Dr Jean-Marie Roussel and chemist Robert Péclet, both with Montreal's *Laboratoire de médecine légale et de police technique*, were able to use an emission spectrograph to identify the specific composition of the explosives which had been used.

The Royal Canadian Mounted Police, aided by the Sûrêté du Quebec and the Quebec City Police Force, therefore began a murder enquiry, questioning everyone connected with the flight. A baggage handler recalled a woman delivering a parcel early on the morning of the flight, who had been adamant that the parcel had to go on that morning's CPA flight to Baie-Comeau and no other. The 28-pound parcel was marked FRAGILE and was addressed to a non-existent person and place in Baie-Comeau; the sender's name was real – but the person involved had not sent a package. A cab driver also came forward, who had taken a woman to the airport and helped her to send a 28-pound parcel to Baie-Comeau.

One of the deceased passengers was Rita Guay, whose husband Albert had bought her ticket, as well as flight insurance in his own favour. The clerk at the Chateau Frontenac hotel who made the sale remembered them well, because Mrs Guay seemed reluctant to go; her husband had been insistent. He had walked her to the taxi then returned to the hotel, where he had been inconsolable after news arrived of the crash. For the funeral, Guay bought an elaborate floral cross, more than three-feet tall, with the inscription: "From your beloved Albert", and had told a friend that he couldn't believe anybody would be "monstrous enough to blow up a plane".

Albert was known to police after his girlfriend, nineteen-year-old waitress Marie-Ange Robitaille, had complained about his behaviour. Some of his neighbours had also told police they were suspicious of Guay's involvement in his wife's death, with one even claiming that Guay had previously tried to hire him to kill her. The police asked Marie-Ange if the description that the baggage clerk and the cab driver had given brought to mind anyone she knew – and it did. It resembled a friend of Guay's, Marguerite Michaud, or as she was now known, Mrs Arthur Pitre.

On 15 September, *Le Canada* newspaper ran a story that the police were looking for the woman who had taken the package to the airport, and Arthur Guay promptly told Mrs Pitre that she had delivered the deadly package and was therefore responsible for the deaths. According to what she later told her brother, Guay suggested that she should kill herself, and leave a note saying Albert was her target, because she owed him money. Mrs Pitre did take the pills Guay left her, but they weren't sufficient to kill her. Her story soon reached the police, who interrogated her and learned that Guay had told her the package contained a statue. That wasn't all, she told them. The previous month she had gone to buy twenty sticks of dynamite, nineteen blasting caps and 30 feet of fuse for Guay, who apparently wanted to help another friend dynamite some tree stumps on her farm.

Guay was arrested on 23 September 1949, and charged with murder. More evidence quickly came to light: a former policeman and dynamite expert, Ovide Cote, revealed that he had inadvertently shown Guay and his watch repairman Genereux Ruest (Mrs Pitre's brother) how to make a time bomb, and Ruest admitted that he had punched a hole in a clock for Guay. Mrs Pitre testified in court that Albert had admitted there was a bomb in the package on the day he suggested she kill herself. Marie-Ange told the court that Guay had tried to rekindle their affair and told her he was glad his wife was dead. Calculations showed that if the DC-3 had taken off on time, the explosion would have occurred when it was over the St Lawrence river, which would have obliterated any trace of the forensic evidence.

The jury took seventeen minutes to return a guilty verdict. Telling Guay that he had perpetrated a "diabolical, infamous crime" which "has no name", the judge was in tears when he passed the sentence of death.

However, Guay wasn't the only person to hang for the murders. Guay sent a forty-page dossier containing his side of the story to the Canadian premier, which revealed that Mrs Pitre and Ruest had been complicit in the murder from the start. They were arrested in June 1950, and Guay's own execution was delayed until January 1951 so he could give evidence at their trials. Both were found guilty – although he claimed not to know anything about the bomb on the plane, Ruest had apparently hobbled out to a terrace at the Chateau Frontenac specifically to watch Flight 108 take off.

"Well, at least I die famous," were Guay's last words to his jailers – although he started to shake uncontrollably as the noose was placed around his neck. Mrs Pitre was the last woman to be hanged in Canada, on 9 January 1953.

Guay's actions may have inspired Jack Gilbert Graham to prepare a highly unusual Christmas gift for his mother: twenty-five sticks of dynamite. "I then wrapped about three or four feet of binding cord around the sack of dynamite to hold the dynamite sticks in place around the caps," he later admitted to the FBI. "The purpose of the two caps was in case one of the caps failed to function and ignite the dynamite." This he wrapped carefully, and presented to his mother.

Totally unaware of her son's matricidal inclinations, Daisie Eldora King boarded United Airlines' DC-6B, Flight 629, travelling from Denver, Colorado, to Portland, Oregon, which set off shortly before 7 p.m. on 1 November 1955. Eleven minutes after take-off, the bomb, which was inside her suitcase in the hold, exploded, and totally destroyed the aircraft. Thirty-nine people, including one child, were killed instantly.

The Civil Aeronautics Board took quick advantage of an offer of assistance from the FBI, and one of the experts from their laboratory helped to examine the wreckage. The tail section had been cleanly severed from the remainder of the airplane "as though cut with a knife", according to the FBI's log of the incident, landing a mile and a half from the other wreckage. After the standard checks were made, it was clear that the explosion had not been caused by anything malfunctioning on the plane, and a week after the disaster, the FBI officially took over the investigation. A full-size "mock-up" of the central part of the DC-6 was created, and treated like a "giant jigsaw puzzle", and from that they were able to deduce that an explosion occurred at station 718 in the rear cargo pit, where grey and black soot-like deposits could be found. This deposit was also on some of the items found at the scene, including a portion of a battery, and confirmed that dynamite had been used.

All of the deceased passengers and crew were investigated, and attention started to be focused on Daisie King – particularly as she was carrying newspaper clippings referring to her son Jack's forgery charge, and his presence on the local "most wanted" list in Denver County. When the FBI realized that there were few signs of her luggage, Jack Graham became a person of interest: he was set to receive a large inheritance on his mother's death; there had been an explosion at the restaurant in Denver that the pair had owned; he had performed demolition work in the US Navy; and he had apparently deliberately wrecked a truck to claim on the insurance.

The stories that Graham and his wife gave the FBI didn't tally, and after further intense questioning, Graham finally admitted the truth to the FBI – not only had he caused the explosion at the restaurant, and wrecked his truck, but he had also been responsible for the crash. He tried to cop a plea of insanity – and even tried to claim that he had only admitted to creating the bomb when he saw a picture of Nazi saboteurs being arrested with a cache of explosives on the FBI office wall. After a suicide attempt, he was tried, and found guilty on 5 May 1956 of murder in the first degree – there was no crime specifically against blowing up an airplane at this point. He was executed in the gas chamber at Colorado State Penitentiary on 11 January 1957.

SUICIDE BY AIRPLANE?

Not every bomb incident in those early days resulted in tragedy. Captain Ian Harvey was awarded the George Medal for his "extreme coolness" in the aftermath of the explosion which took place on his BEA Vickers Viking aircraft on Thursday 13 April 1950. "It required all the strength of the pilot, coupled with superb skill, before the Viking was landed successfully without injury to any of the passengers," read the citation. "In the face of this very grave emergency, the action of Captain Harvey is worthy of the highest praise. The complete loss of the aircraft and all its company was avoided only as a result of his courage, high skill and presence of mind."

Stewardess Susan Cramsie's diary entry for that day read: "Took off at 8pm for Paris – never got there!! Explosion in loo mid-Channel!" With typical British understatement, she failed to add that the explosion nearly cost her her life – she spent over half a year in hospital with serious injuries, one arm almost severed. The force of the blast caused the cockpit door to fly off its hinges and hit the first officer. There were two large holes in the fuselage of the aircraft – one 5 feet by 8 feet, the other only slightly smaller. At the time, Harvey thought that his airplane had been struck by lightning, and realized quickly that it had damaged the fin and tailplane assembly. This meant that the rudder and elevator controls were ineffective, although the ailerons still functioned. All that kept the tail attached to the aircraft was a strip of roof structure and the cabin floor.

Harvey decided that his best bet was to return to the aerodrome at Northolt, and with a great deal of difficulty, he was able to bring the airplane back under a degree of control. The first time that he tried to land, he was unable to, and had to overshoot. The second time, he made a very long, low, flat approach, adjusting the rate of his descent with the engines, and successfully landed.

Investigations by the police, as well as MI5 and MI6, soon showed that the aircraft had not been struck by lightning; there had been an "infernal machine", a "professionally made weapon hidden at the rear of the airliner's convenience", roughly eight inches long, which was "small enough for carrying in a breast pocket". That Sunday's *News of the World* revealed that there had been a time bomb aboard the airplane, and there was much speculation as to which of the twenty-eight passengers was the intended victim – most of them had elected to catch another flight back to France almost immediately. The Director of Naval Intelligence, Rear Admiral Eric Longley-Cook, had been travelling on an earlier airplane, and might have been the target. A key American diplomat, Ralph Straus, was also considered a possibility.

The papers relating to the investigation were sealed under the Official Secrets Act until 2005. No final conclusion was reached by the police, although they suspected a suicide attempt by Alfred Calmet, one of the French passengers. However, they admitted this was a theory made "in the absence of any direct evidence". Calmet was a con man whose wife was having an affair and who had recently insured his life for ten million francs (something he mentioned in passing to one of the other passengers). Most damningly, he spent some time in the lavatory immediately prior to the explosion.

According to the police report; "The motive was suicide, contemplated because of impending financial troubles coupled with domestic unhappiness. There is his statement of new insurance policies to the value of 10 million francs, which would not be payable if suicide was proved. Opportunity exists in France to obtain explosives. By flying over the route in the morning Calmet would know the best time to carry out his plan." However, without any forensic evidence, police were unable to charge Calmet, and the case remains officially unsolved.

ASSASSINATION BY AIRCRAFT

Although there were some people who tried to commit suicide by airplane, selfishly setting off bombs which took everyone on board to their deaths along with them, cases of murder by airplane became more frequent during the 1950s and 1960s. Sometimes the motives behind them were more complicated than they first appeared – and in at least one case, the truth did not become evident for nearly five decades.

On 11 April 1955, seven months before Jack Gilbert Graham gave his mother a lethal Christmas present, a Lockheed L-749 airliner called the *Kashmir Princess* belonging to Air India, on a charter flight from Bombay, India to Hong Kong to Jakarta, Indonesia, was rocked by an explosion. The target – the premier of the People's Republic of China (PRC), Zhou Enlai. Sixteen people aboard were killed, but not Zhou: although both his allies and enemies expected him to be on the airplane, he had changed his plans at the last minute. What seemed at the time to be a stroke of good fortune was anything but that; in fact, the Chinese leader had deliberately, and with malice aforethought, allowed those sixteen people to die. As papers released in 2004 showed, he had been warned that an attempt on his life would be made, but decided to use this to his advantage, and sent lower-level officials than those originally planned, along with journalists, to take the place of his group. He meanwhile travelled by a different route, putting out a cover story about an emergency operation to explain the change. Zhou Enlai later declared that he had made "a minor sacrifice to safeguard a major interest".

Even before Flight 300 took off from Hong Kong on the latest leg of its journey, there were concerns about its safety, because of the nature of its passenger manifest. As far as anyone knew, high-ranking officials from the PRC were travelling on the flight, as a delegation to attend the first Asian-African conference which was being held in Bandung, Indonesia, as well as various journalists and delegates from Vietnam and Eastern Europe. There were rumours that "some persons might molest the passengers on this occasion". The suspects were agents of the Kuomintang, the Chinese Nationalist Party (KMT), led by Chiang Kai-Shek, who were engaged in a cold war with Zhou Enlai's PRC, aided to an extent by the United States, and in particular by the CIA. The KMT maintained a guerrilla unit in Hong Kong, at the time a British territory, between 1954 and 1958.

Guards were posted around the aircraft during its short stay at Hong Kong's Kai Tak Airport, and Air India took extra precautions, with the luggage being taken by the PRC-owned China Travel Service directly to the plane, and the passengers avoiding Customs. Nothing non-essential was allowed on board – Air India didn't carry any post or freight on this flight.

The *Kashmir Princess* departed from Kai Tak at 1.26 p.m. and Captain D. K. Jatar took the plane up to 18,000 feet and settled in for what appeared to be a routine flight. However, precisely five hours after take-off, an explosion shook the plane, and the pilots saw flames streaming from behind the no. 3 engine, on the right wing. As smoke started to fill the cockpit, Captain Jatar shut down and feathered the no. 3 engine, then realized that there was also a fire warning light showing for the baggage compartment. When the fire spread and put the hydraulic system to the flaps and the undercarriage out of service, he had no option but to try to ditch at sea, and hope that crew and passengers could escape in the life rafts.

The last message from the *Kashmir Princess* was a distress call broadcasting their position, but the electrical systems gave out shortly afterwards as the fire spread through the aircraft. The airplane split into three on impact with the surface of the South China Sea: cockpit, cabin and tail section. The cabin, with all the passengers, sank immediately; Jatar's actions did save the lives of three of his crew in the other two sections – but sixteen others died.

Investigations revealed that a time bomb had been set on board the aircraft, with the most likely suspect airport worker Zhou Zhu (also referred to as Zhou Zemin). He was recruited by KMT agents working for the Number Five Liaison Group, who offered him 600,000 Hong Kong dollars and refuge in the KMT home base of Taiwan. Because of the high level of security expected to surround the flight and the airport, the KMT couldn't use one of their own operatives; it had to be someone who would not arouse suspicion by being near the airplane on the tarmac. Zhou had worked for the Hong Kong Engineering Company for five years by this point, since arriving in the British colony, and at that time was an aircraft cleaner.

According to the Colonial Office's report to London, five weeks after the explosion, it was believed that Zhou placed "a small incendiary device with a timer in the starboard wheelbay of the aircraft, where there was a long cavity". The bomb was then moved by vibration down towards the no. 3 engine, and lodged itself against the fuel tank.

Zhou didn't try to flee straightaway; only when the Hong Kong police focused their attention firmly on him, around 18 May, did he decide to try to escape, and managed to hide on a Civil Air Transport aircraft flying to Taipei. Civil Air Transport was operated by the CIA, lending credence to those who believe that the Agency was involved with the plot; the presence of a MK-7 detonator device in the wreckage of the *Kashmir Princess* also pointed at their assistance, since they did provide such devices to the KMT. Certainly, the KMT hadn't warned anyone at Taipei that Zhou was coming. He was arrested at Taipei Airport but when his identity was discovered, the Taiwanese authorities refused to cooperate with any attempts to return him to Hong Kong.

Zhou Enlai wasn't the only leader targeted during the 1950s and 1960s. On 22 November 1966 – perhaps not coincidentally the third anniversary of the death of US President John F. Kennedy – an Aden Airways DC-3, registration VR-AAN, was blown up while en route from Maifa'ah, the capital of the Federation State of Wahidi, to Aden International Airport at Khormaksar. On board were Major Tim Goschen, the Assistant Adviser at Wahidi; Amir Mohammed bin Said, the Prime Minister of Wahidi; and two key members of Shell Oil Company.

The DC-3 was took off as scheduled at midday, but twenty minutes later witnesses on the ground saw and heard a violent explosion. The tail of the airplane came off, and then the nose. The remainder of the aircraft "went into a spin from 6,000 feet", crashing to the ground not far from Ahwar. When the flight crew failed to make a routine check an hour after take-off, air traffic control notified Aden Airways, and their chief pilot, Vic Spencer, flew out from Khormaksar to search for the DC-3, whose pilot was a personal friend.

Spencer found the wreckage strewn over a large area, with body parts and luggage indiscriminately scattered. Managing, with some difficulty, to land near the main part, he discovered that his friend's body was still trapped in the cockpit. Spencer was able to release the corpse with an axe and a jemmy, and brought it, along with the other dead aircrew, back to Aden.

An explosive device was responsible, which had been placed inside an Aden Airways holdall beneath one of the seats. Although terrorism was initially suspected, the investigation showed that Amir Mohammed bin Said's son, 'Ali, was responsible, wanting to take over from his father as Amir. Contemporary reports suggested that 'Ali was a "nasty piece of work but a wimp compared to his evil, but charming, old father who had ruled Wahidi with a rod of iron on behalf of the actual Sultan". Twenty-seven other people died alongside his father; any power bin Said might have gained was short-lived; Wahidi was abolished when it was incorporated into the People's Republic of South Yemen a year later, in November 1967.

FORCEFUL EJECTION

Insurance claims continued to be filed in the wake of air disasters, and, of course, the majority of these were genuine, from the beneficiaries of those who tragically died in accidents or were the unwitting victims of bombings. However, there were those who tried to profit from the tragedies, and even in some cases tried to cause them.

Saul Binstock died, according to the coroner's inquest, of "forceful ejection" on 25 July 1957. Thanks to the skill of Captain Milton L. Shirk, and co-pilot Seth Oberg, he was the only victim of the explosion on board the Convair CV-240 which formed Western Air Lines Flight 39.

The flight was travelling from Rochester, Minnesota, to Los Angeles, with stops at Salt Lake City, Cedar City and Las Vegas. It left the Nevada city at 0255, and was expected to land at Los Angeles seventy minutes later. However, thirty-five minutes before the scheduled arrival, there was a loud noise from the rear of the aircraft.

Retired jeweller Saul Binstock had been sitting in seat 9-A, the second from the rear of the cabin on the left, next to the window. About fifteen minutes after take-off, Binstock went into the lavatory on the right-hand side of the cabin, and remained there. One of the passengers considered asking the stewardess to check on him, since he was concerned about Binstock's state of health on the rather rough flight. The stewardess, Joan W. Hollinger, checked that passengers were wearing their seat belts, then sat down in seat 10-D, in front of the lavatory.

"I looked up and just then I heard a horrible blast, a terrific gush of wind and the cabin filled with a thick fog and an eerie light," she told investigators. "I put my hand to my head as I sat bolt upright. My hat was gone and my hair was flying in my face. I was stunned, shocked, I thought this was the end for a minute . . . I knew there was a hole behind me, but I was not about to move. The window on my right was shattered."

The explosion woke most of the remaining passengers, who had been dozing on the night-time flight. However, a quick head count showed that one of the passengers was missing.

Up front, the first officer was flying the aircraft, and explained that the explosion and the decompression which followed "sounded like someone had fired both barrels of a double-barrelled shotgun behind his head". A quick check of the cabin by flashlight showed a hole approximately two feet by five feet just forward of the right stabilizer, and just aft of the seat where Joan Hollinger had been sitting. The captain then was granted permission to make an emergency landing at George Air Force Base.

There was no question of anything other than an explosive device being responsible for the incident, and a search was carried out along the flight path, which revealed not just parts of the aircraft, but also the body of Saul Binstock "intact but badly mashed". Three fingers from his left hand had been blown away.

A blood-spattered basin from the washroom was found as well, with the flecks of blood looking "as if they had been sprayed from a paint gun," according to W. S. McNamara, the assistant to the chief of Civil Aeronautics' Investigation Division. There also appeared to be four bullet holes in the aircraft's fuselage.

Tests on the wreckage showed that dynamite had been used, and there were also pieces of blasting cap – including one unexploded cap, in the lavatory toilet, along with a number of burned paper matches and pieces of burned paper. It seemed as if it had taken a number of tries before Binstock had managed to light the blasting cap.

Some weeks earlier, Binstock had bought dynamite and blasting caps, and prior to boarding the flight, he had purchased two insurance policies totalling $125,000, with his wife Eva as beneficiary. One of these had a suicide clause that voided payments. Binstock was buried on 14 August.

A NEW TWIST

Two years later, there was a twist on the idea described in the previous chapter. Rather than committing suicide so his family could benefit from an insurance policy, it seems as if a criminal came up with the bright idea of getting someone else to use his ticket on the flight – and then blow the aircraft up so it looked as if he himself had perished in the tragedy. His wife could then claim on the insurance. However, when his wife learned of the deception, she refused to have any part of the money, and vehemently refused to believe that her husband might have been part of such a plot.

Officially the probable cause of the accident that occurred on board National Airlines Flight 967 on 16 November 1959 is "unknown". The DC-7B was scheduled to run between Miami and New Orleans, with a stop at Tampa, Florida. It landed at Tampa on time, and departed there at 2332, with thirty-six passengers on board (although not the thirty-six passengers that the manifest listed). Somewhere between 0051 the next morning and 0106, the plane vanished; it was last spotted by the radar station at Houma, Louisiana, disappearing from the scope in what seemed a perfectly normal move to the scope operator, because it had descended to a lower level than the scope registered, but then it failed to respond to radio messages.

Using the point at which it was last spotted as a starting place, another National aircraft began searching, and spotted floating debris in the water, including several bodies, three life rafts that seemed about three-quarters submerged, and an oil slick around a mile long and 400 yards wide. In the end, nine bodies, a portion of a tenth body (out of a total of forty-two people), five life rafts, five life vests, as well as fragmented bits of upholstery, soundproofing material, cabin linings, seat cushions and backs, metallic parts of seats attached to and buoyed by these cushions and backs, overhead racks and other light items were picked up, as well as a few items of personal effects.

The bodies showed that the passengers had been seated when the DC-7 hit the water, and there was no evidence of fire or smoke in their blood or tissues, although there were signs of burning on the parts of the corpses which had been exposed above the water-line. These signs were also present on some of the debris. According to a coast guard officer, these could have been indicative of an explosion when the plane hit the water; air force fliers involved in the search believed the explosion happened earlier.

However, that was about as far as the Civil Aeronautics Board could take it. Despite assistance from the US Navy, they were never able to locate the wreckage of the plane, so it was impossible to carry out any further tests. They did note that they were aware of the discrepancy in the passenger manifest, even if they were not able to prove any direct correlation between that and the accident.

Robert Vernon Spears, a convicted criminal, was supposed to be on the flight, and was mourned by his wife when the airplane went down. He then hid for two months before being arrested for driving the car belonging to the man who had taken his place. According to Edmund Barker, the journalist who broke the story, William Allen Taylor, one of Spears's former fellow prisoners, used his ticket and "rode to an ocean grave".

Spears's story was convoluted: Taylor had made the bomb so Spears could use it to dispose of a woman witness who was going to testify against Spears in Los Angeles. Taylor was going to take the bomb by car to Dallas, but decided to go by airplane. Spears had a ticket for the flight, which he went into the airport at Tampa and had validated. He then passed it to Taylor, who took his suit-case and the bomb on board the plane. The bomb had a two-hour timer on it. However, Spears denied responsibility for the explosion – he didn't think the bomb had gone off. The only reason Spears was found out was because Taylor had bought an insurance policy; when his wife tried to claim against it, the deception started to unravel.

The FBI thought otherwise, and believed that Spears might well have tricked Taylor onto the plane with the bomb. "Dr. Spears might have had someone travel for him to collect a large insurance for the benefit of his young wife," suggested chief investigator Julian Blodgett, and Taylor's wife felt that her

husband "was unduly influenced by Dr. Spears and betrayed".
By early 1960, Spears's wife was aware of her husband's deception – which she said he had carried out because "he felt he had
been a burden for me" – and he was under arrest for the possession of Taylor's car.

Spears had been in Phoenix with a friend, Dr William A.
Turska, who was horrified to find a case of dynamite hidden near
the desert cabin where Spears had been holed up. Turska told
reporters that the FBI had told him that Spears had dynamite
fuses in his luggage, although this was never confirmed – and
given that the FBI never charged Spears, it would seem likely that
if anything like that was true, it was said in the hope of getting
more information.

Newspapers at the time routinely linked Spears to the crash,
right up to the reports of his death in May 1969. He was one of
the last prisoners sent to Alcatraz before the prison was shut
down in 1963, then dropped out of sight.

The flight on which Spears should have travelled wasn't the only
one to disappear in a suspected bomb blast that year – on 17
April, a Curtiss C-46 carrying twenty-six people that was flying
between the Mexican cities of Mexicale and Guaymas exploded,
catching fire in mid-air. It crashed near Puerto Kino, killing all
on board.

Five months later, on 8 September 1959, a Douglas DC-3
belonging to Compania Mexicana de Aviacion had to make an
emergency landing after an explosion on board the Mexicana
flight from Mexico to Merida, which blew open all the aircraft
doors and sent flames shooting through the cabin. One person
was killed: he either jumped or was blown out of the cabin door,
according to initial reports. The fifty- to sixty-year-old appeared
"nervous and fidgety" according to General Ordonez, a fellow
passenger who saw him go through the open door "at the same
time that flames shot into the cabin".

The co-pilot and the steward were injured fighting the resulting fire, and six of the other passengers suffered second- or
third-degree burns on their arms or heads. Captain David Torre
Lathan was able to bring the DC-3 in to land safely at the oil town
of Poza Rica in south-eastern Mexico – he had originally aimed

for Tuxpan, but given the panic on board, he decided to come down at the first available air field. "It was only about 10 minutes or so before we landed, but it seemed like hours, with all the suspense and the excitement," General Ordonez commented.

At the time, there were rumours that the bomb had been set off to try to kill labour leader Apolinar Jimenez, one of the other passengers, or Jorge Hernandex Ornelas, part of the government bank, although both these theories were "discounted by responsible officials".

TARGETED ATTACKS

A National Airlines DC-6B from New York to Miami fell victim to a bomb on 6 January 1960 – the case was linked at the time to National Flight 967, although it appears that there was no connection. It was, however, confirmed in this case that dynamite had been used – and from the condition of one of the bodies, it was pretty clear who had been using it. (Anyone with a particular desire to know exactly what damage a bomb going off next to the human body will cause is advised to read the Aircraft Accident Report on this incident, which can be found online.)

At around 0238 Eastern Standard Time, the aircraft crashed into a field just north-west of Bolivia, North Carolina, killing the thirty-four people aboard. Flight 2511 was non-stop from New York International Airport (now JFK) to Miami, and had made a routine check with the airline just after 0230. The next anyone knew for certain of its fate was when National Airlines were called by Bolivia resident Richard Randolph, whose son McArthur had gone out to feed the hogs at sunrise and had found wreckage in his field. There were other portions of wreckage at Kure Beach, some 16 miles away, which were determined to be the parts torn away in the explosion.

One of the bodies, that of Mr Julian A. Frank, was not with the others, and was only found three days later. As the Civil Aeronautics Board report put it, "the injuries sustained were significant in nature as they were not of the type normally associated with an aircraft accident . . . Medical experts with extensive experience with battle field (sic) 'land mine injuries' and other injuries resulting from explosives indicate that the injuries sustained by the body found at Snow's Marsh could only have been caused by an explosive blast."

Combined with the forensic reports on the wreckage, the Board determined that a dynamite charge was exploded, which "severely impaired the structural integrity of the aircraft; after making a wide descending right turn, it experienced inflight disintegration and crashed."

Frank was a lawyer from New York City, and was under investigation for embezzlement of over half a million dollars and fraud at the time of his death; in the six months prior to his death, he had taken out nearly a million dollars' worth of life insurance, with his wife and children as beneficiaries, and had boasted that if he died, his wife would be "the richest woman in the world". Investigators learned that he was carrying the sort of bag in which the bomb had been concealed when he boarded the plane. Four of the companies claimed that Frank had committed suicide, and therefore they did not need to pay out; Frank's widow, described as a "blond model" who had advertised Camay Soap on television, was "positive her wealthy husband was either the innocent victim of the explosion or the target of a monstrous mysterious murder plot."

Described by one commentator as "America's first terrorist attack", the explosion aboard Continental Airways Flight 11 was the first bombing of a commercial jet airliner. The Boeing 707 itself already featured in aviation history, since it was the jet whose tyres were shot out by police when Leon and Carl Bearden hijacked it and tried to take it to Cuba as a gift for Fidel Castro (see page 282).

On the night of 22 May 1962, the 707 was heading from Chicago O'Hare Airport to Kansas City, Missouri, and its captain, Fred Gray, had changed routes to avoid a thunderstorm on the direct path. Somewhere around 2117, an explosion went off in the waste bin in the right rear lavatory, which resulted in the tail separating from the rest of the fuselage. The aircraft disintegrated, and the crew desperately tried to bring the plane in safely. They managed to bring the landing gear down, and were trying to implement the emergency descent procedures but the main part of the fuselage hit the ground six miles from Unionville, Missouri. Thirty-six of the thirty-seven passengers died instantly, as did the eight crew; one survivor, Takehiko Nakano, lasted ninety minutes after he was found before expiring.

At first it was thought that the plane had been the unfortunate victim of bad weather – the next day's newspaper stories noted that it was "possibly torn apart by a violent storm" – but once the forensic investigation began, it became clear that explosives were involved. W. Mark Felt, the FBI Bureau Chief in Kansas City (a decade later he was to blow the whistle on the Nixon administration as Woodward and Bernstein's informant "Deep Throat"), began an enquiry, checking into the background of all the passengers.

Thomas Doty soon became the person of most interest. He was travelling with Geneva Fraley, his prospective business partner, and both had purchased life insurance before flying – Doty for $250,000. However, three days later, he was due in court to face first-degree robbery and concealed-weapon charges following an alleged armed attack on a woman. In the days leading up to the flight, Doty had bought six sticks of dynamite for 29 cents each at the Pierce and Tarry Trading Post in Wyandotte County, and had also studied the use of explosives at the Kansas City Public Library. He had hoped that his wife would receive a quarter of a million dollars; instead she was given a premium refund of $12.50.

"Suicide by plane" for insurance purposes continued to plague airlines through the 1960s, with an Aerolineas Abaroa Douglas DC-3 crashing into the Andes on 8 December 1964 following a bomb blast that blew the aircraft's tail off, and Canadian Pacific Airlines' Flight 21, a Douglas DC-6B, impacting in British Columbia after a passenger mixed acid and gunpowder in the aft lavatory, causing an explosion that also ensured the tail broke away. None of the passengers or crew on either plane survived.

However, the idea of bombs aboard aircraft took on a more political aspect as the 1960s ended with the rise of the Palestinian terrorist movement in the wake of the Six Day War in 1967, and members of other organizations emulating their techniques.

POLITICAL BOMBINGS

Although the actions of the People's Front for the Liberation of Palestine (PFLP) are perhaps the best known of the politically inspired aircraft bombings of the 1960s and 1970s, they were by no means the first to try to make their point by such explosions. A Comet operated by British European Airways (BEA) was blown from the skies on 12 October 1967 by a military grade plastic explosive.

Given the problems which had been experienced with the Comets during the early part of their history (see page 193), there was particular interest in this crash, but when the investigators discovered clear signs that a bomb was involved, the decision was taken not to go to the considerable expense and difficulty of raising the wreckage from the seabed.

Cyprus Airways used BEA Comets as part of a long-standing agreement, and the de Havilland DH.106 Comet 4B, registration G-ARCO, had been flown from London Heathrow to Athens International Airport overnight on 11/12 October, arriving around 3 a.m. local time (0100 GMT). After refuelling, fifty-nine passengers and seven crew were on board when it took off as Cyprus Airways Flight 284 an hour and a half later, bound for Nicosia.

The flight was perfectly normal, with the aircraft ascending to flight level 290 (29,000 feet) by 0246 GMT, and one of the last messages suggested that they were expecting to pass abeam of Myrtou in Cyprus just under an hour later. Athens Control handed over responsibility of the flight to Nicosia around 0317, and the crew had just made brief contact with the Cypriot control (they had sent the routine "Bealine Charlie Oscar, over", and an acknowledgement was sent) before the explosion occurred.

According to the official report, around a pound (c.450 grammes) of high explosive was placed beneath seat 4-A or 5-A, which could have been either brought on board within a passenger's hand luggage – Athens Airport being notoriously poor at security, as already noted – or stowed there at some earlier point. The explosion created a hole about three to six square feet in area in the fuselage, with outward "petalling" of the metal, which would then have ripped back in the slipstream of the aircraft. Anyone within direct line of sight of the explosion would probably have been peppered by fragments from the blast, with those directly behind it suffering worse.

Because the aircraft crashed into the sea about 100 miles east of Rhodes, and fell to the seabed, some 7,000 to 9,000 feet below, salvage was finally considered to be impractical, so the black box with the recording of the cockpit was not recovered. However, it seems probable that the damage from the bomb didn't immediately cause the aircraft to disintegrate, although it would have sent it out of control.

The Board of Trade report into the accident suggested that the Comet probably descended to around 15,000 feet with the fuselage substantially complete, but then at around that height, it broke into at least two major pieces, which then fell to the sea, around seven minutes after the last call was made to Nicosia control.

Fifty-one bodies were recovered from the sea within twenty-four hours of the crash, some bearing watches which had stopped as a result of the impact at 0325. The wreckage spread over an area 16 miles in length. Initial reports indicated that thirty-two of the victims were wearing life jackets, but this was later contradicted. One of the seat cushions was found "to have sustained damage . . . consistent with that which would be caused by an explosive device within the cabin at floor level" (the report later noted that the damage was "similar to that seen in cushions used to muffle safe-breaking explosions"), and traces of a chemical were found. By December 1967, it was clear that this was "a kind of plastic explosive normally used for military purposes", but the security services in both Greece and Great Britain were "keeping a strict silence on further details".

As normal, when the official Board of Trade accident investigation report was released, there was no speculation regarding the motives or, on this occasion, the identity of the bomber. However, Cyprus at the time was in a state of turmoil, with United Nations peacekeepers on the ground, and not long after the incident with

Flight 284, there was a spate of bombings in Cypriot government-controlled areas of the island which were blamed on the Turkish Cypriot extremists. It is believed that the head of the Cypriot Army was expected to be on Flight 284, but cancelled at the last minute; he may have been the target. Certainly, whoever blew the aircraft up had access to better quality explosives than those who made the home-made bombs that were used for insurance purposes.

Tragedy struck in Nha Trang Airport in Vietnam two years later, when a Douglas DC-6B came in to land shortly after a bomb had gone off, but the pilot was not able to control the aircraft sufficiently to prevent its impact into a schoolhouse and a cluster of what were described as "slum houses", killing people both on board the plane and on the ground.

On 22 December 1969, the Air Vietnam DC-6 was heading from Saigon to Da Nang, via Nha Trang with sixty-three passengers and seven crew on board. It was about 28 miles south of the stopover airport when an explosion occurred in one of the left-side engines, according to one of the stewards who, like the rest of the crew, survived the crash. The flying metal from the engine injured the pilot and a woman passenger but the pilot was able to keep the aircraft flying, declaring an emergency to Nha Trang.

According to US Air Force security policeman Pat Houseworth, who was coming to the end of his tour of duty at Nha Trang, they were told that the aircraft was still flying, and the pilot was going to attempt to make a landing. The security police were called in to clear the area, and the Air Force Fire Protection Specialists were ready to deal with any fire on board once the airplane was down. From the ground, the gaping hole in the rear passenger side of the DC-6 was clear, but the pilot was able to bring it down.

However, at that point it seemed to onlookers as if the brakes failed, and the airplane sparked and began to come apart, sliding inexorably towards the school house at the far end of the runway and the dwellings near it. The momentum sent the wreckage across the road, hitting a Jeep containing four American service personnel, and into the schoolhouse. Two of the Americans were able to leap to safety, but two others were injured before also vacating the vehicle, which was incinerated in the blast as the DC-6 caught fire. At least thirty people were known to have died: nine on board the aircraft, and twenty-one on the ground, with twelve of those believed to be schoolchildren. After the wreckage was searched, the figure rose to ten on the DC-6 and twenty-four others.

Investigations showed that the aircraft's hydraulic system failed, so the landing gear had to be lowered manually. When the flaps failed to deploy, there was little the pilot could do. Rebel Viet Cong forces were blamed for the bomb, but no particular group claimed responsibility.

THE PFLP STRIKE

There was no question as to who planned and carried out the two explosions which took place pretty much simultaneously on Saturday 21 February 1970, sending one Swissair Convair Coronado plane crashing into the forest, and forcing an Austrian Airlines Caravelle to return to Frankfurt. Although their parent organization officially retracted their claim, the Popular Front for the Liberation of Palestine (PFLP) were responsible; and, as recently declassified FBI documents showed, there were many unanswered questions regarding the possible participation of agents working for the Israelis, particularly bearing in mind that the Swissair flight was heading for Tel Aviv.

Captain Karl Berlinger did not believe that his Swissair Convair CV-990 Coronado Flight 330 was going to crash when he first reported the explosion to air traffic control. It has subsequently strongly been argued that had it not been for smoke within the cockpit preventing him and his crew from seeing their instruments properly, Berlinger would have been able to land safely.

The flight took off from Zurich-Kloten Airport as scheduled, just after midday GMT. Around seven to nine minutes later, a parcel in the rear cargo area exploded. "We suspect an explosion in the aft compartment of the aircraft," the captain radioed back to Zurich calmly. "Everything is ok at the moment but we request descend clearance immediately and firefighting equipment on the ground for landing." Clearance to descend from flight level 140 (14,000 feet) to 100 was granted, and the aircraft was redirected on to a 330-degree course to bring it back. Once the airplane reached flight level 100, a further communication was received from the cockpit asking for the police to investigate the incident.

However, at 1226, it became clear that matters were getting worse. "We have a fire on board – request an immediate landing," came the message, which was followed by an urgent request to descend as quickly as possible because of the fire. "Our navigation is not good," they radioed a few minutes later, and confirmed that they had "electrical power failure". Despite smoke filling the cockpit, they were able to bring the aircraft down to 6,000 feet, but as they came lower, they began to drift off track. "We have . . . smoke on board, I can't see anything," was one of the last messages, before a repeated call of "Goodbye everybody".

One final attempt was made to bring the Coronado in safely: "We cannot see anything; can you give me a low altitude?" was the final message received from the doomed Convair. Despite desperate requests from the control tower for the crew to open a cockpit window (to release the smoke) and increase speed, the aircraft nosedived into the forest at Würenlingen, on the banks of the Aair River, west of Zurich, at an estimated speed of 770 km/h. The tons of fuel on board exploded; no one among the forty-seven people on board had any chance of survival.

The situation could have been worse: the plane hit the ground a mere 200 feet from Switzerland's first atomic research reactor. An investigation commission was sent straight to the scene and it was linked immediately to another event that had taken place earlier that day – the bombing of an Austrian Airlines flight travelling from Frankfurt, Germany to Vienna. A device was hidden inside a package, which was contained in a mailbag bound for Israel; when it detonated within the hold, it's believed that the weight of the letters around it managed to contain the explosion sufficiently that it only created a six-feet square hole (about the size of a manhole cover, according to the Associated Press report) in the bottom of the fuselage, and the pilot was able to return the aircraft to Frankfurt. None of the thirty-eight people aboard was injured.

Packages bound for Israel were severely disrupted as a result of the twin bomb blasts. A temporary ban was imposed by several airlines, and an emergency meeting was called, attended by senior representatives of fifty-three airlines, to discuss increased security measures. The events caused consternation in the Swiss Press, and curbs on Arab entries to Switzerland were enforced.

An offshoot of the PFLP, the PFLP-GC (Popular Front for the Liberation of Palestine – General Command) took responsibility for the bombs, but the *New York Times* reported the following day that a spokesman for the main Palestine Liberation Organization denied that they were involved, going so far as to state that it "condemns such barbaric actions" and claiming that "no commando contingent would have carried out such an action".

Ahmed Jabril's PFLP-GC may have been involved with the bombings, but they may not have been the only ones. Concerns were expressed in the FBI about the escalation of terrorist incidents connected to the Middle East during 1970, and a highly confidential document was prepared by the Bureau, profiling the terrorists involved.

Investigations confirmed that the bombs on both aircraft were wired to an altimeter which triggered a positive electrical contact and explosion when the aircraft reached 3,000 metres. According to the FBI, two West Germans had approached the PFLP-GC headquarters in Jordan in the autumn of 1969, claiming they were sympathetic to the Palestinian cause. One of them was an electrical engineer, who provided some very useful tips for the PFLP-GC.

The pair returned to Europe and in February 1970, the PFLP-GC commandos assigned to carry out the aircraft bombings got in touch with them, seeking advice. It was the West Germans who suggested the devices as used on the Air Austria and Swissair flights. The altimeters were bought in Frankfurt, tested, and then wired to the bombs, which were placed inside hollowed-out radios. These were then packaged up and addressed to Israel. The FBI believed that the two West Germans then took responsibility for mailing the parcels from Frankfurt and Zurich, although they note that one of the PFLP-GC bombers may have taken the Frankfurt parcel.

The last paragraph of the report provides the startling suggestion that the PFLP-GC bomber believed that "the two West Germans were actually Israeli agents who saw to it that the bombs were not placed on El Al planes. He felt that the PFLP-GC had been entrapped into carrying out the bombings by the Israelis in an effort to embarrass the Fedayeen. Subsequent PFLP-GC efforts to locate the two West Germans were negative." (The names of the two West Germans, and the PFLP terrorists were all redacted from the document when it was declassified.)

This could explain why the Swiss authorities were unable to get anywhere with their investigation, and it was formally halted in November 2000. In March 2009, a Swiss MP asked if there were further developments and was told: "There is little hope of bringing the perpetrators to justice, because there are not enough clues to their identity to lead to their arrest. This was already the case in 1970, and in the time since then, traces of the assassination have dwindled, and the chances of a successful prosecution further reduced."

THE GREAT SURVIVOR

A bomb blast which destroyed an aircraft in early 1972 led to what was believed for many years to be the world record for someone surviving the longest fall without a parachute – over 33,000 feet. Vesna Vulović was the only one of the twenty-eight people on board the McDonnell Douglas DC-9-32 aircraft registration YU-AHT who survived.

Vulović wasn't even meant to be working on the JAT Yugoslav Airlines Flight 367, flying from Stockholm to Belgrade via Copenhagen on 26 January 1972. The airline had messed up the schedules, confusing her with a colleague with the same name. The last thing that she remembered about the flight was greeting the passengers as they came on board the aircraft; her next memory was waking up in the hospital, the sole survivor, asking for a cigarette.

The official investigation by the Czech authorities revealed that everything was normal on board Flight 367 before the explosion: the radio communication between the aircraft and the ground, and the voice recorder showed nothing out of place. There were no signs of air turbulence, and all indications were that the aircraft was on course and on time, flying at around 10,500 metres. At 1601 GMT, messages to and from the weather station stopped; the flight recorder ceased functioning at the exact same time.

An explosive device, formed from 2,4,6-trinitrotoluene, 2,4-dinitrotoluene, ammonium nitrate and sodium chloride, had been placed in a brownish-red suitcase. That was then put into a black trunk, and packed all around with newsprint and rags. This was loaded onto the airplane and placed in the forward baggage compartment. At 1601, as Flight 367 was passing over the city of Srbská-Kamenice, an alarm clock fired the detonator, and the bomb exploded. Over the next thirty to forty seconds, a temperature of around 350 degrees caused the wiring near the blast to melt down, and the aircraft frame could not absorb the stress.

JAT Flight 367 broke up into pieces and spent three minutes or so falling to the snowy hills. The rear of the fuselage, with the wings but minus the port engine; the front part of the aircraft with the pilot's cabin; and the port engine and its pylon were found in three separate locations, around a kilometre between each portion. Nineteen of the passengers fell from the aircraft while it was still plummeting; three of them were injured before reaching the ground, so had probably been hurt by the blast. The pilots were still in their seats, and had obviously tried their hardest to control the situation.

One of the first people on the scene was Bruno Honke, a German who had been a medic during the Second World War. He thought he could hear screams among the thud of the bodies hitting the ground and he was amazed to discover that there was a survivor. A young woman, still dressed in her air hostess uniform, was lying half outside of the aircraft; the corpse of one of her colleagues was on top of her, and there was a serving cart pinned against her spine. Vesna Vulović had a fractured skull, three broken vertebrae, two broken legs and a broken pelvis. Paralysed from the waist down, she spent the next few days in a coma, but when she woke, she "nearly died from the shock" of reading the newspaper accounts of what had happened to her.

How she survived was a mystery to everyone: Vulović claimed that she was told that it might have been because her low blood pressure caused her to pass out before her heart burst. The official report noted that she had been in the rear of the aircraft and had thus been slightly protected; this is odd, given that in interviews, both she and the eyewitnesses claimed that she was discovered in the middle part of the airplane – and the sections were sufficiently far apart on the ground, according to the official report, that it would be difficult to make such a mistake.

Vesna Vulović herself has never made claims about what happened. "I am like a cat. I have had nine lives," she told the *New York Times*, and explained in an earlier interview: "I'm not lucky. Everybody thinks I am lucky, but they are mistaken. If I were lucky I would never had [sic] this accident, and my mother and father would be alive. The accident ruined their lives too."

None of the Croatian anti-Yugoslav terrorist groups ever claimed responsibility for the bombing, although the Yugoslav officials said that separatists from the Ustashi fascist movement had taken the action – they had also carried out an assassination that day. Vulović became a national hero, and she used her position to campaign on behalf of the Serbian Democratic Party in 2008.

However, a year later, in September 2009, claims were made that the whole story had been a piece of Communist propaganda. Journalists Peter Hornung and Pavel Theiner said that they had researched the incident, and looked at secret documents compiled by the Czech civil aviation authority. According to them, Flight 367 was flying much lower than reported, and that a MiG fighter from the Czechoslovakian Air Force had fired on the civilian airplane because it was just two minutes' flight time from a sensitive nuclear weapons storage facility. The Soviet and East German leaders Leonid Brezhnev and Erich Honecker were apparently flying back from Prague at the time.

"It is extremely probable that the aircraft was shot down by mistake by the Czechoslovak air force, and in order to cover it up the secret police conceived the record plunge," Hornung said. "The Czechoslovak secret police managed to spread this wild tale throughout the world. No doubts have ever been expressed regarding the fall. The story was so good and so beautiful that no one thought to ask any questions."

Certainly if this version was true, it would explain some of the discrepancies in the stories, since the aircraft wreckage would have been spread over a much less wide area if it had only disintegrated at around 800 metres, as Hornung and Theiner believed. The journalists spoke to villagers who had witnessed the crash, and, albeit thirty-six years later, they recalled seeing the DC-9 intact below the clouds when it broke up, and a second aircraft nearby. The Czech Civilian Authority called their ideas "speculation" and refused to comment on the detail. In the Czech magazine *Technet*, an unidentified military expert pointed out that it would need 150–200 people to remain quiet about what happened, if the conspiracy theory was true, and the wreckage would look very different – "it would look like a sieve".

Either way Vesna Vulović – who also doesn't believe the conspiracy theory – was lucky: while *The Guinness Book of World*

Records may have removed her record from their publications (claiming that "It seems that at the time Guinness was duped by this swindle just like the rest of the media"), surviving a fall of 800 or 10,000 metres is more than most people will ever do.

THE FIRST AERIAL SUICIDE BOMBER

On 8 September 1974, the first recorded instance of an Arab terrorist blowing up an American airplane on a suicide mission took place. At 0940 GMT, TWA Flight 841, a Boeing 707, exploded over the Ionian Sea, around 50 miles west of Cephalonia, Greece, killing all eighty-eight people on board.

The plane was flying the regularly scheduled route between Ben Gurion International Airport in Tel Aviv and JFK Airport in New York, stopping off at Athens and Rome en route. It left Israel forty-three minutes late, at 0613, because of passenger security procedures and landed at 0804 at Athens. Fifty-six passengers left the plane in Greece; a further thirty boarded, bringing the total to seventy-nine. The flight to Rome should have taken one hour forty-eight minutes, assuming that it achieved a cruising level of 35,000 feet (flight level 350).

With Captain Donald H. Holliday at the controls, Flight 841 departed Athens at 0912, and eighteen minutes later, reported that it had reached flight level 280, where it was instructed to remain until told otherwise. Ten minutes after that, at 0940, the captain of Pan Am Flight 110 contacted Athens air traffic control to say he had seen "a four-engine aircraft going down in flames". Olympic Airlines Flight 201 assisted with communications between the Pan Am flight and Athens ATC, and relayed a message back that the Pan Am pilot had been mistaken, and that the aircraft, which he thought was a TWA 707, was not burning, but that it seemed as if an engine had separated from the aircraft. He then clarified that the "aircraft is falling [as well as the engine]. I saw an aircraft pitch up into a steep climb then roll over on its back and start in a dive, then a slow spiral."

When debriefed by the NTSB, the pilot amplified that he had first seen Flight 841 about four to seven miles from him, about 4,000 feet, on a reciprocal heading. When he looked back, he saw it was in "a steep climb altitude" and believed he saw something behind the left wing of the aircraft. When it reached the same altitude as his own aircraft, it "rolled to the left into a steep descent" and continued to do so until it vanished from view. The pilot noticed that the no. 2 engine was missing, and that there was a great deal of debris at a lower flight level, which looked like "pieces of paper fluttering down". There was one large rectangular piece among the twenty-five to thirty pieces of debris. He believed that there was no attempt made by the pilots to recover, and he saw at least one full 360-degree roll as the aircraft went down. All of this took place over a period of a mere twenty seconds.

A Greek Search and Rescue C-47 was dispatched to the scene, and around two and a half hours later, its crew reported spotting debris and bodies. Twenty-four passengers' bodies were recovered from the water from the eighty-eight people on board. Unfortunately neither of the black boxes – the flight data recorder (FDR), or the cockpit voice recorder – was recovered: the FDR sent a locator ping, which suggested that the wreckage was in an area with a depth of 10,380 feet.

The debris on the surface was taken to Athens for preliminary examination by a team which included a member of the UK Accident Investigation Branch. Some of the wreckage was found to be similar to the debris from Cyprus Airways Flight 284's crash in 1967, with a passenger's suitcase, a seat cushion, a floor panel section and aft baggage door parts receiving particularly close scrutiny. Two British explosives experts concluded independently that the various particles and fragments within them showed evidence of the detonation of an explosive device; the FBI agreed.

Post-mortems on the corpses confirmed that all died from impact injuries, rather than from drowning or from the direct effects of the explosion. There was no question of this being a "survivable accident".

The Safety Board examined all the other possible options – Flight 841 was trying to avoid Pan Am 110; an encounter with turbulence; and that one of the aircraft's systems or its structure failed. There was no evidence to point to any of these, and the amount of pilot effort needed to achieve the pitch-up witnessed by Pan Am 110's crew would have been excessive. They concluded that there were "sudden and violent inputs into the rudder and elevator controls in excess of the crew's and the control system's capabilities. Simultaneous mechanical pitch and yaw inputs of that magnitude can be accounted for by the detonation of an explosive device."

This might not have been the first attempt to blow up this particular flight. On 26 August, two weeks earlier, a ramp agent in Rome had noticed smoke when he opened the rear cargo compartment of Flight 841: a suitcase was on fire, and the passenger to whom it belonged, a Chilean named Jose Maria Aveneda Garcia, came forward to collect it. The Italian authorities examined it and believed that the "batteries of a tape recorder caused leaking lighter fluid to ignite". The suitcase was kept; the passenger went on his way. When the suitcase was sent to the FBI, arriving in late September in Washington DC, they discovered particles of C-4 explosive, and "other evidence of an 'improvised explosive device or bomb which malfunctioned, resulting in a fire, rather than the intended detonation'." Garcia could not later be traced, perhaps because by the time the FBI started looking for him, he was one of those already at the bottom of the Ionian Sea.

Initially TWA deemed the idea of sabotage on board their aircraft "highly unlikely" but a youth organization in Beirut connected to the Arab terrorist Abu Nidal, claimed that one of its members had surreptitiously placed a bomb on board. The FBI later believed that Khalid Duhham Al-Jawary, who was behind a number of bomb attacks in the United States and the Middle East, may well have created the device. Given that it was established that it would have been very difficult for anyone to add to the passengers' luggage, it was believed that the suitcase must have been checked in by one of the passengers on board, the first bomber to be killed in this way.

A CANADIAN TRAGEDY

Although the Lockerbie disaster is still the best-known instance of a bomb destroying a plane and killing all aboard, there were other examples earlier in the 1980s. The Air India bombing in 1985 led to major allegations of neglect being made against the Canadian authorities; and the attempt by Nezar Hindawi to blow up an El Al jet, described in the next chapter, saw diplomatic relations broken off between Britain and Syria.

Air India Flight 182 was the first jumbo jet to be bombed when an explosive package detonated inside a Sanyo radio tuner on 23 June 1985; a second device was meant to be aboard Air India Flight 301 from Narita International Airport, Tokyo to Bangkok, to explode around the same time. Instead that bomb went off while the package was still at Narita, killing two and injuring four.

The 747 that formed Flight 182 took off from Pearson International Airport in Toronto at 0015 GMT, 100 minutes late, for the short hop to Montreal. The delay had been caused in part by the time taken to fix a fifth engine (a "spare pod") onto the aircraft which was being taken to India for repairs, and to ensure that the various parts connected with it were stored safely within the hold of the 747. The security on the flight was apparently very tight: passengers were checked with both the door frame metal detectors (the sort you walk through), and also with hand-held devices. Every piece of hand baggage was meticulously searched.

Unfortunately, no one thought to confirm that every passenger who had placed luggage in the hold for onward transit from Vancouver was actually on the plane. A suitcase containing a bulky Sanyo radio unit was simply passed through Toronto Airport's systems – after all, it had the correct tag on it for onward transit to India, and it didn't cause the portable PDD-4 explosive sniffer, which staff at Toronto were using in place of a broken X-ray machine, to give the loud scream that indicated the presence of explosives.

There were 307 passengers and twenty-two crew members on board the 747 when it took off from Montreal at 0218 GMT, with an expected arrival time at London Heathrow of 0833 with Captain Hanse Singh Narendra at the controls. The flight proceeded smoothly, albeit slightly slower than normal because of the increased weight from the extra engine; it was given clearance by Gander, Newfoundland, traffic control with co-pilot Captain Satwinder Singh Bhinder notifying them that they would be cruising at Mach 0.81. The weather didn't cause any problems.

At 0700, with just over ninety minutes of the flight left, the crew were chatting as normal; the purser had asked permission for a young boy to come and look around the cockpit, and was told that it would be possible a little later. There were various jokes about the amount of beer that some of the crew were bringing back to India as presents.

The final check-in was with Shanwick Control, the Irish air traffic control centre. Bhinder contacted it at 0706:39, and confirmed the correct frequency for Shannon. Shannon control then spoke with two other aircraft not far behind Flight 182, TWA Flight 770 and CP Air Flight 282, before Bhinder responded to their request to "squawk 2005". The engineer, Dara Dumasia, then called Bhinder, explaining that the flight purser needed thirty Customs seals for the bar, which London Operations would have to prepare. The last words recorded on the cockpit voice recorder were Dumasia saying, "For their arrival – customs. Bar—"

At 0714:01, the bomb within the suitcase exploded. At Shannon, there was an odd sound on the frequency – it has never been possible to say for certain if it was static, a desperate attempt by the pilots to activate the microphone, or the sound of the explosion itself – and then Air India 182 disappeared from the radar. The traffic controllers desperately called the flight, but there was no reply. "One second it was there, and the next it was gone," one of them later told *Time* magazine.

At 0717, Shannon air traffic control called both TWA 770 and CP 282 to see if anyone on either aircraft could spot any sign of Flight 182. "He won't answer us either," 770 replied. CP 282 could only see TWA 770, so Shannon asked TWA to descend and turn to see if there was any sign of 182, and requested other aircraft in the area to keep an eye out.

With still no positive reply by 0730, Shannon called the Irish Marine Rescue Co-ordination Centre and declared an emergency since Flight 182 had disappeared. They in turn contacted the Valentia Coast Radio Station asking them to alert vessels to look for wreckage, somewhere around 180 miles south-west of Cork. The Irish Naval vessel *Aisling* was 54 miles away, and headed for the site; a Panamanian registered cargo vessel, the *Laurentian Forest*, owned by a Montreal-based company, also made its way there. At 0913, the *Laurentian Forest* reported that it had spotted uninflated life rafts and wreckage from the liner. Twenty-four minutes later, at 0937, the first three bodies were recovered from the water. In the end a giant rescue team worked at the scene, with fourteen helicopters, four reconnaissance planes, and more than a dozen military and merchant vessels. By early evening, sixty-four bodies had been airlifted to Cork – early reports suggested that as many as 144 were recovered, but the final toll was 132 recovered, 197 lost at sea.

Autopsies were carried out on those who were found, most of whom, it was established, had been seated in the rear of the aircraft. The findings were revealed at the inquest held by Coroner Cornelius Riordan in Cork in September 1985. According to Professor Cuimin Doyle, head of the Histopathology Department at Cork Hospital, who carried out twenty-three of the autopsies, "no evidence of an explosion was found. There was no evidence of burning on any of the bodies. There was no evidence of which I know of fire and no obnoxious sign in so far as explosive substances were found." The coroner established that if a bomb had gone off in the front of the aircraft, it would not necessarily show on those bodies.

Many of the deceased showed flail injuries: "My understanding is that flail injury occurs when the body is thrown out of the plane," Doyle explained. "My understanding is that as the body descends it flutters like a leaf and the limbs are thrown about and clothing torn by the air." Many also showed small fragments of plastic and metal, which led credence to the theory that the 747 had broken up, and the pressurized cabin opened during flight. Unfortunately, at least three people survived the fall, but then drowned, including one woman who had been five months pregnant.

There was a strong belief almost immediately that a bomb had been responsible. "It is most likely a bomb," Mike Ramsden, editor-in-chief of the aviation magazine *Flight International* told *Time*. "A bomb is the most likely reason for a catastrophe, so sudden and complete, to an aircraft with a very fine safety record." Ashok Gehlot, the Indian Minister of State for Civil Aviation, was a little more cautious: "Explosion is considered a possibility in view of the fact that the wreckage is spread over a wide area. Sabotage is a distinct possibility."

The black box data was going to be vital, but there were concerns that it might not be possible to retrieve the boxes from the estimated 6,000-feet depth. However, HMS *Challenger* was able to detect their signals, and Air India chartered *Léon Thevenin*, a French cable-laying ship, as well as the *Scarab 1*, a British-made remote-controlled underwater drone, to collect the boxes. They were brought up from 6,700 feet below (deeper than the *Scarab 1* had been designed to operate), and flown to Bombay for examination. An Indian judicial team, with additional members from the US National Transportation Safety Board and the Canadian Aviation Safety Board, were present when they were opened.

According to their report, "From the correlation of the recordings of the Data Recorder and Cockpit Voice Recorder and the Air Traffic Control (Shannon) tape, it is observed that the beginning of the abnormal sounds recorded on ATC Tape (the split-second burst of microphone clicking picked up by Shannon as the plane disappeared from radar) coincides with the timing correlation [and] further shows that the conversations in the cockpit were normal and there was neither any warning nor any emergency declared till the time the flight recorders stopped functioning."

American expert Paul Turner added "[T]he explosive sound on the Cockpit Area Mike occurs prior any electrical disturbances observable on the selector panel signals. Electrical disturbances can generally be seen prior to audio signal when explosive sounds originate at any significant measurable distance from the microphone (15 feet) and in the area where there are significant electrical systems. It is my opinion that an explosive event occurred close to the cockpit . . .

"[T]he cockpit area mike signal that follows the explosive event shows a very much higher noise level than cockpit ambient of 85 decibels, indicating to me that the cockpit area was penetrated and opened to the atmosphere. The selector panel signals show signatures similar to those of an aircraft breaking up and are apparently caused by electrical systems disturbance (circuit breaker blowing, fuse switching etc.) . . .

"The lack of a Mayday call and the apparent inadvertent signal from the cockpit suggest crew incapacitation."

Coroner Riordan wanted to come to the conclusion that an explosion had occurred aboard the flight, but was advised that he could not pursue the matter by a Canadian lawyer present at the proceedings. "I think there is sufficient evidence there to be very suggestive that there was a major violent issue up there, near the nerve centre of the plane," he stated, and then concluded: "In short, if the nerve centre should fail the plane has had a serious stroke, call it what you like. The plane was almost certainly in autopilot and it was traveling at about 600 miles per hour at the time of the incident and it was in the sea five miles ahead so it must have lost altitude very, very quickly. It would do five miles in half a minute. This suggests that the first violent incident put the nerve centre completely out of order and the pilot and co-pilot were rendered incapable."

Part of the reason that so many people – including by this stage, the Royal Canadian Mounted Police, who were in the middle of their investigation – were so convinced that Air India Flight 182 was the victim of a bomb was because of the events at Narita Airport an hour earlier on the same day. At 0620 (3.20 p.m. local time), baggage handlers Hideo Asano and Hideharu Koda were removing the luggage from CP 003, which had arrived fifteen minutes early from Vancouver with 374 passengers and sixteen crew aboard; some of it was destined to be transferred to Air India Flight 301 heading for Bangkok. An explosion killed Asano and Koda, and wounded four others.

The forensic information that was gathered from this incident would be vital to the investigation into Flight 182, since there was little left to examine from the destroyed aircraft. A large task force of officers from the Chiba Prefectural Police spent four weeks collecting the evidence from the debris, which was up to 15 centimetres deep in places. This was sent to either the National Research Institute of Police Science in Tokyo or to the Chiba police department's Scientific Research Institute, where infra-red absorption spectrum analysis, thin-layer chromatography, energy dispersion X-ray analysis and other techniques were used.

Although preliminary reports suggested that a "sophisticated timing device" was believed to have tripped the explosion, the Japanese experts discovered that the high explosive charge used a Micronta car clock as a timer, an electrical relay as a switch, an Ever Ready 12-volt battery as a power source, and a blasting cap as an igniter. Also present were a can of Liquid Fire starting fluid and some smokeless gunpowder, neither of which seemed necessary to make the bomb function, but, police officers eventually believed, might have been part of the bombers' distinctive "signature", and purchase of which became a key piece of evidence against one of the bombers.

The device had been housed inside a Sanyo tuner, model FMT 611K, fragments from which were discovered, along with the cardboard box and the foam packing used to transport it. The tuner wasn't small: it was 16½ x 13¾ x 5⅞ inches; this gave plenty of room inside for the bomb mechanism. The tuner had then been placed in a piece of soft-sided luggage, which had arrived from Vancouver.

On both flights – Air India 182 and CP 003/Air India 301 – there were empty seats, one on the former, two on the latter, all in the name of Singh. One ticket, in the name of A. Singh, was never collected; the other was for Mohinderbel Singh, who was meant to be flying from Vancouver to Narita, and then connecting to Flight 301. His ticket was bought for him on 19 June by a Mr L. Singh, who telephoned through to CP Air in Vancouver to book the tickets, then paid cash for them the next day. Mr L. Singh checked in one piece of luggage onto Flight 003, but never boarded the plane, nor did anyone sit in seat 38H or claim a refund.

The other ticket was purchased for Flight 182 for a Jaswand Singh (later changed to "M. Singh"). On 22 June, CP Air passenger clerk Jeannie Adams checked a passenger in using that ticket. The man was confirmed on the flight from Vancouver to Toronto, but was only on the holding list for the flight to Montreal thence to Delhi. The passenger was adamant that he was properly booked, and had paid extra for business class so he could have his bag checked through to Delhi. This wasn't proper procedure: Singh should have collected his bag at Toronto and then checked it in once more for the onward connection, since he wasn't confirmed. Faced with an obstreperous client, and a queue of people eager to get on their flight, Adams broke the rules. She ripped off the original tag, and replaced it with an "interline" tag: "Vancouver–Toronto on CP, Toronto–Mirabel and Montreal–Delhi as the final destination." By a dreadful happenstance, Adams had also checked L. Singh in for the Narita flight.

For a time, the RCMP did wonder if there was a connection with a plot to assassinate Indian Prime Minister Rajiv Gandhi during his trip to Canada earlier in June, and that the "Singhs" referred to in the reservations were alleged terrorists Ammand Singh and Lal Singh. If they were, no proof has ever been found. What the RCMP was sure of was that it was an incredible coincidence that two people, whose tickets were bought by the same person, both checked in at Vancouver, both failed to board their flights, both had suitcases checked through to their final destinations on Air India airplanes – and there were fatal incidents connected to each of their flights.

The suspects came from the extremist Sikh radical community, who supported the movement to create a Sikh homeland known as Khalistan in the Punjab region of India and Pakistan. The Babbar Khalsa terrorist organization had many members in Canada, notably in the western city of Vancouver. Tensions were stoked by the Indian Prime Minister Indira Gandhi's storming of the Golden Temple in the city of Amritsar, in the Punjab, in early June 1984, which led to her assassination on 31 October 1984. Sikh activists in Canada, including Talwinder Singh Parmar, mill worker Ajaib Singh Bagri, and auto mechanic Inderjit Singh Reyat, began talking openly about revenge against the Indian government. Bagri had called for the deaths of 50,000 Hindus at a speech in New York in July 1984; Parmar had urged a congregation in Alberta to "unite, fight and kill" in revenge.

There has been considerable criticism of the Canadian security forces over their handling of the surveillance of Parmar and Reyat in the weeks leading up to the bombs, but while mistakes were clearly made, it would have been difficult to deduce exactly what was being planned. With hindsight, it's clear that Reyat was preparing a device, purchasing the parts which were recovered from the Narita bombing; there was an incident on 4 June when Parmar and Reyat went into the woods, and there was some sort of explosion. On 9 June, an informer told police that Parmar and Bagri had warned fellow Sikhs not to fly Air India.

Canadian intelligence (CSIS) had a wiretap on Parmar's line, and recorded him talking to Hardial Singh Johal on 20 June, asking, "Did you write the story?" When Johal said he hadn't, Parmar told him to "Do that work first." A few moments later, the reservations were made by Mr Singh for the flights on 22 June – but as was pointed out, by what logic could the CSIS have deduced that "writing the story" equated to "buying the tickets for the planes we're planning to place bombs aboard"? Johal's number was left as the contact phone for the tickets.

When investigations proved that Reyat had bought a tuner that matched the one found at Narita, he was arrested and after initially denying everything, provided enough information to be charged with possession of an explosive substance and possession of an unregistered firearm. Only receiving a fine for that on 29 April 1986, he fled to the UK, but after forensic evidence linked him directly to Narita, he was extradited back to Canada on 13 December 1989, and on 10 May 1991, he was convicted of two counts of manslaughter and four explosives charges relating to the Narita Airport bombing and sentenced to ten years in prison.

Talwinder Singh Parmar was arrested at the same time as Reyat, but there was insufficient evidence against him; he went back to India, and was killed in an exchange of fire between police and militants on 15 October 1992 after he had been in custody for five days. According to one of those who interrogated Parmar before his death, Police Detective Superintendent Harmail Singh Chandi, Parmar claimed that Lakhbir Singh Brar Rode, the head of the International Sikh Youth Federation, had been responsible for the bombing, but that in fact, because Rode was an agent for the Indian government, it was an attempt to discredit the Sikh movement. (This theory was presented to the RCMP, who didn't believe it as it didn't correlate with other information they had.)

Vancouver businessman Ripudaman Singh Malik (who had been observed with Parmar and Reyat in the time leading up to the bombing) and Bagri were arrested in October 2000, and charged with 329 counts of first-degree murder in the deaths of the people on board Air India Flight 182, conspiracy to commit murder, the attempted murder of passengers and crew on the Canadian Pacific flight at Narita, and two counts of murder of the baggage handlers at Narita. Reyat was also re-arrested in June 2001, and charged with murder, attempted murder, and conspiracy in the Air India bombing. He pled guilty to one count of aiding to construct a bomb and received a further five years in prison.

Reyat gave evidence at Malik and Bagri's trial but the judge, the Honourable Mr Justice I. B. Josephson "without hesitation" found him "to be an unmitigated liar under oath" and said, "his evidence was patently and pathetically fabricated in an attempt to minimize his involvement in his crime to an extreme degree, while refusing to reveal relevant information he clearly possesses". He was arrested again, and eventually convicted of perjury.

Malik was accused of being the financier of the operation, but the judge found there was no proof that he bore resentment to the Indian government, and that the key witness against him, a Ms D, who claimed that he had admitted his role in the conspiracy, was not credible. Accordingly, there was "simply no evidence tending to point to the role Mr Malik may have played in the conspiracy to place bombs on Air India planes."

Bagri was accused of transporting the suitcases containing the bombs to the airport. The judge found that he "harboured a motive for revenge so powerful as to countenance participation in offences as horrific as those alleged in the Indictment", unlike Malik. Again, one of the key witnesses against him was Mr C; "his credibility has been examined and found wanting to a very significant degree," the judge stated.

"Words are incapable of adequately conveying the senseless horror of these crimes," Judge Josephson said early in his overall conclusions. "These hundreds of men, women and children were entirely innocent victims of a diabolical act of terrorism unparalleled until recently in aviation history and finding its roots in fanaticism at its basest and most inhumane level." After finding that he was "satisfied beyond a reasonable doubt that the explosive device was located aboard Air India Flight 182 in the baggage area containing the M. Singh bag", he found both men not guilty. "Justice is not achieved, however, if persons are convicted on anything less than the requisite standard of proof beyond a reasonable doubt. Despite what appear to have been the best and most earnest of efforts by the police and the Crown, the evidence has fallen markedly short of that standard."

In light of this, Canadian Prime Minister Stephen Harper set up a public inquiry, headed by retired Supreme Court justice John Major, which uncovered further evidence, notably that a large number of organizations, including Transport Canada and the RCMP, were aware of a high threat to Air India at the time and that trained sniffer dogs should have been at Toronto but were in fact all in Vancouver for training. The inquiry found: "It has often been said that the failures that ultimately permitted the loading of the bomb onto Air India Flight 182 on 22 June 1985, were the result of a series of tragic coincidences and overlapping lapses. While this is true in some respects, the many deficiencies and errors that were observed on June 22, 1985, were also the predictable outcomes of poor regulatory and funding decisions and of a lack of leadership, which combined to create an environment ripe for exploitation by would-be terrorists. Air India's operations in Canada were known to be a 'soft target' and little stress on that system was required to set off the chain of failures that ultimately led to disaster."

What happened afterwards was little better, Judge Major declared. "The level of error, incompetence and inattention which took place before the flight was sadly mirrored in many ways for so many years, in how authorities, governments and institutions dealt with the aftermath of the murder of so many innocents: in the investigation, the legal proceedings, and in providing information, support and comfort to the families."

Even though he knew it was probably too little, too late, Stephen Harper apologized on behalf of the Canadian government. "Some wounds are too deep to be healed even by the remedy of time."

FOILED BY EL AL

Security measures on El Al flights have always been notoriously stricter than on other airlines; the airline is very well aware that they are, and will always be, regarded as a legitimate target by the enemies of Israel, of whom there are many. Their security officers are conscious of the responsibilities on them. When they were presented with an unmarried pregnant Irish girl apparently on her way to Israel with no means of support, there was no question of her being allowed onto the 747 which formed El Al Flight 16.

That was a wise decision. There were 3½ pounds of Semtex explosive in her bag, together with a Commodore calculator which had been rigged to act as a detonator. If Ann-Marie Doreen Murphy had been on the flight on 17 April 1986, the bomb would have been exploded when the aircraft was 39,000 feet above Austria. Unsurprisingly when her lover, Nezar Nawwaf al-Mansur al-Hindawi was on trial, she shrieked, "You bastard you! How could you do that to me? I hate you! I hate you!"

Ann Murphy came from Dun Laoghaire in Ireland, and met Hindawi through a friend in October 1984; they soon became lovers but the relationship faltered when Murphy miscarried. They saw each other sporadically through 1985, and in January 1986, Murphy realized she was pregnant once more. Although Hindawi initially wanted her to have an abortion, he turned up unexpectedly at her flat, saying that he wanted to marry her in Israel. He asked her to book an El Al flight, and gave her money for dresses and a passport – but warned her not to tell anyone they were going. He claimed that his work had bought him a ticket on a different airline, so they would be on separate flights, and was adamant that they would need to travel separately.

Murphy did tell a couple of people – her sisters Heidi and Mary – but was delighted when Hindawi arrived at her flat on 16 April, the night before she was due to travel, bringing her a new holdall suitcase. Since she was about five months pregnant by this stage, he didn't want her lifting anything, and offered to pack for her. She spotted that he added a calculator to the clothing, but he told her it was a present for a friend in Israel. Cautioning her not to put the bag near the fire, he left, returning for her at 7.30 the next morning.

As they travelled to Heathrow in a taxi, Hindawi put a battery into the calculator, then pushed it deep inside the holdall. Once they were at Heathrow, he left her in something of a hurry, before she checked in. Her interview at Gate B23 did not go according to Hindawi's plan, when the baggage agent started to run through El Al's standard questions. When Murphy admitted she had not packed her bag herself, she was regarded with more suspicion. She told them she was heading for a vacation in Israel, travelling alone on her first trip abroad. She did as Hindawi told her and said she wasn't meeting anyone in Israel but was going to be staying at the Tel Aviv Hilton. When the guard asked her whether she had a credit card, she produced her cheque guarantee card (a form of identity to back up cheques, but with no credit usage).

By now highly suspicious, the El Al guard put her unpacked bag through the X-ray machine, but nothing showed up. It felt heavy for a supposedly empty bag; when he examined the zippered bottom more carefully, he pulled out a package of a yellowish-white substance. Murphy denied that it could be her bag, but after they found that the calculator was actually a detonator set to go off three hours into the flight, she realized that her loving Nezar had tried to kill her.

Hindawi was a Jordanian, acting as a Syrian agent, who, at the time that Murphy would have been obliterated along with the other 394 people on board the El Al flight, should have been flying back to Syria, posing as a cabin crew member on a Syrian Arab Airlines flight. He had been working for the Syrians since the start of the decade, personally recruited by the Syrian ambassador to Britain, Loutuf Allah Haydar. The Syrians offered to help Hindawi's struggle against the Jordanian government in return for him attacking an El Al plane.

He was controlled by Lieutenant Colonel Haytham Sa'id, the deputy chief of air force intelligence, who showed him how to prepare the bomb, putting the detonator near the main charge in a false bottom. When the detonator blew, the explosive would

Paul Simpson

combust sympathetically. Hindawi was told to use a female carrier as his unsuspecting victim. Anne-Marie Murphy, who he had initially met perfectly innocently, was the obvious choice and she was carrying a child that he did not want (he already had a five-year-old daughter from a previous marriage).

Once he had abandoned Murphy at Heathrow, Hindawi went back to join the rest of the crew who would be taking the Syrian Arab Airlines flight, but when news of Murphy's arrest reached the Syrians, he was escorted to the Syrian embassy. The ambassador apparently complimented him on his work, and Hindwai was taken to a safe house where his appearance was altered. However, realizing that a failed agent wasn't going to be well-received in the Syrian capital, Damascus, he made a break for it, hiding up in a hotel initially, before giving himself up to the police.

Sa'id had warned Hindawi that a quarter of his relatives in Syria would be killed if he claimed to be anything other than a drug runner should he be captured. Ignoring that initially, Hindawi confessed everything, although he later recanted. That didn't make a difference when he came to trial. "There is convincing evidence," prosecutor Roy Amlot explained, "he was acting in concert with agents of the Syrian government." Anne-Marie Murphy was not put on trial.

The Syrians denied any involvement. "This is merely an allegation without evidence," Syrian President Hafez Assad told *Time* during the trial. "It is logical to conclude that some intelligence services, in the forefront the Israelis, are behind such acts because they benefit from them . . . Israeli intelligence, according to our conclusions, did not plan to blow up the plane. Rather, they planned an operation that would stop before a bombing and enable Israel to use the matter politically, as it is doing now."

The jury believed the prosecution, and Hindawi was given a forty-five-year sentence. British Foreign Secretary Sir Geoffrey Howe told the House of Commons: "It is totally unacceptable that the Syrian Ambassador, members of his staff and the Syrian authorities in Damascus should be involved with a criminal like Hindawi. We have therefore decided to break diplomatic relations with Syria." Israeli Defence Minister Yitzhak Rabin told *Time* that he believed "the decision about this crazy murderous act was taken at a relatively high level". The diplomats Hindawi named were expelled from Britain. Hindawi himself was eventually granted parole in March 2013, but remained in prison until he could be deported to Jordan.

But, most importantly, 395 innocent lives were not lost. Sadly no one acted in time to save those who boarded Pan Am Flight 103 on 21 December 1988.

THE LOCKERBIE BOMBING

On the night of Wednesday 21 December 1988, a bomb exploded inside *Clipper Maid of the Seas*, the Boeing 747-121 operating the London to New York leg of Pan Am Flight 103 from Frankfurt to Detroit. The aircraft was flying over the Scottish town of Lockerbie at the time; in addition to the 259 passengers and crew on board, none of whom survived, eleven further people died on the ground. It was one of the worst aviation disasters in history to that point, and certainly the one involving the most Americans, a dubious distinction which was only surpassed by the events of September 11, 2001. It remains the single worst incident in British aviation history.

To date, only one person has been found guilty of the atrocity, and there remain doubts in many minds over the safety of the conviction on 31 January 2001, of Abdelbaset Ali Mohmed Al Megrahi, an agent for Libyan intelligence, the Jamahariya Security Organization – and indeed whether Libya was responsible for the bombing, or whether it was the work of the PFLP-GC.

Clipper Maid of the Seas had only become Flight 103 at Heathrow; it had previously flown in from San Francisco, awaiting the passengers from the connecting flight from Frankfurt. It was on the ground for six hours before pushing back from the stand at 1804 GMT, and taking off at 1825. It was cleared to flight level 120 and then flight level 310, which it reached at 1856. Seven minutes later, Shanwick Oceanic Control sent through the aircraft's oceanic clearance, but received no acknowledgement, and at the same time, the secondary radar return from the aircraft disappeared from radar screens. Multiple new primary radar returns representing the pieces into which Flight 103 had split could then be seen fanning out downwind for a considerable distance – the trail of debris extended around 80 miles along the east coast of England.

Witnesses to the explosion said that they heard a "rumbling

noise like thunder which rapidly increased to deafening proportions like the roar of a jet engine under power" and which "appeared to come from a meteor-like object which was trailing flame". Two large parts of the wreckage fell on Lockerbie; other major pieces, which included the flight deck, were found in the countryside east of the town. When the wing of the aircraft hit the southern edge of the town, it created a fireball which set fire to nearby houses, leading to twenty-one requiring demolition, and many more needing substantial repairs.

The black boxes were found about fifteen hours after the accident: a mammoth search and rescue operation had immediately been undertaken, which involved police from many neighbouring forces – officers from Northumbria Police were recalled from leave and spent the next few days, including Christmas Day, assisting with the operation. Both the digital flight data recorder and the cockpit voice recorder showed nothing unusual prior to 1902.50; both simply stopped at that time. Examination of the flight deck showed that the controls and switches were in their normal operating positions for cruising flight; there were no signs that the crew had tried to react to the rapid decompression or loss of control, or indeed that there had been any emergency preparations actioned. As forensic investigation would reveal, this wasn't at all surprising: the separation of the forward fuselage from the rear would have been complete within two to three seconds of the explosion, at which point the nose section hit the no. 3 engine intake, causing it to detach from its pylon.

The debris was recovered by the Royal Air Force and taken to the Army Central Ammunition Depot at Longtown, twenty miles from Lockerbie. Around 90 per cent of the hull wreckage was identified, and a reconstruction of the aircraft was made. This showed that there had been an explosion on the lower fuselage left side, in the forward cargo bay area. There was a "star-burst" fracture around the shatter zone immediately adjacent to the explosion, and the panels in this area had a layer of soot, which tested positive for explosive residues.

The debris from the forward cargo was identified; this had been scattered along the southern wreckage trail, while the rear cargo hold container had landed on Lockerbie. This was checked for damage which could have been caused by the explosion, rather than the impact with the ground; two adjacent containers showed the most. One was fibreglass, the other metal: from the parts that remained, the investigators were able to determine that the explosion had occurred within the metal container which was about 25 inches from the skin on the lower left side of the fuselage, and its direct effects were clear from the state of the fibreglass. Inside the folds of the metal container skin was an item from a specific type of radio-cassette player. Forensic scientists at the Royal Armaments Research and Development Establishment were able to show that this had been fitted with an improvised explosive device (IED).

Post-mortems on the bodies recovered at the scene showed that there was no unequivocal evidence that anyone on board had been killed or injured by the blast; however it is likely that some injuries would have been caused. Many of those who died were thrown clear from the aircraft during the plane's disintegration; ten passengers' bodies were never found, and there were only fragmented remains of the thirteen passengers who were in the seats around the wing.

The unequivocal conclusion of the Department of Transport Air Accident Investigation was that "the detonation of an IED, loaded in a luggage container positioned on the left side of the forward cargo hold, directly caused the loss of the aircraft. The direct explosive forces produced a large hole in the fuselage structure and disrupted the main cabin floor. Major cracks continued to propagate from the large hole under the influence of the service pressure differential. The indirect explosive effects produced significant structural damage in areas remote from the site of the explosion. The combined effect of the direct and indirect explosive forces was to destroy the structural integrity of the forward fuselage, allow the nose and flight deck area to detach within a period of two to three seconds, and subsequently allow most of the remaining aircraft to disintegrate while it was descending nearly vertically from 19,000 to 9,000 feet."

A major criminal investigation followed, leading to the eventual trial of two Libyans in 2000 and the conviction of al-Megrahi. The Libyan government admitted its responsibility for the Pan Am disaster in a letter to the UN Security Council in August 2003: "Libya has facilitated the bringing to justice of the two suspects charged with the bombing of Pan Am 103 and accepts responsibility for the actions of its officials."

However, there are many in the international community who believe that they were not responsible – or at the very least, not solely responsible. Some of those doubts might have been laid to rest by the testimony of the former Libyan justice minister Mustafa Abdel-Jalil. On 24 February 2011, in an interview with the Swedish newspaper *Expressen*, he said categorically that he had evidence that the Libyan dictator Muammar Gaddafi personally authorized the attack, and one of the reasons that Gaddafi had pressed for al-Megrahi to be returned to Libya from his Scottish prison was to hide his own complicity in matters. Unfortunately, in the three years since he made the allegation, his proof has never been forthcoming.

But if Gaddafi was the one ultimately behind the attack, why did all the evidence initially point to Syrian and Palestinian involvement – to the extent that in November 1991, most neutral observers who had followed the newspaper accounts were anticipating arrests of agents working for those groups?

Even the families of the victims have queried the procedures followed; Pamela Dix, whose brother died in the disaster, called for a proper public inquiry. In 2009, after al-Megrahi was returned to Libya on compassionate grounds, apparently because he had only months to live, she told the *Daily Telegraph*: "One of the central purposes of a full inquiry would be finally to scotch the many, often outlandish, conspiracy theories that exist around Lockerbie and why and how it happened. To take Megrahi and the criminal investigation: there are those who believe he is innocent, those who believe he is guilty and those somewhere in the middle – like me – who believe that they simply don't know. Our adversarial system means that it all hangs on the balance of reasonable doubt – it is not really about getting to the bottom of the matter."

Two Libyans were put on trial in the Netherlands for the Lockerbie disaster on 3 May 2000: al-Megrahi and Lamin Khalifah Fhimah, who was found not guilty because the prosecution had failed to establish its case against him. Going methodically through the evidence in its judgment, the court found "beyond reasonable doubt that the cause of the disaster was the explosion of an improvised explosive device, that that device was contained within a Toshiba radio cassette player in a brown Samsonite suitcase along with various items of clothing, that that clothing had been purchased in Mary's House, Sliema, Malta, and that the initiation of the explosion was triggered by the use of an MST-13 timer." The entire judgment can be read online: some contemporary US newspaper reports were more than a little selective in their choice of extract, so reading the original is advised.

However, beyond these facts, the court admitted that they had real problems with the evidence. How did the suitcase come to be aboard Pan Am 103? A trail seemed to indicate that an unaccompanied bag with a bomb could have been aboard Flight KM180 from Malta to Frankfurt and then been transferred from Frankfurt to Flight 103, but, the court started, "[t]he absence of any explanation of the method by which the primary suitcase might have been placed on board KM180 is a major difficulty for the Crown case, and one which has to be considered along with the rest of the circumstantial evidence in the case."

The court also wasn't convinced by the evidence of two primary witnesses against al-Megrahi and Fhimah: Jamahariya Security Organization turncoat Abdul Majid Giaka and electronics firm owner Edwin Bollier, whose company made the timer involved. The judges were "unable to accept Abdul Majid as a credible and reliable witness on any matter except his description of the JSO and the personnel involved there". As for Bollier, while some of his evidence "belongs in our view to the realm of fiction where it may best be placed in the genre of the spy thriller", other parts they could accept "despite finding him at times an untruthful and at other times an unreliable witness". The acceptable aspects included his testimony that he had supplied devices to Libya, as well as prototypes to the East German security service, the Stasi.

The owner of the clothing store in Malta, Tony Gauci, "was doing his best to tell the truth," the court found, and the judges believed his account of the clothing sold, even if there were "undoubtedly problems" over his identification of al-Megrahi, as Gauci had identified various different people during different police interviews. "We regard him as a careful witness who would not commit himself to an absolutely positive identification when a substantial period had elapsed," the judges commented.

Discussing the possibility of the previously highly regarded suspects, a cell of the PFLP-GC, which was operating in Germany until October 1988, the court noted: "The evidence which we accept showed that at least at that time the cell had both the means and the intention to manufacture bombs which could be used to destroy civil aircraft." The court then added that "the models [of boomboxes] being used were, however, different from the RT SF-16 used in the PA103 disaster, and the timers were of a type known as ice-cube timers. These were quite different from MST-13s, much less sophisticated and much less reliable."

Khalid Jaafar, a twenty-one-year-old Lebanese-American, was originally believed to have unwittingly carried the bombs onto the airplane, according to federal investigators in April 1989, but the court found there was "no evidence of anything being put in his bags" and pointed out that both his bags were found intact in the wreckage.

The court also discounted involvement by Palestinian Popular Struggle Front (PPSF) member Mohammed Abo Talb, who had been named by al-Megrahi as a possible suspect. "We accept that there is a great deal of suspicion as to the actings of Abo Talb and his circle, but there is no evidence to indicate that they had either the means or the intention to destroy a civil aircraft in December 1988," the judges noted.

"The clear inference which we draw from this evidence," they concluded, "is that the conception, planning and execution of the plot which led to the planting of the explosive device was of Libyan origin. While no doubt organizations such as the PFLP-GC and the PPSF were also engaged in terrorist activities during the same period, we are satisfied that there was no evidence from which we could infer that they were involved in this particular act of terrorism, and the evidence relating to their activities does not create a reasonable doubt in our minds about the Libyan origin of this crime."

However, were al-Megrahi and Fhimah directly responsible? According to the prosecution, Fhimah was to use his role as Libyan Arab Airlines station manager at Lurqa Airport to expedite the passage of the suitcase so it reached Frankfurt and, subsequently, Pan Am 103, but the court found that "it would be going too far to infer that he was necessarily aware that (the luggage labels which he provided to go on the suitcase allegedly carrying the bomb) were to be used for the purpose of blowing up an aircraft, bearing in mind that the Crown no longer suggest that the second accused was a member of the Libyan Intelligence Service." When those facts were added to a lack of evidence placing him at Lurqa Airport on the day the suitcase passed through, the judges ruled that he was acquitted.

As far as al-Megrahi was concerned, though, the evidence stacked up against him. He was in Malta on the date the court accepted that the clothing was bought, 7 December 1988. "If he was the purchaser of this miscellaneous collection of garments, it is not difficult to infer that he must have been aware of the purpose for which they were being bought," said the judges. "We accept the evidence that he was a member of the JSO, occupying posts of fairly high rank. One of these posts was head of airline security, from which it could be inferred that he would be aware at least in general terms of the nature of security precautions at airports from or to which LAA operated. He also appears to have been involved in military procurement." He was again in Malta on 20 December, and "[i]t is possible to infer that this visit under a false name the night before the explosive device was planted at Lurqa, followed by his departure for Tripoli the following morning at or about the time the device must have been planted, was a visit connected with the planting of the device". Therefore, "there is nothing in the evidence which leaves us with any reasonable doubt as to the guilt of the first accused".

Even so, the court accepted that "in relation to certain aspects of the case there are a number of uncertainties and qualifications. We are also aware that there is a danger that by selecting parts of the evidence which seem to fit together and ignoring parts which might not fit, it is possible to read into a mass of conflicting evidence a pattern or conclusion which is not really justified." It was those doubts that fed the conspiracy theorists; at the end of the day, there was simply no direct evidence that the bomb definitely travelled from Malta to Frankfurt to Heathrow, or that al-Megrahi had been the one to send it on its way. There was "a real and convincing pattern" of circumstantial evidence against al-Megrahi, but no hard proof.

Al-Megrahi's initial appeal was turned down on 14 March

2002; an application to the European Court of Human Rights was judged inadmissible in 2003. He therefore applied to the Scottish Criminal Cases Review Commission (SCCRC) for review, and in 2007, the SCCRC "formed the view that there is no reasonable basis in the trial court's judgment for its conclusion that the purchase of the items from Mary's House took place on 7 December 1988. Although it was proved that the applicant was in Malta on several occasions in December 1988, in terms of the evidence 7 December was the only date on which he would have had the opportunity to purchase the items. The finding as to the date of purchase was therefore important to the trial court's conclusion that the applicant was the purchaser. Likewise, the trial court's conclusion that the applicant was the purchaser was important to the verdict against him."

Al-Megrahi was allowed to include other grounds in his appeal, even though these hadn't formed part of the SCCRC's decision to recommend it. However, before the appeal could be heard, he was released from jail on compassionate grounds in August 2009 and returned to Libya. Supposedly having only a few months to live, he actually survived until May 2012.

By the time al-Megrahi returned to a hero's welcome in his homeland, Libya had regained its place on the international stage (prior to the uprising of spring 2011 and the NATO military action begun on 18 March that year) after admitting its responsibility. But was this just a cynical ruse to gain readmittance to the international community and the monies that would flow from Western involvement with Libyan business? In February 2004, the then prime minister of Libya, Shukri Ghanem, suggested in an interview with BBC Radio that Libya wasn't responsible but "had thought it was easier for us to buy peace".

Gaddafi quickly retracted the comments, and Ghanem was fired in a reshuffle two years later. But the idea that the Libyans were simply playing "a game" refused to disappear. Gaddafi's son Saif claimed in an interview with French newspaper *Le Figaro* in December 2007 that al-Megrahi was innocent. He repeated the allegation in a BBC documentary in August 2008, explaining away the apology: "Well yes we wrote a letter to the Security Council saying that we are responsible for the acts of our employees or people. But it doesn't mean that we did it in fact," he said, adding, "I admit we played with the words. We had to. There was no other solution."

So if the Libyans weren't responsible, who was? Some theories propounded over the years can be dismissed simply. For example, the death of the UN Commissioner for Namibia in the explosion led to suggestions that apartheid South Africa had put a bomb in the diplomatic bag. This theory was given some credence by allegations that staff from US embassies were told to avoid the flight, but South African foreign minister Pik Botha made it clear that "had he known of the bomb, no force on earth would have stopped him from seeing to it that Flight 103, with its deadly cargo, would not have left the airport."

Another theory claimed that the Israeli government's intelligence and special operations arm, the Mossad, was responsible – the CIA received an anonymous tip to this effect almost immediately after the incident. Ignoring all the forensic evidence, this theory's proponent, Joe Viallis, who saw the Israelis' hands in everything from Princess Diana's death to the Asian tsunami of 2004, suggested that Mossad had used radio detonation to blow up a bomb that was really closer to the fuselage than evidence suggested.

However, despite its involvement being discounted by the judges at al-Megrahi's trial, the PFLP-GC remains the key suspect for many people, and that Libya was a smoke screen. "Conspiracy theorists have alleged that the investigators' move away from an interest in the PFLP-GC was prompted by political interference following a re-alignment of interests in the Middle East. Specifically it is said that it suited Britain and the United States to exonerate Syria and others such as Iran who might be associated with her and to blame Libya, a country which we know trained the IRA. Accordingly, evidence was 'found' which implicated Libya," the Scottish Lord Advocate, Lord Boyd, said in an address to a conference of law officers in August 2001, seven months after the conclusion of the trial of Abdelbaset Ali Mohmed al-Megrahi.

The Damascus-based group, sponsored by Iran, had warned in 1986 that "[t]here will be no safety for any traveler on an Israeli or U.S. airliner". There's no doubt that the PFLP-GC was working on bombs of a similar nature, even if those bombs were not identical to the improvised explosive device used to such catastrophic effect. However, the group's bomb maker was really a Jordanian intelligence agent, and that agent led to the cell's arrest in October 1988. But were all the devices the cell members created recovered? Was it possible that the two cell members who escaped arrest have been responsible for Pan Am 103?

One theory, supported by former CIA head of counter terrorism, Vincent Cannistraro, suggests that the job was subcontracted to the Libyans after the arrest of the cell's members. The PFLP-GC leader, Ahmed Jibril, is supposed to have received one million dollars personally from the Iranians for the successful completion of the mission, while in 2008, former Iranian president Abolhassan Bani-Sadr said that in the aftermath of the Lockerbie tragedy, Mohtashemi-Pur, from Tehran's interior ministry, had claimed he had personally ordered the bombing of Pan Am 103.

In May 1989, Jabril claimed at a meeting of terrorist groups in Tehran that "the Americans will never find out how I did it", as he accepted responsibility for organizing the attack. Former FBI special agent Richard A. Marquise, the chief of the Terrorist Research and Analytical Center at FBI headquarters in the 1980s, noted in 2008: "Did Iran contract with the PFLP-GC? Probably! But it cannot be proven in court. Did Iran ask Libya and Abu Nidal . . . ? Perhaps, but that too cannot be proven and never will be unless a reliable witness or two comes forward with documentary evidence."

In a report dated 24 September 1989, the American Defense Intelligence Agency claimed it knew that the Iranians paid ten million dollars for the bombing: "The mission was to blow up a Pan Am flight that was to be almost entirely booked by US military personnel on Christmas leave. The flight was supposed to be a direct flight from Frankfurt, GE [Germany], to New York, not Pan Am flight 103 which was routed through London, U.K. The suitcase containing the bomb was labeled with the name of one of the U.S. passengers on the plane and was inadvertently placed on the wrong plane possibly by airport ground crew members in Frankfurt. The terrorist who last handled the bomb was not a passenger on the flight . . . The bomb was designed by Mu'Ay Al-Din (Mughanniya), a Lebanese national who lives in IR [Iran] and who is supposedly Iran's expert on aircraft bombing and high-jacking operations. The bomb was constructed in LY [Libya] and then shipped to GE for placement on the aircraft." However, what's clear is that there wasn't sufficient evidence of an Iranian-plotted attack to be used in court, although the Al Jazeera network claimed in a 2014 documentary that they had tracked down two of the PFLP-GC members to whom the evidence pointed. Sources close to bombmaker Marwan Khreesat, who now lives in Jordan, told the documentary makers that "the attack had been commissioned by Iran, and that the bomb was put on board the plane at London Heathrow". They also interviewed former senior Iranian intelligence official Abolghasem Mesbahi, who said: "Iran decided to retaliate as soon as possible" for the shooting down of Iran Air Flight 655 (see page 426). "The decision was made by the whole system in Iran and confirmed by Ayatollah Khomeini. . . . The target of the Iranian decision-makers was to copy exactly what's happened to the Iranian Airbus. Everything exactly the same, minimum 290 people dead."

There were allegations that the Central Intelligence Agency (CIA) was using Pan Am flights as a drug route, ensuring that the suitcases containing heroin weren't scanned. However, a bomb was switched for the drugs on this occasion. This theory suited Pan Am, since, if the theory were true, it could claim that it couldn't be held responsible for the devastation, as the government had consciously created a situation where such a thing could happen. However, this theory was thrown out of the civil courts for lack of evidence when the airline tried to use it as a defence against the multiple claims brought against it by the families of the deceased.

The presence of American intelligence officers on Pan Am 103 has also given rise to conspiracy theories, particularly when the mother of one, Major Charles McKee, hinted that her son had been acting strangely immediately prior to coming back to the United States. One suggestion was that McKee and his colleague were heading to Washington to blow the whistle on the CIA drug-smuggling operation and had to be eliminated, possibly by a bomb carried by Khalid Jaafar (whose involvement in any aspect of the plot was discounted by the Scottish judges, as discussed earlier).

The placement of the bomb in Malta has also been challenged. It transpired that *Clipper Maid of the Seas* stood on the tarmac at London's Heathrow Airport for around five hours between the time the passengers deplaned on arrival and the new travellers boarded. The Iran Air terminal at Heathrow was next door to the Pan Am terminal, so there could have been an opportunity for someone to place the bomb inside the baggage container from which it exploded; indeed, the Scottish Fatal Accident Inquiry in 1990 had shown that the container stood unguarded for around forty minutes that afternoon.

New evidence was introduced at al-Megrahi's appeal by a retired Heathrow security guard, Ray Manly, who said that he had discovered a break-in at the secured baggage unit at the airport the night before the Lockerbie disaster:

"The padlock was on the floor to the left of the doors and had been cut through in a way which suggested that bolt cutters had been used. In the area on the airside of CP2 [the secure rubber door] baggage containers for several aircraft were left. It was often the case that loose baggage would be left in that area. Such baggage would be tagged for loading. I am also able to say that in the check-in area Pan Am baggage labels of various types were left unsecured at the check-in desk. I believe it would be possible for an unauthorized person to obtain tags for a particular Pan Am flight and then, having broken the CP2 lock, to have introduced a tagged bag into the baggage build-up area."

This break-in was dismissed by the judges as not relevant and not as important as al-Megrahi's lawyers believed. However, it's an incident that Dr Jim Swire, father of one of the victims, has consistently felt needed further investigation. "This break-in must have been known to Lady Thatcher, since the Met[ropolitan Police] investigated it, yet the Crown Office has denied to me in writing that they knew about it. That claim demands further corroboration," he wrote to then Prime Minister Gordon Brown in 2009. "Frankly had that aspect of the case been known to the Zeist [in the Netherlands] court, the trial would have been stopped, or never started in the first place. Unlike Heathrow, where all was documented, there was no evidence of a security breach at the Malta airport."

After much international pressure, Libya paid compensation to the families of those killed at Lockerbie, but as Dr Swire said shortly before al-Megrahi's trial began: "Overwhelmingly, the one thing that matters and keeps coming to the surface is our loss and more importantly Flora's loss. She lost the rest of her life, we've lost her lovely company for the rest of our lives. But, yes, the failure to get to the root of it has kept my anger burning."

The quest for answers is not over. British investigators are still trying to discover further evidence in the post-Gaddafi Libya, and the pieces of the wreckage remain carefully looked after, ready to be examined for any future trial. A joint statement was released by the UK, US and Libyan governments in December 2013: "On the 25th anniversary of the bombing of Pan American flight 103 over Lockerbie on 21 December 1988, the governments of Libya, the United Kingdom and United States of America reiterate their deepest condolences to the families of the victims of this terrible crime. We want all those responsible for this most brutal act of terrorism brought to justice, and to understand why it was committed."

There are many who believe that Pan Am 103 wasn't the only flight that Gaddafi ordered to be brought down. Libyan Arab Airlines Flight 1103 (note the similarity in the flight numbers) apparently was also meant to be blown up in mid-air on 22 December 1992 (the day after the fourth anniversary), with Gaddafi intending to accuse the US Navy of carrying out a revenge attack for the Lockerbie tragedy. When the explosives failed to detonate, he then ordered the 727 to be shot down as it approached Tripoli, then blamed a MiG aircraft for colliding with it. Abdel Majid Tayari, the instructor in the MiG, denied that had happened: "There is no air collision," he told the BBC in 2013. "We were too close to each other, yes. But there were [sic] no air collision." Tayari was imprisoned for forty-two months for something he states he did not do, and was adamant he saw that the tail of the 727 had been detached before it hit his airplane.

The Libyan media blamed the effect of sanctions imposed as a result of Lockerbie, but once the regime had changed, in early 2014, Ali Aujali, the former Libyan ambassador to the United States, claimed that Gaddafi deliberately brought the aircraft down "just to send a message to the world that sanctions had hurt Libyan lives," Aujali told a BBC documentary, "making it look as though the plane crashed because it needed spare parts which weren't available." All bar one of the passengers on board the flight from Benghazi to Tripoli were Libyan nationals; there was one Briton. All 157 passengers and crew were killed. No air accident investigation report was ever published.

THE FIRST 9/11

Not every bomb plan designed by terrorists has succeeded; many plots devised by al-Qaeda have been foiled, or, at the very least, not worked as well as they had hoped. While one passenger's life was lost during the bombing of Philippine Airlines Flight 434 in 1994, the multiple bombings planned for 1995 and 2006 did not materialize, and both the shoe bomber in 2001, and the terrorist who sewed explosives into his underwear did not achieve their aims.

Investigators realized later that the explosion aboard Philippine Airlines 434 was a dry-run by al-Qaeda for a major plot, code-named Opan Bojinka. Their intention was to assassinate the Pope during a visit to the Philippines, and to blow up a dozen airplanes around the world. Al-Qaeda's Ramzi Yousef, one of those responsible for the first attempt by the terrorists to blow up the World Trade Center, was one of the ringleaders of the plot, and came to Manila in 1994, the year after the abortive attack. He drew up the plan, and knew that the delivery mechanism that he had devised for the bombs would need to be tested before the operatives embarked on their deadly mission.

What Yousef had realized was that aircraft were not usually fully cleaned through and inspected during stopovers. If he was able to bring a bomb onto a flight, and leave it under his seat, he could leave at the next stopover, and it could then detonate during the next leg of the journey at no risk to himself. Opan Bojinka – the latter word taken from the Serbo-Croat for "loud bang" – would involve multiple such trips, with the terrorists able to prime twelve devices between them. These would all be on timers so that they exploded as near simultaneously as possible.

However, security was higher following events at Lockerbie and elsewhere, so Yousef had to find a way of getting his explosive past security – they had already tested the device at the Greenbelt cinema in Manila on 1 December 1994, and knew that it worked very well. Several people were injured by the bomb, which was composed of nitroglycerin, glycerin, nitrate, sulphuric acid, as well as minute concentrations of nitrobenzene, silver azide and liquid acetone – all ingredients that Yousef and his co-conspirators had bought in Manila. The timers were Casio wristwatches, which were connected to the explosives. But how could he get these past security?

On 11 December, Captain Eduardo "Ed" Reyes was in charge of Philippine Airlines Flight 434, flying from Ninoy Aquino International Airport, Pasay City in the Philippines to Narita Airport in Tokyo, with a stopover at Mactan-Cebu Airport at Cebu, 300 miles south in the Philippines. One of the passengers solely for the first leg was "Armaldo Forlani", who used the toilet early on in the flight, and then asked the stewardess if he could switch seats to 26K, since there was a better view from there on the Boeing 747-283B. Since the flight wasn't full, there was no objection to this, and Forlani, who had had a drink and a snack during the short flight, was one of the twenty-five passengers who disembarked in Cebu.

Forlani, of course, was the alias Yousef was using, apparently a misspelling of the name of an Italian legislator, Arnaldo Forlani. His desire to sit in 26K may have been based on his belief that it was directly on top of the central fuel tank – by good luck for those travelling later, the aircraft he chose had previously belonged to Scandinavian Airways, and they had their seats configured differently; 26K was two rows too far forward for Yousef's purposes.

He had been able to bring the various elements of the bomb aboard in disguise: the nitroglycerine was contained in his contact lens fluid (since this was a dry run, he was only using one-tenth of the amount that would be used in Opan Bojinka). The digital watch was on his wrist, and the wires to connect it to the bomb, as well as two nine-volt batteries and the filament of a light bulb as an extra detonator, were concealed within the heels of his shoes. Since the detectors at the airports worked from leg-height upwards, they weren't spotted. When he went to use the washroom, he took his wash-kit bag with him, assembled the bomb in private, set the timer for four hours' time then returned to his seat, with the bomb hidden from view. All it then took was a few moments' surreptitious fumbling under the seat to place the explosive device inside the life jacket pocket.

With Yousef safely on the ground, Flight 434 took off from Cebu thirty-eight minutes late, thanks to airport congestion. The ascent to 10,000 metres was normal, and the usual refreshments were served. Halfway through the flight, as it was passing over Minami Daito island, Yousef's device exploded.

Japanese businessman Haruki Ikegami was seated in 26K for the second leg, and was subject to a large proportion of the force of the blast. Those around him were also injured and tried to get as far as possible from the bomb site, although the cabin staff quickly moved to keep them where they were. As the crew tried to help the injured, particularly Yukihiko Osui, whose legs were badly damaged by the blast, one of the stewards examined the situation at 26K – Ikegami's head and upper body were protruding from the hole made by the bomb, and he died a couple of minutes later. Osui needed urgent medical attention.

In the cockpit, as he felt the effects of the blast, Captain Reyes believed for a moment that a total catastrophe was about to ensue, ("It was as if a big rocket exploded right in the room," he would later testify) as the aircraft banked to the right – something which the autopilot automatically corrected – but he then took stock of the situation. His first concern was the fuselage skin, and the dangers of depressurization. Inspection revealed that there was a two-square-foot hole in the cabin floor but none in the outer skin, but damage had clearly been done to the aircraft's systems: the autopilot wasn't functioning properly. Realizing that the injured passengers needed urgent medical attention, he decided to land on Okinawa island.

The co-pilot sent a Mayday message, requesting an emergency landing at Naha Airport, and after Captain Reyes had to literally spell out the problem to the air traffic controllers ("Bravo Oscar Mike Bravo") an American controller, based at the USAF base on the island, took over ground communication. He instructed Reyes to turn towards the island, but the autopilot refused to accept any input from its human counterpart, and continued sending the 747 towards Tokyo.

Reyes was concerned that if he disengaged the autopilot, he would not have any control of the aircraft but when he did so, no major problem occurred beyond what they were already facing – or so he thought. When he tried to turn the aircraft, nothing happened, and he deduced that the explosion had damaged the ailerons – as indeed proved to be the case. Several control cables in the ceiling had been severed, connected to the right aileron, as well as the rudder and elevator cables linked to the pilot and first officer's steering controls.

The QRH (the Quick Reference Handbook – the pilots' guide to what to do in emergency situations) advised using maximum force to try to turn the ailerons, if necessary using both pilots. Nothing happened. Re-engaging the autopilot while he considered his options, Reyes in the end decided to use differential power. This would mean putting more thrust through the engines on one side than the other so that the aircraft turned, in the same way that rowing harder on one side will turn a small boat.

Now on the right heading for Okinawa, Reyes began to reduce the air speed. Flight 434 began to descend, and Reyes was pleased to discover that there was some response from the elevator. To increase their chances, he ordered the flight engineer to dump thirty-six tons of fuel – although this worried the passengers as they saw a smoke trail. Reyes was concerned that the landing gear might not activate, but it did, and he decided to bring the airplane in manually. An hour after the explosion, Flight 434 touched down safely.

The investigation by the Japanese police revealed that the batteries were of Philippine origin, and while enquiries were underway, authorities in the Philippines had a stroke of luck. A fire broke out in an apartment used by Yousef, and when the smoke cleared, the terrorist cell belonging to Yousef was uncovered – his co-conspirator Abdul Hakim Murad was arrested, and bomb-making equipment found, including Casio watches. Murad eventually confessed to the Opan Bojinka plot; Yousef was arrested in Pakistan and extradited to the United States. A laptop found at Yousef's apartment with full details of the Bojinka operation, including flight details, showed how close Bojinka had come to activation.

Yousef conducted his own defence, trying to claim that he was in Pakistan at the time of the bombing, but to no avail: he was found guilty of the Flight 434 bombing, as well as the conspiracy to destroy the twelve other aircraft and the World Trade Center bombing, and was sentenced to 240 years in prison. An appeal on technical grounds was turned down in 2003, and Yousef remains in an ultra-high security Supermax prison.

Despite the revelation of the Bojinka plot, in particular the ability of the bombers to bring explosives on board aircraft disguised within contact lens solution bottles, airlines in the United States elected not to invest in scanners which could detect explosives.

THE FAILED ATTEMPTS

If explosive-scanning machines had been in operation in the immediate aftermath of 9/11, then flight attendant Cristina Jones would not have received a horrendous bite as she desperately battled to stop shoe bomber Richard Reid from setting fire to the explosives contained in his footwear – a method described by US attorney Kasey Warner as "ingenious, simple, hard to detect and deadly".

Jones and Hermis Moutardier were part of the crew on American Airlines Flight 63, travelling from Charles de Gaulle Airport in Paris, France to Miami, Florida on 22 December 2001. Tensions were still high following the events of the previous September 11, particularly on American Airlines flights, given that two of their aircraft had been used by the hijackers. Although passengers were initially more respectful of airline staff in the immediate aftermath of the tragedy, things were starting to get back to normal, although the cabin crew were being more vigilant about suspicious activity – and, as proved to be the case on Flight 63, so were the passengers.

They had very good reason to worry about Richard Reid. The 6ft 4 man, described as "huge" by witnesses at the time, had tried to board the same flight to America the previous day from Charles de Gaulle, but had been prevented from doing so when he failed to answer the security questions adequately. A single young man, travelling to America on a one-way ticket paid for with cash, with no luggage checked in and just carrying a holdall, fit enough of the profiles for them to justify holding him for questioning. However, when the French police discovered that he had a valid genuine British passport, they released him and allowed American Airlines to issue him a ticket for the following day.

Flight 63 departed from Paris a couple of hours late, with Richard Reid seated on the aisle. The attendants noticed that he didn't accept any food or drink – not even water – despite being asked three times by Cristina Jones if he needed anything. Rather than feel that this would lighten her load, she registered that there was something strange about him.

Her colleague Hermis Moutardier was similarly rebuffed, and didn't believe Reid when he claimed he was from Sri Lanka. About three and a half hours into the flight, around the "point of no return" (when the aircraft doesn't have sufficient fuel to return to its starting point, so is committed to the onward journey), Reid allowed the woman seated by the window to go to use the washrooms. He then took her seat by the window.

Moutardier was collecting trays from the aisle while Jones was in the galley, cleaning up, when passengers started to report that they could smell smoke. Moutardier noticed that Reid was trying to light a match. She told him sternly that smoking was not permitted, and he promised to stop, picking at his teeth with the dead match. Moutardier alerted the captain about the suspicious behaviour and determined to keep an eye on Reid.

A few minutes later, Moutardier looked across at the scruffy man again, and saw that he was leaning forward in his seat. Believing that he was trying to have a crafty cigarette, she leaned over to him and asked what he was doing. To her horror, she saw what he was concealing. "He's got the shoe off, between his legs. All I see is the wiring and the match," she told *Time* magazine later. "And the match was lit."

The flight attendant desperately tried to grab him, but twice he pushed her away, the force of his movement sending her into the armrest of the seat across the aisle. Knowing she needed help, Moutardier called, "Get him! Go!" as she ran back to the galley to get some water.

Cristina Jones didn't hesitate. Reid was turned away from the aisle, but he was "very intent on doing something," she recalled. "I didn't talk to him or ask him what he was doing. I just knew it in my mind. I yelled, 'Stop it!' and grabbed him around the upper body. I tried to pull him up. And that's when he bit me."

Jones screamed as Reid's teeth tried to meet through the thumb on her left hand. She cried for help, believing that Reid was intent on ripping her hand apart, and one of the passengers reached from behind Reid and pulled his arm back. He jumped on the man's shoulder, and two other passengers – one of them a professional basketball player – tried to restrain him. "He was almost possessed," Kwame James told the *Daily Telegraph*. "We held his shoulders, held his upper body, held him by whatever we could, but he kept fighting back even with three or four of us on him."

French television journalist Thierry Dugeon was seated ten rows back, but jumped straight in when he saw the fight. "It's three months after September 11," he pointed out. "Of course the first thing you think is something like terrorism."

Moutardier had come from the galley with water and threw it over Reid, then passed bottles of water from the galley for passengers to pour over the shoe bomber. Crew members brought plastic cuffs to tie Reid's hands, and a seat-belt extension, used for cots, to tie his feet. Passengers supplied belts and headphone cords, but Reid continued to struggle.

In the end, the captain called for help from anyone on board who was qualified to use the first aid equipment, and two French doctors agreed to use valium from the kit to sedate him. Even under the sedative, he was trying to gain his freedom – rather an ambitious move, given that in the end he was so tied up that the FBI had to cut him out of the seat to which he was attached when the aircraft finally landed.

No one on board was sure whether Reid was acting alone, or, like the 9/11 hijackers, there was more than one terrorist on the aircraft. A rudimentary security system was set up: as the pilot announced that the flight was being diverted to Boston, and that they were going to be accompanied by fighter jets, everyone was told to sit down in their seats. If they wanted to use the toilets, they had to raise their hand for permission, and were searched before they were allowed into the private cubicle. All male passengers' passports were checked by the crew, one of whom set himself up as a human barricade in front of the cockpit. Passengers were encouraged to chat to the person next to them.

Not realizing exactly what Reid had been intending, one of the crew brought his shoes into the cockpit, perhaps believing that the bomber had been reaching for a knife. When he found wire protruding, and a burn mark, the footwear was placed in a safe place.

To try to keep the passengers calm as they flew to Boston, the crew put on the Reese Witherspoon comedy movie *Legally Blonde*, which was effective, as one passenger wryly noted "until we see F15 fighter jets on starboard". The flight landed at Boston, where a SWAT team in full bulletproof gear boarded and took Reid away. The passengers were allowed to deplane, but their ordeal wasn't over: they were kept for two hours before being interviewed, family by family, by the FBI. Everyone's bags were then meticulously checked for explosives, taking up to fifteen minutes per item. Only then were they released to go on to Miami.

The FBI quickly realized that Reid wasn't the lone nutter who had made the bomb from a recipe on the internet, as he initially claimed. Their investigations – combined with information fortuitously found on a second-hand computer purchased in Kabul, Afghanistan – indicated that, under the name Abdul Ra'uff, Reid had been travelling around Europe and the Middle East looking for terrorist targets throughout the summer of 2001.

Born in London in 1973, he had converted to Islam while in prison in the 1980s and become radicalized at the Finsbury Park mosque, at meetings held by Abu Qatada. He chose the path of jihad, training in Afghanistan. After a summer visiting Israel, Egypt and Turkey, he went to the Netherlands, and from there to Paris, communicating with leaders in Pakistan. In the days before he boarded Flight 63, he emailed a "testament" to his mother talking about his "martyrdom to Islam". When he failed to catch the flight on 21 December, he was encouraged by his contact in Pakistan to try again the next day.

He was initially charged in Boston with interfering with the performance of the duties of flight crew members by assault or intimidation. The FBI analysis of the shoes showed they contained "two functional improvised explosive devices". In fact there were over 100 grams of triacetone triperoxide (TATP) and Pentaerythritol tetranitrate (PETN) hidden within the hollows of each shoe – and the probable reason they didn't detonate when he tried to light them was they had become too damp. If Reid had flown the previous day, chances were much higher that the explosives would have worked, but Reid had walked around with the shoes on for an extra day, and because of his own natural perspiration, the fuse had become too damp to ignite properly. It was also clear that he had received help: there was a human hair in the bomb and a palm print on the paper used to make the detonator which didn't belong to him.

On 16 January 2002, Reid was charged with attempted use of a weapon of mass destruction; attempted homicide; placing an explosive device on an aircraft; attempted murder; interference with flight crew members and attendants; attempted destruction of an aircraft; using a destructive device during and in relation to a crime of violence; and attempted wrecking of a mass transportation vehicle. He pled guilty on 4 October, and was sentenced to three consecutive life sentences as well as 110 years in prison. When Reid told the court he was "at war with your country" and then "You're not going to stand me down. You'll go down. You will be judged by Allah. Your flag will come down and so will your country," Judge William G. Young replied, "You are not an enemy combatant, you are a terrorist. You are not a soldier in any army, you are a terrorist. To call you a soldier gives you far too much stature."

Reid will spend the rest of his life in a Supermax prison. As a direct result of his actions, passengers passing through American airports are required to remove their shoes for scanning.

One of the major restrictions on current-day travel arose as another direct result of a plan to blow up aircraft, as well as threats by at least one airline to sue the British government as a result of the chaos caused by the reaction to the discovery of the plot. Liquids are now only allowed through security in quantities of 100ml or less because a group of terrorists intended to detonate bombs that used liquid explosives which they had brought on board the aircraft in drinks containers.

At the time of the arrest of the suspects in the UK, on 9 August 2006, there were various reports about a widespread conspiracy, which US Homeland Security Secretary Michael Chertoff called "as sophisticated as any we have seen in recent years as far as terrorism is concerned". It was believed at the time that the terrorists were in the "final stages" of a plot to simultaneously blow up as many as ten jets flying between Britain and the US. "We are confident that we have disrupted a plan by terrorists to cause untold death and destruction and to commit, quite frankly, mass murder," Metropolitan Police Deputy Commissioner Paul Stephenson said. "We believe that the terrorists' aim was to smuggle explosives on to aeroplanes in hand luggage and to detonate these in flight. We also believe that the intended targets were flights from the United Kingdom to the United States of America."

There was some considerable doubt thrown over the statements issued at the time – statements which led to no hand baggage being allowed on flights for the next week, full body searches, and major delays at every UK airport (and the threat by Ryanair's Michael O'Leary to sue under the Transport Act 2000 – he was told that the Aviation Security Act 1982 trumped his claim) – particularly since it became clear that the plot was not as imminent as had been claimed. The investigators found evidence on a computer memory stick that the accused suspects had looked up flight schedules, but they hadn't made reservations or bought tickets. Equally, the arrests were made earlier than security services had wanted, after their Pakistani counterparts arrested the putative leader of the plot, Rashid Rauf, without warning them. (The case against Rauf was dropped for lack of evidence; he was believed killed by a US drone strike in Pakistan in November 2008.)

However, what did become clear during the trial of eight of the arrested men at Woolwich Crown Court in 2008 was that there had been a conspiracy, and the intended targets appeared to be United Airlines flights from Heathrow to San Francisco, Chicago and Washington DC; American Airlines flights to New York and Chicago; and Air Canada flights to Toronto and Montreal. As revealed at the trial, the bombs were going to be made using half-litre plastic bottles of Oasis and Lucozade soft drinks. A sugary drink powder, Tang, would be mixed with hydrogen peroxide, used as a hair bleach, and other organic materials to create an explosive mix. This was then injected into a sealed bottle, using a syringe, and the hole resealed. A small quantity of a high explosive would then be hidden inside a AA battery to act as the detonator. That in its turn was detonated by linking it to a light bulb and a disposable camera (inside which the battery could be hidden to bring it on to the aircraft).

Abdulla Ahmed Ali, Tanvir Hussain and Assad Sarwar were

tried twice: at the first trial, they were found guilty of conspiracy to murder involving liquid bombs, at the second the jury found that their plans extended to detonating these bombs on airplanes. In July 2010, Ibrahim Savant, Arafat Khan and Waheed Zaman were found guilty of conspiracy to murder. All were jailed for a minimum of at least thirty years.

THE UNDERWEAR BOMBER

Northwest Airlines Flight 253 was the target of the "Christmas Day bombing" in 2009. The Airbus A330 was heading from Schipol Airport in Amsterdam to Detroit Metropolitan Airport in Romulus, Michigan, when al-Qaeda convert Umar Farouk Abdulmutallab attempted to use explosives sewn into his undergarments to destroy the aircraft. Like Robert Reid, he was unable to get them to detonate properly, and thanks to the intervention of Dutch passenger, Jasper Schuringa, no lives were lost. However, if American passengers had been put through the full-body security scanners that Schipol was introducing at the time, the explosives Abdulmutallab was carrying could well have been detected; unfortunately, according to the Dutch authorities, the American government did not want US-bound passengers to pass through the intrusive scanners, apparently for privacy reasons.

The flight was carrying 279 passengers and eleven crew, and left Amsterdam around 0745 GMT, with an expected arrival time in Detroit of 1640. The flight was uneventful, and Abdulmutallab spent some time in the washroom in the period before the descent, brushing his teeth and putting on some cologne before returning to his seat. He told the people next to him that he had an upset stomach, and covered himself with a blanket. A mere twenty minutes before Flight 253 was due to arrive, after saying his prayers, Abdulmutallab tried to inject chemicals with a syringe into the explosive which he had just retrieved from his underwear (although he initially told police he had it strapped to his leg). "There was a pop that sounded like a firecracker," passenger Syed Jafry told the *New York Times*, which was followed by smoke and a "glow" from Abdulmutallab's seat.

Passengers cried out in alarm, and Dutch film director Jasper Schuringa, who was seated in the same row as Abdulmutallab but on the right-hand side of the aircraft, saw what looked like an object on fire in the Nigerian man's lap and "freaked".

Abdulmutallab wasn't saying anything, and according to witnesses was initially just sitting there in the flames, which were on his leg and the wall of the aircraft.

"Without any hesitation, I just jumped over all the seats," Schuringa explained. "I was thinking, Oh, he's trying to blow up the plane. I was trying to search his body for any explosive. I took some kind of object that was already melting and smoking, and I tried to put out the fire and when I did that I was also restraining the suspect."

Schuringa's hands were burned as he fought with Abdulmutallab, and he shouted for water, particularly as the fire appeared to be getting worse. Schuringa grabbed the terrorist out of his seat, and the flight attendants doused the flames with fire extinguishers. They then helped Schuringa walk Abdulmutallab up to the first-class compartment, where they stripped and searched him, and locked him in handcuffs. He was asked what he had in his pocket, and he replied, "Explosive device."

The pilot declared an in-flight emergency when a fire indicator light came on in the cockpit, and airport rescue, firefighting services, as well as law enforcement officials were put on standby. When the aircraft landed in Detroit, Abdulmutallab was arrested and questioned for nearly an hour before being given hospital treatment. The passengers were deplaned, and then, as the Transport Security Administration explained, "out of an abundance of caution, the plane was moved to a remote area" where the airplane and all baggage were rescreened.

Preliminary analysis indicated that Abdulmutallab was carrying PETN, and he was charged with placing a destructive device in, and attempting to destroy, a US civil aircraft. He was convicted of these plus a further six charges including conspiracy to commit an act of terrorism and attempted use of a weapon of mass destruction on 16 February 2012.

In a recording, Osama bin Laden admitted responsibility for the attack: "If our messages to you could be carried by words, we would not have delivered them by planes," he said on an audio tape, broadcast on Arab television on 24 January 2010. "The message we want to communicate to you through the plane of the hero, the holy warrior Umar Farouk, is a confirmation of a previous message, which was delivered to you by the heroes of [September 11] and which was repeated previously and afterward."

Abdulmutallab confessed that he had been ordered by Anwar al-Awlaki, an American-born radical Muslim cleric, to "wait until the airplane was over the United States and then take it down". The device had been prepared by an al-Qaeda bomb maker, Ibrahim Hassan al-Asiri, who showed him how to use a syringe to inject a chemical that would initiate a fire, which was in turn supposed to detonate the explosive. He received four consecutive life sentences, plus an additional fifty years, on the charges, despite an attempt to claim that would be a cruel punishment, since he didn't kill or seriously injure anyone.

Two further plots were foiled by authorities: in 2010, explosives were brought on board aircraft inside printer cartridges (whose workings would have masked the circuitry of the bombs). Two devices were found on 29 October, one containing 400 grams of PETN, the other 300 – both considerably larger than that used by Abdulmutallab. Both had been transported by cargo planes and passenger jets; however it seemed as if al-Qaeda intended them to explode once the aircraft were in American airspace, and thus would have been with couriers. One was found at East Midlands Airport in the UK; the other at Dubai.

At the end of April 2012, a further plot was uncovered, which would have used a device created by al-Asiri with no metal parts and a different sort of detonator, according to American officials. The would-be suicide bomber was arrested before he could go to an airport; however, as one anonymous official told the *New York Times*: "If they built one, they probably built more. That's the scary part."

Part 9:
Shootdowns

THE USTICA MASSACRE

During wars in the twentieth and twenty-first centuries, pilots have been pitted against pilots, with the victors often the more skilled flyer, or the one with better technology at their disposal. But there are numerous incidents where unarmed commercial aircraft have been shot down, either by other aircraft or by a missile attack.

English actor Leslie Howard was the victim of one such incident during the Second World War, while the shooting down of a Cathay Pacific Douglas C-54 in July 1954 led to delays in the People's Republic of China being allowed entrance to the United Nations. An El Al flight that strayed into Bulgarian airspace the following year was shot down by Bulgarian MiG-15 jets at the height of tensions in the Cold War – some believed that the El Al pilots tried to make a run for it when they were challenged – while the Israelis were responsible for the downing of a 727 operated by Libyan Arab Airlines in February 1973, an act described by Israeli Minister of Defence Moshe Dayan as "an error of judgement". During the conflict in Rhodesia (as it was at the time), the Zimbabwe People's Revolutionary Army shot down two flights belonging to Air Rhodesia using Strela 2 missiles in September 1978 and February 1979; at the first, ten of the survivors were killed by the guerrillas at the crash site; at the second, everyone was killed. (Strela 2 missiles would continue to be used nearly a quarter of a century later by militant groups; two were fired during the 2002 Mombasa attack on Israeli airline Arkia.)

One of the most contentious incidents occurred on 27 June 1980 when Aerolinee Itavia Flight 870 crashed into the Tyrrhenian Sea near the island of Ustica – an incident referred to by the Italian media as the Ustica Massacre. No one knows exactly what happened: the DC-9 was heading from Bologna to Palermo, with seventy-seven passengers, two pilots and two flight attendants on board. At 8.59 p.m. local time, it simply disappeared off the screens of Italian ATC – there were no reports of trouble, maydays or other evidence.

But the investigation, such as it was, seemed dogged by difficulties: recordings went missing, key witnesses died. The first investigation stated that "All available evidence considered unanimously confirms that the DC-9 incident was caused by a missile that exploded near the nose of the plane. At the present time, the evidence is insufficient to specify the type, origin and identity of the missile." In 1989, the Italian Parliamentary Commission on Terrorism issued a statement regarding Flight 870 claiming that it occurred "following a military interception action, the DC-9 was shot down, the lives of eighty-one innocent citizens were destroyed by an action properly described as an act of war, real war undeclared, a covert international police action against our country, which violated its borders and rights."

Five years later, an investigation was carried out jointly by the British Air Accidents Investigation Branch and Italian investigators, who examined the wreckage and found evidence that a bomb had exploded in the rear lavatory. Both theories couldn't be true, although it seemed as if the wreckage supplied evidence to back both up. (*Air Crash Investigation*'s episode *Massacre Over the Mediterranean* firmly backed the bomb theory, despite the later revelations.)

Documents discovered in Libya following the fall of Muammar Gaddafi suggested that the 1989 report may have had validity after all. That night, Gaddafi was due to travel back from Europe to Libya in his personal Tupolev jet, and the French considered that this was a good time to assassinate him. Mirage fighters could shoot the aircraft down, and there would be one less dictator to deal with.

Gaddafi didn't travel, after being tipped off by someone from the Italian secret service of the plan. He landed in Malta, but failed to notify the Libyan Air Force of his change of plans, and a MiG-23 fighter was sent to escort him back. Not able to find the leader on his prescribed route, the pilot tried to search for him – and found himself picked up as a potential hostile target by the Italian Air Force and the US Navy, who sent fighters up. That meant that there were now representatives of four nations in the skies above Sicily – as well as the unsuspecting crew of Itavia Flight 870.

Then followed a catastrophic series of errors. The MiG pilot assumed that the jet was Gaddafi's, so went into close formation with it. The French Mirage pilots saw a jet and a fighter together, and assumed that they were the Libyans – they were flying in the direction of North Africa – so fired a missile, blowing Flight 870 out of the sky. A dogfight between the Libyan MiG pilot and the Mirages followed with the MiG eventually crashing into the Sila Mountains in Castelsilano, Calabria, where it was found on 18 July 1980, three weeks after the incident. The links between the two were hastily covered up but in 2008, the former Italian President, Francesco Cossiga, confirmed that French fighter jets had been responsible, and three years after that Italian courts ordered the Italian government to pay $127 million to the families of those aboard the jet for failure to protect the flight and concealment of the truth. In January 2013, the Italian Supreme Court ruled that there was "abundantly" clear evidence of the missile strike.

THE BRINK OF WAR

Perhaps one of the most famous shootdowns occurred on 1 September 1983, when a Soviet Su-15TM fighter fired on Korean Air Lines Flight 007, with US congressman Larry McDonald aboard. According to US President Ronald Reagan, this was a "crime against humanity", and "an act of barbarism" – and the escalation that followed between the United States and the Soviet Union brought the world very close to war. The aircraft might not have been from an American airline, but it had left from American territory, and was carrying at least sixty-one American passengers. For some of McDonald's fellow congressmen, the attack was on a par with attacking a school bus, and that sentiment was shared by their allies. "Would Washington or our government ever dream of launching killer missiles? Never in a million years," proclaimed the British *Sun* newspaper.

KAL 007 was thirty-five minutes late leaving JFK in New York on the night of 30 August, bound for Seoul (the flight crossed the international date line, which is why it would appear to be a two-day journey). Two hundred and sixty-nine people, including twenty-three crew, were aboard the flight, which was due to stop over at Anchorage Airport in Alaska. This it duly did after a seven-hour flight, and the aircraft left Anchorage at 1300 GMT on 31 August, with Captain Chun Byung-in in charge. The flight wasn't full – at least one key person, former president Richard Nixon, had decided not to travel that day.

The route from Alaska to Seoul took the 747 along Red Route 20, the most northern of the five NOPAC (North Pacific) routes that ran between Alaska and Japan. The 3,800 miles should have taken about seven and a half hours to complete, passing by the Kamchatka Peninsula (part of the Soviet Union), about 30 miles from the Kuril islands, and then down over Honshu and west into Seoul. The maps were very clear about the dangers of straying off course: "Aircraft infringing upon non-free flying territory may be fired on without warning." The Soviets monitored all flights near their territory, and in their turn the Americans monitored the Soviet radar stations' communications.

Unfortunately for Captain Byung-in and everyone else on board Flight 007, the autopilot wasn't working in the correct mode. Instead of keeping the 747 within Red Route 20, it was allowing the aircraft to start drifting off course – northwards, towards the Soviet Union. Twenty-eight minutes after Flight 007 left Anchorage, it was 5.6 miles north from where it should have been; when fifty minutes had elapsed, it was 12.6 miles off course. This divergence kept increasing, and the aircraft strayed into the North American Air Defence buffer zone, as it eventually found itself 160 miles north of where it should be ... and heading directly for the Kamchatka Peninsula.

At 1551 GMT, KAL 007 entered the Soviets' restricted air space zone, which extended 120 miles from the Kamchatka coastline. When it was 80 miles from the coast, a MiG and three Su-15 Flagon fighters were scrambled by the Soviets. The elderly fighters tried to keep up with the 747, as it crossed the peninsula, and then re-entered international airspace over the Sea of Okhotsk. But when it reached the island of Sakhalin – an area which held highly secret Soviet military equipment and personnel – the Commander of the Soviet Far East District Air Defence Forces, General Valery Kamensky, ordered that it should be destroyed even if it was in international airspace, as long as it was not a passenger craft. His subordinate, General Anatoly Kornukov, the commander of Sokol Air Base, was adamant that it couldn't be civilian: "I am giving the order to attack if it crosses the State border," he announced.

The lead Su-15 fighter pilot, Major Gennadi Osipovich, fired warning shots – around 200 rounds of armour-piercing shells – but on board the 747, Captain Byung-in seemed unaware of the peril he was in. He was in contact with Tokyo ATC asking if he could climb to a higher level to eke out the fuel a bit more. He started to climb towards flight level 350, and the Su-15 overshot him.

With no access to KAL 007's communications with Tokyo ATC (despite later claims that he had spoken with the 747 prior to the attack), the Soviet pilot assumed that this was an evasive manoeuvre. The 747 was heading out of Soviet airspace once more, and he was ordered to fire at the aircraft. Two Kaliningrad K-8 air-to-air missiles were released, and seconds later Japanese fishermen saw a "glowing orange-coloured, expanding fireball".

The explosions didn't destroy the aircraft. The Soviet pilot claimed that he had taken off half of the 747's left wing, but in fact the data recorder showed that it was intact at that point. Instead the missiles damaged it, and Captain Byung-in started a slow and painful descent, levelling off at 16,424 feet, and trying to turn north. However, he couldn't keep control as the aircraft rapidly decompressed, and the 747 descended over Moneron Island. What happened after that was open to speculation: the last ten minutes of the flight weren't recorded by either of the black boxes.

For a time, the Japanese Civil Aviation Bureau, who were tracking it, informed the FAA that "Japanese self-defence force radar confirms that the Hokkaido radar followed Air Korea to a landing in Soviet territory on the island of Sakhalinska and it is confirmed by the manifest that Congressman McDonald is on board." For five hours, relatives of the passengers waited for news, and then were told that the aircraft had landed safely; it was a further thirteen hours before the truth came out as the American intercepts of the Soviet transmissions were revealed. "The Soviet pilot reported that he fired a missile and the target was destroyed," Secretary of State George Shultz announced. The Soviet Union said nothing for a couple of days, but eventually the official news agency TASS admitted that there had been an "unidentified plane" which "violated the state border and intruded deep into the Soviet Union's airspace", implying that the 747 had been on a spying mission. President Ronald Reagan was incandescent with rage: "What can we think of a regime that so broadly trumpets its vision of peace and global disarmament and yet so callously and quickly commits a terrorist act to sacrifice the lives of innocent human beings?"

The full story of KAL 007's final flight took many years to come out. Key pieces of evidence – such as the CVR transcript – were kept under wraps by the Soviets, and it was only after the fall of the USSR and the rise of the Russian Federation that the information was shared with the rest of the world. The Soviets carried out their own search and rescue operation, as did the Americans and Japanese, acting on behalf of the aircraft's owners, the South Koreans. The Soviets found the wreckage quickly (although they didn't tell the Western powers they'd done so) but they did pass over some effects which drifted to shore.

No NTSB enquiry was carried out, on State Department orders since it wasn't an accident, and the International Civil Aviation Organization (ICAO) took over responsibility for the investigation. The ICAO couldn't force parties to divulge information, so their preliminary report on 2 December 1983 was based on simulations; they deduced that an autopilot error was responsible for the accidental violation of Soviet airspace. An amendment to the Convention on International Civil Aviation made it clear: "The contracting States recognize that every State must refrain from resorting to the use of weapons against civil aircraft in flight and that, in case of interception, the lives of persons on board and the safety of aircraft must not be endangered."

Russian Federation President Boris Yeltsin assisted with the transfer of materials to the South Koreans and the ICAO, including transcripts of the Soviets' own activity, and a fresh inquiry was opened. The Russian Federation carried out their own investigation and concluded it was a case of mistaken identity; the new data helped the ICAO to confirm their own original theory. Contrary to the many conspiracy theories which have grown up around the flight, the truth was horribly simple: at a time of heightened world tensions, KAL Flight 007 had inadvertently been in the wrong place at very much the wrong time.

"THE OTHER LOCKERBIE"

If KAL 007 had been in the wrong place at the wrong time, much the same could be said about Iran Air Flight 655, whose fate showed that it wasn't just the USSR who could make fatal mistakes – the Airbus A300 was shot down by the US Navy ship USS *Vincennes* on 3 July 1988, while it was over Iran's territorial waters. Two hundred and ninety people were killed in an incident that the BBC described as "the other Lockerbie".

It was a time as "tense, volatile and uncertain", to quote Admiral William Crowe, as the Cold War: the Iran-Iraq war was underway, and US navy personnel were in the Persian Gulf, engaging periodically with Iranian forces. On 29 April, that year the Navy's protection was extended to all friendly shipping outside declared exclusion zones, and USS *Vincennes*, which had the state-of-the-art Aegis Combat System fitted, was rushed to the Gulf, arriving in Bahrain on 29 May. Its captain was William C. Rogers III.

On the morning of 3 July, Captain Mohsen Rezaian was preparing to take his Airbus A300 on the twenty-eight-minute second leg of his flight from Tehran to Dubai via Bandar Abbas, an airfield in southern Iraq that, like many in that part of the world, was used by both military and civilian aircraft. He should have taken off at 0950 local time (0620 GMT) but there was a short delay, and eventually the Airbus was on its way at 1017.

Like all Iran Air aircraft, the Airbus was equipped with a transponder which was set to squawk Mode III, the civilian frequency (as opposed to Mode II, which was used by the military), and the specific code 6760 – the 6700-series meant it was a commercial, not military, aircraft. Captain Rezaian was using air corridor Amber 59, the 20-mile wide lane direct to Dubai, climbing to a cruising altitude of 14,000 feet as he gained speed. He was still climbing through 13,500 feet when the Airbus was hit by two SM-2ER anti-aircraft missiles which had been fired by USS

Vincennes. The aircraft tumbled in flames near Qeshm Island into the waters of the Persian Gulf, where its black boxes disappeared for ever. There were no survivors.

The *Vincennes* crew believed that they had destroyed an F-14 fighter belonging to the Iranian Air Force which was diving towards them intent on their destruction. The discrepancy in size between an Airbus and the fighter would seem to make that almost impossible to believe. As with the truth about Korean Air Lines Flight 007, it took some time before the whole story of what went on that day became public – in part because the US Navy, understandably, did not necessarily want to release operational information to the media while they still had service personnel in the Gulf. There were also some serious discrepancies between the recollections of the personnel on the *Vincennes* and the electronic records which were being automatically generated by the ship's systems; as the *New York Times* pointed out: "Without Aegis, we would undoubtedly be reading for years to come articles about the great Iranian kamikaze plot."

At the time of the attack, USS *Vincennes* was actually within Iranian territorial waters (something which wasn't immediately apparent in the coverage of the incident when it was being portrayed as the United States protecting itself). The guided missile cruiser was part of Operation Earnest Will, and earlier that day one of its helicopters had taken small arms fire from patrol vessels belonging to the Iranian Revolutionary Guard (whether the helicopter should have been that near to the patrol vessels is a matter of debate). The *Vincennes* pursued the vessels, initially into Omani waters – where all participants in the chase were ordered to leave by an Omani Navy warship – and then into Iranian waters.

Nearby were two other Navy warships, the USS *Sides* and the USS *Elmer Montgomery*. The *Sides* remained some miles away, with its systems automatically linked to the *Vincennes'*, but the *Elmer Montgomery* was with the *Vincennes* within the 12-mile line that delineated the Iranian waters. Shots were being exchanged between the *Vincennes* and the Iranians as the Airbus took off from Bandar Abbas, and on the *Sides*, the captain was informed that there was an F-14 coming out from the airport. It was given track number 4131, and since the *Vincennes* and the *Sides'* systems were linked, Rogers' ship used the same designation.

Both the *Vincennes* and the *Sides* tried to contact 4131 on the International Air Distress and the Military Air Distress frequencies, and Captain Carlson on the *Sides* ordered his men to "light him up" – this would indicate to a military pilot that he was being tracked by missile fire control radar, and, if he had any sense, he'd turn around and go back to base rather than risk being fired at. However, 4131 didn't make any sort of change to its flight pattern, continuing to accelerate slowly and climb.

However, on the *Vincennes*, people were making mistakes. The Mode III squawk was being misreported up the chain of command as a Mode II, and the challenges were directed to an unidentified "Iranian F-14". Somehow the fact that a commercial aircraft might be flying directly overhead was missed, even though Navy listings of scheduled flights was checked (the multiple time zones in the region, particularly with some of them half an hour out from normal may have contributed to the error). A warning that the flight might be a "COMAIR" (commercial aircraft) was ignored.

More challenges were issued ("Iranian fighter, you are steering into danger and are subject to United States naval defensive measures") although not over the air traffic control frequency which the Airbus had recently been using to communicate with the tower. The most recent IFF (Identity, Friend or Foe?) query of the transponder showed that it was military – although it seems that whoever was working it hadn't recalibrated the range on the IFF device, so it was reacting to a real F-14 on the ground at Bandar Abbas. According to what Rogers was being told by his men, the aircraft was coming straight at him, and was descending.

Believing that he was acting in self-defence, to prevent harm to his ship and his people, Rogers made the decision to fire, but almost as soon as the missiles had made contact, it started to become obvious that the target which had been destroyed was bigger than an F-14. On the *Elmer Montgomery*, they saw the wing of the Airbus plummet into the sea. And on the *Sides*, Carlson and his crew were horrified when his radar people confirmed that it was a commercial aircraft.

Initially, the American public were told that the Iranian jet had been outside the commercial air corridor, and had only been fired upon when it had failed to respond to warnings, and was descending towards the *Vincennes*. That day, President Reagan issued a statement describing it as "a proper defensive action . . . The course of the Iranian civilian airliner was such that it was headed directly for the USS *Vincennes*, which was at the time engaged with five Iranian Boghammar boats that had attacked our forces. When the aircraft failed to heed repeated warnings, the *Vincennes* followed standing orders and widely publicized procedures, firing to protect itself against possible attack." A letter from the president to the Speaker of the House of Representatives and the President Pro Tempore of the Senate the next day confirmed that "USS *Vincennes* and USS *Elmer Montgomery* were operating in international waters". However, by 11 July, the president had decided that "the United States will offer compensation on an ex gratia basis to the families of the victims who died in the Iranian airliner incident . . . consistent with international practice and is a humanitarian effort to ease the hardship of the families. It is offered on a voluntary basis, not on the basis of any legal liability or obligation."

Admiral William Fogarty conducted a "Formal Investigation into the Circumstances Surrounding the Downing of Iran Air Flight 655 on 3 July 1988", which concluded that "The data from USS *Vincennes* tapes, information from USS *Sides* and reliable intelligence information, corroborate the fact that [Iran Air Flight 655] was on a normal commercial air flight plan profile, in the assigned airway, squawking Mode III 6760, on a continuous ascent in altitude from take-off at Bandar Abbas to shoot-down." The ICAO reported in December 1988, confirming that the *Vincennes* was in Iranian waters, something the Navy had sought to keep quiet for operational reasons, and noting that Captain Rezaian probably assumed that the calls from the *Vincennes* and the *Sides* were directed at a different aircraft.

Iran took the US to the International Court of Justice in 1989, and seven years later, President Bill Clinton authorized the payment of $61.8 million ($300,000 per wage-earning victim, $150,000 per non-wage-earner, the rest for the aircraft) as compensation, explicitly on the "ex gratia" basis which his predecessor had mentioned.

THE MISSILE THAT WASN'T

Many apparently unexplained incidents have been attributed to missile fire; there are even those who believe that some of the aircraft hijacked during the 9/11 attacks were fired upon, and that's why they crashed. Aer Lingus Flight 712, a Vickers Viscount, disappeared off County Wexford, Eire, in March 1968; some people were adamant that it had been hit by an experimental missile sent from the test station at Aberporth in West Wales. And there are those who are equally certain that the explosion of TWA Flight 800 over Moriches Inlet in New York was caused by a missile, despite numerous pieces of evidence to the contrary.

"We just saw an explosion up ahead of us here something [like] about sixteen thousand feet [altitude] or something like that. It just went down – to the water." Eastwind Airlines' Captain David McClaine was an eyewitness to the death of TWA Flight 800 on 17 July 1996. He wasn't the only one: there were dozens of people – some sources suggest as many as 244 of them – on Long Island, to the west of the aircraft's trajectory, who believed that they had seen something that resembled a flare or a firework ascend, which culminated in an explosion. Accordingly, the FBI and the CIA became involved in the investigation alongside the NTSB; as FBI Assistant Director James K. Kallstrom noted: "A lot of people saw things in the sky. And a lot of people saw what we think is the same thing. Those witnesses, they're good people, and they told us what they saw."

TWA 800 had arrived at JFK in New York around 1631 Eastern Daylight Time on 17 July, after a transatlantic trip from Athens, Greece. It was refuelled, and a new crew, comprising Captain Ralph G. Kevorkian, Captain/Check Airman Steven E. Snyder, Flight Engineer/Check Airman Richard G. Campbell, and flight engineer trainee Oliver Krick, took over. The flight should have left JFK for Charles De Gaulle Airport in Paris, France, around 1900, but it was delayed, because of a broken-down vehicle which was blocking it in at the gate. By the time the correct equipment to tow that out of the way was found, and some concerns about a possible mismatch between a passenger and luggage were resolved, it was one second before 2000 that the cockpit door was shut, and the crew prepared to depart.

The 747 pushed back from the gate around 2002, and five minutes later, after three of the engines had been started and the various checklists completed, the aircraft was ready to taxi. The final engine, no. 3, was started during the taxi to the departure runway. Captain Kevorkian was at the controls for take-off at 2019. The flight was initially directed to climb and maintain 19,000 feet, but then at 2026.24, the clearance was amended to 13,000 feet.

They reached that level at 2027.47. A minute and a half later, at 2029.15, Kevorkian said, "Look at that crazy fuel flow indicator there on number four – see that?" A minute after that, Boston ARTCC told them to climb to 15,000 feet, which Captain Snyder acknowledged. At 2030.25, Kevorkian confirmed "climb thrust", and Engineer Campbell replied, "Power's set." Forty-seven seconds after that the CVR recording ended after picking up an unintelligible word, and then a very loud sound. At the same moment, 2031.12, the flight data recorder lost power. The sound on the CVR was similar to recordings from other aircraft that had experienced structural break-ups.

Just over half a minute later, Captain McClaine on Eastwind Flight 507 made his initial report to the ARTCC that he "just saw an explosion out here". Over the next few minutes, the 747 fell from the sky into the Atlantic Ocean, eight miles south from East Moriches, New York. In addition to the four crew, fourteen cabin crew and 212 passengers lost their lives.

As the CIA report on their investigations noted: "The crash of TWA Flight 800, potentially one of the most lethal international terrorist acts ever perpetrated against the United States, touched off the most extensive, complex, and costly air disaster investigation in US history. Had it been the result of state-sponsored terrorism, it would have been considered an act of war." Very quickly, the NTSB and the FBI focused their attention on three possible causes: a bomb, a missile or mechanical failure. With CIA help, the FBI investigated the terrorism-connected possibilities; the

NTSB began rigorous tests on the wreckage, and, once they were found a week after the accident, the black boxes.

Structural failure was dismissed: there were no signs of fatigue or other damage that would be sufficient to cause the disaster, and the cargo doors were intact and had been in position. A fuel/air explosion in the centre wing fuel tank was debated, as it was believed likely, based on the locations of the various pieces of recovered wreckage, that the first parts to depart from the aircraft had been around its wing centre section. Tests carried out both in the United States and Great Britain suggested that such an explosion could have broken apart the tank, with catastrophic results.

But how was the explosion ignited? The most obvious way seemed to be that energy could have entered the tank via the fuel quantity indication system wiring, but the investigators looked into every other possibility, from malfunctioning parts to lightning or meteorite strike (the latter two both considered "very unlikely", although a meteorite expert did present expert testimony on the subject). The wreckage didn't support the possibility of an explosion, and tests indicated that the other causes were unlikely – including electromagnetic interference from radios and personal electronic devices.

Once the explosion had taken place, the front part of the aircraft separated from the remainder of the fuselage, and the rear kicked up abruptly and climbed for several thousand feet. As it then fell, it produced an increasingly visible fire trail, and about forty-two seconds after the explosion, the left wing separated from the fuselage, releasing unburned fuel which then exploded. That produced a dramatic cascade of flames that was even picked up by an infra-red sensor on a satellite in space. That debris took seven seconds to hit the water.

In the end the NTSB determined that "the probable cause of the TWA flight 800 accident was an explosion of the center wing fuel tank (CWT), resulting from ignition of the flammable fuel/air mixture in the tank. The source of ignition energy for the explosion could not be determined with certainty, but, of the sources evaluated by the investigation, the most likely was a short circuit outside of the CWT that allowed excessive voltage to enter it through electrical wiring associated with the fuel quantity indication system."

A large number of people refused to believe this was the case. The FBI formally ended its sixteen month investigation into the crash in November 1997: "No evidence has been found which would indicate that a criminal act was the cause of the tragedy of TWA flight 800," FBI Assistant Director Kallstrom told a news conference. "We do know one thing. The law enforcement team has done everything humanly possible, has pursued every lead, has looked at every theory and has left no stone unturned."

Kallstrom was not impressed when he was pressed about this. "Nothing is absolutely zero, but it's as close to zero as you can get in my estimation," he said of the chances of it being a missile strike. He was even less impressed with the idea that there was some form of cover-up going on of a so-called "friendly fire" incident, in which a US missile, fired from the USS *Normandy*, was responsible. "The notion that this did happen and we, hundreds and hundreds of F.B.I. agents and police officers and all the other folks, are covering this up is nonsense. It's just not true and it's an outrageous allegation." He later commented that the *Normandy* had been too far away, didn't shoot any missiles that night, and if it had done so, the 747 would have been blown to "smithereens".

The theory had not been helped by President Kennedy's former press secretary, Pierre Salinger, who claimed, three months after the event, that he had verifiable evidence. "It's a document I got about five weeks ago – came from France – from an intelligence agent of France. He had been given this document from an American Secret Service agent based in France," Salinger explained to CNN at the time. "He had been doing an inquiry and had some contacts with the U.S. Navy." The document was a fake. Other evidence Salinger found included videos of radar screens that apparently showed a blip approaching the 747 but which didn't actually connect with it.

The CIA went so far as to produce an animation which was broadcast on various news outlets, which explained what the various witnesses, both on Long Island and in some cases on other aircraft had seen ("Not a Missile" flashes up on screen periodically). A detailed analysis of exactly what people saw and heard was also produced, which can still be read on the CIA website, which concluded: "Any eyewitness who thinks he may have seen a missile shoot down Flight 800 needs to have seen something that occurred more than 42 seconds before the aircraft broke into 'two distinct fireballs' and more than 49 seconds before the plane hit the water. CIA analysts are not aware of any eyewitness who did."

The theories won't go away. A new documentary aired in July 2013 which rehashed many of the same arguments (as well as the common sort of conspiracy theories that arise whenever the CIA is involved with something), and as a result the NTSB refuted everything once more, even showing reporters the wreckage of the aircraft. Joseph M. Kolly, director of the NTSB Research and Engineering division was clear: "There is no evidence of high energy penetration," he explained. "It's very clear to us that this was a central wing tank explosion and not anything else."

A DIRECT HIT

The pilots of a DHL A300 cargo plane were rather luckier than many who have encountered missiles mid-flight. They were hit by a surface-to-air missile shortly after they left Baghdad Airport in Iraq on 22 November 2003, but were able to return to the airport safely. "The rulebook had gone out the window," flight engineer Mario Rofail noted ruefully later.

The original US military briefing on the incident gave no indication of the drama that had unfolded. "A DHL plane took off from Baghdad Airport this morning and was hit by a SAM-7 surface-to-air missile," an unnamed military official said. "It caught fire, it turned around and came back to the airport where it safely landed. The fire was taken out. There are no injuries."

By chance, both sides of the incident were recorded: Claudine Vernier-Palliez from French magazine *Paris-Match* was embedded with the Fedayeen unit who fired the missile, while the three flight crew on the DHL aircraft described their perilous descent in detail to *Flight International* magazine a year later.

The Fedayeen unit had kept their SAM-7 missile hidden overnight ready to strike at the DHL aircraft. They were fighting the Americans because they believed that the occupying force which had been in Iraq since the fall of Saddam Hussein wasn't respecting their people. They only fired on the civilian couriers because they were transporting the GIs' mail, and on the morning of 22 November, they loosed two missiles. The first one hit the Airbus's wing; the other missed.

One was enough for Captain Eric Genotte, First Officer Steeve Michielsen and engineer Rofail. They had been climbing rapidly, as was standard practice, given the dangers of surface-to-air missiles, and were at 8,000 feet when the missile hit the wing. The hydraulic systems were seriously compromised: all pressure went from two of them immediately, the third lost pressure and hit zero within seconds. The horizontal stabilizer became frozen in position; the actuators drained on the primary flight control surfaces and spoilers, and they went limp. Unsure if they'd been hit by a missile or another aircraft, they declared an emergency and then tried to take control of the aircraft, which, unknown to them, was trailing a 50-metre flame from the left wing.

"The aircraft was like a piece of paper in the air," Rofail recalled. "We went through a series of steep banks and dives – you could not leave your seat." The men remained calm as they looked for a way to get their speed under control: the control yokes and rudder pedals were useless, and eventually they devised a way to pilot the aircraft using the throttles alone – all that they basically had available to them, since at least the engines hadn't been damaged by the missiles – and often having to act in a way that was counter-intuitive to all of their training and gut reactions. It took ten minutes before they could turn the aircraft around towards the airport.

They were now at about 4,000 feet, and Rofail used the emergency gravity system to lower the landing gear, which gave them an extra degree of stability. The difference in lift and drag between the left wing and the intact right wing was increasing as the damaged wing continued to disintegrate.

Because the fuel tank had been full when the missile hit, there had been no fuel-air vapour inside, so there was no possibility of an explosive ignition when it was destroyed, which would have blown the wing off the aircraft. However, to add to their problems, one of the other fuel tanks had been pierced, and was losing fuel.

The pilots brought the aircraft round to make a long final approach, with co-pilot Michielsen reminding Gennotte not to retard the throttles before touchdown or the nose would drop. Gennotte needed to retard the right throttle slightly to line up the aircraft, but otherwise was able to keep them open as he touched down, despite the turbulence they encountered at 400 feet – and the moment that he did, Rofail slammed the throttles into reverse, as the sand on the left-hand side of the runway was put to good use to brake the Airbus. The three men exited down the slide, and started to run from the aircraft, thinking that the fuel tanks could explode. And were urgently told to stay exactly where they were by soldiers approaching. They were in the middle of a minefield!

The pilots were presented with the Hugh Gordon-Burge Award from the Guild of Air Pilots and Air Navigators in recognition of their outstanding airmanship in saving an aircraft.

Part 10:
Your Life in Their Hands –
Suicidal Pilots

OUT OF CONTROL

While the most famous suicidal hijackers are those who took over the United and American Airlines aircraft on September 11, 2001, they were by no means the first people to try to kill themselves while at the controls of an aircraft. Thankfully, though, the many psychological tests which pilots have to undergo are designed to weed out those with such thoughts – whether they've come through religious fervour or a desire to self-harm – but inevitably there have been a few occasions when people have slipped through the net. When pilot suicide (or deliberate actions by the pilot which put the aircraft in peril) is listed as a probable cause of an incident by the various accident investigation departments around the world, chances are that the findings will be challenged – often by friends and family of the pilot in question. However, there are some incidents which, on the balance of probabilities, can be ascribed in this way – and in this section, we'll also look at another incident which might as well have been suicide, when a pilot allowed his adolescent children to sit at the controls of an aircraft in flight . . .

"Captain, what are you doing? Please stop it," came the anguished voice of the co-pilot on Japan Airlines Flight 350 on 9 February 1982. For some reason known best to himself, Captain Seiji Katagiri had engaged the thrust reversers in flight – trying to achieve deliberately what would happen accidentally a few years later to Lauda Flight 004, and crash the DC-8.

The JAL flight was on its way from Fukuoka to Haneda Airport in Tokyo, and was on its approach across Tokyo Bay. There were 166 passengers as well as a crew of eight aboard the jet, with Captain Katagiri assisted by First Officer Yoshifumi Ishikawa, and flight engineer Yoshimi Ozaki. The cockpit voice recorder showed that Katagiri was "in an abnormal state, crying out loud in the cockpit", as the aircraft was coming in to land, and during what he later referred to as a "loss of consciousness" he engaged the thrust reversers on engine nos. 2 and 3. This threw the aircraft into a sharp descent.

While flight engineer Ozaki grappled with the captain, Ishikawa tried to pull back on the controls to bring the aircraft out of the nose-dive. However, because the reversers had been engaged, the control lever was extremely heavy, and Ishikawa had real problems. In the end, he was unable to rectify the situation, and the aircraft came down in the bay, 350 yards short of the runway at Haneda. Twenty-four people were killed, 150 others were injured. To cap it all, the captain was then one of the first people to climb on board a rescue boat – photos showed him with a bland expression, wearing a cardigan and not his uniform, both in a lifeboat next to one of the flight attendants and then later aboard a bus carrying survivors, after he had apparently told officials he was an office worker.

According to Katagiri's statement to police later, he had felt ill on the morning of the flight. Then, as they were coming into Haneda, "[a]fter I switched from auto to manual operation just before landing, I felt nausea, then an inexplicable feeling of terror, and completely lost consciousness". He also claimed that he "pushed forward the control stick when the plane was in a landing position", and said that he didn't remember if he had put the engines into reverse.

Japan Airlines faced some considerable backlash when it was discovered that he had been allowed to fly, despite the fact he suffered from hallucinations and feelings of depression, and had been urged to see a psychiatrist on no less than three occasions. He had been given one month's leave fifteen months before the crash for a "psychosomatic disorder", and some reports suggested that he had been grounded for as much as a year before resuming flight duties in August 1981.

Three psychiatrists were brought in to examine him after the crash, and he was prosecuted, although eventually he was deemed not guilty by reason of insanity. JAL president Yasumoto Takagi visited the families of the crash victims to apologize personally.

A dozen years later, on 21 August 1994, Royal Air Maroc Flight 630 crashed after the autopilot was disconnected not long after take-off. The pilot, Younes Khayati, was held responsible. The last thing on the cockpit voice recorder was co-pilot Sofia Figugui screaming for "Help, help! The captain is—"

The twin-turboprop ATR 42 was flying from Agadir, Morocco, to Casablanca when it came down with an extremely violent impact at Douar Izounine, 20 miles north of Agadir, ten minutes or so after its 7 p.m. take-off. All forty-four people on board were killed, including Kuwaiti Prince Ali al-Mahmoud al-Jabir al-Sabah, the brother of the Kuwaiti Defence Minister, and his wife.

The Moroccan Association of Navigators claimed that as soon as Khayati began positioning himself for take-off, he signalled to the control tower that he had a technical problem and wanted to return to the parking area. However, the flight proceeded, and ten minutes into the flight, the auto-pilot was disconnected. The Moroccan commission of enquiry said that the recorders showed that Khayati did that deliberately "and aimed the aircraft toward the ground". There was nothing irregular about the aircraft, which had received regular maintenance and equipment checks.

They were setting up a panel to uncover why Khayati had committed suicide, although news reports suggested that he "was in despair over his love life" – some later reports even suggested that this was a lovers' quarrel with his co-pilot. As the commission stated: "The behaviour of the pilot is all the more inexplicable considering he was an experienced pilot with 4,500 hours of flying time and with confirmed professional aptitudes and physical condition." The suicide verdict was eventually not challenged further.

A GAMBLE TOO FAR?

There was considerable dispute over the cause of SilkAir Flight 185's crash, with the Indonesian National Transportation Safety Commission saying they could not determine what had happened, because the evidence was inconclusive, while the American National Transportation Safety Board stated, in their additions to the NTSC's report, that the crash had occurred because of deliberate flight control inputs, most likely by the captain. A civil jury, not allowed access to the official investigations, came to yet a third conclusion. However, as a former Australian investigator told the *Sydney Morning Herald* when the paper ran a feature on the incident: "The only possible way for an aircraft to behave in this way is for the pilot to hold the control stick firmly forward. Even if the wings fell off, the aircraft couldn't descend that fast." And it was certainly extremely suspicious that neither the Cockpit Voice Recorder (CVR) nor the Flight Data Recorder (FDR) were operating at the time of the crash – first one then the other seemed to have been switched off deliberately.

The flight from Jakarta to Singapore should only have taken eighty minutes, and was set to leave at 0830 GMT, 3.30 p.m. local time, on 19 December 1997. The Boeing 737-36N was piloted by Captain Tsu Way Ming, with First Officer Duncan Ward, five flight attendants and ninety-seven passengers on board. The 737 took off normally, and was cleared to climb to flight level 350, which it reached at 0853, sixteen minutes after take-off.

At 0905.15, the CVR stopped recording, shortly after it registered the captain saying: "Go[ing] back for a while, finish your plate", but five minutes later, the ATC transcript showed that someone on the flight deck acknowledged receipt of instructions to maintain flight level 350, and to contact Singapore Control at the appropriate time. One minute later, the flight data recorder also stopped operating.

Fifty seconds later, between 0912.09 and 0912.17, the 737

descended 400 feet, and by 0912.41, it was at flight level 195 –
15,500 feet below where it should have been. A few seconds later,
villagers in the Musi River delta heard a jet's engines increasing in
intensity. As they rose in a crescendo, there were two thunderous
booms as the aircraft broke through the sound barrier. The 737
plummeted to earth, and seemed to be upside down before it
plunged into the Musi River and disintegrated into myriad fragments, which penetrated into the mud of the riverbed. There were
no survivors; in fact, most of those who died couldn't be identified. The aircraft had come down so hard and so fast that it had
only travelled 3.4 nautical miles forward during its descent from
35,000 feet.

Because of the magnitude of the destruction of the aircraft,
there were very few clues as to what happened. However, both the
CVR and the FDR were found. The sounds on the CVR were
consistent with the recorder being switched off manually: if it had
malfunctioned, because of a short circuit, a hum would have been
heard on the recording. There was no hum. If it had malfunctioned because of an overload, then there would have been a
"snap" of the circuit breaker on the recording – the CVR operates
for a fraction of a second after power is removed. There was no
snap.

It therefore seemed as if someone had deliberately switched it
off. And one of the two men on the flight deck had a history of
doing this: on a previous flight, Captain Tsu had been in an argument with that trip's first officer, Lawrence Dittmer, after Tsu
had flown an aircraft in to land with "violent rolls". The first officer had been requested to submit a report as a result, which was
negative towards Tsu, and the next time they flew together, Tsu
raised the matter. On their way to taxi for take-off, he pulled the
CVR circuit breaker, which was on a panel behind the command
seat. Tsu explained that he wanted to preserve their conversation
to present to management; if the CVR continued to operate, then
the conversation would have been wiped. The first officer refused
to fly without the CVR operative, and Tsu eventually gave in and
reconnected it.

That wasn't the only blemish on Tsu's record, by any means.
He was relieved of his line instructor pilot status as a result of that
argument with the first officer, but there were already concerns

that he was unsafe, and rumours that he had nearly crashed. Other pilots were concerned about the cavalier way in which he seemed to treat his aircraft, and management were not happy that he failed to file reports after incidents (Tsu thought that the company was making a fuss about a "minor issue" and was invited to outline his concerns to them – but he never did).

Investigations also showed that Tsu had personal problems outside the aviation industry. He was losing heavily on the Singapore stock exchange, and his account had been suspended for failure to pay debts. The day of the crash, he had promised to make a payment when he got back from Jakarta – but he had no money with which to do so. He also took out a new insurance policy which became valid on 19 December, the day of the crash – the day which was also the eighteenth anniversary of a crash in which four of Tsu's colleagues in the Republic of Singapore Air Force died, a crash for which he blamed himself. He may even have been disturbed to see that supermodel Bonny Hicks was on the flight: she had been married to a friend of Tsu's, and divorced him for an American, who was accompanying her on the flight.

First Officer Duncan Ward was also investigated – after all, according to the CVR, he was at the controls. Ward was a well-respected pilot, who had told a friend he would see him a few days later "if I make it". By contrast, no skeletons were discovered in his closet.

The Indonesian NTSC report almost seemed determined to avoid the evidence of Tsu's behaviour, noting simply that "the technical investigation has yielded no evidence to explain the cause of the accident". The American NTSB were almost dismissive of this, noting that there was great concern about the NTSC's inability to "find the reasons for the departure of the aircraft from its cruising level of FL 350 and the reasons for the stoppage of the flight recorders". They were blunt: "The conclusions presented by the NTSC regarding the stoppage of the CVR are not in full agreement with the evidence" (the NTSC said that the possibility of a broken wire couldn't be ruled out). "It is probable that the airplane was likely responding to sustained flight control inputs from the cockpit," the Americans wrote; the NTSC wouldn't be drawn: no information from either black box meant to them that you simply couldn't say what had happened. "There was no evidence to positively conclude that the departure from cruise flight was an intentional maneuver," the Indonesians replied. Those reading the reports can judge for themselves which seems more likely, but it's worth noting that a Singapore High Court judge ruled that "the onus of proving that flight MI185 was intentionally crashed has not been discharged".

As mentioned, a third theory was promoted by the jury sitting in the Superior Court in the United States in 2004: they believed that defects in the rudder system caused the crash, and blamed the Parker Hannifin Corporation, the makers of the rudder. Without accepting responsibility, the company paid compensation.

PILOT NOT IN CHARGE?

The fate of EgyptAir Flight 990 on Halloween, 31 October 1999 has been as controversial as the SilkAir crash. Two hundred and seventeen people died when the Boeing 767-300 crashed into the Atlantic Ocean; the Egyptian Civil Aviation Authority (ECAA) maintained it was due to mechanical failure. The American NTSB, brought in by the Egyptians because they had resources that the ECAA lacked, believed it had been brought down deliberately by Relief First Officer Gameel al-Batouti, and that even if the ECAA theory was right, the aircraft would have been recoverable thanks to the 767's elevator control system. Misinformed speculation, though, on why al-Batouti brought the aircraft down did much to harm American-Egyptian relationships for a time, and there were some who believed that the ECAA knew that al-Batouti was responsible but could not allow that verdict to be revealed.

EgyptAir Flight 990 was bound from Los Angeles International Airport for Cairo, with a stop off at JFK in New York. The flight across the continental United States was normal, and it arrived at JFK shortly after midnight on the morning of 31 October Eastern Standard Time. As was normal practice because of the length of the flight, there were two crews rostered for the journey, each consisting of a captain and a first officer. Relief Captain Raouf Noureldin and Relief First Officer Gameel al-Batouti joined Captain Ahmad al-Habashi and First Officer Adel Anwar at JFK; also on board was Captain Hatem Rushdy, EgyptAir's main pilot on the 767, who was deadheading back to Cairo.

In principle, al-Habashi and Anwar would fly the aircraft for the first portion of the trip, and would then be relieved by Noureldin and al-Batouti. Al-Habashi oversaw the take-off at 0120 and the start of the ascent to the climb to their assigned flight level, 33,000 feet. At about 0140, al-Batouti came into the cockpit and suggested that he started his portion of the trip early.

"I'm not going to sleep at all," he told Anwar, and told him to go back and get some rest. Anwar argued that he should have been told al-Batouti wanted to work his shift first, but eventually, seeing that al-Batouti was set on taking the right-hand seat, he asked the captain for permission to leave. Muttering to himself about al-Batouti's habit of doing what he pleased ("Some days he doesn't work at all"), Anwar left the cockpit.

EgyptAir 990 levelled out at flight level 330 at 0144, and the last transmission from the aircraft was received at 0147.39, acknowledging a change of radio frequencies from the New York ARTCC. As soon as this had happened, Captain al-Habashi told al-Batouti that he was heading to the toilet while the passengers were eating, "before it gets crowded". Al-Batouti told him to "go ahead please", and at 0148.18, the captain left the cockpit.

Eleven seconds later, al-Batouti made a comment that no one could later make out from the CVR recording. It might have been something like "control it" in Arabic, or "hydraulic" in English. Either way, ten seconds after that, at 0148.40, he stated quietly, "Tawakkalt Ala Allah" ("I rely on God"). This is a phrase that can often be used by Egyptians to ask for God's assistance on the task in hand; it was originally translated as "I place my fate in the hands of God", which gave al-Batouti's next actions overtones which may not have been intended.

The evidence from the FDR and the CVR shows what happened next. At 0148.19, there was the sound of an electric seat motor, and twenty-seven seconds after that, the autopilot was disconnected – with no automatic tone generated to indicate that this wasn't done manually. The 767 stayed level for about eight seconds, and then al-Batouti repeated his Arabic phrase quietly. Five seconds after that, at 0149.53, the throttle levers were moved from the cruise power setting to idle, resulting a second later in an abrupt nose-down movement.

Over the next ten seconds, as the aircraft began to descend rapidly, al-Batouti said "I rely on God" seven more times. At 0150.06, Captain al-Habashi burst into the cockpit, demanding to know what was happening. Al-Batouti didn't reply: he simply kept repeating that he relied on God. The aircraft was accelerating past its maximum operating airspeed, and the master alarm started to blare.

At 0150.08, al-Batouti declared his reliance for the eleventh and final time. The captain was getting no sense from him, and tried to pull the aircraft out of the dive. The elevator surfaces began to move in opposite directions – suggesting the pilots were giving contrary instructions. At 0150.21, the engine start lever switches were moved to the cut-off position, and then the throttle levers were moved to full throttle. "What is this? What is this? Did you shut the engine?" Captain al-Habashi asked incredulously. "It's shut," al-Batouti told him at 0150.29 – the only words that he spoke other than his trust in God the entire time the aircraft was accelerating towards the Atlantic Ocean.

"Pull with me!" the captain repeated over and over during the last six seconds of the recording, but the indications are that al-Batouti refused – the elevator surfaces remained in a split condition. The CVR and FDR stopped recording at 0150.38 and .36 respectively, but the aircraft stayed in the air for a further 114 seconds – as the CVR stopped, the 767 was seen on radar climbing to about 25,000 feet, but then it started a second descent. One can only speculate that for a few seconds the captain was able, somehow, to keep the first officer away from the controls. But it was far too late: all aboard the 767 died on impact with the Atlantic Ocean off Nantucket.

Analysis of the black boxes revealed what had happened in the cockpit, but the NTSB were careful in their announcement of the findings. NTSB chairman Jim Hall held a news conference on 19 November, and suggested that the accident "might, and I emphasize *might*, be the result of a deliberate act . . . No one wants to get to the bottom of this mystery quicker than those investigating this accident, both here and in Egypt, but we won't get there on a road paved with leaks, supposition, speculation, and spin. That road does not lead to the truth, and the truth is what both the American people and the Egyptian people seek." He was trying to keep a lid on any potential difficulties, particularly since newspapers such as the *Washington Post* had headlined stories on the crash with: "Pilot prayed, then shut off jet's autopilot". Some papers translated al-Batouti's prayer as: "I have made my decision. I put my fate in God's hands."

The Egyptian investigators, however, were pursuing other theories. Originally they had suggested there might have been a bomb in the forward lavatory. Now, they claimed that the NTSB was trying to make al-Batouti into a scapegoat (a theory promulgated by the Islamist-oriented *Al Shaab* newspaper in Egypt which claimed that "America's goal is to hide the truth by blaming the EgyptAir pilot"), and hinted that the head of the NTSB's investigations might be a Zionist biased against Egyptians. They also believed that al-Batouti's prayers had been a response to something wrong with the flight rather than preparing to die. They came up with multiple theories, any of which would absolve the relief first officer from responsibility.

The FBI, involved since it seemed to be a criminal investigation, discovered that al-Batouti had a reputation for sexual impropriety, but it seemed as if EgyptAir was already aware of this, and the pilot had been cautioned for his behaviour – although the man responsible for that disciplining was the captain deadheading back to Cairo. There seemed to be no real motive for al-Batouti acting as he had.

The Egyptians suggested that the actuators on the 767's elevators had failed, and that was what al-Batouti was trying to fix. The NTSB and Boeing tested the Egyptian theories, and found that if this had happened, all the pilots needed to do was pull back hard on the controls: a natural reaction to any pilot. The Americans also couldn't understand why, if he was desperately trying to save the aircraft rather than destroy it, al-Batouti gave no hint at all on the CVR of any potential problem – not even when the captain re-entered the cockpit.

The NTSB report was finally released on 21 March 2002 (at a time when relations with the Arab world were difficult in the wake of 9/11): "The probable cause of the EgyptAir flight 990 accident is the airplane's departure from normal cruise flight and subsequent impact with the Atlantic Ocean as a result of the relief first officer's flight control inputs. The reason for the relief first officer's actions was not determined." The ECAA concluded the opposite: "The Relief First Officer (RFO) did not deliberately dive the airplane into the ocean . . . There is evidence pointing to a mechanical defect in the elevator control system of the accident . . . Although this evidence, combined with certain data from the Flight Data Recorder (FDR), points to a mechanical cause for the accident, reaching a definitive conclusion at this point is not possible because of the complexity of the elevator system, the lack of reliable data from Boeing, and the limitations of the simulation and ground tests conducted after the accident... Investigators cannot rule out the possibility that the RFO may have taken emergency action to avoid a collision with an unknown object. Although plausible, this theory cannot be tested because the United States has refused to release certain radar calibration and test data that are necessary to evaluate various unidentified radar returns in the vicinity of Flight 990."

When the story featured on *Mayday/Air Crash Investigation*, the American theory was followed; al-Batouti's family disputed these theories on air.

One of the most recent cases where pilot suicide has been suspected took place in Namibia on 29 November 2013 when Mozambique Airlines Flight TM470 went down in Bwabwata National Park in the remote northern part of the African nation. The preliminary report from the Moçambicano de Aviação Civil (Mozambican Civil Aviation Institute) was issued on 21 December, and suggested that Captain Herminio dos Santos Fernandes had a "clear intention" to crash the jet.

The Embraer 190, which had only been inspected the day before the crash, was on a scheduled flight from Maputo Airport in Mozambique to Quatro de Fevereiro Airport in Angola. It left Mozambique at 0926 GMT (1126 Central African Time), and should have arrived at 1310 GMT with six crew and twenty-seven passengers (original reports suggested there were twenty-eight). When it failed to arrive, search teams were alerted, and there were fears that the pilots might have had problems with lightning and thunderstorms in the region.

At some point during the flight – at the time of writing, the CVR transcript, or the specific timings have yet to be released – the first officer left the cockpit to use the lavatory. Captain Dos Santos Fernandes remained alone on the flight deck. He shut the cockpit door to prevent the first officer from re-entering, and reset the altitude three times, from the cruising flight level of 38,000 feet down to a final reading of 592 feet, which was below ground level. Despite the alarms that were going off, and the first officer (and probably others) banging on the cockpit door, the captain operated the throttle, and the speed brakes to ensure that the aircraft dived for the ground. Only one body was recovered intact.

"The plane fell with the pilot alert, and the reasons which may have given rise to this behaviour are unknown," said Joao Abreu, chairman of the Mozambican Civil Aviation Institute. "All these operations required detailed knowledge of the plane's controls, and showed a clear intention to crash the aircraft." An investigation into Captain Dos Santos Fernandes got underway. There were rumours that he may have had marital problems, or suffered a bereavement.

The FAA has very clear guidelines with regard to pilots' mental health, and any problems – particularly if they require medication – have to be alerted to them as soon as possible. No one suffering from psychosis, severe personality disorder, manic-depressive illness or substance dependence can fly an airliner, and captains are evaluated every six months. Thankfully, that means that instances such as those in this chapter are few and far between.

However, there will always be those who exercise their judgement wrongly. Captain Yaroslav Kudrinsky, the pilot of Aeroflot Flight 593, paid for that misjudgement with his life, as well as those of his family and seventy-two other people on board the Airbus A310.

Flight 593 should have been a routine run from Sheremetyevo International Airport, Moscow to Hong Kong's Kai Tak, and on 23 March 1994, Captain Kudrinsky brought his two children – twelve-year-old Yana, and sixteen-year-old Eldar – with him. It was their first international flight, and they were brought into the cockpit while he was on duty. The autopilot was on, so when Yana "flew" the aircraft, nothing actually happened – a fact the young girl guessed.

Her older brother replaced her in the seat, but the pressure that he put on the column was enough to disengage the autopilot – which triggered a warning light, but not an audible alarm. The first time anyone realized there was a problem was when Eldar asked why the aircraft was turning to the right. The co-pilot and Eldar tried to turn the controls back but the aircraft was already descending steeply. Eldar scrambled to get out of the seat to allow his father to take control but precious seconds were lost as he got up, catching his foot in the right pedal. As Kudrinsky repeatedly screamed at his children to "Get out!" the two pilots started to pull the aircraft out of a spin and get it back on a level – but the altitude was too low to recover. "Everything's fine," Kudrinksy said moments before the aircraft hit a wooded hillside.

Until the black box data was analysed, there were concerns that the aircraft had been sabotaged, or there had been a sudden decompression, since no one could understand how it had suddenly dropped in the way it had. No technical malfunctions could be found in the wreckage, with Rudolf Teimurov, chairman of the Russian flight-safety committee of the Inter-State Aviation Committee noting: "We have doubts that the crew had followed the operational procedures defined by the manuals." They so nearly managed to save everyone on board – but there simply wasn't time.

Part 11:
Take-Off to Disaster

ENGINE DEPARTURE

As has been demonstrated elsewhere in this volume, the time around take-off and landing can be the most perilous for the pilots (as well as those in their charge). This section looks at three take-offs which went disastrously wrong, leading to some of the highest death tolls in aviation history.

The last word recorded on the cockpit voice recorder of American Airlines Flight 191 was a brief "Damn" from First Officer James Dillard just after a thud was heard. A few seconds later, the DC-10 he was piloting plunged into a field half a mile from the runway at Chicago's O'Hare Airport. It was just after 1502, Central Daylight Time on 25 May 1979; 273 people – including two on the ground – died, making this the worst aviation accident to occur on American soil. (The 9/11 attacks are not included in this calculation, since they cannot under any definition be termed an "accident".)

The DC-10 had arrived as scheduled from Phoenix, Arizona, but was running just slightly behind time when Captain H. Lux began his take-off roll. No one had any reason to suspect there was anything wrong with the aircraft – but just as Lux reached take-off speed, 6,000 feet down the runway, the left engine lost power. White vapour began to pour from the engine and the leading edge of the wing, and it looked to observers as if the engine was bouncing up and down. Then just as Lux started rotation, the engine came off.

The engine and its pylon, as well as a three-foot section of the leading edge, went forward, almost as if they had lift and were climbing along with the aircraft, and then came back over the rest of the wing, not touching it, and landed on the runway. It was presumably at this point that Dillard gave his mild expletive – unfortunately the CVR lost power when the engine separated, so no more was recorded.

American Flight 191 reached for the sky, and it seemed to onlookers as if it was going to be alright. ("Do you want to come back?" the tower enquired, but received no reply.) However, when it reached a height of about 300 feet, twenty seconds into the flight, it began to bank to the left. It carried on with that roll until the wings were past the vertical position (as the photograph of the incident shows in which it looks as if the aircraft has been placed on its side as it goes over the O'Hare building). The engine separation had severed the hydraulic fluid lines that controlled the leading edge slats on the left wing – which made the outboard slats, the ones near the tip of the wing, retract. That had caused the wing to stall, and the aircraft entered a steep dive.

First Officer Dillard was the only one who had been able to do anything, since the generator for the captain's instruments was powered by the engine which was now hundreds of feet below them on the runway. The slat disagreement system wasn't operative because of the engine loss, nor was the stick shaker, so they didn't realize how bad the situation was. Dillard was in control of the aircraft for the take-off, and (it is presumed in the absence of the CVR recording) he was working on the assumption that they had undergone an engine failure, rather than it disappearing altogether. The first officer tried his hardest to pull the aircraft out of the dive, but there was no chance of recovery. The electrical and the hydraulic systems had both failed – at the time the DC-10 was certified for service eleven years previously, engineers had calculated the odds of such a simultaneous failure at 10 billion to 1.

On the ground, near Interstate 90, at the police canine centre, police officers watched in horror. "We could see all the fuel was spouting out the left side where the engine would be," Patrol Officer Michael Delany told reporters. "And then as he got over our compound, the other engine shut off. So there was complete silence in the air. And then the plane turned, perpendicular to the ground, with the left wing facing down and the right wing facing up."

The DC-10 slammed left wing first into a field, with debris flying into the nearby Oasis Mobile Home Park, destroying five trailers and several cars. It then careered into an old storage hanger at the edge of the airport, and blew up. Two residents of the mobile home park were killed.

What puzzled the NTSB investigators initially was why the loss of one engine had led to disaster – the DC-10 should have been able to return to O'Hare with its two remaining power plants. However, when they discovered how much damage there was to the wing – and the fact that that information was not available to the pilots – the situation made far more sense. The photographs taken of the disaster were invaluable; digital analysis (a discipline which was in its comparative infancy in 1979) was able to show the position of the flaps, as well as the state of the landing gear. It wasn't the other engines that had failed but the wing, which had stalled as a result of the loss of the engine.

But what had caused the engine and pylon to detach? Every piece of metal from the jet was examined and it appeared initially that a broken bolt, 3 inches long and $3/8$ of an inch in diameter, found by the runway was responsible – it was even nicknamed "the murdering bolt" by one of the investigators. It was one of the five bolts that attached the pylon to the wing, and it looked as if it had snapped because of metal fatigue. However, once it was under the electron microscope, scientists saw that it had been broken by a sudden strain put on it. Add to that the discovery of a 10-inch fracture on the rear bulkhead of the pylon assembly and a much wider problem became evident. All DC-10s were then inspected, and within two hours of another DC-10 in Chicago being found with 27 fasteners missing or sheared and a cracked spar web on its pylon, the FAA grounded the entire fleet of DC-10s. Of 138 aircraft, thirty-six had faults.

So what had caused the bolt and plate to crack like that? With a bitter irony, it turned out that this had happened as a direct result of an attempt by American Airlines (in common, it should be noted, with others including Continental and United) on safety grounds to reduce the number of times that the engine was removed from the pylon, with all the associated disconnects and reconnects of systems such as hydraulic and fuel lines, electrical cables and wiring. The engine manufacturers, McDonnell Douglas, recommended that the engine should be detached from the pylon before the pylon was then detached from the aircraft; the airlines' maintenance crews took them off in one piece – and American and Continental were using a forklift truck for the procedure. (McDonnell Douglas pointed out that they did not have "the authority to either approve or disapprove the maintenance procedures of its customers".)

Further detective work revealed that the removal of the pylon and engine from American 191 had run into problems. For the forklift method to work properly, everything had to be aligned correctly, and the forklift operator was guided by hand and voice signals. However, during a procedure to replace spherical bearings at the American Airlines maintenance facility in Tulsa, Oklahoma, nearly two months before the crash, which required the engine and pylon to be removed from the wing, the forklift lost hydraulic pressure. (Different accounts state that there was an argument between two of the personnel, there was a shift change around this time, or the forklift simply ran out of fuel, either of which caused the forklift to be switched off.) The pylon assembly dropped, and had to be rammed back into position. A witness to a similar remounting noted that when the engine/pylon assembly was reinstalled on the aircraft, the impact of inserting the pylon fitting into the wing caused an extremely violent reaction from the aircraft – shaking, vibration, and loud noise – which should have indicated there was possible damage.

The forced reassembly caused a fatigue crack in the rear pylon mount which got worse over the next eight weeks. Eventually, on 25 May, it ceased being able to support the pylon, and without that support, the engine rotated upwards on the forward mount, which couldn't take the strain and also failed.

As a result of the accident, the FAA issued airworthiness directives which required "installation of two autothrottle/speed control computers, each of which received information from the positions of both outboard wing slat groups, and installation of a stick shaker at the First Officer's position, in addition to that previously required at the Captain's position, with both stick shakers actuated by either autothrottle/speed control computer". If these had been available to the first officer in those precious seconds after the engine fell off, he would have been aware of the problems with the wings.

American Airlines were fined half a million dollars for improper maintenance procedures, and more than 200 lawsuits were filed after the crash. The airline and McDonnell Douglas had paid out more than $70 million in damages within the first ten years.

THE LUCKIEST PASSENGER

Eight years later, on 16 August 1987, McDonnell Douglas were in the headlines again, with the news that one of their DC-9s had crashed at Detroit Metropolitan Wayne County Airport, shortly after take-off. Captain John R. Maus and First Officer David J. Dodds' flight had lasted mere seconds; all but one of the 156 people on board died – four-year-old Cecelia Cichan miraculously survived – and there were two fatalities on the ground.

The DC-9 that formed Northwest Airlines 255 had already been flown that day by the same flight crew from Minneapolis, Minnesota, to Saginaw, Michigan, via Detroit Metropolitan Wayne County Airport, and it was now a flight from Saginaw to Santa Ana, California, with stops at Detroit and Phoenix, Arizona. It arrived at its gate at Detroit around 1942 Eastern Daylight Time – for some reason, the pilots missed the gate and taxied by it initially, so had to perform a 180-degree turn to reach it.

The preparations for departure seemed to go according to the book – Captain Maus carried out a visual walk around inspection of the aircraft; a mechanic reviewed the airplane and cabin maintenance logbooks, which showed no discrepancies; and the first officer received the flight release package on the captain's behalf. The flight left the gate about 2032, and during the push back, they went through the Before Engine Start part of the aircraft checklist. At 2033.04, they began to start the engines. Less than a minute later they were cleared to taxi, and given various other instructions, which they acknowledged.

However, when they were given clearance to taxi to the runway, and told to change radio frequencies to speak to the ground controller, First Officer Dodds only repeated the taxi clearance; he didn't repeat the frequency, nor did he tune the radio to it. Although earlier Dodds had confirmed that the crew had the most up-to-date Automatic Terminal Information Service (ATIS) information, the CVR recording showed that they in fact had not received it before they started to taxi. ATIS gives pilots data they need, such as temperature, ceiling, visibility, wind strength and direction, as well as notes on the runways in use, and whether there are any wind shear advisories in effect – all information vital to ensuring that the aircraft is configured properly for take-off.

Maus and Dodds had been given figures in their dispatch package based on using a different runway (runway 21 rather than runway 3), so they had to confirm that they were within the limits for the one they had been allocated. Checking with North-west's Runway Takeoff Weight Chart Manual confirmed that they were within the permitted weight.

Somehow Captain Maus missed the turn-off for the taxiway to the runway – the second such error that day. They were reminded to change frequency, which they still hadn't done, and then given a new taxiway route to the runway. At 2044.04, they were cleared for take-off.

Engine power began to increase at 2044.21, but the autothrottle didn't engage at first. It did, at 2044.38, and seven seconds later they had reached 100 knots. At 2044.57.7 Dodds called "Rotate" – and eight seconds later, the stall warning stick shaker started to operate. Over the next few seconds, the supplemental stall recognition system also activated – but at no time did the Central Aural Warning System (CAWS) sound, telling the crew that the aircraft was in the wrong configuration for take-off.

The take-off roll seemed longer than normal to those watching, with rotation beginning only 1,200 to 1,500 feet from the end of the runway. The DC-9 also rotated at a higher angle than DC-9s normally did, which meant that the tail of the aircraft came close to striking the runway. Watching from the aircraft behind Flight 255 in the queue, it seemed as if the flaps were extended, although none of the witnesses could be sure to what degree.

Flight 255's journey lasted just twenty-two seconds from take-off to first impact. As soon as the DC-9 became airborne and reached about 48 feet, it started to roll from left to right. The wings seemed to level for a brief moment, but then banked to the left. The left wing hit a light pole in one of the airport's car rental lots severing 18 feet of the wing, and igniting the fuel within – an orange flame started to emanate from the left wing tip as the

DC-9 carried on rolling to the left, then continued across the lot into an adjoining Avis facility, where it knocked a jagged piece off the roof of the enquiries building. It then hit the road outside the airport, ricocheted off the embankment of an access road to Interstate 94, and then began disintegrating into chunks of metal which erupted into flames, destroying cars and killing two people. The CVR registered seven separate impacts in the space of 5.3 seconds before it ceased operating.

Initially nobody could believe that four-year-old Cecelia Cichan found still belted in her seat was a survivor of the crash; they assumed that somehow she must be connected to the cars the DC-9 had encountered during its final moments. However, firefighters John Thiede and Dan Kish found her just feet from the bodies of both her parents and her six-year-old brother, and she was identified by her grandfather who recognized her purple nail polish and chipped front tooth.

The NTSB investigation discounted any evidence of fire or early disintegration of the aircraft, and wind shear was seriously examined – a gust of wind can cause serious problems for pilots, and the activation of the stall warning stick shaker and the flight's failure to achieve its predicted climb profile strongly suggested that it could have encountered a strong downdraught or a rapidly decreasing head wind shear. However, analysis of the digital flight data recorder showed that the aircraft was still accelerating during its climb rather than decelerating as would be the case if it had been caught in a wind shear. The only way that the stall warnings could have been activated at the speed the aircraft was going was if the slats and flaps were in the wrong configuration – that they were set up as if the aircraft was cruising, rather than taking off. The flight data recorder showed that they were indeed always retracted.

That led to two questions: how could two experienced pilots such as Maus and Dodds have made such an error? And why didn't the computerized systems warn them that the aircraft wasn't in the correct take-off configuration? The latter was easier to answer: the unit that supplied power to the CAWS didn't operate properly. The NTSB couldn't state exactly what caused this because of the extensive damage caused by the accident, but the relevant circuit breaker could have been intentionally opened by however, she was not put off flying: "I have this mentality where if something bad happened to me once on a plane it's not going to happen again," she told a documentary about sole survivors of crashes. "The odds are just astronomical." Or, as the NTSB report, put it: "The survival of the 4-year-old female child can only be attributed to a combination of fortuitous circumstances."

floor between the two pilots; that wasn't the case. He was standing between them, with one throttle in each hand – because no. 2 was frozen in place, all three couldn't be operated together. The coordination between the three pilots had to be exact to try to keep the aircraft level.

They were able to get the gear down, but as they began what they hoped would be a final approach, they were still too far north, and needed to try to make one final turn. "You're gonna have to widen out just slightly to your left, sir, to make the turn to final, and also it'll take you away from the city," controller Bachman advised. "Whatever you do, keep us away from the city," Haynes agreed. They tried to make a left turn, but it wasn't feasible, so they started one final right turn. As they did so, Dvorak offered his seat to Fitch who was now having to finesse the throttles all the time; Dvorak then took the jump seat.

As they did so, Bachman offered them a four-lane highway as a potential place to ditch but they were able to line up with the airport. "Won't this be a fun landing!" Haynes said, to general amusement in the cockpit. To everyone's amazement, he was able to tell Bachman a few moments later, "We have the runway in sight."

They continued easing the aircraft down, and when Bachman formally told them, "You're cleared to land on any runway," Haynes couldn't help but quip, "You want to be particular and make it a runway, huh?" Warned by the first officer that they were two minutes from touchdown, the flight attendants shouted at the passengers to get their heads down. As they were on the final approach, Bachman advised that they were approaching a closed runway, which had "wide open field" at the end. The plan, such as it was, was to land, hopefully staying upright on the landing gear, go off the end of the runway – since they had no hydraulic braking – shear the gear and keep going on their belly until they stopped.

And then, fifty feet above the runway, the luck which had kept the aircraft going for the last three-quarters of an hour ran out. Not totally, but just enough. ("If we'd had ten more seconds, we could have put it on the runway," Bill Records would later say.) Fitch kept manipulating the throttles and the aircraft was lined up pretty well – the right wing tip was in the centre of the runway, with the right main gear off to the side. But then another phugoid

motion began. Fitch applied a final burst to the throttles, but the
left engine spooled up faster than the right, so the aircraft banked
right. Flight 232 touched down at Sioux City on its right wing at
about 1850 feet per minute – six times faster than the normal rate
of descent.

Over the next few seconds, the right wing sheared off, along
with its engine; the fuel from that spilled out and caught fire. The
right main gear separated from the aircraft, although the left
stayed on as the rest of the aircraft hit the ground. The tail section
broke off, and the rest of the fuselage slid along sideways on the
left main gear and the right wing stub for about 2,000 feet. Then
the left wing came up, and the aircraft went up on its nose, and
bounced on the runway, turning upside down and crashing down.
(Contrary to persistent newspaper reports, it didn't cartwheel.)
The cockpit and the first-class cabin both separated.

"The flames were coming in the airplane while we were skid-
ding down the runway," passenger John Transue recalled. "We
started to roll and while we were rolling it seemed to me the flames
shot into the cabin . . . the whole nose section of the plane just
disappeared."

All of the flight crew were injured – Records had broken ribs,
hips and pelvis, as well as internal injuries; Fitch dislocated one
shoulder and broke the other, as well as his hand and rib; Dvorak
smashed his right angle and got a large burn on his arm; Haynes
got fourteen lacerations in his head, and needed ninety-two
stitches in his scalp, and surgery to restore his left ear which was
almost severed. To begin with, no one checked the cockpit wreckage for survivors – they thought it was part of the avionics
compartment, not the cockpit itself. In the end they had to lift the
wreckage off them to get them out. All of them were back at work
within weeks; Haynes retired at the mandatory retirement age in
1991, and continued to lecture about the crash for many years.

There were 111 fatalities in the accident, with one person
dying a month later (so technically he was classified as a survivor). One hundred and eighty-five people survived, many from
the central piece of the fuselage; some of them were so disoriented by the crash that they started to walk away from rescuers
across the corn fields. One baby died from asphyxia, placed on
the floor at the request of the flight attendants to be held down by

his mother – the recommended procedure in those days. As a result, Jan Brown became a campaigner for changes in federal safety regulations. One young boy was happy to have received an injury; according to his father, Rabbi Avrohom Brownstein, nine-year-old Ysrael had always wanted a broken arm like his friends, and now he had one.

Court cases inevitably followed, with the Aluminum Company of America (ALCOA) charged with faulty forging of the titanium, General Electric with not detecting the metallurgical flaw in making the fan disc from the forgings, McDonnell Douglas with failing to provide a backup to the all-hydraulic flight controls, and United with missing the crack on the fan disc in its inspections. They settled the first batch as the case came to trial in January 1992. The last of hundreds of cases was settled seven years later; approximately $200 million was paid out.

The NTSB concentrated on the source of the engine failure, and after a key piece of the fan disc was located in a cornfield three months after the crash, they were able to complete their investigations. In their findings they noted: "The airplane was marginally flyable using asymmetrical thrust from engines No. 1 and 3 after the loss of all conventional flight control systems; however, a safe landing was virtually impossible." Luckily, 103 years of combined flying experience in the cockpit of Flight 232 ensured that the impossible was achieved.

AFTERWORD

"I certainly hope this little incident hasn't put you off flying, miss. Statistically speaking, of course, it's still the safest way to travel." (*Superman: The Movie*, 1978)

During the writing of this book, family and friends have all wondered if it's made me more or less frightened of flying – particularly since, partway through, I was making a transatlantic trip during some of the worst weather that we've seen in many years. I've never been the world's happiest flyer but have always subscribed to the theory that once you're on board the aircraft (or "plane" as I used to think of them), there's very little you can do. If something's going to go wrong, then your fate is completely in someone else's hands.

That's not totally true, as I've realized from researching the accounts you've just read, and talking to aviation professionals. Whether they're on the flight deck or out in the cabin, they are constantly monitoring what's going on – things that may look random at first glance are anything but – and the amount of training that they all go through is reassuring. But as passengers we have a part to play as well, and if we spot something, they'd rather know about it than not.

One of the other reassuring elements is that there have not been anywhere near as many serious incidents in the past few years – the loss of Malaysia Airlines Flight MH370 on 8 March 2014 for reasons that are, at the time of writing, still unknown, notwithstanding. Yes, there are still runway incursions; yes, a bird strike can hit at any time. However, as technology has improved, so the level of safety seems to have risen. Accidents can and will happen. But so long as we continue to learn from them, hopefully they won't be repeated.

ACKNOWLEDGMENTS

First and foremost, my thanks to those many aviation professionals who have posted their thoughts online about some of the incidents described in this book; and to those who for reasons of professional courtesy I can't name but who provided me with valuable insight into what goes on during a flight – particularly the many areas which members of the public might not be aware of. It's certainly given me a very different perspective on certain things.

Also, special thanks to: Duncan Proudfoot and Clive Hebard at Constable & Robinson for inviting me on board this project, and to Iain Coupar and Tash Siddiqui for their invaluable assistance in the preparation stages.

Mihai Adascalitei for his translation skills, which helped me avoid some unforced errors; Brian J. Robb, Scott Harrison and Iain Coupar again for their excellent proofing and helpful comments; and as ever, Gabriella Nemeth, my copy editor, who has helped ensure stupid mistakes haven't marred the text – any that remain are strictly my responsibility.

Fellow writers Sarah Lotz and Sarah Pinborough for encouragement at exactly the right time when this project looked as if it might be overwhelming.

Carol Matthews for helping to spread the load and freeing up some extra time to work on this; Geraldine Rowlands and Nick Hancock for sterling musical assistance; and the members of the Hurstpierpoint Singers and All the Right Notes for the opportunities to unwind from the intricacies of this project.

Caitlin Fultz, Clare Hey, Emma Capron, Lee Harris, Amanda Rutter and Emlyn Rees for the usual help keeping the wheels of commerce going.

Monica Derwent, Amelia Holland, Sam Dorset, Adina Mihaela Roman, and Patricia Hyde for research help.

The staff of the Hassocks branch of the West Sussex Libraries

Service, who once again assisted with tracking down rare items and exemplified why we need a library service to continue. As writer Joanne Harris recently said: "A library is a civic space and a physical reminder of the value our society places on books and literacy. A secular church for readers." Long may they continue to draw in worshippers!

And, most importantly, my partner Barbara and my daughter Sophie for their love and support even when I'm getting frazzled, and our terriers Rani and Rodo who don't care what I'm writing about, so long as I stop somewhere between 12 and 1 each day to take them out!

GLOSSARY

ACC (see **ARTCC**)

Air Traffic Control (see **ATC**)

Airway systems The ICAO define these as "a control area or portion thereof established in the form of a corridor". They are the designated routes which aircraft use to travel from point to point, established as a result of a collision in 1922. Airways can be at different heights on the same routes for going in different directions (so odd numbered flight levels go East–West; even-numbered go West–East, for example).

Airworthiness Directives These are issued by the FAA to correct an unsafe condition in a product – an aircraft, engine, propeller or appliance. They are legally enforceable.

Area Control Centres (see **ARTCC**)

Area Regional Traffic Control Centers (see **ARTCC**)

ARTCC Area Regional Traffic Control Center. This is the American term for an Area Control Centre (ACC): it's the facility which is responsible for controlling aircraft as they travel through a particular volume of space (a Flight Information Region). The FAA notes that it is there to "provide air traffic control service to aircraft operating on IFR flight plans within controlled airspace, principally during the en route phase of flight. When equipment capabilities and controller workload permit, certain advisory/assistance services may be provided to VFR aircraft." The areas can be subdivided.

ATC Air Traffic Control. The primary purpose of this is "to prevent a collision between aircraft operating in the system and to organize and expedite the flow of traffic".

Attitude The way an aircraft is oriented with regard to the Earth, so whether it's climbing (pitching), cruising or descending.

Backtrack An aircraft is doing this when it is using a portion of a runway as a taxiway, rather than taxiing on a separate route to the end of the runway. (See the Tenerife disaster, page 98.)

At controlled airports, this is authorized under specific instruction from air traffic control. At uncontrolled airports, this may happen, and pilots are recommended to broadcast that they're doing so.

BFU Bundesstelle für Flugunfalluntersuchung: The German Federal Bureau of Accident Investigation; the country's equivalent of the NTSB. It is responsible for the investigation of civil aircraft accidents and serious incidents within Germany.

Black box This is a misnomer for two reasons – firstly, it's not black, it's orange, so it can be found more easily. Secondly, there isn't just one black box, there are two: one contains the flight data recorder, the other the cockpit voice recorder. They are now sited at the rear of the aircraft, in the hope that they will survive a nose-down crash more easily. They are designed to withstand massive forces, and temperatures up to 2,000 degrees Fahrenheit; if they're submerged, they should be able to send signals from depths up to 20,000 feet.

CENIPA Centro de Investigação e Prevenção de Acidentes Aeronáuticos: The Brazilian Aeronautical Accidents Investigation and Prevention Centre, which is part of the Brazilian Air Force.

CAB The Civil Aeronautics Board, which was the predecessor of the NTSB in America. It was set up by President Roosevelt in 1940 as an independent part of the Department of Commerce. It was superseded by the NTSB in 1967 when the various American transportation agencies were combined into the new Department of Transportation.

Cockpit voice recorder (see **CVR**)

CVR The cockpit voice recorder: one of the black boxes, which records everything that happens on the flight deck. It has channels for each of the pilots, as well as other crew, air traffic control and a microphone in the cockpit roof. Currently, the minimum requirement is for recordings to last thirty minutes, but the NTSB has been pushing for this to be increased to two hours, and for video recordings to be made as well.

Empennage The proper name for the tail assembly of the aircraft – this normally includes the horizontal and vertical stabilizers, which are used to control pitch and yaw, the elevator, and the black boxes.

FAA The Federal Aviation Administration: Their continuing mission is to provide the safest, most efficient aerospace in the world. The Federal Aviation Agency came out of the Civil Aeronautics Authority following the Grand Canyon Disaster in June 1956 (see page 19), and was made responsible for civil aviation safety. It became the Federal Aviation Administration in 1967. It regulates everything that takes place which is to do with aviation in the United States – and because that affects a great many other countries, its rulings have an effect on most airlines, particularly if they wish to fly into the United States. They provide Advisory Circulars, Airworthiness Directives and Regulations, as well as Notices to Airmen.

FDR Flight data recorder: one of the black boxes, this monitors everything to do with the flight, from the fuel levels, the engine noises, the use of all of the instruments. All it doesn't do is record what the crew are saying to each other – for that, see **CVR**.

Feathering This occurs on propellers where the blades are rotated parallel to the airflow – it's like closing an umbrella, so the blades don't obstruct the airflow. If the engine isn't producing enough power to contribute to thrust, then some propellers would autofeather, and assume this position. A feathered or autofeathered propeller will extend a glide range; if a propeller autofeathers when the pilot isn't expecting it, though, it means he loses the thrust from that engine.

Flaps These are pieces of the wing, which are mounted on the trailing edge (the other side from the leading edge) which help to reduce the speed of the aircraft, and also help to increase the angle of descent for landing. Extended, they help to increase the drag and slow the aircraft down.

Flight Data Recorder (see **FDR**)

Flight Information Region A volume of airspace under the control of a particular ACC/ARTCC.

Flight level The level at which the aircraft is travelling. Flight levels are specific barometric pressures, and are calculated using a sea-level pressure of 29.92 inHg. Thus flight level 350 is a nominal 35,000 feet above the ground, even if the ground happens to be considerably higher than sea level. Some authorities note that flight levels are not used beneath flight level 180.

Horizontal stabilizer Part of the empennage. One of the control surfaces of an aircraft which keeps it in trim.

ICAO International Civil Aviation Organization. This is a United Nations specialized agency, created by the Convention on International Civil Aviation in 1944. It works with the signatories to develop internationally recognized standards and recommended practices which can then be used by the states when they are developing their own legally binding civil aviation regulations.

IFR Instrument Flight Rules. These are the rules and regulations established by the FAA to govern flight under conditions in which flight by outside visual reference is not safe. IFR flight depends upon flying by reference to instruments in the flight deck, and navigation is accomplished by reference to electronic signals. The whole of the continental United States is covered by IFR rules.

ILS Instrument Landing System. This is a radio beam transmitter that provides a direction for approaching aircraft tuned to its frequency. It comprises the localizer for lateral guidance, and the glide slope for vertical guidance.

Leading edge The part of the wing of the aircraft that first contacts the air.

NOTAM Notices to Airmen – advisories of potential hazards along a route are filed with the relevant authority (the FAA in the US) and then forwarded to those who indicate that they are going to be using that particular route.

Notices to Airmen (see **NOTAM**)

NTSB The National Transportation Safety Board. The independent American federal agency charged by Congress to investigate every civil aviation accident in the US and significant accidents in other modes of transportation. Because of the range of expertise at its disposal, it is often called in by other countries' accident investigation boards. It was set up in 1967 as part of the Department of Transportation, but was given complete independence outside the DOT in 1974, since Congress reasoned that they couldn't carry out their functions unless they were totally separate. They have no formal authority, but rely on their reputation for thorough, accurate and independent investigations, and hope that the transportation industry will follow their recommendations.

Pan pan pan If this call is made, then something urgent has happened but at the time isn't causing immediate danger to life or the vessel. The next step up is Mayday.

Phugoid When an aircraft enters a phugoid, it is pitching up and climbing, then pitching down and descending. The pilots need to act counter-intuitively to deal with this (see JAL 123, page 203 and United Airlines 232, page 209 and 473).

Pilot flying This is the pilot who is actually in command of the aircraft: if the first officer is in control of the take-off, he is the pilot flying, even if he is not the aircraft commander. The opposite is the "pilot not flying".

Pitch The degree to which the aircraft's nose goes up or down.

Plane A toy model of an aircraft – although the word is used colloquially to denote the actual aircraft.

RA Resolution advisory: an instruction given by a collision alert system to help pilots avoid collisions. They will be issued simultaneously to both aircraft, with opposing instructions to help maintain the distance. They override air traffic control instructions.

Roll The rotation about the axis aligned with the direction that the aircraft is flying.

Rotation (See **V speeds**)

Rudder The control surface on the trailing edge of the vertical stabilizer which controls yaw.

Runway numbers These are designated by degrees of the circle divided by ten – so runway 27 is a runway in a 270-degree (West) angle. Since some runways can be used in either direction, a strip of land can be referred to as Runway 9 and Runway 27.

Slats These are surfaces on the leading edge of the wing which are used to help an aircraft travel at a slower speed without risking stalling.

Stabilizer The control surfaces on the empennage.

Stick shaker This is a mechanical device which makes the control yoke of the aircraft shake to warn the pilot that the aircraft is in imminent danger of stalling.

Take-off (For speeds relevant to this, see **V Speeds**)

TCA Terminal Control Area. An area of controlled airspace around an airport which is formed of various layers of increasing size, making it resemble an upside down wedding-cake.

TCAS Traffic Collision Avoidance System. An automatic system which uses the transponder transmissions from other aircraft to ensure that the area around the aircraft is safe. It operates separate from Air Traffic Control, and will issue traffic advisories of nearby traffic, and resolution advisories to make sure the pilots keep their aircraft the prescribed distance apart.

Whip stall A stall during a small aircraft's vertical climb; the aircraft pauses then drops nose downwards. The nose appears to move like a whip, hence the name.

V speeds The various speeds at which an aircraft needs to travel for safe flight. V_1 is the maximum speed in the take-off at which the pilot can stop the aircraft safely. V_{ROT} is the rotation speed – the speed at which the nosewheel leaves the ground. V_2 is the speed at which the aircraft can safely become airborne with one engine inoperative. These are set by the pilots prior to take-off.

VFR Visual Flight Rules. This is when a pilot is operating by sight rather than by instruments. There are very clear times now when this is permitted (as developed following a large number of incidents charted in this book).

VORTAC VHF omnidirectional range beacon with a tactical air navigation system beacon. These provide pilots with positional information.

Yaw Rotation in a horizontal plane around the vertical axis – so turning to left or right. This is controlled by the rudder.

SOURCES

Part 1: Mid-Air Collisions

Flight, October 8, 1910: "Milan Flying Meeting"

Popular Mechanics, January 1911

Mortimer, Gavin: *The First Eagles* (Zenith, 2014)

New York Times, April 7, 1922: "Americans Die in French Air Crash"

Associated Press, April 7, 1922: "No Passengers in British Machine"

Flight, April 13, 1922: "London-Paris Machines Collide"

Historic Wings, April 7, 2013: "The First Midair Airline Disaster"

Associated Press, November 25, 1942: "Army Pilot Acquitted of Manslaughter Charge"

Time, November 2, 1942: "CATASTROPHE: Weather Clear, Altitude Normal"

Civil Aeronautics Board, January 28, 1943: File No. 2362-42, Docket no. SA 74

The State, July 13, 1945: "Airliner, Army Plane In Mid-Air Collision: Two Soldiers And One Child Killed in Crash" (reprint of statement from Florence Army Air Field)

Civil Aeronautics Board, June 12, 1946: File No. 2773-45: "Accident Investigation Report (revised)

New York Times, April 6, 1948: "Soviet-British Plane Collision Kills 15; Russian Apologizes"

The Spectator, April 15, 1948: "News of the Week"

New York Times, April 6, 1948: "Britain is Stirred by Plane Incident"

Hansard, April 26, 1948: Vol. 450 c5W "Gatow Air Disaster"

Flight, February 3, 1949: "York and DC-6 Collision Report"

Flight, July 8, 1948: "The Northolt Disaster"

The Times, September 21, 1948: "Air Collision Inquiry – Last Instruction to Pilots"

The Times, September 28, 1948: "Air Crash Inquiry – Ministry Official's Theory"

The Times, November 11, 1948: "Airport Control – Wider separation of aircraft"

Flight, February 24, 1949: "Dakota-Anson Collision"

Flight, October 6, 1949: "Dakota-Anson Collision"

Aviation Safety Network, report number 19490219-0 (quote from official report)

Roosevelt, Eleanor: *My Day*: (November 5, 1949)

Civil Aeronautics Board, September 22, 1950, File No. 1-0138

Time, November 14, 1949: "DISASTERS: Bolivia 927! Turn Left"

Washington Post, November 2, 1949: "Planes Collide Near National Airport Killing 55; D.C. Loses Home Rule Advocate"

New York Times, November 2, 1949: "55 Killed in Worst U.S. Civil Air Crash"

Arlington Fire Journal, February 11, 2005: "DAYS OF DISASTER – 1949 & 1982"

Associated Press, November 1, 1949: "Planes Crash In Midair; 23 Killed"

Wings, August 2006: "Lessons from Tragedy over the Grand Canyon"

Around Arizona, July 15, 2012: "Grand Canyon Collision" (includes numerous quotes from contemporary *New York Times* reports)

Los Angeles Times, June 3, 2006: "Crash Set a New Course"

Arizona State University, 2008: "1956 Airline Crash"

Time, July 30, 1956: "Aviation: Crash Program"

Time, July 9, 1956: "Disasters: Painted Desert: 11:31"

Time, September 24, 1956: "Corporations: Genius at Work"

Civil Aeronautics Board, SA-320, File No. 1-0090, April 17, 1957

New York Times, July 2, 1956: "ALL 128 ON 2 AIRLINERS FOUND DEAD; CAPTAIN PRESUMED TO HAVE COLLIDED BEFORE CRASHING IN GRAND CANYON."

New York Times, July 5, 1956: "Airlines Seeking Collision Alarm"

New York Times, July 3, 1956: "Removal of Air Victims Starts; Wreckage in Canyon Is Studied,"

New York Times, April 18, 1957: "CANYON AIR CRASH TERMED MYSTERY"

Life Magazine, April 28, 1957: "Collision and Air Safety: The

Lessons of Grand Canyon, reconstruction of crash" (includes Mel Hunter's illustration based on the CAB findings)

Deseret News, June 30, 2006: "Vestiges of '56 collision still imbedded in Grand Canyon"

Aircraft Accident Report, July 1, 1956: "Big Airliners Dive Into Canyon: 127 Believed Killed"

AAP, July 1, 1956: "Find Wreckage Of Planes In Which 128 Perished"

Deseret News, April 22, 1958: "Stop Those Mid-Air Collisions"

Time, December 26, 1960: "Disasters: Death in the Air"

British Pathe News, December 1960: "Sky Disasters: New York – Munich"

New York Times, December 16-22, 2010: "Park Slope Plane Crash" (series of features)

New York Times, October 15, 2004: "Pillar of Fire"

New York Times, March 24, 2002: "The Day the Boy Fell From the Sky"

New York Times, December 17, 1960: "127 Die As 2 Airliners Collide Over City"

Cause & Circumstance blog, May 3, 2004: "A Legacy of Superb Airmanship"

Props, Pistons, Old Jets And the Good Ole Days of Flying blogspot, September 4, 2009: "EASTERN FLIGHT 853 AND TWA FLIGHT 42 MIDAIR COLLISION DECEMBER 4, 1965" This includes excerpts from: *Reader's Digest*, May 1967: "Ten Minutes to Live"

CAB Aircraft Accident Report SA-389 File 1-0033, December 20, 1966

CAB Aircraft Accident Report SA-361 File 1-0083, June 12, 1962

GoUpstate, June 12, 2006: "NTSB to re-examine cause of 1967 midair collision"

NTSB, September 5, 1968, Doc. NTSCB AAR 68 AJ

Blue Ridge Times-News, July 19, 2007: "Flight 22 – Views from Hendersonville"

News-Leader, December 4, 2005: "Feds reopen probe of 1967 crash"

GoUpstate, July 16, 2005: "'I've never been to the crash site. Would you take me?'"

Aero-News, February 12, 2007: "NTSB Says No Change In Findings On 1967 Piedmont Airlines Midair"

Times-News, September 27, 1968: "Piedmont Airlines Cleared Of Blame In Air Crash Here"

Associated Press, July 20, 1967: "Navy Secretary Among Victims"

Eller, Richard E. *Piedmont Airlines: A Complete History, 1948-1989* McFarland, 2012

Spartanburg Herald-Journal, February 10, 2007: "NTSB Stands By Decades-Old Conclusion"

NTSB, July 15, 1970, Doc. NTSB-AAR-70-15 SA-417 File No 1-0016

McGlaun.com blog: "The Story of Flight 853" (detailed eye-witness testimony, and photos from the crash site)

NBC, October 10, 1969: *Huntley-Brinkley Report* (uploaded to YouTube at https://www.youtube.com/watch?v=aSBRZJqLp5)

Time, September 19, 1969: "The Air: Death in the Skies"

Examiner.com, February 26, 2013: "Allegheny Flight 853 (Photos)"

United States District Court, S. D. Indiana, Indianapolis Division, October 13, 1976: ALLEGHENY AIRLINES, INC. v. UNITED STATES

United Press International (UPI), September 10, 1969: "No Survivors in Air Crash Over Indiana"

Vincent v. Hughes Air West, Inc., 557 F. 2d 759, Court of Appeal

Associated Press, June 7, 1971: "Marine Jet, Civilian Plane Collide"

Associated Press, June 7, 1971: "Safety Agencies Fight; Collisions Continue"

UPI, June 7, 1971: "Navy Jet, Airliner Collide, 49 Killed" [At the time they believed that the pilot had parachuted to safety]

Associated Press, June 8, 1971: "Airline Hit Marine Jet, Survivor Says"

UPI, June 8, 1971: "50 died; nobody blamed"

UPI, June 9, 1971: "Flight Rules That Led To Crash Criticized By Federal Investigator"

UPI, June 9, 1971: "Crash Stirs Rule Probe"

Milwaukee Journal, June 10, 1971: "Air Crash Linked to Acrobatics"

UPI, June 11, 1971: "Crash clues may be held by recorder"

Deseret News, June 17, 1971; "10 More Feet – 50 Lives"

UPI, June 18, 1971: "Probe reveals faulty radar"

Associated Press, June 18, 1971: "Don't Place Blame for 2-Jet Crash"

NTSB, August 30, 1972, Report No. WTSB-AAR-72-26, SA-426, File No. 1-0005

UPI, July 30, 1971: "161 Die in Worst Aviation Disaster"

Time, August 9, 1971: "DISASTERS: The Worst Ever"

Haine, Col. Edgar A.: *Disaster in the Air* (Cornwall Books), 2000

BBC News On This Day 1950–2005: "5 March: 1973: Mid-air collision kills 68"

Flight International, March 15, 1973: "Iberia DC-9 Crash Repercussions"

Hansard, April 3, 1979: "Nantes Aircraft Crash"

French Secretariat of State for Transport, reprinted by Department of Trade, Accidents Investigation Branch, July 1975: Aircraft Accident Report 7/75

Time, September 20, 1976: "Disasters: Look Up In Horror"

Yugoslav Federal Civil Aviation Administration Aircraft Accident Investigation Commission Report, reprinted by DOT Aircraft Accident Report 5/77

Yugoslav Federal Committee for Transportation and Communications Second Commission of Inquiry with United Kingdom Addendum, Aircraft Accident Report 9/82

AirDisaster.com, "British Airways Flight 476"

Associated Press, April 12, 1977: "8 on trial for Zagreb air collision"

The Age, December 6, 1979: "Reconstruction of air tragedy"

Weston, Richard with Ronald Hurst, *Zagreb One Four: Cleared to Collide?*: (HarperCollins, 1982)

FAA Historical Chronology, 1926-1996 (at the FAA website, www.faa.gov)

Time, October 9, 1978: "Nation: Death over San Diego"

San Diego Magazine, August 1998: "This is It!"

NTSB, April 20, 1979, Report NTSB-AAR-79-5

Time, June 24, 2001: "Collision in the 'Birdcage'" (reprinted from 1986)

Cenovich, Marilyn: *The Story of Cerritos: A History in Progress* (online at Cerritos Library, 1995)

New York Times, September 1, 1996: "California Jet Crash Led to Sweeping Changes"

Reuters, April 15, 1989: "Jury Fixes Blame for Crash That Killed 82"

Los Angeles Times, September 8, 1986: "Accounts of Terror in Lives of Six Families: Cerritos Crash: View From Ground Zero"

Long Beach Press-Telegram, August 26, 2011: "Cerritos plane crash left its scars"

Los Angeles Times, September 1, 1986: "70 Die as Planes Collide in Air"

Associated Press, August 30, 1987: "Fears linger in Cerritos one year after air crash"

Flight International, November 20, 1996: "Collision raises doubts on ATC routeings"

Court of Inquiries, 1997, "CIVIL AVIATION AIRCRAFT ACCIDENT SUMMARY FOR THE YEAR 1996"

New York Times, November 13, 1996: "Two Airliners Collide in Midair, Killing All 351 Aboard in India"

New York Times, November 14, 1996: "Indian Officials Gather Evidence on Midair Collision"

CNN, November 14, 1996: "Pilot error focus of India collision investigation"

Rediff, May 15, 1997: "Communication gap caused Charkhi Dadri mishap: ATC guild"

Rediff, May 26, 1997: "Charkhi Dadri collision occurred in "heavy clouds": US pilot"

Director General of Civil Aviation, India, June 15, 1999: "OPERATIONS CIRCULAR NO.3 OF 1999"

Independent, 13 November 1996: "Human error is blamed for crash"

New York Times, May 5, 1997: "One Jet in Crash Over India Ruled Off Course"

Independent, 14 November 1996: "THE INDIAN AIR CRASH: Tapes point blame at Kazakh pilot"

Inquirer Wire Services, November 13, 1996: "Search Begins After Midair Crash 351 Feared Dead As Jets Collide Over India"

Flight Safety Australia, November-December 2006: "Mid-Air Disasters"

Flight Global, November 9, 2010: "Japanese air traffic controllers lose appeal in JAL near-miss case"

Yomiuri Shimbun, March 21, 2006: "Court clears air controllers in near miss"

Japan Airlines, January 31, 2001: "TOKYO: JANUARY 31, 2001 - FLIGHT JL907 INCIDENT"

CBS, January 31, 2001: "Close Call For JAL Jets"

Associated Press, January 31, 2001: "At least 35 airline passengers injured in near miss"

Associated Press, February 3, 2001: "Japanese police pursuing possibility of negligence in planes' near collision"

Japanese Investigator-General, June 12, 2005: "Accident Investigation into a Near Mid-Air Collision"

BFU, May 2004, "Investigation Report AX001-1-2/02" (Quotes from the official English translation)

BBC News, 2 July 2002: "Crash planes dived to disaster"

BBC News, 3 July 2002: "Air crash safety device switched off"

BBC News, 13 July 2002: "Controller admits mid-air crash"

BBC News, 26 February 2004: "Grieving father held for killing"

BBC News, 19 May 2004: "Swiss firm admits air crash blame"

BBC News, 4 September 2007: "Four guilty over Swiss air crash"

The Age, February 29, 2004: "Did father's grief lead to murder?"

New York Times, June 30, 2012: "Plane Crash Remembered; One Mourner Not Welcome"

Daily Mail, 3 July 2002: "Children die in mid-air collision"

Guardian, 26 October 2005: "Russian tells of air crash grief that led to killing"

Aviation International News, August 2002: "German collision was the first of the TCAS era"

ABC News, July 2, 2002: "52 Kids Among Dead in Midair Collision"

New York Times, October 3, 2006: "Colliding With Death at 37,000 Feet, and Living"

New York Times, December 10, 2008: "Brazil Lays Some Blame on U.S. Pilots in Collision"

Associated Press, October 1, 2006: "Brazilian Authorities Suspect No Survivors From Jet That Crashed Carrying 155 People"

New York Times, November 8, 2006: "U.S. pilots charged in Brazilian plane crash"

Aviation International, December 11, 2008: "NTSB, Cenipa at Odds over Midair Accident Report"

Time, December 21, 2006: "Are U.S. Pilots Being Made Scapegoats in Brazil?"

Xinhua press agency, January 13, 2010: "Brazilian court overturns acquittal of U.S. pilots in 2006 air disaster"

New York Times, May 16, 2011: "Pilots Avoid Jail in Brazil Crash"

Reuters, October 15, 2012: "Brazil upholds U.S. pilots' convictions in 2006 air disaster"

Time, April 3, 2007: "The Chaos in Brazil's Blue Skies"

Terra, December 11, 2013: "STJ reduz pena de pilotos condenados pelo acidente com avião da Gol"

CENIPA, December 8, 2008: Final Report A-00X/CENIPA/2008 with Appendix 1 and 2 from NTSB

AeroSafety World, February 2009: "Midair over the Amazon"

Part 2: Ground Collisions and Near Misses

Associated Press, December 21, 1972: "11 Are Killed in Crash of Airliner in Chicago" (in fact there were only 9 fatalities on the day)

National Transportation Safety Board: Aircraft-Accident-Report File 1-0017 (now AAR73-15)

Hansard, April 8, 1974: "Luton Airport – Oral answers to Questions – Trade"

Department of Transport, February 26, 1975, Aircraft Accident Report 3/75

Subscretaria de Aviacion Civil, Spain, October 1978: Report into the Collision at Tenerife Airport Spain on 27 March 1977.

Netherlands Aviation Safety Board, ICAO Circular 153-AN/56: Final Report and Comments of the Netherlands Aviation Safety Board of the Investigation into the Accident

Flight International, January 20, 1979: Tenerife: The Last Analysis

Time, April 11, 1977: "Aviation: '. . . What's he doing? He'll kill us all!' (The quote was meant to have been said by Captain Grubbs)

Flight Safety Australia, Sept-Oct 2007: "Tenerife: A Survivor's Tale"

Los Angeles Times, March 27, 1987: "Jet Crash Lingers in Memory: Survivor Recalls Horror of Disaster That Killed 582"

Cockpit Voice Recorder transcripts from KLM and Pan Am aircraft at Project-Tenerife.com (where many original source documents have been uploaded)

Flight International, December 17, 1983: "Madrid cleared?"

Spanish Civil Aviation Accident Investigation Commission, May 1986: "Informe Técnico: Accidente occurrido el 07 de Diciembre de 1987"

Reuters, December 8, 1983: "Madrid airport crash death toll set at 92"

NTSB Aircraft Accident Report AAR91-05, June 25, 1991

New York Times, December 4, 1990: "COLLISION IN DETROIT; At Least 8 Die in Collision On Detroit Airport Runway"

Flight Safety Foundation, *Flight Safety Digest*, December 1990: "Lessons Learned From Hijacking"

Time, October 15, 1990: "China: Deadly Bouquet"

New York Times, October 3, 1990: "127 Killed in Jetliner Collision in China"

New York Times, October 10, 1990: "Hijacking Prompts Beijing Shake-Up"

AirDisaster.com: Special Report: Xiamen Airlines Flight 8301

National Transportation Safety Board, October 22, 1991: Aircraft Accident Report AAR91-08

People, February 25, 1991: "The Fire This Time"

Los Angeles Times, May 8, 1991: "Controller Says Her Error Caused Runway Collision"

NTSB docket LAX04IA302

PR Newswire, June 29, 1999: "Incident at JFK Airport Sparks FAA Investigation."

Newsday, June 23, 1999: "Near miss for passenger plane, jet"

Chicago Sun-Times, October 15, 2000: "Close call on O'Hare runway"

St Petersburg Times, June 14, 2000: "Planes urged to stop at runway intersections"

FAA Animation: Runway Incursion Providence, Rhode Island (YouTube http://www.youtube.com/watch?v=qUDFY5qlTSA/ Unofficial video: using the tape: http://www.youtube.com/watch?v=QrzpvcKoRyw)

Providence Journal, August 13, 2000: "Near-Miss: An NTSB Recreation"

Providence Journal, September 15, 2005: "T.F. Green Airport's Airfield Ground Radar System Acts as Eyes in Fog"

NTSB, July 6, 2000: Safety Recommendation

NTSB, March 22, 2000: "Testimony of Jim Hall"

Associated Press, October 8, 2001: "Jets collide on Milan runway; 118 killed"

Agenzia Nazionale per la Sicurezza del Volo, January 20, 2004: "Final Report"

New York Times, October 9, 2001: "Milan airport crash kills 118 / Cessna strayed into big jet's path"

Flight International, April 27, 2004: "ATC body blasts Linate verdicts"

New York Times, March 15, 2005: "4 convicted in 2001 Milan plane crash"

AvioNews, February 20, 2008: "Linate massacre: tomorrow the Cassation sentence"

Associated Press, February 21, 2008: "Court upholds convictions in Italian air crash"

Cineflex, *Mayday / Air Crash Investigation,* March 23, 2012: "The Invisible Plane"

Aviation Herald, January 10, 2012: "Incident: Southwest B737 at Chicago on Dec 1st 2011, ATC error causes runway incursion"

New York Times, September 24, 2012: "Safer Flights, but Risk Lurks on the Runway"

Part 3: Death Comes on Swift Wings: Bird Strikes

Daily Times (Chattanooga, Tennessee). April 4, 1912: "Aviator C.P. Rodgers Almost Instantly Killed. His Biplane Falls Distance of 200 Feet" (wire report)

Civil Aeronautics Board, July 31, 1962: Aircraft Accident Report SA-358, File No. 1-0043

Time, October 17, 1960: "Disasters: Electra's Tragedy"

Kalafatas, Michael: *Bird Strike: The Crash of the Boston Electra* (Brandeis University Press, 2010)

CAB, March 22, 1963: Aircraft Accident Report File No. 0-0034

Associated Press, November 24, 1962: "All On Board Viscount Are Found Dead"

UPI, November 24, 1962: "Engine Failure Believed Cause of Maryland Crash"

US Court of Appeals, February 16, 1983: "Marilyn Joyce SELLFORS, Etc., Plaintiff-Appellant, v. UNITED STATES of America, Defendant-Appellee. No. 80-7897."

Associated Press, February 27, 1973: "Birds Possible Cause of Crash"

UPI, February 26, 1973: "7 die in plane crash"

Associated Press, February 26, 1973: "6 Killed in Jet Crash; Birds Possible Cause" (only 6 bodies were initially found)

University of Nebraska, November 3, 2006: "Bird and Other Wildlife Hazards at Airports: Liability Issues for Airport Managers"

New York Times, November 12, 1975: "Jet at JFK Hits Birds & Burns; All 139 Safe"

Overseas National Crew website: testimonies regarding 1975 bird strike

NTSB, December 16, 1976; Report No. NTSB-AAR-76-19

New Scientist, April 28, 2006: "The Space Vulture Squadron"

Guardian, November 10, 2008: "Ryanair jet makes emergency landing in Rome after birds sucked into engine"

Flight Global, November 10, 2008: "Ryanair cites multiple bird-strike as 737 overruns at Rome"

BBC News, November 10, 2008: "Bird-hit jet in emergency landing"

Aviation Herald, November 18, 2008: "Accident: Ryanair B738 at Rome on Nov 10th 2008, engine and landing gear trouble, temporarily departed runway"

GAPAN, January 22, 2009: "US Airways Flight 1549 Crew receive prestigious Guild of Air Pilots and Air "Navigators Award"

New York Post, January 17, 2009: "Quiet Air Hero is Captain America"

NTSB, May 4, 2010: Aircraft Accident Report NTSB/AAR-10/03, PB2010-910403

US Airways, January 15, 2009: "Press Release"

Daily Telegraph, 21 August 2013: "Bird strikes damage three aircraft a week"

Bird Strike Committee USA website: www.birdstrike.org/

CBS: *60 Minutes*, February 8, 2009: "Flight 1549: A Routine Takeoff Turns Ugly" / "Saving 155 Souls In Minutes"

ABC News, January 17, 2009: "Miracle on the Hudson"

New York Times, January 17, 2009: "1549 to Tower: 'We're Gonna End Up in the Hudson'"

Associated Press, February 24, 2009: "Controller Thought Plane That Ditched Was Doomed"

New York Times, February 5, 2009: "Was Flight 1549's Pilot Fearful? If So, His Voice Didn't Let On"

FAA, February 2, 2009: "Full Transcript, Aircraft Accident, AWE1549"

NTSB, May 4, 2010: Aircraft Accident Report NTSB/ AAR-10/03, PB2010-910403

Part 4: A Fatal Icy Touch

Flight International, June 19, 1969: "Fay Vindicates Thain" (worth seeking out for the beautiful photo of Concorde over London above the report)

Flight International, November 2, 1967: "Munich – Second Report Disputed"

Daily Mirror, 5 February 2008: "Munich Air Disaster: The pilot who was wrongly blamed for the crash"

Sporting Intelligence, April 25, 2011: "JOHN ROBERTS: 'The pilot for United's fateful flight from Munich was unfairly blamed. One twilight in 1974, he told me his story'"

Morrin, Stephen R: *The Munich Air Disaster* (Gill & Macmillan, 2007)

Associated Press, February 17, 2014: "Plane crashes into mountains in Nepal, killing all 18 passengers"

Scientific American, February 17, 2009: "How does ice cause a plane to crash?"

Skybrary: "In-Flight Icing"

Newsweek, April 5, 1992: "An Icy Night Is No Time To Wing It"

CAB, January 16, 1945: File No. 4889-43, Docket No. SA-84

Associated Press, October 16, 1943: "Plane Crashes Seeking Landing Area"

Saginaw News, April 6, 2008: "Michigan's third-worst plane crash killed all 47 aboard 50 years ago today in Freeland"

Michigan Daily News, March 24, 2008: "47 perish: Easter Sunday plane crash at Tri-City Airport remembered 50 years later"

Civil Aeronautics Board, February 17, 1965: Revised Aircraft Accident Report File No. 1-00, SA-331

Civil Aeronautics Board, September 20, 1961: Aircraft Accident Report File No. 1-0001, SA-353

New York Times, January 19, 1960: "50 Lost in Viscount Crash"

Associated Press, January 20, 1960: "Airliner Crash Kills Fifty"

New York Times, August 4, 2002: "Afterward"

NTSB, August 10, 1982: Aircraft Accident Report no. NTSB-AAR-82-8, PB82-910408

Sun-Sentinel, January 13, 2002: "Lessons Learned From A Deadly Crash"

Washington Post, January 13, 2012: "The 30th anniversary of the Air Florida plane crash"

Washington Post, January 12, 2007: "A Crash's Improbable Impact"

Time, January 17, 1982: "Plane Crashes into River"

New York Times, February 10, 1984: "Relative Of 2 Victims In Air Crash Still Angry"

New York Times, January 27, 1982: "2 MISSING FROM JET IN BOSTON HARBOR"

UPI, January 27, 1982: "2 victims hunted in wake of airliner crash in Boston"

NTSB, July 10, 1985: Aircraft Accident Report NTSB/AAR-85/06, PB85-910406, replacing NTSB-AAR-82-15

New York Times, March 27, 1992: "Canadian Judge Calls Air Crash Avoidable"

Commission of Inquiry into the Air Ontario Crash at Dryden, Ontario: Final Report. March 1992

Canberra Times, January 7, 1993: "Dryden Disaster, Three Years Later A Look Back On The Crash Of Air Ontario Fokker F28"

Canadian Press, March 9, 2009: "Feelings still strong 20 years after Dryden plane crash"

Phoenix New Times, January 29, 2009: "Three US Airways Flight Attendants Are Paying the Price for Speaking Up When They Thought Their Plane Was at Risk"

New York Times, March 29, 1992: "The Ordinary Turned to Instant Horror for All Aboard USAir's Flight 405"

New York Times, March 23, 1992: "At Least 19 Killed in Crash at Snowy La Guardia"

Associated Press, March 26, 1992: "Co-pilot in fatal crash saw no ice on wings"

FAA, Report of the FAA International Conference on Airplane Ground Deicing Held in Reston, Virginia on May 28–29, 1992

NTSB, Aircraft Accident Report, NRSB/AAR-93/02, PB93-910402

Statens haverikommission, Board of Accident Investigation, Report C 1993:57, Case L-124/91

Daily Telegraph, February 8, 2008: "My escape from BA038 was damn fun"

Daily Telegraph, October 3, 2012: "Out of court settlement reached between British Airways passengers and manufacturers"

BBC News, 17 January 2008: "Eyewitnesses on Heathrow incident"

BBC News, 20 January 2008: "BA pilot 'feared all would die'"

BBC Hereford News, 24 March 2010: "Air crash: '30 seconds to impact'"

Department of Transport, February 9, 2010: Aircraft Accident Report 1/2010

Time, July 5, 2012: "Air France Flight 447: Pilot Errors Mounted in Tragic Crash, Report Finds"

Popular Mechanics, December 6, 2011: "What really happened aboard Air France 447"

Daily Telegraph, April 28, 2012: "Air France Flight 447: 'Damn it, we're going to crash'"

New York Times, July 29, 2011: "Report on Air France Crash Points to Pilot Training"

Bureau d'Enquêtes et d'Analyses pour la sécurité de l'aviation civile, July 27, 2012: Final Report on F-GZCP (and preliminary reports issued from June 1, 2009 onwards)

Part 5: Explosive Decompression

Australian Associated Press, May 3, 1953: "Comet Jet Crashes in 'Tempest'"

Ministry of Transport, February 1, 1955: "Report of the Public Inquiry into the causes and circumstances of the accident which occurred on the 10th January, 1954, to the Comet aircraft G-ALYP"

Flight International, October 29, 1954: "The Comet Accidents; History of Events"

Flight International, February 18, 1955: "Report of the Comet Inquiry"

New York Times, April 10, 1954: "Second Comet Jet Crashes"

NTSB, January 15, 1975: Aircraft Accident Report File No. 1-0043, NTSB-AAR-75-2

El Defensor Chieftain, June 5, 2010: "Aircraft Down"

United Press International, March 4, 1974: "Bomb blast suspected in 345-death jet crash"

Department of Trade, February 1976: "Report on the accident" LTS/2291/75 FRENCH/JHB (translated from the original French)

Chicago Tribune, June 2, 1985: "Failure Analysis"

Time, August 26, 1985: "Disasters: Last Minutes of JAL 123"

Aircraft Accident Investigation Commission, June 19, 1987: Aircraft Accident Investigation Report

Associated Press, August 13, 1985: "Jet Crash Kills Over 500 In Mountains of Japan"

Guardian, 13 August 1985: "524 killed in worst single air disaster" (at the point the story was filed, none of the survivors had been found)

New York Times, November 8, 1985: "J.A.L.'S POST-CRASH TROUBLES"

Honolulu Advertiser, January 18, 2001: "Engineer fears repeat of 1988 Aloha jet accident"

Disaster City website (Matt Austin): www.disastercity.info

Time, May 9, 1988: "The Plane Was Disintegrating"

NTSB, June 14, 1989: Aircraft Accident Report NTSB/AAR-89/03, PB89-910404

Congressional Record, May 10, 1989: "Honoring the crew of United Airlines Flight 811"

NTSB, March 18, 1992: Aircraft Accident Report NTSB/AR-92/02, PB92-910402 replacing NTSB/AAR-90/01, PB90-910401

New York, February 1, 2009: "Crash Diary No. 1"

New York Times, February 26, 1989; "Aboard Flight 811: Passengers' Routine Dissolves Into Terror"

Los Angeles Times, February 25, 1989: "Jumbo Jet Rips Open Off Hawaii; 9 Killed, 18 Hurt : UNITED AIRLINES FLIGHT 811"

Sunday Star Times, February 27, 2009: "Flight 811: The Untold Story"

Associated Press, October 3, 1990: "Half of Door From Stricken Jetliner Recovered Off Hawaii"

Airdisaster.com, Eyewitness Report: United Flight 811 http://www.airdisaster.com/eyewitness/ua811.shtml

Seattle Times, January 5, 1992: "Terror In The Sky – Flight 811 Lost A Cargo Door And Nine Lives – Boeing Is Still Wrestling With Solutions And Settlements"

Department of Transport, February 1992: Aircraft Accident Report 1/92

New York Times, June 11, 1990: "4 Miles Over Britain Pilot Is Sucked Out; Crew Holds On Tight"

Sydney Morning Herald, February 5, 2005: "This is your captain screaming"

Hellenic Republic Ministry of Transport & Communications Air Accident Investigation & Aviation Safety Board, November 2006: Aircraft Accident Report

New York Times, August 16, 2005: "Crash inquiry focuses on oxygen mask use"

BBC News, 23 December 2008: "Five charged for Helios jet crash"

Flight International, October 17, 2006: "Investigation dispels myths around Helios Airways crash"

Cyprus Daily, August 14, 2013: "Helios Remembered"

Part 6: Fire!

Flight, October 7, 1926: "Another Cross-Channel Air Service Disaster"

Ottaway, Susan: *Fire over Heathrow, The Tragedy of Flight 712* (Pen and Sword Books, 2008)

Associated Press, August 21, 1980: "Did stove cause disaster?"

A. Haine, Edgar: *Disaster in the Air* (Associated University Press, 2000)

UPI, August 21, 1980: "Jetliner fire started by stove; death toll set at 301."

Presidency of Civil Aviation, Jeddah, January 16, 1982: Aircraft Accident Report

Flight Safety Foundation, "FSF Heroism Award"

Guardian, 23 August 1985: "54 killed as Boeing bursts into flames"

Air Accidents Investigation Branch, December 15, 1988: Aircraft Accident Report 8/88

Time, May 27, 1996: "Does Air Safety Have a Price?"

Time, May 20: 1996: "Death in the Everglades"

Time, December 2, 1996: "Tragedy Retold: ValuJet Crash"

Time, August 19, 1997: "Verdict Is In on ValuJet Crash"

Atlanta Journal-Constitution, March 1, 1997: "Closed case, loose ends"

CNN, June 17, 1996: "ValuJet timeline"

ValuJet Flight 592 Remembered, July 12, 1999: "Press Release: U.S. ATTORNEYS' OFFICE IGNORES CRITICAL EVIDENCE IN THE VALUJET CRASH"

Tampa Bay Gazette, May 11, 2006: "10 years after tragedy, AirTran flies on"

Department of Transportation, October 13, 1999: "Mechanic in SabreTech Case Indicted for Contempt of Court"

NTSB, August 19, 1997: Aircraft Accident Report, NTSB/AAR-97/06, PB97-910406

Royal Aeronautical Society, March 2013, "Smoke, Fire and Fumes in Transport Aircraft"

Time, November 9, 1998: "Playing Deadly Games?"

Time, September 14, 1998: "No Safe Harbor"

Nova, February 17, 2004: "Crash of Flight 111"

CBC News, September 14, 2011: "Swissair crash may not have been an accident: ex-RCMP"

USA Today, February 16, 2003: "Doomed plane's gaming system exposes holes in FAA oversight"

Transportation Safety Board of Canada, March 2003, Aviation Investigation Report A98H0003

Nova, January 27, 1998: "Supersonic Spies"

Time, June 18, 1973: "Disasters: Deadly Exhibition"

New Scientist, June 7, 1973: "Concordski and Concorde"

Time, August 7, 2000: "The Concordski"

Observer, 13 May 2001: "Doomed: The Real Story of Flight 4590"

New York Times, February 1, 2010: "Trial Opens in Concorde Disaster"

BBC News, 25 July 2000: "Concorde crash kills 113"

ABC News, September 4, 2000: "Metal Part Maybe Came From Continental Jet"

Bureau Enquêtes-Accidents, January 2002: Accident Report f-sc000725

Part 7: Hijackings

Time, August 8, 1948: "HONG KONG: Pilots & Pirates"

Macau Business, November 1, 2008: "Flights of Fancy"

Fortnight Journal, December 8, 2011: "The First Hijacking Myth"

Associated Press, November 2, 1939: "Flying Murderer Given Life Term"

Associated Press, November 2, 1939: "Earnest Pletch is Given Life Term In State Prison" [NB DATES ARE THE SAME – later report same day]

Press-Democrat, Hennessey, Oklahoma, August 18, 1911: "What the World is Doing"

Ogdensburg Journal, August 10, 1911: "'Joy Fliers' Appear"

Bloom, October/November 2000: "The Killer Who Fell From the Sky"

Associated Press, December 28, 1921: "Aero Thief Injured"

Sydney Morning Herald, February 11, 1933: "Two Years For Receiving"

New York World, June 22, 1917, reported in *The Argus* (Melbourne, Victoria, Australia), June 23, 1917: "Joyflight Ends Fatally"

Sydney Morning Herald, September 23, 1930: "Stolen 'Plane"

Free Czechoslovak Air Force website: "They Flew to Exile 1950"

"The Flight to Erding by Dr Miloš Vitek" at http://freespace. virgin.net/daj.mipivo/english.htm

Orizont Aviatic 34, 2005

Film Reporter.Ro: March 1, 2011: "EXCLUSIV: Destinul lui Vasile Ciobanu, pilotul primei curse aeriene deturnate vreodată"

Associated Press, March 5, 1976: "First Hijacker Sentenced"

UPI, March 5, 1976: "Skyjacking originator sentenced"

Koerner, Brendan I.: *The Skies Belong to Us: Love and Terror in the Golden Age of Hijacking* (Random House, 2013)

Miami Herald, November 7, 1975, "Hijacker: Cuba Suspected Spying"

Associated Press, July 7, 1954: "Youth Tries To Take Over Airliner, Killed By Pilot"

AP, July 7, 1954: "Pilot Kills Boy To Save Lives"

Washington Report on Middle East Affairs, November/December 1994: "Israel Was First Nation to Skyjack a Civilian Airliner"

Foreign Relations of the United States, 1961–1963, Volume X, Cuba, January 1961–September 1962, Document 252

McWhinney, Edward: *Aerial Piracy and International Terrorism: Illegal Diversion of Aircraft and International Law (International studies on terrorism)* Kluwer Academic Publishers, 1987

Beartooth NBC, June 27, 2011: "A Look Back July 1961: Hijacked Airliner"

Ohio County Times, April 12, 1973: "You Can't Keep a Good Man Down"

Associated Press, August 4, 1961: "Fantastic Scheme to Hijack Jet Foiled"

Associated Press, August 10, 1961: "JFK Assigns Plane Guards"

Associated Press, August 10, 1961: "File Charges in Hijacking"

Associated Press, August 11, 1961: "Three Hosiers Resume Travels After Hijacking"

Associated Press, August 14, 1961: "Mexico Calls on Castro to Extradite Hijacker"

Associated Press, November 26, 1961: "Hijacker to be sent to Mexico"

Walter Winchell on Broadway, April 16, 1963

UPI, March 14, 1968: "Dateline: Mexico"

Time, August 4, 1961: "Aviation: Gift for Castro"

Time, December 6, 1968: "Travel: What to Do When The Hijacker Comes"

Time, September 21, 1970: "World: Drama of the Desert: The Week of the Hostages"

Time, August 2, 1968: "Algeria: Skyway Robbery"

American Experience: Hijacked (PBS, broadcast February 25, 2006; transcript on their website)

Foreign Service Journal, December 1969: "The Hijacking of TWA Flight 840"

Foreign Relations of the United States, 1969–1976, Volume E–1, Documents on Global Issues, 1969–1972: Israeli Attack on Beirut Airport and Hijacking of TWA Flight 840, January-December 1969

Guardian, 26 January, 2001: "'I made the ring from a bullet and the pin of a hand grenade'"

UPI, December 26, 1968: "Two Killed by Arabs on New York-Bound Jetliner"

Skyjack Database at www.skyjack.co.il (caution advised as there is some erroneous data here)

Mickolus, Edward F.: *The Terrorist List A-K* (ABC-Clio, 2009)

Aviation Security, March 24, 2006: "Leila Khaled In her own Words" (interview carried out in 2000)

Middle East Quarterly, Fall 2007: "Terror in Black September: An Eyewitness Account"

Boston Globe, June 22, 2010: "Obituary: John Ferruggio, at 84; hero of 1970 Pan Am hijacking"

Baldwin, James Patrick, Kriendler, Jeff with Giles, Lesley: *Pan American World Airways – Aviation History Through the Words of its People* (Bluewater Press, 2013)

BBC, 1 January 2001: "UK Confidential: Black September"

Time, July 12, 1976: "TERRORISTS: The Rescue: 'We Do the Impossible'"

Dunstan, Simon: *Entebbe: The Most Daring Raid of Israel's Special Forces* (Rosen, 2011)

Ynet News, July 7, 2006: "Special: Entebbe's Unsung Hero"

Ynet News, July 1, 2006: "Special: Mossad took photos, Entebbe Operation was on its way"

Jewish Telegraph, July 1, 2006: "Entebbe: Miracle on the Runway"

Time, July 26, 1976: "TERRORISM: Vindication for the Israelis"

Flight International, July 17, 1976: "Entebbe postscript"

McNab, Chris: *Storming Flight 181: GSG-9 and the Mogadishu Hijack 1977* (Osprey, 2011)

Time, October 31, 1977: "The World: Terror and Triumph at

Mogadishu" (NB certain pieces of operational information about the hijack were not known when this was written)

Mogadishu: The Documentary: (German television) uploaded to YouTUbe at http://www.youtube.com/watch?v=KItCN0PT5Vo

Somali Archive: Lufthansa Flight 181 (contemporary footage) https://www.youtube.com/watch?v=fun4dL601T0

Time, June 24, 2001: "Terror Aboard Flight 847" (NB This is a reprint of a contemporary article)

New York Sun, June 13, 2010: "Thinking of Robert Stethem"

New York Sun, January 11, 2006: "The Feeling of Betrayal"

Associated Press, July 1, 1985: "The Ordeal of Flight 847"

Chicago Tribune, July 3, 1985: "Hostage Diary: 'I Thought I Was Dead'"

Associated Press, June 17, 1985: "Passenger List of TWA Flight 847"

Associated Press, June 17, 1985: "Letter Urges No Military Action"

NBC News, February 13, 2008: "Bomb kills Hezbollah militant wanted by U.S."

Jewish Telegraphic Agency, December 2, 1985: "The Ordeal of Egyptair Flight 648 Eyewitness Accounts of the World's Bloodiest Hijack"

United States Court of Appeals, District of Columbia Circuit. – 134 F.3d 1121, United States of America, Appellee, v. Omar Mohammed Ali Rezaq, A/k/a Omar Marzouki, A/k/a Omaramr, Appellant, Argued Nov. 21, 1997. Decided Feb. 6, 1998

Associated Press, December 1, 1985: "Victims of hijack return to Egypt"

Pflug, Jackie Nink with Kizilos, Peter J. : *Miles to Go Before I Sleep* Hazelden Foundation, 1996

Time, June 21, 2005: "Terrorism: Massacre in Malta" (Again, a reprint of a contemporary article)

Flight Line Malta website, March 7, 2006: "Egypt Air Flight 648 Hijack in Malta" http://www.flightlinemalta.com/airaccidents/SU-AYH/

New York Times, October 7, 1996: "U.S. Sentencing Due Today in 1985 Hijack"

New York Times, November 25, 1985: "Attack 'Was Our Only Hope,' Pilot of Flight 648 Declares"

Washington Post, October 8, 1996; "Airline Hijacker Gets Life for Incident That Killed 58"

The 9/11 Commission Report .

History Commons Complete 911 Timeline and the various newspaper articles referenced therein (www.historycommons.org/timeline.jsp?timeline=complete_911_timeline&day_of_9/11)

Part 8: An Explosive Situation: Bombings on Board

Time, April 17, 1933: "Foreign News; Dr. Voss"

Fairbanks Daily News-Miner, April 4, 1933: "Demented Man May Have Set Plane Ablaze"

Sydney Morning Herald, April 5, 1933: "Mr. Albert Voss; Postponement of Funeral"

Sydney Morning Herald, April 29, 1933: "Mr. Albert Voss: Open Verdict Returned" (The story was followed in Australia, as an Australian citizen was one of the victims)

Straits Times, September 16, 1933: "Mrs. Albert Voss Drowned"

FBI files on the 1933 Indiana crash can be read at:
http://media.nbcchicago.com/documents/fbi+file+1.PDF and
http://media.nbcchicago.com/documents/fbi+file+2.PDF

Associated Press, October 11, 1933: "Seven Killed in Crash of Giant Transport Plane"

Associated Press, October 12, 1933: "Suspects Bomb Wrecked Plane"

Jackson Center, Indiana, October 11, 1933 "Giant Plane Crashes – 7 Die" (transcribed at http://www3.gendisasters.com/indiana/961/jackson-center-in-airplane-crash-oct-1933)

Time, October 23, 1933: "Aeronautics: Death on No. 23"

Historic Wings, October 12, 2012: "An Act of Air Sabotage"

Star-Ledger, September 30/October 14, 2013: "United 23 took off from New Jersey 80 years ago; its midair explosion remains a mystery"

Chesterton Tribune, December 4, 2013: "Jackson Township plane crash of 1933 still remains a mystery"

NBC Chicago, October 8, 2013: "80 Years Later, Plane Crashes Remains a Mystery"

Chicago Tribune, September 9, 2011: "United Flight 23 to Chicago: The First Airline Terrorism?" (NB the graphic on this is not accurate)

Associated Press, May 7, 1949: "Airline Overdue with 12 Aboard"

Associated Press, May 8, 1949: "Planes Search for Missing D.C."

Associated Press/Reuters, June 2, 1949: "Air Deaths By Bomb"

Associated Press, February 7, 1960: "Experts Say Luggage Checks Won't Halt Airline Bombs"

Associated Press, March 14, 1950: "Guay to Die For Murder Of Wife by Plane Blast"

Montreal Gazette, October 3, 1981: "Murder in Quebec"

Greenwood, F. Murray Greenwood and Boissery, Beverley: *Uncertain Justice: Canadian Woman and Capital Punishment 1754-1953* (Dundurn Group Ltd, 2000)

Simon, Jeffrey David: *The Terrorist Trap* (Indiana University Press, 2001)

Mellor, Lee: *Rampage: Canadian Mass Murder and Spree Killing* (Dundurn Press, 2013)

Ottawa Citizen, February 23, 2009; "Your crime . . . has no name"

Canadian Virtual Museum: "The Albert Guay Affair" http://www.museevirtuel-virtualmuseum.ca/sgc-cms/expositions-exhibitions/detective-investigator/en/timeline/mcq/guay.html

Woodley, Charles: *The History of British European Airways* (Pen and Sword Aviation, 2006)

Harding, John: *Flying's Strangest Moments* (Robson Books, 2006)

Daily Telegraph, 27 July 2004: "Obituary: Captain Ian Harvey"

Associated Press, April 16, 1950: "Viking Airliner Explosion: Possible Intended Victim"

FBI official website: "Famous Cases & Criminals: Jack Gilbert Graham"

United Nations Security Council, December 8, 1967: "Report by the Secretary-General on the United Nations operation in Cyprus"

Flight International, October 19, 1967: "The Safety Record Worsens"

Flight International, October 26, 1967: "Comet Restrictions"

Flight International, November 2, 1967: "New Comet Clues"

Flight International, November 30, 1967: "No Salvage for Comet"

Flight International, December 7, 1967: "Sensor"

Flight International, September 5, 1968: "Comet Sabotage? – the Evidence"

Associated Press, December 22, 1969: "30 Dead in South Viet Plane Mishap"

PRH: A Day in the Life (blog), December 6, 2007: "Air Vietnam Crash 12/22/69"

PRH: A Day in the Life (blog), January 25, 2010: "The Plane Crashes at Nha Trang Air Base 1969" (*N.B. the report he links to is at http://www.planecrashinfo.com/1969/1969-89.htm and not as stated in either of these blog entries.*)

Ensalaco, Mark: *Middle Eastern Terrorism: From Black September to September 11* (University of Pennsylvania Press, 2007)

The History and Death of EVAS website: Flight 330 transcript

Associated Press, February 21, 1970: "Swiss Air Crash Claims 47 Dead"

Federal Bureau of Investigation, June 1970: "The Fedayeen Terrorist – A Profile"

Reuters, February 23, 1970: "Ban on air freight to Israel"

Associated Press, February 23, 1970: "Swiss clamp tight restrictions on Arabs"

20 Minuten, February 19, 2010: "We are crashing – goodbye, everybody"

Technet, January 26, 2012: "Seriál: Teroristický útok nad ČSSR přežila jen letuška, padala z 10 km"

New York Times, April 26, 2008: "Serbia's Most Famous Survivor Fears That Recent History Will Repeat Itself"

Czech Aviation Authority report: http://www.nacr.cz/Z-files/znasichfondu_II_2.pdf

New Zealand Herald, January 27, 2012: "Heroic hostess living under shadow"

Guardian, January 13, 2009: "Woman who fell to earth: was air crash survivor's record just propaganda?"

Daily Telegraph, January 26, 2012: "40 years on, woman who survived 33,000 foot fall still faces questions"

National Transportation Safety Board, March 26, 1975: Report Number NTSB-AAR-75-7.

Associated Press, January 24, 2009: "Terrorist Who Plotted Attack on New York City to Be Released"

New York Times, June 25, 1985: "Japanese Look for Explosives in Airport Bombing"

Jiwa, Salim: *The Death of Air India Flight 182* (as updated on website www.flight182.com)

Time, July 29, 1985: "Disasters: Unraveling Taped Secrets"

Time, July 1, 1985: "Disasters: Two More Strikes for Terrorists?"

Time, July 8, 1985: "Disasters: A Case of Global Jitters"

Time, April 12, 2005: "Disasters: Deep Grab" (originally printed July 15, 1985)

Vancouver Sun, May 11, 1991: "Portrait of a bomber"

In The Supreme Court Of British Columbia, R. v. Malik and Bagri, 2005 BCSC 350, Reasons for Judgment, published March 16, 2005.

Tehelka, August 4, 2007: "Kanishka Tragedy: Operation Silence"

Commission of Inquiry into the investigation of the Bombing of Air India Flight 182, June 2010, "Air India Flight 182: A Canadian Tragedy"

Israel Security Agency website: "Anne-Marie Murphy Case (1986)"

People, October 27, 1986: "With the Promise of Happiness, She Became a Bomber's Pawn"

National Interest, Spring 1989: "Terrorism: The Syrian Connection"

Time, June 21, 2005: "Terrorism: Questions About a Damascus Connection" (reprinted from October 1986)

Time, November 3, 1986: "Terrorism: Making the Syrian Connection"

Time, December 8, 1986: "West Germany Verdict Against Damascus"

Time, June 21, 2005: "An Interview with Hafez Assad" (reprinted from October 1986)

Time, May 19, 1986: "The Road From Damascus"

The Times, 28 March 2013: "Plane plot bomber Nezar Hindawi released on parole"

Expressen, February 23, 2011: "Khadaffi gav order om Lockerbie-attentatet"

AAIB, February 1990, "Report No: 2/1990 - Report on the accident to Boeing 747-121, N739PA, at Lockerbie, Dumfriesshire, Scotland on 21 December 1988"

Defence Intelligence Agency report, 2003 (redacted version at http://web.archive.org/web/20080308085805/http://www.dia.mil/publicaffairs/Foia/panam103.pdf)

The Opinion of the Court in the case against al-Megrahi on http://www.scotcourts.gov.uk/

Scottish Criminal Cases Review Commission, June 28, 2007: "News Release: ABDELBASET ALI MOHMED AL MEGRAHI"

Radio 4, *Today* programme, February 24, 2004

De Braeckeleer, Dr. Ludwig: "Diary of a Vengeance Foretold" (to be found at http://english.ohmynews.com/articleview/article_view.asp?menu=c10400&no=384534&rel_no=1) (The complete series examines and gives credence to many of the conspiracy theories involved, even if some of them are mutually exclusive.)

Time, April 27, 1992: "Pan Am 103: Why Did They Die?"

American Radio Works, March 2000: "Shadow over Lockerbie" (transcript at http://americanradioworks.publicradio.org/features/lockerbie/story/printable_story.html)

Storyville, BBC Four, February 3, 2014: "Mad Dog – Gaddafi's Secret World"

BBC News, January 4, 2013: "Calls to re-open Libya plane 'crash' investigation"

Flight International, January 6, 1993: "Boeing 727 crashes in Libya"

Al Jazeera, March 11, 2014: *Lockerbie: What Really Happened*

Cineflex: *Mayday/Air Crash Investigation*: Season 3, Episode 6: "Bomb on board (interviews with Captain Reyes and crew)

Los Angeles Times, September 6, 1996: "Jury Finds Three Guilty of Plot To Blow Up a Dozen US Planes"

CNN, September 6, 1996: "Plane terror suspects convicted on all counts"

Los Angeles Times, September 1, 2002: "Sunday Report: The Plot"

United States Court Of Appeals For The Second Circuit, April 4, 2003; UNITED STATES OF AMERICA, *Appellee*, v. RAMZI AHMED YOUSEF, EYAD ISMOIL, also known as EYAD ISMAIL, and ABDUL HAKIM MURAD, also known as SAEED AHMED, *Defendants-Appellants*, MOHAMMED A. SALAMEH, NIDAL AYYAD, MAHMUD ABOUHALIMA, also known as Mahmoud Abu Halima, BILAL ALKAISI, also known as Bilal Elqisi, AHMAD MOHAMMAD AJAJ, also known as Khurram Khan, ABDUL RAHMAN YASIN, also known as Aboud, and WALI KHAN AMIN SHAH, also known as Grabi Ibrahim Hahsen, *Defendants*.